THE TWILIGHT LABYRINTH

Other Books by George Otis Jr.

The Last of the Giants: Lifting the Veil on Islam and the End Times
Strongholds of the 10/40 Window: An Intercessor's Guide to the
 World's Least Evangelized Nations
Unleashing the Power of Informed Intercession: A Guidebook on
 Spiritual Mapping and Community Transformation

THE TWILIGHT LABYRINTH

Why Does Spiritual Darkness Linger Where It Does?

GEORGE OTIS JR.

A Division of Baker Book House Co
Grand Rapids, Michigan 49516

Published by Chosen Books
a division of Baker Book House Company
P.O. Box 6287, Grand Rapids, MI 49516-6287

Printed in the United States of America

Library of Congress Cataloging-in-Publication Data

Otis, George, 1953–
    The twilight labyrinth : why does spiritual darkness linger where it does?
/ George K. Otis Jr.
        p. cm.
    Includes bibliographical references and index.
    ISBN 0-8007-9255-6 (paper)
    1. Demonology. 2. Spiritual warfare. 3. Mythology—Comparative studies.
4. Occultism—Religious aspects—Christianity. 5. Occultism—Controversial
literature. 6. Otis, George, 1953– I. Title.
BT975.O85   1997
235'.4—dc21   97–15171

Unless otherwise noted, Scripture quotations are taken from the HOLY BIBLE, NEW INTERNATIONAL VERSION®. NIV®. Copyright © 1973, 1978, 1984 by International Bible Society. Used by permission of Zondervan Publishing House. All rights reserved.

Scripture marked NASB is taken from the NEW AMERICAN STANDARD BIBLE ®. Copyright © The Lockman Foundation 1960, 1962, 1963, 1968, 1971, 1972, 1973, 1975, 1977, 1995. Used by permission.

Scripture marked NKJV is taken from the New King James Version. Copyright © 1979, 1980, 1982 by Thomas Nelson, Inc. Used by permission. All rights reserved.

Scripture marked RSV is taken from the Revised Standard Version of the Bible, copyright 1946, 1952, 1971 by the Division of Christian Education of the National Council of the Churches of Christ in the USA. Used by permission.

Scripture marked KJV is taken from the King James Version of the Bible.

For current information about all releases from Baker Book House, visit our web site:
http://www.bakerbooks.com

This book is dedicated to the memory of Tom Dologhan,
former director of the Navajo Gospel Mission
and one of God's choicest heroes.
I wish we'd had more time, Tom. See you soon.

"What is the way to the abode of light?
And where does darkness reside?
Can you take them to their places?
Do you know the paths to their dwellings?"

Job 38:19–20

CONTENTS

PREFACE

Reflections on a Journey

A common complaint among American voters these days is that political campaigns have become dull and uninformative. While the candidates themselves bear much of the blame for this,[1] the news media are also partially responsible. This is especially true of television, a medium whose high costs and rapid pace inhibit a thorough airing of the issues. Solutions to complex societal problems simply cannot be unpacked in thirty-second sound bites.

To get around this seemingly intractable problem, a Seattle-area candidate by the name of Joe King produced a novel television ad recently. Instead of dispensing the typical vague platitudes, King used his half-minute spot to highlight the complexity of current issues and to encourage viewers to write in for more details. Those who did so were provided with a copy of the *Joe King Plan*, a thoughtfully prepared digest of the candidate's analyses and proposals.

Although Mr. King's bid for office ultimately came up short, his rejection of superficiality did not. In the weeks following the election, many voters hailed his initiative as a refreshing departure from modern campaign tactics.

The same attitude has been emerging of late among Western rank-and-file Christians. Challenging the popular notion that they can endure only twenty-minute sermons and newsletter-length books, many believers are displaying a formidable appetite for substance. Unfortunately a high percentage of pastors, authors and publishers are still wedded to the old paradigm.

In addressing this problem, *The Twilight Labyrinth* jettisons intellectual one-night stands in favor of conceptual courtships. Instead of rushing toward dubious conclusions, it allows readers to linger over rich nuances and intricate interrelationships. As the distillation of many years of hard work, it is my version of the *Joe King Plan*—a book intended for believers fed up with both the narrow-minded rationalism of some evangelicals, and the simplistic pop culture that has grown up around certain charismatics.

The primary purpose of *The Twilight Labyrinth* is to help Christians arrive at a more complete understanding of the modern spiritual battlefield. To reach this goal, readers are taken on a journey that winds through ancient civilizations, the inner workings of the human mind, and God's eternal Word. It is a quest whose departure point is a single, riveting question: Why does spiritual darkness linger where it does?

My own seven-year investigation into this matter has taken me into nearly fifty nations of the world. Along the way, I have ascended the summits of sacred mountains, plumbed the depths of university libraries and paddled down the holy Ganges River at dawn. I have ventured into crowded festivals, dank temples and remote monasteries. I have listened to the stories of Tibetan Buddhist lamas, Native American medicine men and the leading theorists of the New Age movement. I have compared notes with missionaries and national pastors, interviewed anthropologists and prehistorians, and picked the minds of experts on everything from shamanism and ancestor worship to folk Islam and religious initiations. The book you are now holding in your hands is the culmination of this fascinating and instructive journey.[2]

Diligence in record-keeping has proven critical. It is amazing how quickly an epic quest such as this can shrivel into a handful of memories, a few stories to tell. The visceral experience of standing atop Japan's Mount Ontake, or watching Tibetan pilgrims circumambulate the Jokhang Temple, begins to seep away. While most tourists avoid this dissipation by purchasing canned, prepackaged memories in souvenir shops, I managed to keep the whole sprawling adventure alive on microcassettes and dog-eared notepads.[3]

Perseverance is another virtue in research. Putting this book together has reminded me of the little slide puzzles I used to play with as a youngster in the church pew. Sometimes I thought I had finally solved the puzzle, only to discover a single, out-of-place tile hidden under my thumb. Although these oversights are common to man, this does not make them any less frustrating. The only antidote to their paralyzing effect is tenacity. As Garth Henrichs counsels, "The man who is waiting for something to turn up might start on his shirt sleeves."[4]

Some challenges, of course, cannot be met by perseverance alone. A good example is a nasty encounter I had with the Adversary back on July 15, 1993. About four in the morning I was startled awake by the most intense presence of evil I had ever experienced. Darker than the night itself, it hovered over my bed in icy silence. The fear was suffocating. My heart began racing like a greyhound, and the hairs on my arms and neck stood at military attention. There was no doubting that this incorporeal intruder was a sentient force—a force whose intentions and power were utterly malevolent.

The visitation was the spiritual equivalent of a Mafia warning. By launching a multi-year investigation into the dark side of the spiritual dimension, I had stuck my nose where it did not belong. Even worse, I had sent detailed outlines on the project to my publisher earlier that very day. With things clearly getting out of hand, the powers of darkness apparently felt it was time to raise the stakes. While there was no audible interchange with the night visitor, his threat was all too clear: *If you proceed with this project, I will touch your children.*

The follow-through on this threat (detailed in chapter 9) is but one of several such incidents that occurred during the course of this project. It is apparent in retrospect that these episodes were God's way of ensuring that my theories on spiritual warfare were seasoned by personal battlefield experience.

The Twilight Labyrinth deals with things that are real, but not seen; with things that are hinted at, but not broadcast. While non-Western readers will nod knowingly at the following stories and concepts, those from rationalist-oriented cultures will occasionally stumble. Taught to avow a clear split between the spiritual and the material, most Westerners are uncomfortable with the supernatural as an everyday companion. As the late writer Anaïs Nin once said, "We don't see things as they are, we see them as we are."

Our own experiences (or lack of them) have a profound effect on the way we view the external world. As the torrent of daily life rushes past us, we use these experiences to filter out an astonishing volume of ideological flotsam and jetsam. Reality is whatever gets through.

Since the following pages contain information alien to Western experience, portions of the book will inevitably end up on the refuse grates of reader worldviews. There is little that I as an author can do about this, other than to heed Roger Andersen's sage advice to "accept that some days you're the pigeon, and some days you're the statue."[5]

Nevertheless, I am hopeful that *The Twilight Labyrinth* will provoke many readers to expand their catalog of life experiences.

George Otis Jr.
Seattle, Washington
March 1997

ACKNOWLEDGMENTS

During its seven years in development, *The Twilight Labyrinth* was touched by literally hundreds of hands. Many delivered essential raw material in the form of articles and interviews. Others dug into the project's wet clay and helped to sculpt stories and ideas. Still others brushed off extraneous words and punctuation. Now that the book is complete, a few of these gracious hands deserve special recognition.

Major Interviews: Pete Gray Eyes, Stephen Hishey, Robert Kayanja, Randy and Marci MacMillan, Thomas Muthee, Dawa Sandrup, Herman and Fern Williams, and several whose names cannot be mentioned.

Travel Companions and Interpreters: Robert Dayzie, Thomas Hemingway, Mike Hendricks, K. M. John, Dr. Billy Ogata, Dr. Rana Singh, Dick Speer.

Research Support: Mark Albrecht, Brooks Alexander, Margy Brink, Harold Caballeros, Dr. Barry Chant, Kunzang Delek, Ed Delph, Tom and Betty Dologhan, Susan Drake, Matthew Hand, Hallett Hullinger, John Hutchinson, Douglas Layton, Sheryl McLaughlin, Chris Van den Assem, Hassanain Hirji-Walji, Dr. Eisuke Kanda, Filiberto Lemus, John Robb, Hector Torres, Derrick Trimble, Tashi Tsering, Wendell and Francis Tsoodle, Asbjørn Voreland, Dr. C. Peter Wagner, Steve Watters.

Special Support: Ken and Roberta Eldred, George and Virginia Otis.

Editorial and Publishing: Jane Campbell, Bill Petersen.

I also want to offer a special word of thanks to my wonderful wife, Lisa, and our four children—Brendan, Brook, Daron and Jenna—for their patience, companionship and counsel over the course of this lengthy project. May God reward each of you according to your faithfulness!

CHAPTER ONE

ENCOUNTERS WITH
THE WORLD NEXT DOOR

I n the Calle Villares, the so-called magic market of La Paz, Bolivia, are hundreds of remedies for sale that will, depending on one's need, keep evil spirits at bay, cure vexatious diseases or facilitate journeys to the Otherworld. While native herbs like *ayawasqua* and *estingo* are especially popular, more serious customers, including shamans and sorcerers, tend to favor potent ritual ingredients like flamingo feathers and mummified llama fetuses.[1]

Half a world away, in the Voudon fetishers market of Ouidah, Benin, equally discriminating patrons browse through an exotic emporium of turtle skulls, dried chameleons and dark monkey hands—the latter displayed in a beseeching row, palms up. Here the shopping lists include magic charms *(gris-gris)* assembled to promote personal success, and various items to be used in worship of ancestral spirits known as *orisha*.[2]

Scenes like these may appear to have been ripped out of an eighteenth-century travel journal. But in truth they are just as likely to have been captured on some German tourist's high-powered videocamera. On any given day or night, spiritual business is being transacted in literally hundreds of international locations. From the labyrinthine shadows of Taiwan's Snake Alley to the magic circles of Marrakech's Djemaa el-Fna, the desperate, fearful and curious of the earth seek out keys to the supernatural. And these esoteric bazaars, colorful as they may be, are only part of today's strange landscape.

In another kind of spiritual staging area, tourists are bedding down, courtesy of a Romanian tour company, in Castle Dracula, a gloomy stronghold in Transylvania's Borgo Pass. What sets this enterprising scheme apart from the magic markets is the notion that visits to the Otherworld (or spiritual dimension) can be arranged merely by selecting vacation dates and paying the requisite tariff. Then again, it is possible these intrepid travelers have discovered that, given the proper setting and expectations, the slightest tap is often enough to open enchanted doors.

To those who think such doorways are nonsense, I commend the following accounts. Drawn from settings on five continents, this diverse collection of strange places, mystic rituals, evil powers and miraculous deliverances offer an authentic peek into the world next door.

A Visit to Dharamsala

It was not the best time to fly. India's infamous hot season was in full swing, and the superheated air rising off the plains below had produced decidedly unfriendly skies. Almost from the moment the packed Air India flight lifted off the runway in New Delhi, a combination of powerful updrafts and hidden air pockets transformed our aging Boeing 737 aircraft into a turbulent aerial roller coaster. So in the midst of sudden lurches and sickening free falls, I found myself engaged in serious conversation with God.

The unstable sky was not the only issue on my mind. There was also my mission. I had come to the Himalayas in April 1992 in search of an explanation for the potent spiritual darkness that blankets this region, and had scheduled three weeks of meetings with a select list of gurus, lamas (high-ranking Buddhist monks), scholars and missionaries. The complicated logistics, which included rendezvous in national libraries, private homes and remote monasteries, proved a blessed distraction from the turbulence.

My traveling companion was Dick Speer. It was nice to have him along. A former military adjutant and seminary graduate, Dick was a man seasoned not only by years of world travel and structured disciplines but by life's school of hard knocks. In the mid-1980s Dick's parents had been murdered at home by a family acquaintance who had suddenly lost control of his senses.

After touching down in Jammu, in northern India, none the worse for wear, Dick and I found a taxi willing to take us on the five-hour, 215-kilometer trip to Dharamsala, the mountain home of Tibet's Buddhist god-king, the Dalai Lama. We had a reservation for the night at the nearby Kashmir Cottage.

We ran into a hitch, however, when Raina, our driver, asked whether we were going to upper or lower Dharamsala. I did not know. Shrugging off my ignorance, Raina responded with characteristic Indian politeness: "No problem, sir." After the ordeal of getting here, I sincerely hoped he was right.

If necessity is the mother of invention, India is its best showcase. At every turn in this trying land, basic human ingenuity prevails in the form of jury-rigged protection from the merciless sun and astonishing methods of conveying the commodities of life. Pulsing beneath the seeming chaos of the streets—often a tangled maze of pedestrians, three-wheel taxis, sacred cows and horse carts laden with everything from textiles to stoves—is a purposeful rhythm of survival.

Somewhere beyond the Swastika Poultry Farm, we ventured into the true countryside. It was dusk, and small cooking fires were being kindled in the villages. There was just enough light to see the resigned, stubbled faces of old men hastening their camels along with canes, or attending, with small cans of tar, to the Sisyphean task of repairing the highway's ubiquitous potholes. In the distance, colorfully dressed women, their hair pulled into tidy ponytails, could be seen towing gaggles of children in from the fields. Other weary villagers loitered under the huge branches of ancient pipal trees, hoping, perhaps, for some day-end enlightenment.

Leaving the provincial border post at Lakhanpur, we proceeded into the foothills. The road was badly deteriorated and at various points crisscrossed deep river washes that, in the rainy season, carry torrents of precious water to the sun-scorched plains below. Hillside homes made of stone and baked bricks were set among artistically contoured wheatfields and rice paddies. It was cooler now, and I could see a full moon rising over the silhouetted Shivali Range.

For the first time I felt a twinge of foreboding. It was almost as though we had crossed an invisible border.

As we wound higher through stands of fragrant tali and jasmine trees, Dick asked Raina about his life. It had not been a happy one—or fair. Still shy of his thirtieth birthday, Raina had already felt the rough edges of India's caste system. He lamented the recent loss of his one true love—a girl whose companionship was forbidden him by virtue of his lower social status. But efforts to improve his lot through education had failed. Although he had earned a law degree at Jammu University, he remained consigned to the life of a cabby. "It is a shame for India!" he exclaimed.[3]

Moments later Raina drew our attention to a cluster of shimmering lights that seemed to hover mysteriously on the dark heights above us. We were finally nearing Dharamsala. Within a few kilometers the road narrowed and began a steep ascent facilitated by a series of switchbacks. Not fond of heights, I was glad we were doing this at night.

I could hear the sound of drums and deep bass chanting reverberating out of some unseen monastery. It was sure evidence we had entered the realm of Tibetan Buddhism, and I was eager to see what secrets the morning light would reveal.

Our biggest problem at the moment was finding accommodation. A clerk at the Kashmir Cottage informed us he had no record of our booking—and, unfortunately, no vacant rooms either. Inquiries at the Hotel Tibet and government-run Bhagsu proved equally fruitless. At midnight, after two exhausting days of travel, Dick and I were beat. Now, it appeared, Dharamsala was battening down for the night without us.

Just when we were beginning to wonder if there was any room in the proverbial inn, Raina turned onto a side street to question a small cluster of Tibetans. They suggested we investigate a private residence on Bhagsu Nath Road that rented out guest rooms occasionally. A quick check at the door revealed that they, too, were filled up for the night—but, being devout Buddhists, they were not keen to turn us away. Instead, the patriarch of the family motioned us to bring our bags inside.

We were met at the front door by a young woman who guided us through a warren of cubicles that served as living quarters for at least three generations of family members. Most were already asleep. Lifting a curtain of beads attached to the threshold of yet another room, she gestured us inside. The dimly lit chamber was filled with pungent incense and flying insects. There was something strange about it.

In no time a parade of family attendants furnished us with blankets, juice and Tibetan butter tea. At one A.M. they finally withdrew and we got a chance to take better stock of our surroundings. Only then did we discover that we had been accommodated in the family idol room. Strange indeed! But after taking time to thank God for His provision and protection, Dick and I drifted off to sleep.

In the wee hours of the morning, I sensed something on my face. Ascending out of a placid dreamscape, I could barely discern the vague outline of a man hovering above me. Who was he? What was he doing here? Fumbling for my glasses, my senses went on red alert.

The first clue was a waft of potent incense. No stale leftover from the night before, this offering had been freshly lit. With my glasses firmly in place, I realized that the ambiguous, hovering form of a moment ago was none other than the family patriarch, Tsering Dorje. Having moved our luggage quietly away from the altar, he was busy preparing "breakfast" for his honored gods. Their meal consisted of water, which Tsering poured carefully into silver chalices stationed before each image, and dried rice grains ritually tossed at the altar. I watched the rice ricochet off the idols in all directions and realized my alarm clock had been the undigested food of the gods![4]

Tsering Dorje, with dangling turquoise earrings and ebony hair tied back into a waist-length ponytail, could easily pass for a Navajo medicine man. In fact, strong evidence suggests that both Tibetans and Navajos emerged from the same genetic and spiritual seedbed.[5]

As chanted prayers began to fill the room, my musings quickened. Tsering, having fed his gods dutifully, was moving into his morning worship routine. After agitating an elaborate silver bell and two-headed drum for several minutes in the direction of the altar, he bent down to light an incense stick.[6] As the smoke streamed lazily toward the ceiling, he cupped his hands reverently toward the idols, prostrated himself and rose again—all the while chanting mantras he hoped would bring him into harmony with the universe.[7]

As Tsering continued his obeisance, I began to feel uncomfortable. Our presence now felt voyeuristic. Although our host had exhibited no shame or embarrassment, I was wondering if we should try to slip quietly out.

Then Tsering's son Tashi, as if he had been reading my mind, poked his head into the room and invited Dick and me to breakfast. His father, we were told, would carry on for another three hours—a daily ritual he had maintained without fail since fleeing Tibet in 1959. Given the anemic prayer lives of most Western Christians, Dick and I felt chastened by what we had seen and heard.

◻   ◻   ◻

Our first stop in Dharamsala was a meeting with Tenzing Atisha, a young and politically savvy environmental desk officer with the Dalai Lama's exile government. After a summary review of our research priorities, Atisha graciously offered to escort us on a private tour of the Tibetan national oracle room at Nechung Monastery. "When we're finished," he added, "I'll give you directions to a cottage above Dharamsala where you can seek an audience with the Ling Rinpoche."

The Ling Rinpoche, I knew, was the recently identified boy many Tibetans believe is the reincarnation of the Dalai Lama's late religious mentor, Kyabje Ling Dorje Chang.

"It's a bit of a climb," continued Atisha, "but well worth the effort. And while you're busy with that, I'll try to ring up one other person you should definitely see before you leave."

No rituals were underway when we entered the national oracle room, but the spiritual oppression within the walls was palpable. This was the place, after all, where Tibetan Buddhist contact with the spirit world reaches official heights. The current medium, or *kuden,* is the thirteenth to serve the Tibetan State Oracle—a territorial spirit that author John Avedon indicates "has been consulted by the nation's leaders on virtually every key decision of state for the past 1,300 years."[8]

The actual event, according to our guide, begins with twenty Nechung monks seated in a circle. Some blow blasts on long cylindrical horns, while others strike brass gongs and lacquered drums. The kuden, riding the sound of the music, goes into a trance and invokes the spirits. As possession occurs, a quiver runs through his body. His breathing becomes labored and his eyes take on a wild, startled look. This is replaced by a piercing, distant stare as he begins to visualize himself as a tutelary deity standing at the center of a celestial mansion. His own consciousness cast aside, he has become Dorje Drakden, the chief spirit minister and bearer of counsel for the State Oracle of Tibet.[9]

"Whenever His Holiness visits Nechung," Atisha told us, "he sits here." He pointed to a sacred perch from which the Dalai Lama whispers secret questions into the ear of the possessed *kuden.* "The lamas and people's deputies consider the oracle infallible. They take by faith whatever he says."

▣   ▣   ▣

Taking leave of Atisha, we headed back up the hill in search of the boy deity. It was, as Atisha had warned, a bit of a climb. The trail to the Ling Rinpoche's residence, also known as the Chopra House, took us past stands of weather-beaten prayer flags and chattering red-faced monkeys that scampered around with furry little ones clinging to their undersides.

At the top Dick and I were met by the Rinpoche's wary caretaker, who explained that the search for the boy had involved divinations performed by the Dalai Lama to determine the location of the rebirth. On the basis of these tests, senior Buddhist officials had been dispatched in 1987 to the village of Bir, where four children born in the specified year and showing positive signs were each presented with several rosaries, one of which had belonged to the Dalai Lama's late mentor.

A solitary child, nineteen-month-old Tenzin Chöpak not only selected the correct rosary but immediately turned 21 beads on it. Then, when he was presented with a tray of sweets, the toddler spontaneously distributed the contents among those present and gave a hand blessing.

Now the young Rinpoche, age seven, was alone inside the Chopra House sitting ramrod-straight. With his shaved head and burgundy robes, he looked like a junior version of the initiate monks who populate all Tibetan monasteries. Dick and I could discern a clue to the boy's unique status, however, in a sprawling collection of toys—supplied entirely by doting pilgrims—that would almost put F. A.O. Schwarz to shame.

He was a precocious lad who seemed willing to assume the role expected of him. When I inquired into the whereabouts of his father, another visitor pointed to the caretaker and exclaimed, "He is the boy's father." Without missing a beat, the Ling Rinpoche snapped back, "He's not my father, he's my servant!"[10]

Back in Dharamsala we learned that Atisha had scored on our next appointment. Tashi Tsering, a brilliant documents specialist with the Library of Tibetan Works and Archives, was waiting to meet us at the Hotel Tibet.

With his long hair and wispy beard, Tashi reminded me of a venerable master of the Shaolin Temple. As I quickly learned, however, this appearance belied a thorough understanding of modern research techniques. Tashi Tsering was a genuine scholar, and his excellent command of English allowed me to delve into early Tibetan history, exploring in particular the influence of a pre-Buddhist religion known as *Bön*. The *bön-po,* as the religion's followers are called, are deeply superstitious and inclined toward magical practices.

So it was eerie, to say the least, to find ourselves plunged into darkness, via power failures, every time we raised a related inquiry. "Perhaps," Tashi suggested, "we can talk further in the morning. If you come by the library, I can give you additional material on Bön, as well as on a derivative Buddhist ritual called *chöd."* Known as the mystic banquet, chöd is a gruesome visualization rite in which practitioners invite demons to feed on their dismembered body parts.

It was, I agreed, a subject that would be better discussed in the morning.

Outside on the street, fluorescent bulbs and kerosene lanterns flickered to life, heralding the arrival of sunset. It was a magical hour in which the sharp lines of the Himalayas dissolved into brooding shades of teal, and the dusky plains, suddenly sprouting countless pinpricks of light, were transformed into a carpet of stars. As the heavenly orbs took their appointed places, Dharamsala was suspended in a kind of middle earth.

This surrealistic setting—embellished with chanting monks, pungent incense and endlessly rotating prayer wheels—reminded me how far I was from home.

Suspension of Belief

October 19, 1993, was a day to remember. Besides marking my fortieth birthday, it was my first full day in the 150-year-old British hill station of Mussoorie. I was back in northern India, and although it had been only eighteen months since my journey to Dharamsala, the memories flooding my mind were from another, far earlier visit to the region.

It had been in this dusty land of idols back in 1962, when I was traveling with my parents, that God first seeded my heart with a passion for the lost—an event that would lead me into a lifetime of service to unreached peoples. This call, though not as dramatic as that experienced by Saul of Tarsus, did come on a highway—a pot-holed ribbon of asphalt between Delhi and Agra.

The heat on that particular day was oppressive. In fact, the only thing that sustained me was the knowledge that our driver had packed a case of Coca-Cola in the trunk. When he finally pulled off the road to open this refreshment, I was ready.

What I was not prepared for were the hordes of Indian children who suddenly appeared, seemingly out of thin air, and began to form a tight semicircle around our open trunk. They were a ragged lot, obviously undernourished and, like me, very thirsty. It was their eyes, however, that got to me—deep brown pools of longing that reflected back an image of a well-fed American boy in freshly pressed light blue shorts and crisscross suspenders. A boy so overwhelmed by the need before him that he never downed a drop of soda.

This 32-year-old memory, more than anything else, had brought me back to petition God for a visitation of grace on this land. My traveling companions were seventeen Christian intercessors from across the United States and Canada. All of them, including my older son, Brendan, were here as active participants in a month-long prayer campaign for the 10/40 Window called "Praying through the Window."[11]

I had included Mussoorie on the itinerary for two reasons. First, the Mansuri Ridge (upon which the community is built) offers an outstanding intercessory vantage point over the rugged Garwhal— a series of shrine-infested valleys that are sometimes referred to as the "Land of the Demons." For anyone interested in praying over the strongholds of northern India, this hilltop platform is hard to beat. At the same time, Mussoorie offered us a chance to meet with Stephen Hishey, a keen Tibetan Christian based in nearby Dehra Dun.[12] I had wanted to interview Stephen for more than two years about an encounter he had reportedly had with a levitating Tibetan oracle.

Our group met Stephen at the Savoy Hotel, an outworn lodging house built by the British in 1902 that once rivaled the famous Raffles Hotel in Singapore. The Savoy's registry is filled with names like Indira Gandhi, Haile Selassie, Queen Mary, Rudyard Kipling, Pearl Buck and Lowell Thomas.

Following Stephen's informative briefing in the hotel lounge, he and I took leave of the team to chat privately. Positioning ourselves on the grass beneath two enormous deodars—trees old enough to have witnessed the entire history of Mussoorie—Stephen began to unfold a fascinating story.[13]

"In our neighborhood," he explained, "a young boy recently became quite ill. His parents took him to several doctors, but none of them seemed able to formulate a workable diagnosis. In fact, the only thing anyone could agree on was the fact that he was dying. Prescribed medications had no effect, and each day the life force seemed to drain from the boy's body. After eight months his parents became desperate.

"One day about this time, my wife and I noticed that a large crowd had gathered around our neighbors' home. We wondered if perhaps it had something to do with the boy. Out of concern and curiosity, we decided to walk over. Working our way through the crowd and peering through the doorway, we saw two Buddhist monks. One was banging on a brass plate, while the other sat cross-legged in front of a small mound of red coals. The latter was a thirty-year-old medium who had been brought in to ascertain the source of the boy's physical problems. We recognized him immediately as a weak-willed monk whose life was a revolving door for demonic spirits.

"Moments after our arrival, this medium became possessed by various spirits, including house gods, that were being invoked by the lama. As the demons settled into his body, we watched in amazement as he plucked a live coal out of the fire and placed it into his mouth. There was a sickening hissing sound as the red-hot ember came in contact with the moist tissue.

"As he chewed on the live coals, the monk suddenly levitated six feet into the air. Still seated in a cross-legged posture, he began to fly in a circular pattern just over the heads of the crowd. As he moved about the room, the people bowed in awe, crying, 'God, god, god.' This lasted for about two minutes before my wife and I, unable to tolerate this perversion any longer, began to invoke the name of Jesus."

Then Stephen showed a hint of a grin.

"Do you know what happened next?" he asked. "The oracle dropped to the floor! After a few moments, the lama asked the medium to explain his sudden and unflattering reintroduction to the law of gravity. As he surveyed the room, the monk's gaze came to rest on my wife and me, standing near the doorway. Pointing a finger in our direction, he exclaimed, 'These are the people.' It was clear to me that this knowledge had been given him by a supernatural power.

"At this point the lama came over and stood directly in front of us. With his hands clasped together, he bowed politely. This was not an act of reverence, mind you, but a gesture beseeching us to go away. And we did. For although our prayers had interrupted the devil's show once, it was obvious the crowd was still in his sway. I have learned that when Satan loses control in one area, he often uses other avenues.

"As we were in the process of leaving, the medium spoke again. This time I heard the spirit exclaim, 'I am going to take life from this family.' Immediately the people began to cry out to the deity. Many of them begged for mercy and forgiveness. While this was taking place, the lama asked the trembling oracle why sickness had come to the family. In an unnatural, guttural voice, the spirit replied, 'Because you have not kept my place holy.' This response was, to us, terribly revealing."

As our conversation drew to a close, I asked Stephen what he knew about the outcome of this bizarre episode. Had the boy's condition improved or were the lamas still laboring to diagnose the malady?

"From what I understand," Stephen replied, "the family was required to make a sacrifice of some kind. Once this obligation was met, the boy emerged from his coma and recovered fully. The medium, however, was another matter. I saw him about three days after this encounter and he looked like a skeleton. It was as if the blood had been drained out of him. He was very, very sick, completely unable to walk. But that's what the spirits do—they drain you."

The Girl Who Married a Snake

Another remarkable encounter with the spirit world was recorded a few years ago by documentary researcher Douchan Gersi. Born in Czechoslovakia during the late 1940s, Gersi moved with his family to southern Africa, where he gained firsthand exposure to the mysteries of the Otherworld. Provoked by his experiences, Gersi spent the next three decades on a global quest for answers. The results of this journey were packaged in a fascinating PBS documentary entitled "Faces in the Smoke."

One of Gersi's investigations took him into the sweaty, secretive world of Haitian voodoo, a world in which driving drumbeats, bloody sacrifices and hidden societies are rooted in the fertile religious soil of West Africa. The animating spirits of Voudon, called *loas* or *guédés,* were carried to the New World originally in the hearts and minds of slaves. In time the myths were contextualized and embellished by local topography and adaptations from Roman Catholicism.

At the top of the Haitian pantheon is Djamballah-Wedo, a spiritual composite of Ayida Wedo the Rainbow and Djamballah the Serpent. The latter is viewed by Haitians as the father of falling waters and reservoir of all spiritual wisdom; and it is his fusion with Ayida Wedo that gives birth to the spirit that animates blood. Every year thousands of Voudon pilgrims are possessed by the spirit of Djamballah the Serpent as they stand in the spray of waterfalls located in Haiti's mountainous interior.

In his best-selling book *The Serpent and the Rainbow,* Harvard-trained ethnobotanist Wade Davis admits that possession is a phenomenon that science can well observe but poorly explain. "For the nonbeliever," he writes, "there is something profoundly disturbing about spirit possession. Its power is raw, immediate, and undeniably real, devastating in a way to those of us who do not know our gods."[14]

It was this kind of raw power that Douchan Gersi encountered when he was granted permission to film a "marriage" between a twenty-year-old Haitian woman named Marie and the great Djam-ballah-Wedo. Gersi noted in retrospect that "as far as possession phenomenon is concerned, her wedding ceremony was perhaps the most impressive and disturbing of all the Voodoo ceremonies I have witnessed." Such marriages, which are based on the same dedicatory principles that might lead a Catholic woman to become a nun, are rare, for the simple reason that marrying a loa requires onerous obligations that few are prepared to assume.

Marie, however, was undeterred. As a nineteen-year-old initiate, she had begun to see a snake in her dreams that obsessed her. When she turned twenty, she dreamed the snake wanted to marry her.[15]

As Gersi positioned his photographic equipment prior to the ceremony, he was joined in the Voudon sanctuary, or *peristyle*, by two highly skeptical American friends—Steven Ball and his former wife, Virginia. Together they watched as two chairs were set near the altar for the intended husband and wife. The audience started drifting in from the surrounding community, and soon the peristyle was filled with the intoxicating resonance of voodoo drums and earthy Creole chanting.

As the ceremony began in earnest, Marie, decked in a colorful dress and large straw hat, paraded about the peristyle with the *houngan* and two *mambo* assistants (the priest and priestesses of the Voudon faith). When the divine bridegroom failed to show after three hours, the houngan sent the mambos to fetch a potent lure. When they returned to the peristyle, one priestess was bearing a bowl of milk, while the other carried a cup of barley syrup and three chicken eggs—a feast no snake could resist for long.

Two more hours passed. Then one elderly, milk-bearing mambo lurched spasmodically into the air as if hit by lightning. Just as suddenly she collapsed to the ground, hissing like a snake, and slithered across the floor with her tongue darting in and out. Moving with remarkable speed, she forced the houngan and the other mambo to retrieve her from the midst of the panicked crowd. As she wriggled in all directions, the serpentine force made it difficult for them to hold onto her body.

"Only five minutes earlier," marveled Gersi, "this old woman had barely enough strength to carry her own tired body. Now she wasn't even a woman, but a snake moving with a woman's body."

Finally subduing her, the houngan and his assistant placed the old woman—the manifestation of Djamballah-Wedo—next to the bride-to-be. The possessed mambo was calmed down considerably but continued to hiss and flick her tongue. Both parties now faced the altar, where a civic representative was waiting to preside over the exchange of vows. (Astonishing as it seems, the local legal system actually recognizes these mystic marriages.) Holding the incarnation of Djamballah-Wedo by the hand, Marie looked every bit the enraptured bride.

Besides obligating Marie to promise obedience and fidelity, the official wedding contract required her to give herself to her husband every Thursday for 24 hours. This yielding of body and soul was to be accomplished in a specially dedicated room within her house. Djamballah-Wedo's part of the bargain: to assure Marie's protection and secure practical provision for her everyday life.

Many Westerners scoff at such ideas, but one French businessman has adopted a more sober view. His story, which Gersi recorded in Paris, came spilling out after a screening of Gersi's documentary on voodoo.

The man, a frequent traveler to Haiti, had persuaded a young maid on duty at his hotel, through great persistence and the lure of a considerable sum of money, to share his bed. On returning to France, however, he began to experience nightmares in which he was attacked by a man with a serpent's head. These nightmares not only persisted but were compounded by a series of misfortunes in the real world. Within a few days the man lost his job, saw his wife leave for another suitor, and experienced a variety of health-related problems, including a nervous breakdown. At no time did the Frenchman connect these problems with his earlier infidelity in Haiti.

One month later, however, he had a new nightmare in which the maid herself appeared behind the protective stance of the serpent-headed figure. With nothing to lose, the businessman decided to go back to Haiti and try to clear up the matter.

The former maid had been released from her hotel job because of a health problem. But after several days of searching, the Frenchman finally located the girl and learned she was married to the great spirit Djamballah-Wedo. Having resolved her own difficulties through a series of purification rituals, she agreed to direct her erstwhile lover to a powerful houngan who could exorcise his troubling spirits. Submitting to this spiritual shell game, the Frenchman saw his wife, job and health restored as quickly as they had been removed.[16]

Pete Gray Eyes and the Owls

The first time I heard Pete Gray Eyes' story was during an April 1992 visit to Tom and Betty Dologhan's lovely, cabin-like home in Flagstaff, Arizona. Leaning across the dinner table, Tom held my wife, Lisa, and me spellbound with a remarkable narrative that included human "shapeshifters,"[17] talking owls, paralytic curses and supernatural deliverances. I had never heard anything like it before. And were it not for Tom's well-deserved reputation as a man of integrity, and his thirty years at the helm of the Navajo Gospel Mission, it would have been easy to dismiss the entire account.

Five months later Tom made arrangements for me to meet Pete Gray Eyes face to face. At NGM headquarters he introduced me to Mike Hendricks, an experienced mission worker who would drive me out to Pete's hogan in the rugged Navajo mountain area.

Our first objective out on the reservation, although it was getting late in the evening, was to rendezvous with the third member of our team, Navajo Alliance pastor Robert Dayzie. A long-time friend of both Mike and NGM, he had agreed to serve as our local guide and interpreter.

Robert's church was situated in a small box canyon carved out of hundred-foot brown sandstone cliffs. Although they were difficult to see at night, I could feel their presence.

After being ushered into a small room that served as the Dayzies' kitchen, sleeping quarters and living room, I was questioned by five Navajo Christians who had gathered to hear about our mission. When I explained that the research would provide Anglo believers with a better understanding of the spiritual dimension, they nodded approvingly. Bolstered by an assortment of high-calorie refreshments, we spent the next three hours exploring the touchy subject of Navajo witchcraft. It was a disturbing discussion, especially revelations about a shapeshifting cult known as "skinwalkers."

By seven the next morning Mike, Robert and I were off to find Pete Gray Eyes. The scenery was magnificent. Great vistas replete with multi-hued buttes and mesas opened up around every bend. The scent of sage and juniper filled the vehicle through my open window. Overhead a squadron of hawks, unfettered by gravity, described majestic circles in the air.

Around 8:30 A.M. we arrived at Pete Gray Eyes' hogan. It was a resourceful home site. Nearly all the gnarled branches of nearby piñon trees had been converted into makeshift shelves accommodating a collection of fiber ropes, tin cans, rubber tubes and wooden boxes. One box, suspended just out of the reach of wild animals, contained chunks of chewy-looking cornbread and sheep fat from a recent butchering. During the winter, Robert explained, the box served as an inexpensive refrigerator. A sheepskin was drying on the roof of the octagonal hogan, along with blue corn and apricots.

After exchanging greetings in Navajo, Pete, a small, handsome man in his early seventies, invited us to gather under his *cha ha óoh*, or shade house. Well-preserved except for some missing front teeth, and sporting a long, gray braid and baseball cap, he had a storytelling face and lively, blue-gray eyes. His frequent gestures revealed dark, weathered hands and a silver watchband embellished with two turquoise horseshoes.

For the next 45 minutes or so, while Mike, Robert and I listened, Pete unfolded his story in characteristically clipped Navajo phrases. Listening to him speak, I could understand why this peculiar assemblage of sounds so bedeviled enemy code-breakers during the last World War. But Robert, wearing his translator's hat, had no such difficulty. Absorbing the story impassively, he interrupted only rarely with what I assumed were clarifying questions. Finally, after what seemed an eternity, he leaned forward to translate.[18]

"In the early 1970s," he related, "Pete was doing traditional medicine work on the reservation. His healing ministry was so effective that he began to draw business away from some of the other medicine men. Out of spite, they decided to cast an evil spell on his family. To do this, they bundled up some of Pete's personal effects with baling wire and buried them as witchcraft fetishes.[19]

"About that time, Pete and his wife became seriously ill. Her symptoms included blood clots, lung lesions and partial paralysis, while

Pete contracted painful sores in his throat. In addition to their physical problems, the Gray Eyes also lost seventy goats to coyotes, and watched their sheep corral catch fire spontaneously and burn halfway to the ground. All the while, Pete and his wife were tormented by a flock of owls that loitered at night outside their hospital window and around their hogan."

The owl, I knew, is a notorious messenger of death and darkness. Owls reportedly screeched before the deaths of Julius Caesar and the emperor Augustus. Even then the bird was associated with witchcraft. In Scotland the owl has long been known as the "night hag" and the "corpse bird."[20] Much of this historical uneasiness is undoubtedly due to the creature's nocturnal habits, mournful cry and semi-human face. But the Navajos have an added concern. They believe the owl is a favored form assumed by members of the demonically empowered skinwalker cult.

"When Pete couldn't cure his wife," Robert continued, "he turned to other medicine men. Most of them operated out of the Paiute Mesa area. They performed many ceremonies, but none of them produced any results.[21] With growing concern, Pete extended his search for help into the Hopi reservation, and finally into the Kayenta area. Some of these medicine men were able to retrieve the buried witchcraft bundle, but his wife continued to deteriorate. As a last resort, Pete took her to the hospital in Tuba City. Unfortunately, this also proved fruitless.

"By now Pete had begun to despair. It got to the point where he just wanted to get drunk and drive off a cliff, which he saw as preferable to the agony of these spells. The owls that were flocking around his hogan at night began speaking to the family. They screeched obscenities and taunted, 'These people are going to die. These people are going to die.'

"In fact, death did come to their home. One of their daughters, thirty-year-old Lina, passed away here."

"Was her death linked to the curse?" I asked quietly.

Robert nodded. "She got sick and died very quickly. To this day Pete doesn't know what the illness was.

"One night in the wintertime, things got really bad. The dogs started barking as if someone were outside, but when Pete went to look around, no one was there. Then the coyotes started howling and the owls began screeching their death threats. Mrs. Gray Eyes' condition became so desperate that Pete called the Adventist hospital near Monument Valley to pick her up in a helicopter. From there she was transferred to Fort Defiance, and finally to see specialists in Albuquerque.

"Fortunately, Pete's wife came in contact with some Christians who began to intercede on her behalf. As a consequence of this prayer support, her condition improved, to the extent that she was allowed to return to Paiute Mesa. The bad news was, dark forces were still bewitching their home site.

"About this time the Gray Eyes met an itinerant Navajo evangelist named Herman Williams. After a few months of visitation, they decided to attend one of his camp meetings. There the entire family came under the conviction of the Holy Spirit and gave their lives to Christ. When the service ended, Pete asked what he should do about all the commotion still plaguing his household. Brother Williams responded that he should just preach to those owls."

An interesting piece of advice. But what did it mean?

⊡   ⊡   ⊡

A few months after my encounter with Pete Gray Eyes, I decided to contact Herman Williams, the Navajo evangelist, to get his perspective on this amazing story. After twice missing him at his home in Tuba City, we finally connected by phone in June 1994. Herman was able, as I had hoped, to add rich detail to the account.

"We first visited Pete's home around 1974," he began. "His wife was still quite ill at the time, but being traditionalists, they never told us exactly what was wrong. She would get up and make us coffee, while Pete just sat there not saying much. Still, we came around every month or so to see how they were doing. Mostly we prayed and read the Word. We also talked to them about the Great Medicine Man who has great powers—greater than all the medicine men on the reservation. Speaking to them in Indian terms, I said, 'Jesus can be your Chief, and also your Great Medicine Man.' That's the way I put it.

"A few weeks later, on a Sunday night, we were winding down a long service at the Navajo Mountain Alliance Church. It was almost 11:30 P.M. when, lo and behold, Pete and his whole family walked into the meeting. Since there were no other seats left, the ushers escorted them up to the front row. I had nearly completed my message and was in a bit of a quandary over what to do. Finally I decided to read the message over again briefly, then give an invitation. To my surprise, Pete and his whole family stood up. Our womenfolk took Pete's wife and the girls to one room, while the elders counseled with Pete.

"When they returned to the sanctuary, I asked Pete, 'Can you tell us what happened tonight?' Taking the microphone, he said, 'You people all know me. I've been a medicine man for many years. I've gone to many homes and doctored their families. But lately my family has been suffering. I've realized that I need the Great Physician, the Great Chief. For this reason my family and I have come tonight—to dedicate our lives to the Lord.'

"Hearing this, I tell you, the people began to celebrate and praise the Lord! After everyone was dismissed, Pete asked if he could come over to the parsonage for a little while. When we sat down, he shared with me that for many months he had been visited by owls that spoke to him in Navajo saying, 'We are going to kill you.' This occurred not only with the owls, but also with coyotes. It is very possible that skinwalkers were tormenting the family.

"Pete said to me, 'I know when we go home tonight, those owls are going to be there. What can I do?' So I thought a while. Finally I said, 'You go right back and speak to them. Give them your testimony. Tell them what happened to you tonight.' Pete and I looked at each other, nodded, and then he left.

"When they arrived back at their hogan, sure enough, the owls were sitting in the trees—a bunch of them. So Pete stepped out of his pickup and said, 'Hey, you owl people, we've got some good news to tell you. This evening we went to church and heard about the Great Chief. And I'll have you know that we have all given our lives to this Great Chief. We belong to Him now. I have given up my medicine bag. I'm not going to do that anymore.'

"Then Pete proceeded to outline the specific boundaries of his property that were being dedicated to the Lord. The way it sounded, he must have talked a whole hour or so to those owls, explaining that his land, grass, hogan, family, sheep, cats and dogs had all been given to the Lord. When he completed his list, Pete told the owls directly, 'You have no business here. Every one of you must leave and never come back—in the name of the Great Chief, Jesus Christ.'

"After he said this, Pete told me he couldn't hear a thing. It was completely silent. Then all of a sudden, high in the tree, he heard an owl take flight. And then another, until they had all gone. To this day they have never returned.

"Shortly after this, two things happened. First, the sores and paralysis that had been plaguing Pete and his wife vanished completely. This was something our elders had prayed for fervently, and it was quite dramatic to witness the symptoms disappear.[22]

"The second shoe in this amazing story dropped when the medicine men who had bewitched Pete's family all died! After this," Herman concluded, "divine fear struck the area. People streamed forward day and night to get saved. I strongly believe these developments marked the beginning of the great Navajo revival."

Sticks and Stones *Will* Hurt You

In the early afternoon of January 11, 1982, four Hopi Indian men walked into the Smithsonian Museum of Natural History in Washington, D.C. Shortly afterward, according to *Science* magazine reporter Jake Page,

> The Hopi were met by Associate Curator of North American Ethnology William Merrill and escorted to the fourth floor where a nondescript door was unlocked. At the flick of a switch, fluorescent lights revealed nearly endless racks of earthenware pots and a row of cabinets . . . bearing names of Indian tribes from every corner of North America. The racks and cabinets housed the Smithsonian's Indian artifacts, collected mostly around the turn of the century.

For nearly a thousand years, the Hopi have lived atop sun-scorched mesas in what is now northeastern Arizona. In this arid realm that Page calls "a cruel patchwork of sandtraps," Hopi farmers have developed elaborate and productive techniques of dry farming. At the core of their interventionist philosophy, however, lies an ardent belief that the surrounding environment can be controlled through ritual and ceremony.

For the Hopi, few things are taken more seriously than the business of summoning rain. The ceremonies provide high drama, and every other year during the month of August, visitors from around the world gather to watch painted members of the tribe's Antelope and Snake Societies engage in what the U.S. Bureau of Indian Affairs once called "a loathsome practice."

Filing into the dusty plazas of Oraibi, Hotevilla or Walpi, two dozen dancers break the anticipatory silence with resonant and mesmerizing stomping. Once they are fully entranced, the performers squat in front of an evergreen shelter, or *kisi*, to pick up their sacred cargo. As the audience gasps nervously, clan members return to the ritual circle with rattlesnakes and other serpents clenched firmly in their teeth.

The Hopi also call on a panoply of spirits, called *kachinas*, to bring rain. Increasingly familiar to tourists as elaborately hand-carved dolls, the kachinas are actually part of a highly complex religious construct in which they appear alternately as divine intermediaries, the spirits of Hopi ancestors, or the vapor emitted by water on a cold morning. Although the kachinas dwell six months out of the year on the San Francisco Peaks that tower over the nearby town of Flagstaff, they spend the rest of their time on the Hopi mesas where, embodied in masked dancers, they descend into sacred plazas and *kivas* (underground ceremonial chambers) like a swarm of bees.

But the Hopis' survival, like that of all Indian tribes, also depends to a considerable degree on decisions made in Washington.

The four Hopi visitors to the Museum of Natural History—including a young clan priest and a recently elected tribal chairman, Ivan Sidney—were visiting the nation's capital to see various officials. About 4:00 P.M., however, the delegation spilled out of the Smithsonian into the freezing January winds—"badly shaken," according to Page. Just prior to their abrupt departure from the fourth-floor storage room, the Hopis had seen a drawer full of elongate witchcraft fetishes.

"These," explained Sidney to associate curator Merrill, "were used to do bad things." Drawing back a few paces, he added: "They should never have been made, [and] they shouldn't be in this city."

Adding to the Hopis' concern was a bulbous-eyed, black kachina mask wrapped in a clear plastic bag. Shaking their heads, they requested that the bag be opened so the mask could "breathe." As Merrill obliged, the tribal chairman, a former police chief at home with sophisticated anti-crime technology, issued a warning. With the kachina mask's long pent-up energies now released, he said, there would be a tremendous rain or snowstorm in Washington. It was nothing to fool with.

Then the Hopi, extremely uneasy, decided to cut their trip short by two days. "Something bad," they said, "is going to happen in this city."

In fact, Page relates in his *Science* magazine article, the delegation

> left in a heavy snowstorm, taking the city's Metro to the airport since surface traffic was at a near standstill. Twenty minutes after they passed underground near the Natural History Museum, another Metro train derailed there. When they arrived at National Airport, it had just been closed down: An Air Florida jet had taken off and crashed into the 14th Street Bridge, plunging into the ice-bound Potomac River.[23]

My own brush with the power of Hopi ritual objects came in the spring of 1992. Having read a good deal about the tribe and their kachinas, I decided to record some observations firsthand. My initial destination for this field work was the ancient village of Walpi perched atop the western edge of the First Mesa in Arizona. The climb up was steep and hot, and I was glad to reach the welcoming shade of the community center.

Because their colorful rituals have attracted so many tourists, the Hopi have been forced to post signs asking visitors not to pilfer religious articles. Not only do the Indians object to their space being turned into an exotic flea market, but they are acutely aware of the supernatural forces associated with these items. Unfortunately, many sticky-fingered tourists are not so illumined. I noticed a letter to this effect pinned to a community center bulletin board. The short, hand-scrawled note had been sent to the tribe accompanied by a stolen prayer stick.[24] The writer explained that his life had been visited by a series of catastrophes almost from the moment he took possession of the illicit item, and it ended with a desperate apology.[25]

I had been warned by a Taos-Kiowa Indian, Wendell Tsoodle, about another object to be avoided—the "trip stick." Wendell, a former medicine man, was well acquainted with these potent bundles that are stuffed into the rafters of Hopi dwellings as protection against foreign intrusion.

"Be sure to plead Jesus' blood," he admonished me as I left his suburban Albuquerque home for the Hopi mesas.

Whether it was a chink in my spiritual armor or merely a viral coincidence, two days after visiting Walpi I found myself in the emergency room of St. Joseph's Hospital in Phoenix. In the middle of a miserable night, doctors hooked me up to an IV in order to replace fluids I had lost during a violent bout of vomiting.

◻   ◻   ◻

Another incident illustrating this kind of object-related spiritual power took place in Apache, Oklahoma, in the spring of 1983. James and Judy Goombi's three children, looking for something to do, began rummaging through a box of memorabilia they discovered packed away in an outdoor storage shed. Fascinated by a collection of old photos depicting their grandparents' involvement with traditional Indian medicine ways, the children brought the entire box—which their mother had inherited from her deceased father—into the house. Afterward it was placed in a bedroom closet and promptly forgotten.

A few nights later, the Goombis' three-year-old son Jason wandered into the master bedroom. "There was a man in my door," he said, "but he just disappeared."

Chalking this up to youthful imagination, the Goombis responded by tucking the little fellow back into bed. But when he returned later in the night with the same report, he was allowed to bunk down with his parents.

Fifteen-year-old Melissa was also having difficulty sleeping. In an attempt to relieve her fitfulness through a change of location, she shifted quietly into her brother's empty bedroom. Once again, bad dreams took over, and on awakening from one of them, she was startled to see an old Indian man with long, gray hair standing over her. Too afraid to scream, she pulled the covers over her head and prayed. As she did so, the old man vanished.

When Melissa reported her experiences the next morning, the Goombis began to suspect something out of the ordinary. James was forced to abandon the mystery until after work, but Judy faced no such constraints. Something had violated the sanctity of her home, and she wanted desperately to know who or what it was. Mulling the events of the previous night over in her mind, she suddenly remembered the memorabilia box. Pulling it out of the closet, she began to pick through its sentimental treasures—until she spied something that made her heart skip. It was no larger than a silver dollar, but Judy recognized it immediately as her father's medicine bundle. She also remembered that it was meant to be passed on to her son Jason.

Realizing that evil spirits were trying to extend their foothold into the next generation, Judy swung into action. She asked her brother, Essie, and his wife, Phyllis, to join her in a vacant field, where they built a fire to destroy the medicine bundle. But as the smoke spiraled into the sky, it released one final spasm of hate. In a scene worthy of the late Alfred Hitchcock, scores of scissortail birds suddenly swooped out of the sky and began attacking the group, until the last of the bundle had been consumed.

The scissortail, it turned out, was the father's medicine bird.[26]

Strong evidence suggests that the potency of certain ritual objects is linked to empowerment rites in which designers and owners invoke the presence of relevant spirits.[27] Zuni Indians, for example, hold an annual "Council of the Fetishes" in which gathered tribal fetishes are worshiped and energized by special night chants and offerings of prayer-meal.[28] In New Ireland, a thin, zucchini-shaped island off the northeast coast of Papua New Guinea, spiritual artisans service the elaborate funerary festivals of the culture by manufacturing wood carvings known as *malagans*. Once completed, the malagans are arranged in a display house behind a screen made of coconut leaves. There the carvers begin a chant that will attract a supernatural presence into the figures. Once this is accomplished—and until such time as they are destroyed—the malagans are considered dangerous.[29]

A similar process is followed in the fashioning of the *kris*—an embellished, wavy-bladed dagger found throughout southeast Asia.

According to Sutikno Timur, a practitioner of traditional magic in East Java, the power of the dagger depends on the *empu,* or craftsman. Declares renowned artisan K. R. T. Hardjonagoro: "You can't make a kris with your eyes. You must create a link with the person who orders it." You need spiritual strength to fill the kris with balancing forces. The purpose is to pass on this power to the person who will own it. True artisans are said to take the blade red-hot in their fingers from the forge. The pressure helps form the design and adds to the aura of the talisman.[30]

In some instances, the power of ritual objects seems to accumulate over time. One expert who believes this is Dr. Yoshihiro Tanaka, founder and president of the Nagoya-based Matsuri Society, an organization that facilitates the study of Japanese religious festivals. "In many cases," Tanaka told me, "folk objects have special powers that do not exist in the same objects in their newer forms."[31]

Another Asian scholar sees a direct correlation between sacred objects and protective deities. Mina Tulku, who serves as curator of Bhutan's fortress-like National Museum, laid out his thoughts on the subject in May 1992 when I visited his poorly lit office in Paro.

I knew that his title of *tulku* designated him the reincarnation of a high lama, but his rotund frame and jovial countenance reminded me more of a Buddhist Friar Tuck. During the course of our conversation, Mina Tulku mentioned that while religious law permitted him to marry, he had elected to remain single so as not to expose others to the hazards of his job. When I looked at him quizzically, he went on to explain that, as curator, he was responsible to determine the history of artifacts offered to the museum. Since many items originated from sites like temples and monasteries that are under the dominion of guardian deities, the evaluative process requires great care. Assuming custody of objects that have been stolen or otherwise wrongfully obtained, he explained, could be fatal.[32]

A sobering confirmation of Mina Tulku's point is provided in Mickey Hart's recent book, *Drumming at the Edge of Magic.* A longtime percussionist with the famed rock band The Grateful Dead, Hart is also a drum collector whom his New Age comrades often think of when they browse through markets and curio shops overseas.

A few years ago one of these friends set a little skull drum in front of Mickey. "It's called a *damaru*," he said. "It's a power drum. Only the most enlightened lamas have them. I just had to buy it for you."

"I set the skull drum on the table," Hart recalls, "and felt a kind of creepy fascination."

After playing his macabre instrument for fifteen minutes or so, he placed it back on the shelf and then promptly threw up.

> I had no reason to associate my nausea with the *damaru*. But I soon began bumping into things, falling down when I shouldn't have, injuring myself in minor but annoying ways; it gradually felt as if everything in my life was starting to unravel. It was only after several weeks of such uncharacteristic misfortune that I suddenly remembered the odd little Tibetan drum that [my friend] had given me. *It's a power drum!*

When Hart tried playing the drum again, he felt so awful that he telephoned psychologist Stanley Krippner and asked him to examine it. Krippner acknowledged its obvious potency but declined to pursue further studies.[33] Then Hart phoned bandmate Phil Lesh, who agreed to take the drum off his hands. But before long he, too, experienced the object's malevolent effect. Two weeks later he phoned back frantically: "Mickey! I want you to come over and get this drum right now. I don't want it here another minute."

The two bandmates finally resolved their dilemma by driving down to Berkeley to meet with Tarthang Tulku, a senior lama in town to dedicate a new Tibetan Buddhist center. When the musicians handed the power-imbued crania to the diminutive Tibetan, he looked at the drum and whispered, "So you've come home at last." Then, turning to his guests, he said, "I hope you have been most careful, Mickey Hart. This is a drum of great, great power. It wakes the dead, you know."

"Not long after this," Mickey wrote in his book, "I drove my car over a cliff. It snagged on a tree halfway down, saving my life, but not all my bones."[34]

Something Is Out There

There is something profoundly disquieting about the prospect of a world riddled with haunted drums, levitating monks, cursing owls, serpent marriages and mountain spirits. Most of us would prefer to dismiss such things out of hand—and we likely would do so, were it not for those nagging, half-suppressed doubts we carry around. *After all,* our inner voice whispers, *what if the tale is true?*

Sometimes these suspicions are pulled to the surface in spite of our sensible, linear-thinking belief systems. This, at any rate, is what happened to *Newsweek* commentator Dan Greenburg. In a June 1976 article, Greenburg described a series of encounters with forces he could not explain away—encounters that tempered his open mockery of the occult. Greenburg insisted in his article that he had "come too far and seen too much" to go back to his comfortable old beliefs.[35]

British writer Harold Owen also talks about brushing up against the supernatural in his three-volume autobiography, *Journey from Obscurity.* During childhood his elder brother, the famed World War I–era poet Wilfred Owen, amused himself by asking the younger children to wait in dark rooms while he disguised himself in a sheet and descended on them with a shaded candle. This was frightening enough, but a trifle compared to an incident that took place during one of these games on a dark upstairs landing:

> It was when I was halfway along the tiny passage that I became petrified, standing where I was with one foot off the ground. An unseen thing was there; something . . . so utterly unphysical and unheard of and, with my awareness of the uncanny, so terribly, terribly dangerous, that I felt with clear and absolute knowledge that here was something far beyond any nonsense of Wilfred's. . . . It was as if I had plunged out of this world.[36]

To those who are not expecting them—and even to some who are—encounters with the world next door can be nerve-rattling. Describing a dream in which he was visited by a spirit, one of Job's comforters declared:

> "Now a word was brought to me stealthily, my ear received the whisper of it. Amid thoughts from visions of the night, when deep sleep falls on men, dread came upon me, and trembling, which made all my bones shake. A spirit glided past my face; the hair of my flesh stood up."
>
> Job 4:12–15, RSV

The power around spiritual doorways—be they temples, caves or magic markets—is especially palpable. During a May 1993 visit to the Bahadur Saeed shrine in Varanasi, India, I was riveted by the raw intensity surrounding dozens of female supplicants, most of whom were inviting spirit possession by swaying back and forth, their braided hair loosened and describing circles in the air. As the trance state became fully developed, previously attractive faces contorted, eyes rolled back into sockets and bodies began to slither across the tiled courtyard like hungry serpents.

Missionaries and anthropologists have observed similar scenes in literally every corner of human society.[37]

On occasion the spiritual energy has even been known to affect electronic equipment. After making a movie in Indonesia, filmmaker Eros Djarot recounted to *Asiaweek* correspondent Keith Loveard the details of just such an incident:

> While the crew was shooting a scene in a graveyard, their camera wouldn't work. They tried a new one, then another. Back in their hotel, they could find nothing wrong with the cameras. Finally, a village elder explained that the spirits of the graveyard had to be mollified with whiskey, rice and a chicken. After the offering was made, filming went ahead without a hitch.[38]

This problem, according to Douchan Gersi, the documentary film producer, is common to sacred sites and supernatural feats. "[The phenomenon] is strange, mysterious and powerful," he concludes. "Something that defies all scientific logic."[39]

It is the quest of this book to try to define this disturbing "something" that causes us to turn on the porch light of our souls. Are we dealing merely with charlatans and large-scale hallucinations? Or, as C. S. Lewis seems to suggest in his *Chronicles of Narnia,* do wardrobe passageways to other dimensions actually exist? And if the latter prove real, what role, if any, do we play in the world next door?

Such questions are not new, of course. Variations on this theme, as we will discover shortly, have dominated human thought and discourse from the dawn of time. This is because there is an innate sense in each of us that we are not fully of this world; that our origin and destiny are linked to a realm that is perceived only dimly. We want to go home but are not entirely sure how to get there.

The other issue is safety. If we do find our way into the world next door, what adversaries or obstacles might we encounter there? How will we recognize them? Avoid them? Fight them? Do any maps exist that can help us navigate the mysterious labyrinth that men and women call the spiritual dimension?

Part One

Under the Overworld

Illuminations from the Basement of Reality

Chapter Two

Navigating the Labyrinth

alk of passageways and quests and the mind inevitably conjures images of intrepid adventurers probing their way through a vexing maze. For centuries these mysterious, convoluted realms have commanded the attention of kings, pilgrims and recreationalists alike. Monarchs found the inherently confusing nature of the labyrinth useful for hiding councils and protecting tombs. Penitents sometimes took ritual journeys through churchyard labyrinths in lieu of pilgrimages to distant shrines. Hobbyists saw the maze as a puzzle to be solved, either by negotiating their way to the center and back, or by locating the shortest route between entrance and goal.[1]

While the modern labyrinth is almost always a garden maze of paths bounded by hedges, in classical times it was a structure, at least partly underground, of intentionally perplexing architecture. The Egyptian labyrinth at Crocodilopolis, for example, contained three thousand chambers, half of which were subterranean. It was here, according to the Greek historian Herodotus, that sacred crocodiles guarded the tombs of the kings. Even more famous was the labyrinth at Knossos on the island of Crete. Purported to be the haunt of the legendary Minotaur—a half-man, half-bull creature that consumed human sacrifices—the actual labyrinth was more likely a rambling palace or grotto attended by masked Minoan priests.[2] Other architectural labyrinths have been found in Roman, Celtic and Asian settings.

The labyrinth expressed symbolically through paint, carving and dance presents even more interpretive options. Spirals, for example, are widely seen as the body of the Earth Mother. The Hopi Indians link the symbol to their kivas, the womblike sanctuaries out of which they believe their nation emerged.

The builders of the ancient Maltese temple complex at Tarxien evidently saw things much the same way. In the view of feminist art historian Elinor Gadon, a labyrinthine, underground sanctuary known as the Hypogeum served as "the womb and the place of burial where the dead returned to the Mother."[3] Similar interpretations have been found at sites from Central America to Siberia.

The most universal definition given to the labyrinthine form, however, is that of a symbolic journey into the Otherworld. It is a passage millions have taken and countless more are working up the courage to attempt. Their goal, of course, is paradise. Unfortunately, paradise is situated in the midst of an unfamiliar realm in which getting lost is a distinct possibility. It can be a wearing and perilous pilgrimage that, in the end, holds no guarantees. The hub of this elaborate and confounding web may, according to ancient traditions, host not paradise but a devouring spider.

A Conversation in Marrakech

For most of my life, the question of *how* I might go about navigating the Byzantine realm of the Otherworld was buried under a stack of what I considered far more salient questions. Why, for example, would I would want to bother investigating its secrets in the first place? What exactly would I be trying to find? And what destination would I be trying to reach?

Not until the summer of 1990 did I come to understand why I needed to probe the heart of the labyrinth. When the unexpected revelation arrived, I was sipping tea on the Tichka Hotel patio in Marrakech, Morocco.

Marrakech, situated on the Haouz Plain under the High Atlas Mountains, is a city whose Moorish architecture, snake charmers and elaborate fantasias[4] remind first-time visitors that they have journeyed well beyond Palm Springs or the Italian Riviera. As the undisputed heart of Morocco's deep south, Marrakech has become a gathering place of disparate centuries, cultures and races, a red clay citadel whose combined verve and mystery remain unparalleled throughout North Africa.

I had not sat down to tea alone. Seated in the chair across from me was a young tentmaker missionary I had met previously in the United States. Greg (not his real name) had been serving in Morocco for several years.

In the course of our time together, Greg bared his soul. After nearly seven years of ministry, most of them in the Berber-dominated highlands of Morocco, he had yet to see any fruit. Assuming that his calling obligated him to more than mere attempts at disciple-making, he was left deeply frustrated and confused by his apparent lack of evangelistic success. As far as commitment, training and integrity were concerned, Greg was a class act. Besides being an all-around nice guy, he was cross-culturally savvy and linguistically proficient—the very characteristics that generally make a successful missionary. I knew we were missing something—but what?

I heard myself giving Greg the standard line from Ephesians 6 about the futility of wrestling with flesh and blood. All appeared to be well on the natural plane in terms of his training and commitment, but I reminded him that a fierce battle was raging in the spiritual realm. He was up against personalities without bodies, invisible forces that had burrowed deep into the prevailing culture and that opposed his mission bitterly.

As I paused to let these words sink in, a strange thing happened: The message suddenly reversed direction and penetrated my own spirit. In that special and slightly uncanny moment, I caught my first glimpse into the awesome import of the labyrinth.

That night, and for many nights to follow, I reflected on my own experiences accumulated over decades of worldwide travel. Like a bleary-eyed patron at a movie marathon, I sat mesmerized by countless long-forgotten scenes projected onto the screen of my memory. The details—which in some instances included vivid smells, textures and feelings—were phenomenal. Only in the exquisitely engineered human mind is it possible to hear the bark of a dog long dead or relive the terrifying sensation of being a child lost in an amusement park. No other device can recover both the events themselves and our intimate responses to them.

My season of mental globetrotting made one thing crystal-clear: Greg's experience was anything but unique. In virtually every corner of the world there are certain neighborhoods, cities, cultures and nations that embrace more idolatry, manifest greater spiritual oppression and exhibit more resistance to Gospel light. This much is observation. The real question is, Why?

Certain travelers have described instances in which the prevailing spiritual atmosphere changed one way or the other at the very instant they crossed a particular territorial threshold.[5] Richard Cavendish, referring to the dark side of this phenomenon, speaks of an "atmosphere of appalling menace which often clings to a place and impresses itself on strangers who know nothing of its history."[6]

Dr. Gary Kinnaman documented such an experience after visiting a three-hundred-year-old Massachusetts bed-and-breakfast with his wife a few autumns back. Despite being welcomed into a home that was decorated gorgeously with period antiques, Kinnaman reported that "the feeling inside was almost more oppressive than I could bear." Although no ghosts or demons actually materialized during their brief stay, the Kinnamans left with a conviction that "there was an unmistakable spiritual presence in that home."[7]

While this kind of anecdotal evidence gives weight to the proposition that spiritual darkness is palpable and geographically concentrated, it is not as helpful in offering a rationale for the phenomenon. Once again we are left to ask, Why are things the way they are?

The variations on this basic inquiry are virtually endless. Why, for example, is the island nation of Haiti the premier social and economic eyesore in the Western hemisphere? Why do the Andean nations consistently rank as global leaders in per capita homicide rates? Why has Japan remained such a thorny challenge for Christian evangelists? Why is there so much overt demonic activity in and around the Himalayan Mountains? Why has Mesopotamia put out such a long string of tyrannical rulers?

While obvious sociopolitical factors must be considered, any investigation limited to this arena is certain to leave some vexing loose ends.[8]

In the months that followed my conversation with Greg in Marrakech, I decided to recast and tighten my core question. The updated version asked, *Why does spiritual darkness linger where it does?* I was convinced that this profoundly simple inquiry possessed universal relevance. And while I recognized that it would consume my attention, I did not realize how radically that single question—which, once asked, begged for answers—would alter my own vision and career.

I was comfortable with the prospect of international travel but less certain about navigating the labyrinth. This was a realm that tested veterans, and I was an amateur. Inside the maze, few things are as they appear; and since I had little desire to traverse the twisting diversions of the dark side, I knew I needed some kind of map, and preferably a guide, to keep me on track.

The Descending Staircase

A few weeks after my visit to Morocco, my wife, Lisa, and I checked into an idyllic Welsh bed-and-breakfast for some much-needed recuperation. What we got was a dose of Murphy's Law. In the wee hours of the morning, we were abruptly roused from sleep by the voice of a BBC newsman booming out of a preset radio alarm on our nightstand. As I groped to shut off the radio and restore the peace, my senses were reignited by the news: The Iraqi military had mounted a full-scale invasion of Kuwait. Saddam Hussein had just played the first hand in what was to become an extraordinary round of high-stakes poker—one that would illustrate just how many false entrances the labyrinth can present.

As the months wore on, a steady flow of allied troops and materiel into the region suggested that the United Nations, and George Bush in particular, were prepared to call Saddam's bluff. By the end of 1990, heavily loaded military transports were swarming over the Arabian Peninsula like a plague of apocalyptic locusts. And with each successive touchdown, the world inched closer to the "Mother of All Battles."

Western television networks covered the buildup with an intensity normally reserved for the Super Bowl or Academy Awards. The entire afffair took on a surreal quality. For the first time in history, television viewers could toss some popcorn into the microwave, pull out their easy chairs and settle down to watch a war.

It was more than macabre voyeurism. Most viewers, especially in America, watched because they had a vested interest. These were not scenes, after all, generated by television actors or nameless foreign participants. Intimate friends and family stood in harm's way, and every community was anxious to rally around.

Recognizing the exceptional level of personal interest, the major networks scrambled to feed the public hunger for detail. In addition to hiring ranks of expert commentators, several broadcasters transformed their studios into elaborate walk-in maps of the Persian Gulf. Standing inside these battlefield mockups, military savants like ABC's Tony Cordesman helped viewers visualize the evolving conflict by maneuvering electronically superimposed icons of war.

Eventually the networks decided to supplement these lessons on military strategy and tactics with commentary on Middle Eastern politics. Provided mostly by academics and retired politicians, the message was simple. Troop buildups and border incursions, viewed outside the larger context of regional politics, would remain as enigmatic as they were disconcerting. If we wanted to comprehend the Arabian battlefield, we would have to look beneath the immediate dust and din.

A third wave of scholars soon joined the fray to argue that since politics are nourished by historical roots, the only way to understand the Gulf tensions was to descend into the annals of the past. It was a persuasive assertion that would go virtually unchallenged— at least for a week or so. By then a fresh set of network experts came forward to insist that local history and politics were merely the offspring of prevailing cultural values.

Put on the move again, the truth-seeking public would eventually encounter a final group of sages who maintained that authentic understanding lay deeper still. From their perspective, the real bottom line was etched deeply in the region's all-pervasive religion. It was Islam, and Islam alone, that offered the Rosetta stone to decipher the mystery of the Iraqi conflict.

Listening to these urgent and contradictory voices in the months prior to the Gulf War—taking us from military strategy and Middle East politics to history, culture and religion—I began to wonder if anyone really knew where this descending staircase led. Was there, in fact, an ultimate basement of reality?

Once again I found my thoughts drifting back to the labyrinth. But instead of wondering about some mysterious center, now I was asking where I needed to go in order to get to the bottom of things. Either way, I realized, it was a matter of locating the source, or origin, of what *is*—the terminus where one discovers why things are the way they are.

The majority of Christians has long seen this basement of reality as synonymous with the spiritual dimension or supernatural world. And judging by the amount of time we spend talking, singing and reading about this realm in which we say reality is rooted, one would expect its labyrinthine passages to be as familiar to average believers as the sea is to mariners. Unfortunately, confident observations on the location and characteristics of the Otherworld are surprisingly hard to come by.

Western Christianity and the Supernatural

The late Dr. Francis Schaeffer presented a pleasant exception to this trend in his 1972 book, *Genesis in Space and Time.* As he saw it, the supernatural world is the intriguing half of the universe, one that stands "not somewhere far off, but immediately before us almost as a fourth dimension." To Schaeffer, this fact carries significant implications. Not only does humanity live in the fold of the supernatural realm, he believed, but there is "a cause-and-effect relationship between it and our own visible world at every existential moment."[9]

C. S. Lewis saw things much the same way. To him the supernatural, far from being "remote and abstruse," was a matter of daily and hourly experience, a present realm "as intimate as breathing."[10]

If these thinkers are correct, it means the danger and beauty of the spiritual dimension are always immanent, lying just above, below, beyond or within the immediate center of the present moment. We can no more escape this fact than we can turn ourselves inside out, and our only rational response is to commit more time to learning the lay of the labyrinth. If we are diligent in this pursuit, the resulting knowledge can provide a powerful paradigm for interpreting events and priorities in the material world.

But not everyone is prepared to accept Schaeffer's premise that a cause-and-effect connection exists between the spiritual dimension and our daily lives. And many who *are* willing to admit as much see the relationship as abstract and removed, one in which a deterministic and primitive Sovereign does little more than maintain life support.

In fact, despite protestations to the contrary, the worldview of most Western Christians is more rationalistic than spiritual. We suspect what we cannot see and verify empirically, which is why many churchgoers prefer to deal with their deity (if they believe in one) through text and form. Most view intimate dialogue and other forms of sensory contact with the supernatural as wishful or superstitious behavior.[11]

A person's prevailing worldview—which Fuller Seminary professor Charles Kraft defines as the "culturally structured assumptions, values, and commitments underlying a people's perception of REALITY"—is more influential than theology in determining his or her perception of ultimate reality. Why? Because, according to Kraft, not only are we taught to view reality in socially prescribed ways, but we are "constantly under pressure from the other members of our society to maintain those perspectives."[12]

The effect of this pressure was demonstrated in experiments begun in the 1960s by Columbia University scientist Eric Kandel. When the siphon of an Aplysia, a sea snail, was tapped, the creature withdrew its gill automatically. But if the tapping continued, the reflex weakened slowly until the mollusk ignored the stimulus altogether. This phenomenon, called habituation, resembles the ability of the human being to adapt to traffic noise[13] or, in terms of worldview, of the Western Church to accommodate to rationalism.

We have been desensitized in our intuitive responses to supernatural stimuli by the drumbeat of socially correct science. As Walter Wink put it in *Review & Expositor,* "The more ably clergy are educated, the more likely they are to be enculturated into reductionistic scientific attitudes and to ignore their own tradition."[14] The Acts of the Apostles has given way to the Enlightenment.

It is with no small measure of consternation, then, that these same Western clergy have found themselves lately engulfed in reports (most with origins in the developing world) suggesting that supernatural forces may be on the prowl after all. Rather than process these tidings as confirmation of biblical teaching, many see them as a direct threat to their rationalist assumptions. Some leaders have gone so far as to muzzle veteran missionaries until their claims of supernatural occurrences can be substantiated with *prima facie* evidence.

Such responses are not merely cautionary but frank disbelief— and the disbelief is telling. As C. S. Lewis remarked, "The mind which asks for a non-miraculous Christianity is a mind in the process of relapsing from Christianity into mere 'religion.'"[15]

One of the most notable of today's "doubting Thomases" is anti-charismatic flame thrower John MacArthur Jr. While insisting he is "not by nature a skeptic" and "by no means one of those whom C. S. Lewis called 'naturalists'" (people who assume miracles cannot happen), MacArthur's book *Charismatic Chaos* reads like the latest issue of *Skeptical Inquirer.* In an effort to validate his contention that reports of modern-day miracles are unreliable and ephemeral, MacArthur refers to the fleshly nonsense promoted by some charismatics and to what he considers a lack of documentation. "The truth is," he proclaims with an air of decisive finality, "those who claim miracles today are not able to substantiate their claims."[16]

After citing several contemporary signs and wonders reported by John Wimber and Dr. C. Peter Wagner, MacArthur declares:

> Frankly, I find all those accounts preposterous. It is difficult to resist the conclusion that they are either utter fabrications or yarns that have grown with the telling. . . . Those who are credulous about claims of modern miracles—especially those who are the most zealous defenders of contemporary signs and wonders—often seem reluctant to deal with the possibility, or rather the likelihood, that those marvels may actually be authenticating a diabolical variety of "revelation."[17]

Responding to this kind of cynicism, theological writer Paul Thigpen notes that people are more often accurate about the things they affirm than the things they deny. This is because affirmations are often based on what we have experienced ourselves, while denial typically accompanies what we have not experienced. "In short," Thigpen explains, "we tend to measure life's possibilities by our own limited experience . . . [something that] is nowhere more obvious than in the matter of spiritual gifts and the miracles they accomplish."[18]

Inherent in all worldviews, including MacArthur's, is the assumption that our way of seeing the world is right. But we act not according to the way things are, but according to how we expect them to be, believe them to be, imagine them to be. The hazard, as Winkie Pratney points out in *Healing the Land,* is that "with the right facts and a false premise, you can for all the right reasons come to the wrong conclusion. And you may never even know why you are wrong."[19]

Several years ago my editor, Jane Campbell, shared a memorable anecdote about faulty perspective. Attending *The Marriage of Figaro* at New York's Metropolitan Opera, she found herself seated in the alpine "Family Circle" section where opera glasses are more a necessity than a status symbol. As the lights lowered, she eased the mini-binoculars out of their case and endeavored to focus on the distant stage. For several frustrating moments, the performers remained undefined phantasms trapped in a blurry twilight zone. Finally, realizing the show was going on without her, Jane decided to perform a quick equipment check. Then she noticed, with some chagrin, that she had been looking through the wrong end of the glasses.

Could it be that Western Christianity has likewise been viewing reality through the wrong end of the interpretive lens? Some leaders think the answer is a resounding *yes.* They argue that, like the blind men and the elephant, we have been dealing with the right facts from the wrong premise.

One of the voices urging recovery of a biblical view of the spiritual dimension is Anglican theologian Michael Green. A former professor of evangelism and New Testament at Regent College in Vancouver, British Columbia, Green sees the Western Church as

> preoccupied with its own survival, its petty concerns, its tradition, its canons and its revised worship books—or else coming out with dicta about many of the contemporary problems of our society without getting to the heart of the matter. It scratches at the spots caused by measles without getting down to the disease itself.[20]

Green's is not the only voice on the subject, nor the first. "Back in 1951," he notes, "Professor James Stewart made a plea in the *Scottish Journal of Theology* for a recovery of the dimension of the cosmic battle in our theology." According to Green,

He concludes this short but important article by pointing out that our real battle is not "with Communism or Caesarism, but with the invisible realm where sinister forces stand flaming and fanatic against the rule of Christ."[21]

Some of Green's strongest support, surprisingly, comes from the ranks of evangelical liberals. In *The New Face of Evangelicalism,* for example, Rene Padilla writes of the need to "understand man's situation in the world in terms of enslavement to a spiritual realm from which he must be liberated."[22] To Walter Wink it is a matter "of formulating a new paradigm of reality . . . capable of integrating nonreductionistic science with the actual spiritual experiences of people."[23]

This missing paradigm is also the focal point of an astute article by Trinity Evangelical Divinity School professor Paul Hiebert entitled "The Flaw of the Excluded Middle." In it Hiebert observes that the worldview of most non-Westerners is three-tiered: the cosmic, transcendent world on top; a middle layer featuring supernatural forces on earth; and the empirical world of our senses resting comfortably on the bottom. He concludes the article by exploring the unique tendency of Western society to ignore the reality of the middle zone, an all-important crossover realm that hosts such phenomena as magic and witchcraft, territorial deities and divine signs and wonders.[24]

I encounter this myopia frequently. During a July 1994 interview with the Dutch TV network Evangelische Omroep, I was asked if I could offer scriptural justification for Christian involvement in what has become known as spiritual warfare. Although the question was asked without hostility, it struck me as odd—a revelation, perhaps, of just how far Western Christianity has drifted from the worldview of our biblical forefathers. Human involvement in the cosmic battle is a deep presumption of Scripture. From Genesis to Revelation, no other alternative is even hinted at.

It is helpful in this regard to recall the context in which many of the biblical authors contributed their inspired thoughts. Moses, we are told, "was educated in all the wisdom of the Egyptians" (Acts 7:22),[25] a schooling that presumably would have included exposure to the solar mysteries and to the worship rites associated with Osiris and the satanic prototype deity Seth. Daniel as a young man was tutored by Ashpenaz in "the language and literature of the Babylonians" (Daniel 1:4), an education designed to prepare him for service in one of the most notoriously idolatrous regimes in history. The apostle Paul, on his missionary journeys throughout Asia Minor, was addressed by superstitious philosophers in Athens, practicing sorcerers in Cyprus and Philippi, and rabid goddess worshipers in Ephesus.[26]

Even in these oppressive, supernaturally charged settings, God's sovereign hand of blessing rested on these men. Daniel was accorded the ability to "understand visions and dreams of all kinds" and Nebuchadnezzar found him "ten times better than all the magicians and enchanters in his whole kingdom" (Daniel 1:17, 20). Moses was empowered to perform "miraculous signs and wonders," some of which the local magicians were unable to duplicate "by their secret arts" (Exodus 7:11; 8:18). Paul was involved in numerous extraordinary miracles, ranging from the resuscitation of Eutychus to the infliction of temporary blindness on Elymas the sorcerer.[27]

We see further evidence of human interaction with the spiritual dimension in Elijah's power encounter with the prophets of Baal, the apostle Philip's supernatural teleportation to Azotus, and Ezekiel's dramatic description of the glory of God departing from Jerusalem escorted by multi-faced cherubim and whirling chrysolite wheels.[28] In fact, points out Oscar Cullmann, superhuman forces of some sort are mentioned in almost every place in the Bible where Christ's complete Lordship is discussed.[29]

The ancients' preoccupation with the demonic has been cited by both Michael Green and Heinrich Schlier. In his book *Principalities and Powers,* for example, Schlier catalogs the vast number of names used by the New Testament writers to describe this infernal pantheon. Among the more notable appellations: principalities, powers, thrones, dominions *(kuriotetes),* lords, princes *(archontes),* gods, angels, spirits, unclean spirits, wicked spirits and elemental spirits *(stoicheia).* These are in addition to the many synonyms for Satan himself. "In some way," Schlier adds, "revelation absorbed these phenomena from the tradition of universal human experience."[30]

Frog Eyes and Flatlanders

In the modern world, of course, assumptions have changed. Having escaped the influence of planets, the gods and evil spirits, we have turned to the religion of science. It is science, Kraft notes, that gives us control over the material world, which has become the central focus of our lives.[31] In such a world, data reigns as king; logic is the prevailing creed; and what we cannot explain, we dismiss with euphemisms.

So conditioned are we by scientific rules of rational evidence that we presume to say, with remarkably close-minded certainty, that we should ignore particular recurring phenomena because they are impossible. Yet, as Philip Slater observes in *The Wayward Gate,* "Never, since science first began to enforce its rule that certain kinds of events must not be treated as real, have there been so many challenges to that rule."[32]

Investigations into black holes and other oddities of the universe are edging science toward ideas that considerably overlap the psychic—and spiritual—realm. Accompanying each new revelation is, in Slater's words, "a growing sense of urgency about the tininess of the small corner of reality we're aware of—a sense of how little we see and hear and know, and how vast the dimensions."[33]

Human sensory experience occurs in a universe of four dimensions: length, width, height (or depth) and time.[34] Scientists suspect, however, on the basis of mathematical calculations, that the universe contains ten dimensions. Beyond the observable four in which we live are six additional theoretical dimensions that physicist Michio Kaku calls hyperspace.[35] The word *hyperspace* means "over, above or beyond the present dimension." If these "higher" dimensions actually exist, the implications are potentially mind-boggling. Among other things, UFOs and time travel would no longer be confined to the realm of science fiction. Any being that was able to harness the six extra dimensions of hyperspace would find it an easy task to move in and out of conventional space-time, while earthbound observers would find such actions nothing short of miraculous.

This is because the concept of higher dimensions is so wickedly difficult to comprehend. As Christian apologist Brooks Alexander observes, "We can't conceive of something we can't experience (or extrapolate *from* experience)."[36] The only way of envisioning interventions from hyperspace, Alexander believes, is to imagine how we would interact with a world of *fewer* dimensions than our own.

It was just this line of reasoning that prompted nineteenth-century British novelist Edwin Abbott to introduce his famed two-dimensional world called Flatland—a realm, as its name suggests, where there is no up or down.[37] Its flatter-than-pancake inhabitants, appearing in two-dimensional shapes like squares, triangles and circles, are incapable of visualizing height. Imagine the astonishment resulting from the passage of a three-dimensional object through their level plane, or even from the simple act of lifting one of their inhabitants up and placing him or her down somewhere else.

They would consider both of these events supernatural. In the latter instance, the Flatlander "disappeared" and then, just as suddenly, "rematerialized." In the former instance, the mysterious object, appearing as if from nowhere, changed in form from moment to moment (or at each point along its trajectory). The three-dimensional form would occur in Flatland not as a thing, but as a process.

The Flatlanders' experience, which Alexander sees as analogous to the recent rash of UFO sightings, "is completely and authentically tangible within the realm of the observers . . . but it is also inexplicable in that realm."[38] Limited by their perspective, lower-dimensional creatures are left to draw conclusions about higher reality from incomplete and transient clues. Clues in the scriptural record might include the radiance on Moses' face after he spoke with God (Exodus 34:29–35), the transfiguration of Christ (Matthew 17:1–9) and Jesus' ability to pass through walls after His resurrection (John 20:19, 26; see also Luke 24:37). Unfortunately, these momentary traces reveal frustratingly little about the world that has left them.

Higher-dimensional beings, on the other hand, are in a position to observe lower realms in an unhindered and absolute manner. Coupled with their superior perspective is their ability to manipulate virtually at will. The options, which are many, include violating the lower dimension's laws of cause and effect, invading and inhabiting familiar images and intervening in the vulnerable inner lives of its inhabitants.[39]

These options contain obvious potential to deceive, but the deception need not be exercised. Most Christians would argue that God Himself has adopted these techniques without malice in our present world. The calming of a Galilean storm, the incarnation of Christ and the conviction of the Holy Spirit are all examples.

Far from denying "supernatural" intervention, then, science's own thesis—the existence of higher dimensions—offers a platform for its confirmation.[40] Even previously-snickered-at concepts such as omnipresence are being retrieved by science from the "mythological" domain.

The contemporary term for this godlike characteristic is *nonlocality*, a concept rooted in the strange but exhaustively tested theory at the heart of modern physics known as quantum mechanics. Every unit of matter or energy, according to the conventional interpretation of this theory, exists alternately in wave and particle form. Matter and energy, as particles, behave more or less like little billiard balls. But in a wave state, things get bizarre. Here each bit of matter or energy is considered to exist simultaneously in a virtually infinite number of locations. Weirder still, scientists proclaim that it is the act of human observation that somehow causes the quantum mechanical wave to collapse, thereby allowing matter and energy to revert to the particle state.

If you find this perplexing, you are not alone. As science editor David Freedman notes, "The question of exactly how observation causes matter and energy to make the transition from wave weirdness to well-behaved particle is one that most physicists don't even ask."[41]

Current physics is, at best, a strained way of describing reality. Many things implicit in human experience we miss altogether. The fact is, as William Poundstone points out in *Labyrinths of Reason,* "There are things going on out there that we will never appreciate."[42] And in this respect, our limited vision is almost froglike.

Robert Ornstein cites research on the eye of the frog showing that it discards all except four available stimuli: fixed contrasts delineating the general shape of the environment; sudden moving outlines; abrupt decreases in light; and small, dark objects close to the eye. Except for these bits of information that help the frog stay alive, it is blind as a bat.

And so, in many respects, are we. The difference between us and the frog is only a matter of degree. We see a tiny fragment of reality—one that allows us to master our physical environment—and little more. What we mean by "reality" is not what exists, but merely what we need.[43] The question, in the words of Isaac Asimov, is this: "How far are our assumptions justified, and to what extent are they merely careless, or self-serving, misinterpretations of reality?"[44]

The relevance of this question first surfaced in my own mind during an in-studio radio interview in the early 1990s. My host was a popular figure at a large Christian station in southern California. Despite his success on the air, he was depressingly cynical in private. When a commercial break interrupted our conversation about contemporary supernatural phenomena, he leaned back in his chair, removed his headphones and shook his head. "I just don't know," he said disbelievingly. "I just don't know." After pausing for a long moment, I replied: "It's all right not to know something. But the real question is, How badly do you want to find out?"

Like Elisha's servant in Dothan (2 Kings 6:8–18), Western Christianity has clung to its millpond discriminations of reality so tenaciously that it has nearly lost all ability to recognize the spiritual dimension. To quote William Irwin Thompson:

> We are like flies crawling across the ceiling of the Sistine Chapel: we cannot see what angels and gods lie underneath the threshold of our perceptions. We do not live in reality; we live in our paradigms, our habituated perceptions, our illusions. . . .[45]

Considering the hour, this is a dangerous flaw—perhaps fatal. Merely acknowledging our blindness, however, is not enough. We must go on to personalize the cry of Elisha: "O Lord, open our eyes so we may see."

Demon Theory No. 16

Having examined what the labyrinth is, and why it merits investigation, we are left with one more preliminary question: How do we go about navigating this extraordinary realm? Some philosophers insist the goal is hidden in the journey itself. So Cathy Johnson seems to suggest in her contemplative book *On Becoming Lost: A Naturalist's Search for Meaning:*

> There is an art to wandering. If I have a destination, a plan—an objective—I've lost the ability to find serendipity. I've become too focused, too single-minded. I am on a quest, not a ramble. I search for the Holy Grail of particularity and miss the chalice freely offered, filled and overflowing.[46]

Nothing is more paralyzing, on the other hand, than limitless possibility. As Poundstone warns thoughtfully: "In an infinite maze, one cannot afford to wander aimlessly through parts unknown."[47]

Not only are there places in the spiritual labyrinth that ought not to be visited, but such wandering is highly inefficient. Venturing up alleys merely to see if they are blind is scattershot research. If we are going to do it, we should at least be aware of its limitations.

To illustrate, philosopher of science Hilary Putnam offers his own tongue-in-cheek "demon theory." The theory (really a hypothesis) is this: A demon will appear before your eyes if you put a flour bag on your head and rap a table sixteen times in quick succession. Putnam calls this Demon Theory No. 16. Demon Theory No. 17 is the same, except there have to be seventeen raps, and so on. There is an infinite list of demon theories.[48]

Putnam's point, of course, is that researchers must be selective about the theories they quarry. It is possible to spend one's entire life digging into implausible theories and get nowhere. The trick is to winnow out the "possibly true" hypotheses from those not worth bothering with. If science and elements of Western Christianity are misled in their wholesale distrust of the supernatural, others err in their wholesale appropriation of it. This is particularly true of certain charismatics and "demon chasers" who all too often define the modern spiritual warfare movement.

A fourteenth-century Franciscan monk named William of Okham offered what may be the best tool for slashing away at the abstract "realities" propounded by gullible individuals. His principle, known as "Okham's Razor," states: "Entities are not to be multiplied beyond necessity." In other words, the simplest explanation that accords with the evidence is usually the best. We should not resort to new assumptions or hypotheses except when necessary.

"If," writes Poundstone, "a footprint in the snow *might* be explained by a bear, and *might* be explained by a previously undiscovered manlike creature, the bear hypothesis is favored." This is not simply a matter of choosing the less sensational explanation. "One favors bears over abominable snowmen only when the evidence (such as a half-melted footprint) is so deficient that both the bear and the yeti theory account for it equally well."[49]

Sometimes the best alternative *is* sensational. UFO landings, for example, offered a more plausible explanation at one time for Britain's mysterious crop circles than an opposing theory that vast herds of hedgehogs had trampled them out.[50] But Okham's Razor is not infallible. Sometimes the principle discounts hypotheses that appear extravagant but are correct nevertheless. Misplaced skepticism in the past, for example, has diverted attention from realities like the true shape of the earth and the role of microorganisms in causing disease. Keeping an open mind, therefore, is something we must learn to do, for while extraordinary claims require extraordinary proof, sometimes the evidence we seek is nestled right under our noses. As Sherlock Holmes observed, "There is nothing more deceptive than an obvious fact."

More Questions for the Quest

Open-mindedness is not the only requisite for successful exploration. We also need guidance—in the form of maps and clues, or else an experienced escort.

In the Tudor and Stuart eras, British garden maze designers often incorporated a key or clandestinely marked clues, so that the initiated could find their way in and out without difficulty. The initiated in this case were kings and aristocrats who sought to avoid getting dangerously lost within their own hedges.

Navigating a spiritual labyrinth is, of course, a far more serious undertaking. It is probed not for sport but to gain a balanced picture of reality. Getting lost is easy. Not only is the terrain unfamiliar, but it is haunted by forces intent on distracting human travelers from their mission.

But the risks are proportionate to the potential reward, and it is comforting to know that God has left a friendly trail of clues to direct us through the labyrinth's myriad nodes and branches. That He would do this is evidence of both His justice and His great affection for truth-seekers.

Despite God's benevolent intent, however, navigational success requires our cooperation. Many of the hints He has strewn along our pathway are discernible only as we stay observant and inquiring. But even these traits will not lead us home. For while clues to spiritual realities may be discovered by honest inquiry, they become valuable only when they are interpreted by the Holy Spirit. He alone illumines to us that magnificent guidebook to the spiritual dimension known as the Bible.

The primary purpose of our investigative journey, once again, is to gather intelligence for the spiritual battle described in 2 Corinthians 10:3–5 and Ephesians 6:12. If we accept the biblical premise that the battle is real, we must also accept that our adversary is authentic. And as every successful businessman, coach, politician or military commander understands, we ignore our competition at our own peril.

One would think the majority of Christians would know in both theory and practice what the apostle Paul was talking about when he spoke of the battle being waged against spiritual hosts of wickedness in the heavenly places. Unfortunately, this is not the case. For many believers, the concept of "heavenly places" is an abstraction that ranks somewhere between gravity and the ozone layer.

Paul speaks of "the heavenlies," according to Michael Green, not merely as the dwelling place of God, but as the surroundings of the material world. It is a place, according to this more expansive definition, that encompasses "the abode both of the principalities and powers (Eph. 6:12) and of the God who in Christ exercises his reign over them (Eph. 1:20)."[51] And here we arrive at a critical point. Since God is a primary inhabitant of the spiritual dimension, any investigation that fails to consider His attributes, intentions and actions is grossly deficient. Confining ourselves to the dark side of the labyrinth will guarantee an unbalanced picture of reality.

Reflecting the nature of its dual tenants, the labyrinth is both luminous and shadowy. The devil and his minions have had their lease canceled, but full eviction has not yet occurred. Their influence over men and women remains strong and malevolent. It is in the twilight where the children of light and the forces of darkness share a common terrain. It is also the realm in which the godly in Christ are called to battle.

As we enter the twilight passages of the labyrinth, our quest to solve one of the great puzzles of life begins. Why spiritual darkness lingers where it does is no shallow mystery. But we have not been left to our own devices. In the next six chapters of this section, we will examine some of the broken twigs and arrows in the dust that point to the heart of the labyrinth. Careful readers will discover these clues in the form of heights, imaginations, gateways, rebellions, traumas, pacts, traditions, festivals and technology. Each of these signal themes comes with its own steamer trunk of revelations, and those patient enough to unpack them in proper order will find their way.

As we begin our journey, our initial action will be to consider the evidence for an objective devil and any master plan that might lie behind human suffering, worldviews, mythological motifs and religious systems.

Chapter Three

Faces of the Dragon

Over the centuries, popular opinion about the devil has shifted nearly as steadily as the undulating dunes of the Sahara Desert. At one moment he looms as a fiend of dark and terrible power, while in the next he is transformed into a buffoon. Still other times he is perceived only as the contrivance of a fearful imagination.

To those who consider Satan a tangible danger to be reckoned with, he and his retinue are everywhere active. Capable of causing untold mental and physical harm, they are seen to take possession of their victims not only through transgressions and explicit pacts, but by stealthy entry through unguarded physical orifices. This has led some societies to view yawning, sneezing and other, more private activities as occasions for concern. Nor do worries stop with what might come *in.* Germans and Transylvanians in earlier days shared the belief that it was dangerous even to sleep with one's mouth open. They feared the sleeper's soul might escape, in the form of a mouse, through the open mouth and be harmed on its travels.[1]

The ancient Mesopotamians were among the first to perceive malevolent spirits as ubiquitous. In addition to Lamashu, the dreaded she-spirit that threatened women in childbirth and stole infants from the breast, there was Namtaru, the dreaded plague demon. There was also Rabisu, the Croucher, who lurked in door-ways and dark corners, and his opposite, the evil *utukku* demon, who haunted open spaces.[2]

In later centuries the evil one attracted a host of popular nicknames, some of which have carried over into the modern era: Black Bogey, Old Hairy, Gentleman Jack, Lusty Dick, Old Gooseberry, Old Horny, the

Good Fellow, Old Nick and Old Scratch. These appellations, for all their whimsy, seem to have served a purpose. As Jeffrey Burton Russell, history professor at the University of California at Santa Barbara, points out, "Giving the Evil One an absurd name was a popular antidote to the terror he struck."[3]

In more recent years, however, the devil's credibility has taken a beating. In the words of Walter Wink, "Demons, in polite society, are simply 'out.'"[4] Debunked by rationalists, exorcised by psychotherapists and demythologized by theologians, the devil is no longer the chief suspect behind much of the mischief that goes on in contemporary society. As Robert Frost wrote of Satan: ". . . Church neglect and figurative use have pretty well reduced him to a shadow of himself."[5]

In the headlong rush to relegate the devil to metaphor and euphemism, secular skeptics have often found themselves taking a back seat to Judeo-Christian clergy. In the words of one American Catholic scholar, "No up-to-date theologian believes that Satan is a person."[6] To George MacRae, a Bible scholar at Harvard Divinity School, "The Old Testament simply does not contain a personal Devil who is the principle of evil and God's adversary."[7] Echoing this observation, Rabbi Menachem Brayer declares bluntly, "There is no such thing as a Satanic force."[8]

Positioned as we are, in Walter Wink's words, between the rock of rejection and the hard place of hysteria,[9] it is increasingly difficult to locate the demonic on our current world or mental maps. The question is, What are we left with when we abandon the extremes of rejection and hysteria?

Most people, despite the encroachments of liberal theology, still think of darkness as more than the absence of light. They see it as something malevolent, active and often palpable. In 1972 Pope Paul VI referred to demons as "the invisible presence of an obscure enemy," an evil that is "not only a spiritual deficiency, but an efficiency. A live spiritual being that is both perverted and perverter; a terrible reality, mysterious and fearful."[10]

Others, while prepared to acknowledge Satan's dark presence in the world, are persuaded that Christians either need not, or should not, spend their time bothering with him.

The problem with this, of course, is that the Scriptures *do* bother with him. Presented as "the god of this world," the devil and his entourage figure in the New Testament nearly twice as often as the Holy Spirit.[11] And as well-known University of Chicago researcher Andrew Greeley cautions, "If Satan is still in business, then it behooves us to be prepared to greet him with proper respect. . . ."[12]

Winged Luminosity

Although the prospect of mistaking the identity of the evil one would seem rather high, suggestions to this effect are often greeted with a knowing smile. According to those who have had flagrant dealings with him, he is not a being one has difficulty recognizing the second time around. In the early fourteenth century, for example, a Cistercian brother (named, ironically, Adam) met the devil near Chevreuse, France. Not only did the adversary give off "a stench of corruption," but his eyes reportedly gleamed "like polished copper cauldrons." St. Theresa of Ávila, after an encounter with the evil one, added that "a great flame seemed to issue from his body." During Martin Luther's ten months at Wartburg Castle, the monk experienced continual poltergeist phenomena and heard Satan grunting audibly like a pig.[13]

While it would be easy, and certainly desirable, to dismiss these stories as the products of overburdened minds, their sheer numbers make this considerably more difficult. What is more, the descriptions of suspect and scene are chillingly consistent: a hideous or lecherous countenance, the rotting odor of death, a suffocating sense of oppression. There is also the terror that arises from the knowledge that one has attracted the attention of a supernatural psychopath.

But as disturbing and widespread as these incidents are, they do not tell the whole story. Many souls have, for whatever reasons, encountered the devil without a hint of the mortal danger that stood before them. This is testimony, of course, to Satan's well-known but rarely discerned ability to appear as an angel of light (see 2 Corinthians 11:14).[14]

Aside from the nasty descriptions mentioned above, two of the most common features associated with the devil and his demons might be expected of fallen angels: wings and a luminous countenance. And although these characteristics are often construed to be part of a diabolical disguise, they are more likely genuine endowments. If we accept that the devil employs deceptive devices primarily to cover his allegiance and intent, it follows that he can masquerade as an angel of light while at the same time *being* one.[15]

At least one Old Testament passage seems to indicate Lucifer may have served at one time as heaven's appointed guardian cherub, or "light-bearer," on the earth. As the presumed subject of Ezekiel 28:11–15, he was, we are told, a "model of perfection . . . in Eden, the garden of God." Verse 14 informs us he was "anointed as a guardian cherub." The name *Lucifer* in Hebrew is *Helel ben-Shahar,* or "day star, son of the dawn" (see Isaiah 14:12). The morning star was identified in the ancient world as male and called, in Latin, *Lucifer.*[16]

Given the passages in John's Gospel presenting Satan as the prince of this world,[17] Francis Schaeffer wondered if he occupied this role "prior to man's revolt or even prior to man's creation."[18] This was the view favored by C. S. Lewis, who in his famous space trilogy imagined each planet ruled by a powerful angel called an Oyarsa. Earth itself has fallen under the power of a "bent Oyarsa," or an evil *archon.*

But this angle raises questions of its own. If Lucifer did inhabit Eden when he was "the model of perfection" (Ezekiel 28:12) and "blameless in [his] ways" (verse 15), what prompted his fall? Moreover, if this fall occurred after he walked in Eden, why is he portrayed in Scripture as falling from heaven (see Isaiah 14:12; Luke 10:18)?

The typical response to the first question—What prompted Lucifer's fall?—centers on his jealousy[19] over man's unique nature and the special attention Adam elicited from God. Jealousy, in turn, led to prideful comparisons and exalted thoughts—and the rest, as they say, is history. As to the second question—How could Lucifer have fallen from heaven if he rebelled on earth?—the leading theory is that Lucifer, as an appointed cherub, traveled the dimensional highway between heaven and earth routinely. His initial sin may have taken place on earth, but his rebellion was eventually carried to heaven, whence he was ejected along with one-third of the angelic host.

Did Lucifer inhabit Eden prior to his fall from heaven? The specifics are conjecture, but the hypothesis is supported by generous evidence.[20]

Insofar as Lucifer's angelic form is concerned, it is worth noting that history, both ancient and contemporary, is punctuated with examples of human interaction with luminous beings. One early incident involved Manes, the founder of the Manichaean religion that once attracted St. Augustine. At twelve years of age, Manes reportedly received a revelation from an angel dispatched by the King of the Gardens of Light. Other examples of luminous beings are Mithra, a deity extolled in the Zoroastrian scriptures as the god of heavenly light, and the legions of heavenly light beings described in the sacred writings of the Mandeans.[21]

The radiant, diaphanous spirits that inhabit the experiences of many near-death survivors are also referred to typically as "light beings." In his book *Fire in the Head,* author Tom Cowan points out that shamans tend to have at least a few helping spirits composed of light or brilliant colors. He writes about an Irish mystic interviewed in the early twentieth century who claimed to be able to distinguish various orders of light beings: "those which are shining, and those which are opalescent and seem lit up by a light within themselves."[22]

Then there is the widespread "earth lights" phenomenon that offers a striking correspondence to angelic encounters documented in Scripture. In describing the arrival of divine beings over Babylonia, for example, the prophet Ezekiel refers to "an immense cloud . . . surrounded by brilliant light." Emerging from the core of this brilliance, which Ezekiel suggests resembled "glowing metal," the creatures themselves "sped back and forth like flashes of lightning." As if this were not enough, the prophet concludes his "close encounter" report with the disclosure that each creature was accompanied by gyroscopic-type wheels whose "rims [are] high and awesome."[23]

Here we must consider the disturbing possibility, bolstered by both Scripture and human experience, that fallen angels are capable of emulating the appearance and performance of their divine counterparts.[24] If true, this means that the devil's potential to deceive is considerable. It also means that, for our own good, we really ought to break the habit of equating luminosity with goodwill.

In his 1926 novel *Under Satan's Sun,* French author Georges Bernanos wrote of a lonely but spiritually devoted vicar named Donissan. Finding himself hopelessly lost one night on a country road, the priest encounters a pleasant little man who offers to help him. As they journey together, the good fellow's sympathy and insight eventually bring him into Donissan's confidence. At the same time, he drops hints, purposefully or otherwise, as to his real identity: He lives "nowhere," he is "married to misery" and he interrupts with a particularly obnoxious laugh. It gradually dawns on the pious Donissan who his new friend really is, and the diminutive man reveals at last the strange and terrible truth: "I am Lucifer, the light-bearer—but the essence of my light is an intolerable coldness."[25]

The words, despite their fictional origin, are insightful. Cold light, or luminescence, is borrowed light, the afterglow of energy absorbed from a radiant source. The frigidity of the evil one is a mark of his solitariness, a sad revelation of just how far he has fallen from the incandescent presence of his Maker. Lucifer, the bearer of light, has become Satan, the prince of darkness.

But despite his tragic and sordid circumstances, the enemy is still a versatile creature. There is nothing, so far as we know, that limits him or his followers to the guise of a little man or even a glowing specter. Author Michael Harner, after journeying into the Otherworld with shamans in the Amazon, reveals that he met hideous beings who threatened him and claimed to be the "true masters of the world." They appeared, according to Harner, as "large, shiny, black creatures with stubby pterodactyl-like wings. . . ."[26] To the Araucanian Indians of central Chile, Harner's description might fit the demon Pihuecheyi, a dreaded, winged snake with a vampire's taste for blood.

While they are not always this hideous, demonic spirits and protective deities have appeared in winged form almost from the beginning of recorded history. In early Mesopotamia and Persia, winged gods and genies were depicted routinely on pottery and bas-relief, and as the forbidding stone guardians of temple portals. Many Asian cultures have long associated the flying serpent or dragon with power, wealth and esoteric knowledge.[27] Ditto the Hindu and Buddhist deity Garuda. As the golden-feathered sun bird of heaven, he is considered the embodiment of air and a dominator of earthly snake energies.[28]

The Bejeweled Guardian

According to international folklore and religious tradition, spiritual forces are typically associated with animals. Satan himself is often seen as a horned goat, although his most common image is that of a dragon or serpent. Fearful and mysterious, the serpent is respected above all other beasts for its ability to move quickly and silently between various realms.[29]

The Bible, too, identifies Satan with the dragon-serpent (see Job 26:12; Psalm 74:13; Revelation 12–13; 20:2). Passages about the titanic strength of Leviathan have been cited consistently as descriptions of the devil. Martin Luther, for example, drew inspiration from Job 41:33–34 when he penned some of the original words to "A Mighty Fortress Is Our God":

> Upon earth there is not his like, a creature without fear.
> He beholds everything that is high; he is king over all
> the sons of pride.

The harmony between biblical images and religious folklore is, in some cases, striking. Take, for example, the depiction in Ezekiel 1:17 of the four-faced cherubim whose attendant wheels moved "in any one of the four directions the creatures faced." The imagery presented is comparable to the Chinese dragon king "who issues his commands by moving in all four directions simultaneously," and to the Indian god Varuna who "faces the four directions simultaneously from his home in the City of Starry Night." The palace of that latter deity is surrounded by serpents, and his name, *Varuna,* means "the binder," "the encompasser" and "the concealer."[30]

Another tie-in between Scripture and religious mythology is found in the association dragon-serpents purportedly have with jewels and esoteric knowledge. According to the Chinese sage Li Shichen, "The dragon's nature is rough and fierce, yet he likes beautiful gems and the Stone of Darkness. . . ." Most cultural traditions, moreover, see this affinity extending beyond mere fondness for magic baubles. To the Maya, the very power of the Celestial Iguana, or dragon-lord of fire, is embodied in a blue-green stone. Other societies relate the gems of the serpent to consciousness itself. In these systems, the first stirring of the mind is known as the dragon's precious stone or wish-fulfilling jewel—a treasure that, from the beginning, has been placed right in the dragon's jaws. Resting in this precarious position, the gem of knowledge is called, suggestively, "the Morning Star."[31]

This very title, of course (along with "son of the dawn"), is accorded in Isaiah 14:12 to Lucifer—a name given presumably because he was intended to bear the light of God's Kingdom and character on earth. In Ezekiel 28:12–14 this selfsame cherub is encountered as the wise and bejeweled guardian of Eden:

> "'You were the model of perfection,
> full of wisdom and perfect in beauty.
> You were in Eden,
> the garden of God;
> every precious stone adorned you:
> ruby, topaz and emerald,
> chrysolite, onyx and jasper,
> sapphire, turquoise and beryl.
> Your settings and mountings were made of gold;
> on the day you were created they were prepared.
> You were anointed as a guardian cherub,
> for so I ordained you.'"

Can it be that the ubiquitous dragon-serpent of religious mythology is none other than the jewel-encrusted morning star of Scripture? Is it possible that the very prevalence of this motif is evidence not only that the creature lives, but also of an active master plan to sow deceptive pseudo-wisdom throughout the world?

Chasing the Dragon

"The King of Meditation" honored at Tibetan Bonpo death rituals is presented as "the great turquoise dragon of spiritual vision [which] soars in mid-air."[32] Speaking of this dragon, the master in the *Book of Changes* declares, "It furthers one to see the great man." When asked what this might signify, he replies, "Things that accord in tone vibrate together. Things that have affinity in their inmost natures seek one another. . . ."[33]

In her outstanding book *The Catalpa Bow*, Cambridge professor Carmen Blacker recounts an August 1972 meeting with a Mrs.

Sasanuma in the Japanese village of Fukakusa. At the age of five, Mrs. Sasanuma's only son developed what was apparently an incurable sickness. When the medical specialists finally gave up hope of his recovery, she embarked on an urgent round of pilgrimages to various shrines, to no avail. Then, at the point of despair, she experienced a visitation by the radiant goddess Kishibojin, who promised to save the boy. By the next day, all trace of sickness had vanished.

As Blacker tells it, "Mrs. Sasanuma then found herself completely taken in charge by Kishibojin." In addition to having to pursue a fearful regime of austerities, the entranced mother somehow managed to erect a temple to the goddess and collect a body of disciples. During this time, "Kishibojin would appear to her frequently in snake form, with such vividness that she sometimes felt that she had become a snake herself."[34]

Similar appearances have been recorded over the years in countless other locations. One can only suspect that the devil, given his early success with Eve, has developed a special affection for this cunning reptilian emissary. And why not? Judging by the serpent's prominence in sacred architecture around the world, theirs has been an effective partnership. The lintel above the doorway at Cambodia's fabulous Angkor Wat, for example, is adorned with two *makara* dragons with garlands for bodies. These serpents also serve as the suggestive foundation for a second door designated for the imagination. Elsewhere throughout the country, each irrigation reservoir has its own temple where local divinities are worshiped in dragon form.[35]

In the celebrated Mayan city of Palenque, set in the steaming lushness of Mexico's Chiapas state, the Temple of the Inscriptions harbors the sarcophagus of the great seventh-century Mayan priest-king Pacal. Near the sarcophagus, located in a limestone chamber deep beneath the jungle heat, a serpent molded of plaster slithers along the floor to the threshold of the chamber. There it is transformed into a stone pipe that ascends along the edge of a hidden staircase to the temple floor above. Through this conduit, the Maya believed, Pacal's spirit could rise to the world of the living.[36]

Besides Mesoamerica and the Orient, serpent images can be found in the architectural landscape of Egypt, West Africa and the Andes, as well as in select parts of the South Pacific and Caribbean. In Europe the motif is widespread in Mediterranean and Celtic lands, and has shown up in wood carvings on the roofs of Norwegian stave churches.

The snake has also been widely adopted in personal ornamentation, perhaps more so than any other object in nature. Among the Egyptians, serpent's head amulets were thought to repel the attacks of Set and Apophis. Several of these amulets have been found resting with mummies. Grecian women commonly wore bracelets fashioned in the form of serpents, a practice that did not set well with Clement of Alexandria:

> The women are not ashamed to place about them the most manifold symbols of the evil one; for as the serpent deceived Eve, so the golden trinket in the fashion of a serpent misleads the women.[37]

In addition to the immediate protection ostensibly provided by snake eyes, Greeks believed that the serpent's vision extended into the future. Thus, the "wise" serpent was sought out regularly as an oracle. Every household in ancient Greece kept a snake fed with milk and honeycakes in order to coax it into bestowing protection, offspring and oracular advice.[38] There is also evidence that the Maltese culture at Tarxien used the snake for divination, albeit in a different manner. According to Goddess historian Elinor Gadon, the focal point for this activity was an underground sanctuary known as the Hypogeum. Carved out of living limestone, it contained an Oracle Room replete with a two-meter-deep pit well suited for snakes. Here, she believes, human priests or priestesses invited serpent bites as a way of entering into altered states of consciousness. Feminist author Merlin Stone similarly speculates that

> the sacred serpents, apparently kept and fed at the oracular shrines of the Goddess, were perhaps not merely the symbols but actually the instruments through which the experiences of divine revelation were reached.[39]

In most cultures the snake has enjoyed an even more exalted role. For thousands of years, and in myriad forms and settings, serpents have been viewed not only as revelatory instruments, but as the revelation itself. Among the more prominent of these reptilian deities: Mexico's Coatlicue, otherwise known as the "Serpent Lady" or "She of the

Serpent Skirt"; Haiti's Djamballah, sometimes viewed as the African equivalent of the Mesoamerican plumed serpent Quetzalcoatl; and the Great Rainbow Snake who, according to Australia's aboriginal peoples, was the principal activist during the primordial creation known as the Dreamtime.[40] In the Andes both shamans and mountains are frequently identified with serpent spirits, while in Benin the Yoruba worship the Python deity by kissing the dust of its path.

In Tantric Buddhist iconography, the consort of the Guardian of the North is the green, snake-headed Kinkinadhari; while Yamantaka, the "Conqueror of Death," or "Guardian of the South," is bedecked in a garland of snakes. (He also holds a skullcap full of blood and a white staff impaling a fresh-cut yellow head.) The national flag of the Himalayan kingdom of Bhutan features a jewel-clutching dragon; while the nation's primary ethnic group, the Drukpa, refer to themselves proudly as the "People of the Dragon."[41]

In the Gyasumdo region of Nepal, local Tibetans live in a delicate relationship with sensitive underworld serpent deities known as *klu*. With their ability to bestow both harm and blessing, these deities resemble the more familiar *nagas* of India. Both demand, and get, regular offerings to placate their wrath and solicit their help.

Indian worshipers during the midsummer Naga festival flock by the thousands to ancient serpent shrines.[42] In some parts of India, barren women use the occasion to visit snake holes where they hope to find fertility by laying out ritual offerings of milk, eggs and burning camphor. Out on the streets, in a scene one observer called "reminiscent of the crucifixes carried by cathedral choirboys," celebrants parade with poles bearing live monitor lizards smeared with vermilion. Other marchers bear earthen pots containing recently captured cobras considered to be a manifestation of the Lord Shiva.[43]

Earlier in the year, Indians honor Manasa, Queen of the Snakes, by painting images of serpents and birds on the walls of their houses. The observance inevitably summons up a well-known story about a merchant named Chanda who not only refused to worship Manasa, but professed a profound contempt for her. In time, so the story goes, six of his sons died from snakebite.[44]

Halfway around the globe, America's Hopi Indians (as we have seen) also honor the snake. At the beginning of their snake-antelope ceremony, designed to bring rain to the sun-parched lands of

northeastern Arizona,[45] about 24 painted men file into the plaza rat-
tling gourds and seashells. With their right feet, they stomp on a
pochta, or resonator board, that covers the small hole representing
the place of the Hopis' mythological emergence from the underworld. It is a powerful sound that vibrates at the seat of the soul. As
Frank Waters describes it in his 1972 *Book of the Hopi:*

> There is no mistaking its esoteric summons. For this is the manda-
> tory call to the creative life force known elsewhere as the Kundalini,[46]
> latently coiled like a serpent [waiting] to ascend to the throne of her
> Lord for the final consummation of their mystic marriage. [And] the
> power *does* come up. You can see it in the dancers . . . swaying to the
> left and right like snakes, singing softly and shaking their antelope-
> testicle-covered gourds as the power makes its slow ascent. Then their
> bodies straighten, their voices rise. . . . So it goes on in a kind of mes-
> meric enchantment in the darkening afternoon.[47]

From Chaos to Panic

Wisdom is not the only trait, or even the dominant one, attributed
to the dragon-serpent. A careful review of serpent lore turns up at
least two other equally prominent associations—fertility and fear,
especially fear of death. By loitering conspicuously at the primary
intersections of human existence, the great usurper has created a
reputation for himself as the ultimate arbiter of life and death.
Depending on the requirements of any given moment, he can appear
to his subjects as either a creative genius or a fearful terminator.

To be credible as a prime mover, of course, the serpent must possess great antiquity. And as far as the gnostic Ophites were concerned, this was precisely the case. The snake was God, they insisted,
because it came before all.[48] The Egyptians expanded this vision to
include an entire brood of serpents. From temple to village the warning went forth: "Whatever you do, wherever you go, tread carefully—
beware of the Oldest of the Old!"[49]

In the *Popol Vuh,* the sacred book of the Maya, Quetzalcoatl first
appears as Gukumatz, a glittering celestial serpent of the primordial waters.[50] This linkage of the dragon-serpent with a turbulent,
murky sea is widespread in religious mythology. It is a symbolic

union that has become metaphorical for primal beginnings. Unlike the controlled sequences recorded in Genesis 1–2, however, the creative process is often dark and chaotic.

In the Babylonian creation epic *Enuma elish,* chaos is personified as Tiamat, a primeval sea that is at once swelling and restless, bitter and foul. A Babylonian priest of Marduk writing in the third century B.C. said that, in the beginning, "all was darkness and water," and in this murky chaos strange beasts came into being—beasts like men with wings. To the Greeks, Chaos was a god that characterized yawning emptiness; the formless, undifferentiated state. Early Mesoamericans added countless devouring mouths to the definition, while Hindus simply called it *tad ekam,* Sanskrit for "That One." Many other traditions describe the flux as an abyss of water stirred by a fiery spirit whose light allows it to see. Thus illumined, say the Hindu Upanishads, the spirit looks about itself hungrily—the very activity (in Greek, *derkesthai,* "to glance dartingly") that gives the dragon its name.[51]

The dragon of the Old Testament is also a creature of the waters. In addition to the Hebrew *tannin,* literally "sea serpent," there is that aquatic reptile known as Leviathan:[52]

> In that day, the LORD will punish with his . . . fierce, great and powerful sword, Leviathan the gliding serpent, Leviathan the coiling serpent; he will slay the monster of the sea.
>
> Isaiah 27:1

Since the waters of the abyss are considered too deep for the earth to contain, the dragon has often been sought out in the heavens. It is here, high above the earth, that his illusions of immortality are most clearly seen and admired. As Francis Huxley notes in *The Dragon,* "The Druids believed that every spring equinox a concourse of snakes created a glass egg out of the interweaving of their eyes."[53] A symbol of immortality, this egg was shaped like a celestial ring— a ring that modern science has since identified as the Milky Way. To the Akkadians, this glowing heavenly train was known as the Snake River, or River of the Abyss; to the Greeks, as the World Stream; to the Norse, as the Worm of Middle Earth; and to the Indians, as the Path of the Snake and the Bed of the Ganges. In Borneo the Dayak people still believe the world is enclosed in a circle formed by the water snake biting its tail.[54]

The dragon-serpent, however, is not always so beneficent. Like most creatures, it has its dark side. Undoubtedly aware of this, the oracular witches in Shakespeare's *Macbeth* make a point of including "fillet of a fenny snake" and "Adder's fork and blind-worm's sting" to their sinister black cauldron brew.[55]

The serpent's dark side is equally manifest in the nonliterary world. To the inhabitants of the Melanesian island of New Ireland, the *masalai* snake is not only kindred to malevolent spirits, but has the frightening ability to transform itself into multiple configurations.[56] At the Calle Villares in La Paz, images of the devil can be purchased that depict him with a fanged serpent coming out of his head. To the Mapuche Indians of southern Chile, this image is akin to a feared, multiheaded snake spirit named Chinufilu. In *The Highest Altar*, Patrick Tierney tells of one man with a crippled leg who saw this serpent gnawing away at him in his dreams for more than sixty years.[57]

In medieval France dragons were widely believed to have a taste for young children and virgins. Huxley points out that "at least four of them are to be found in Provence: one at Aix, where it was burst asunder by St. Margaret; one at Draguignan, where the town mayor has the right to have any of his godchildren christened 'Drac'; a third at Beaucaire, that specialized in forcing nursing mothers to suckle baby dragons; and the most famous at Tarascon . . . [that] guarded the entrance to the Celtic Tartarus."[58]

Sometimes imaginary dragons come to life with terrifying and destructive consequences. Such was the case with Belinda, a bright, artistic 32-year-old patient at UCLA's Neuropsychiatric Institute. According to her physician, Dr. Ronald Siegel, when she was a child, she "talked and played with the dragon in his imaginary castle for periods of fifteen minutes to three hours. These visits were the height of her pleasure." As Belinda grew older, however, she spent more and more time exploring the dragon's domain, sometimes withdrawing from the real world for weeks on end. Although some imaginary companions function as Freudian superegos, speaking to the child as a parent would, Siegel reports that Belinda's dragon became powerful enough to rule most aspects of her behavior in the real world:

Belinda consulted her dragon about every decision, from where she should go during the day to what she should say. She was caught in a tug-of-war between the dragon, who wanted her to spend the rest of her life painting murals on castle walls, and her therapists, who were trying to keep her grounded in reality.

Eventually Belinda became suicidal and was hospitalized. Although she was kept from killing herself, she remained trapped inside the dragon's world. Siegel's description of a painting she gave him at this time is chilling: "It showed a world of gray shadows and ominous tones. A dragon flew overhead. In its claws it carried a cocoon with Belinda's naked body inside."[59]

In addition to dread and desperation, most people have also experienced the undirected terror that the Greeks named *panic* after the god Pan. Reflecting his domain and character, these attacks are especially common in lonely and desolate places. Tuareg nomads who ply the vast expanse of the Sahara Desert are particularly vulnerable. Many report being tormented by spirits that materialize at night to haunt and mislead—invisible beings that are also believed responsible for causing echoes and whirlwinds.[60]

Coleridge captured this numinous state of affairs in *The Rime of the Ancient Mariner:*

> Like one, that on a lonesome road
> Doth walk in fear and dread,
> And having once turned round walks on,
> And turns no more his head;
> Because he knows, a frightful fiend
> Doth close behind him tread.

As Richard Cavendish observes,

The age-old belief in hostile spirits is not fully accounted for by putting them in pigeonholes according to their social functions and historic origins. Behind it is an uncalculated and universal human experience—the recognition of an evil presence, like the sense of something following you silently along a lonely road, when you know that you must not run from it and you must not look back to make sure it is not there, because if you do either, you will acknowledge it and let it in on you.[61]

The early Christians associated all pagan deities with demons, but Pan more than the others. He was feared for his connection with the wilderness, the favorite haunt of hostile spirits, and for his unrestrained sexuality. Hairy and goatlike, Pan's horns and cloven hooves eventually became the prototype for Christian images of Satan.[62] He exerted power over those who preferred emotion over reason as a guide to truth. The early twentieth-century British occultist Aleister Crowley was strongly attracted to Pan, whom he viewed as the inspirer of lust, cruelty and divine madness.[63] Each of these earthy contributions was duly hailed in Crowley's infamous "Hymn to Pan."

In his playful aspect, Pan, who liked to blow haunting tunes on a reed pipe and chase animals, is associated with a number of well-known literary works, including Robert Browning's *Pied Piper of Hamelin*, Sir James Barrie's *Peter Pan* and "The Piper at the Gates of Dawn" in Kenneth Grahame's *Wind in the Willows*. In Grahame's beloved children's story, Rat and Mole find themselves drawn by an unearthly piping to the Master of Animals.[64] Standing there, Mole whispers to Rat, "Are you afraid?" To which Rat replies: "Afraid! Of *Him?* O, never, never! And yet—and yet—O, Mole, I am afraid."[65]

Plying the Nether Gloom

Guided by rumor and their own superstitious inclinations, medieval cartographers routinely embellished the maps of their day with fantastic creatures and dire warnings. It was a popular and expedient way of dealing with *terra incognita*, and explorers, both armchair and deckside, spent long hours fantasizing about mysterious deeps inscribed with the words *Here Be Dragons*. Many clearly believed this advisement.

The question of where the dragon makes his lair is still alive today. In fact, it is central to our understanding of one of the devil's most important and widely recognized aspects. In addition to his well-documented association with luminosity, gems, wisdom, chaos, death and moral baseness, he is closely related to power—specifically, the power of the air.

The King James Version of Ephesians 2:2 refers to him as "the prince of the power of the air." In this passage, the Greek word for air (*aer*) refers not to a direction (up, or heavenward) but to a place (the atmosphere). The distinction is important. The fact that the great dragon rules a place reminds us that he is an objective, created personality. While his interests are often pursued inside the human mind, he is not an imaginary creation.

To the Sumerians he was known as *Enlil*, or "Lord Air." In addition to serving as the tutelary deity of Nippur, the holiest of all Babylonian cities, Enlil was considered the "King of the gods" and the original custodian of the Tablet of Destinies. Elsewhere in the Middle East, the Semitic god Adad,[66] whose symbol was forked lightning, rode the clouds with a thundering voice. The Bible acknowledges the importance of Adad in the Syrian context by such names as *Ben-Hadad* and *Hadad Rimmon* ("Hadad is the thunderer").[67] Other atmospheric deities include the Greek god *Typhon,* believed to be the source of the stormy winds that wreak havoc on land and sea, and *Huracan,* the dragon of the Caribbean said to be responsible for hurricanes and earthquakes. The dragon was also seen as a weather-maker by the ancient Olmecs and the seafaring Norwegians.[68]

It would be easier to dismiss these examples as little more than the fanciful musings of superstitious societies, were it not for recent testimony of veteran space shuttle astronaut Story Musgrave. With six missions under his belt, the recently retired Dr. Musgrave is considered the dean of the modern shuttle program. Admitting that he "still [doesn't] have an explanation," this elite scientist recounts that on two separate missions, he clearly observed a serpent, some six to eight feet in length, following the shuttle around the upper reaches of the earth's atmosphere.[69]

Indeed, there is something strange about the atmospheric abode of the fallen angels. In some mysterious manner it serves, as 2 Peter 2:4 and Jude 6 reveal, more as a prison than a home. The fallen angels are confined by God to a realm of nether gloom called Tartarus,[70] not simply a faraway dimension but a place *within* a dimension that happens to surround the earth.[71] While it effectively prohibits fallen angels from wandering unrestrained within their own dimension, nothing prevents them from descending, like Christ, "to the lower, earthly regions" (Ephesians 4:9). In fact, the one Paul refers to as "the prince of the power of the air" (Ephesians 2:2, KJV), John calls "the prince of this world" (John 12:31; 14:30; 16:11).

The Implications of Radical Evil

One further piece of evidence suggests to us not only the presence of a real devil (but an active diabolical master plan) We discover this evidence not within a religious context but through indicators offered by natural reason. It is found in what Jeffrey Russell calls "radical evil." Westerners must break out of the narrow limitations of materialistic reductionism, he argues, and deal with the traditional prince of darkness—a prince "whose energies are bent on the destruction of the cosmos and the misery of its creatures."[72] As Andrew Greeley once said, "There are more powers under heaven than philosophy and sociology can dream of—although anthropology knows them well."[73]

History's path is littered with people who have given themselves to evil—men and women who, as Jesus put it, "loved darkness instead of light" (John 3:19). Besides defiling their own spiritual houses, they employed cunning manipulation and cruelty to extend their ruin to countless other lives and institutions. In those instances in which such people managed to attain positions of great power— Genghis Khan and Adolf Hitler are two examples—the very foundations of the earth have been shaken.

There are those who insist on sanitizing human vileness by wrapping it in scientific definitions, but the fact of radical evil remains. In the end there is nothing clinical about the Hell's Angels making sacraments out of urine and excrement, or the Nazis manufacturing tobacco pouches out of the breasts of young women, or the disciples of Charles Manson jabbing knives and forks into the stomach of a pregnant Sharon Tate.[74]

There is evil in each of us, but combining even large numbers of individual evils does not explain Auschwitz, Rwanda or Cambodia under Pol Pot. Confronted with such monstrosities, we can only agree with Russell that "evil on this scale seems to be qualitatively as well as quantitatively different. It is no longer a personal evil, but a transpersonal evil. . . ."[75] At the same time, Russell worries that "the flat, materialistic assumptions of contemporary Western society have effectively censored concern with radical evil by expressions of contempt for transcendent views."[76]

Catholic evangelical Peter Kreeft agrees. In response to those who insist it is psychologically unhealthy to believe in demons—a regression into medieval fear and superstition—Kreeft asks:

> If wild animals exist, is it unhealthy to believe they exist? Isn't it much more unhealthy to pretend that they don't? If our ancestors tended to make the mistake of overemphasizing the devil (and this was indeed unhealthy), we tend to the opposite mistake: forgetting that life is spiritual warfare, that there *is* an enemy. . . .[77]

Here we are asked to confront two facts: first, that the devil exists, and second, that he is a ruler. (Jesus Himself acknowledged the reality of Satan's empire in Matthew 12:26: "If Satan drives out Satan, he is divided against himself. How then can his kingdom stand?") If Satan is a ruler, it follows naturally that he has servants. Michael Green points out that their ranks comprise not only "the hosts of evil spirits whom he drew with him from heaven (cf. Rev. 12:4, 9)," but the human co-conspirators who march in lockstep with the world rulers of darkness.[78]

The recognition of the dragon's existence, as important as this is, is still a prologue to our quest to understand why darkness lingers where it does. The labyrinth yet holds many secrets. From here we must locate the path that leads us toward an understanding of how and when this evil empire was established.

CHAPTER FOUR

ANCIENT MYSTERIES

For most humanistic visionaries, history, especially ancient history, holds little interest. Like young adults embarrassed by photos of their own infancy or awkward adolescence, these individuals are willing to acknowledge the past as a matter of record, but not to admire it.[1] As shapers of the future, they are impressed not with means but with ends; with what will be, not what has been.

The reasoning of contemporary humanists is simple: Since knowledge is cumulative, the front end of the human story is a poor place to seek answers. (Garden tenders, cave painters and ark builders simply do not offer much to progressive societies.) Rather than wade against the tide of history, therefore, we must pivot into its momentum and allow it to carry us to our destiny. "Progress is not an accident," Herbert Spencer once argued, "but a fact of nature."[2] The only thing we need to realize the promise of perfection (so goes the argument) is to keep our eyes fixed firmly on the future.

This thinking, despite its general acceptance and happy tone, is burdened by a serious flaw: While knowledge does indeed accumulate with time, wisdom is not always a fellow traveler. As evidence, we have only to consider the recent advent of interactive pornography, saline abortions and biological weapons. The long-observed principle of moral entropy dictates that, apart from the preservative of godly wisdom, mankind gets worse, not better, with time.

Popular assumptions about the future, then, are not likely to lead us to any model of perfection. For that we must look to the deep past, drawing back the curtain of time to apprehend a creation pulled fresh from the divine forge—a creation still radiating the purity and pleasure of the Almighty.

While the Bible does not linger long on the genesis of human history, its insights into the nature of the original mold, and what caused it to be broken, are sufficient to keep a careful reader occupied for some time. In the pristine context before the Fall, and in the eventful centuries surrounding the Flood and Dispersion, even seemingly trivial details are loaded with import. It is here in the deepest archives of human history that we discover why the labyrinth became an alien and confusing place.

The Dimensional Gate

After the first man was animated by the breath of God, he was placed in a Garden called Eden. In this lush and magical environment, life was sustained, secrets were shared and relationships flourished in primal purity. It was God's handiwork, and it was magnificent.[3]

Attempts have been made throughout history to recreate this numinous context. Although the most popular building materials have been words, resulting in literary efforts like Frances Hodgson Burnett's turn-of-the-century classic *The Secret Garden,* others have used bricks and seeds, fashioning places like Babylon's famous Hanging Gardens and the utopian Findhorn community on Scotland's northeast coast.

Christian theologians, for their part, tend to be more cautious in their depictions of Eden. While allowing that the Garden presented imposing dimensions, life-giving fruit and remarkable harmony between the species, they are leery of attempts to extend this list of features. From their perspective, Eden is simply the backdrop to man's creation and the high moral drama that surrounded the Fall. The plot, not the set (as they rightly remind us), should capture our attention.

There is ample evidence, however, that Eden was more than an elaborate garden. According to Genesis 3:8, God not only designed this special place; He *visited* it. Eden was intended as a place of communion between man and his Maker, and the interactions recorded in Genesis 2:15–22 and 3:8–13 were apparently consistent with an ongoing routine.

Even so, Eden was not the Creator's primary abode. When He appeared to walk with Adam and Eve in the cool of the day, *He came from somewhere else.* And since God is a Spirit, the fact that He was manifest in a material context can mean only that He descended from a higher realm. Whatever else Eden may have been, it was clearly a dimensional gateway.

The reality of interdimensional travel is addressed in several biblical passages. In Genesis 28:10–19, for example, Jacob was given a vision of a stairway or ladder extending between earth and the heavenly realm. As he beheld this extraordinary stairway, he noted that it was filled with angelic traffic "ascending and descending." Awakening from his experience, the overwhelmed patriarch declared: "How awesome is this place! This is none other than the house of God; this is the gate of heaven."

The apostle Paul spoke with equal amazement of "the surpassingly great revelations" he received when he "was caught up to the third heaven" (2 Corinthians 12:2). In another letter (Ephesians 4:9–10) he described Christ Himself ascending and descending through "layered" dimensions[4]—an almost surreal capacity that is also alluded to in Matthew's brief but fascinating account of the Transfiguration (17:1–9).

There is the additional theory, introduced in the previous chapter, that Lucifer frequented Eden's dimensional gateway, too. Support for this idea is provided by the prophet Ezekiel, who places the anointed cherub at both ends of the celestial ladder. At one moment we find the cherub "in Eden, the garden of God" (28:13), while in the next he is described as being "on the holy mount of God" (verse 14). Until Lucifer was expelled from that mount, he walked among—or up and down—"the fiery stones" (verse 14).[5]

In the incipient days of human history, then, we find God (and possibly Lucifer) shuttling between earthly Eden and an abode of higher dimensional beings that the prophets call the "holy mount of God" or "mount of assembly" (see Isaiah 14:13).[6] While the exact location of this dimensional gate is not specified in Scripture, some scholars have speculated that it may have been linked to the Tree of Life at the center of the Garden (assuming that the portal was territorially fixed). Wherever it was, this gateway between heaven and earth would have held far more impressive possibilities than today's Star Trek–style transporters and worm holes!

Nearly all of Hollywood's recent portrayals of dimensional travel, including the intriguing 1994 motion picture *Stargate,* represent what we might term "lateral journeys." On such journeys, movement is limited to standard space-time dimensions. (Even when alien forces are involved, they are invariably based in some quadrant of the physical universe.) While the facility of these missions in exploring the full range of the space-time continuum is dramatic enough, they offer no comparison to the "vertical travel" suggested in Scripture.

Scientists like to theorize about higher dimensions but are at a loss when it comes to describing them. Most simply fall back on the term *hyperspace,* the word we introduced in chapter 2 meaning "over, above or beyond the present dimension." To actually glimpse the realms hinted at by science's arithmetical calculations, we must turn once again to the prophet Ezekiel. After taking one of history's longest peeks at angelic comings and goings, he offers us a scene so exotic, so unearthly, it can only be the top of Jacob's stairway:

> Spread out above the heads of the living creatures was what looked like an expanse, sparkling like ice, and awesome.
>
> Ezekiel 1:22

In a similar incident recorded in the book of Exodus:

> Moses and Aaron, Nadab and Abihu, and the seventy elders of Israel went up and saw the God of Israel. Under his feet was something like a pavement made of sapphire, clear as the sky itself.
>
> Exodus 24:9–10

Many aspects of the mount of assembly remain clouded in mystery, but it is clearly a site of power (which Satan in Isaiah 14:13 covets) and an important arena for discussion and debate. In the book of Job we read that the angels (literally, *beneha elohim,* or "the sons of God") come here "to present themselves before the LORD" (Job 1:6; 2:1). Satan was permitted to join them and take advantage of his access to accuse God of showing favoritism to Job.

Who are these privileged "sons of God" who gather to dialogue with the Almighty on the mount of assembly? While we cannot be certain, it seems likely they are a select group of high-ranking angels.[7] Perhaps the best candidates for this role are the 24 elders mentioned in Revelation 4:4. Gary Kinnaman equates their title with governance and suggests they are angelic beings whose service in God's created order is along the lines of "heavenly senators."[8]

A cosmic mount of assembly is also found at the center of many of the world's ancient religious myths. While we may agree that the majority of these accounts possess dubious authority, their tendency to coalesce around one motif is intriguing. As far away as the Altai region of western Siberia, religious nomads have spoken earnestly of a mountain at the heart of the world, above which is found the upper world (Ezekiel's expanse?). These nomads also embrace notions about the duality of divine presence. At the dawn of time, according to their myths, the Creator sat on a golden mountain in the midst of the sky. After forming the earth out of emptiness, he lowered the mountain onto solid ground.[9]

Equipped for Success: Adam in Wonderland

A careful examination of the Genesis record reveals how marvelously equipped the first human citizens were for life, communion and leadership. God clearly had big plans for Adam and his wife. As they exercised dominion over the earth, their joyful obligations were to grow in wisdom and to multiply their kind.[10]

To maximize their experience, God instilled in Adam and Eve something unique. Although presumably He had formed millions of living species prior to man, in no other instance did He quicken that life by His breath. But when He breathed life into Adam's elemental frame, the gateway was opened for mankind to enter the dimension of the spirit. As the late Andrew Murray wrote in *The Spirit of Christ*:

> The spirit quickening the body made . . . a living person with the consciousness of himself. The soul was the meeting-place, the point of union between body and spirit. Through the *body*, man, the living

soul, stood related to the external world of sense; he could influence it, or be influenced by it. Through the *spirit* he stood related to the spiritual world . . . [where] he could be [both] the recipient and the minister of its life and power. Standing thus midway between two worlds, belonging to both, the *soul* had the power of . . . choosing or refusing the objects by which it was surrounded, and to which it stood related.[11]

Murray's description of the soul as a meeting place is helpful, but it leaves another question unanswered: What is the relationship between the soul and mind? Despite Murray's silence on the subject, the consensus is that, rather than standing in relationship, soul and mind are simply interchangeable terms for the seat of consciousness.[12]

And what of the role of the brain in consciousness? Here a feud exists between Cartesian notions of a "directive soul" and Gilbert Ryle's proposition that the brain is simply a physical organ. Neurologist Richard Restak sees folly in both camps. Resorting to analogy, he tells of an eight-year-old boy who travels to Washington, D.C., expecting to see the United States government. On the first day he visits Congress; on the second he tours the White House; and on the third he is shown the Supreme Court. At this point the puzzled boy asks, "But where's the government?" The problem, of course, is that the young man has confused entities located in space and time with a process that describes the interactions of these entities.

So are consciousness and the brain the same? The famed British biologist Sir Julian Huxley observed:

> The brain alone is not responsible for mind, even though it is a necessary organ for its manifestation. Indeed, an isolated brain is a piece of biological nonsense as meaningless as an isolated individual.[13]

As neurobiology has been perfecting its notion of what consciousness is, quantum theorists led by famed Oxford physicist Roger Penrose have been making remarkable claims about what it may do. Quantum theory contends (as we noted in chapter 2) that unwatched electrons and other subatomic particles inhabit a twilight zone between mass and energy. In some inexplicable way, they settle into one state or the other only as impressions are registered in the mind of an observer.* The mind-boggling implication here is that consciousness may actually *define* reality, at least in the sense that observation apparently has a literal effect on the structure of the physical world.[14] When one considers this extraordinary phenomenon, according to the late particle physicist James Jeans, "The universe begins to look more like a great thought than like a great machine."[15]

If consciousness defines external reality, however, it also depends on interaction with the outside world. The mind cannot function properly apart from stimulating contact with things and people. Experiments with volunteer students at McGill University and other institutions have demonstrated conclusively that sensory deprivation leads to confusion, panic and restlessness. Severe deprivation, such as that produced by special immersion tanks, can lead to the disintegration of consciousness.[16]

These design truths shed light on God's intent in Eden. By creating Adam as a living soul with the power of conscious observation, God prepared him to operate as a genuine creative force in the physical universe. To facilitate Adam's extraordinarily high level of consciousness, God began by opening up a vast array of natural sensory channels. He augmented these by instilling in the man the capacity for spiritual communion. Finally He placed His finely tuned creature in the midst of a wondrous environment, which He graced routinely by His own presence. Thus was Adam empowered, through constant stimulation, not only to exercise effective dominion in the physical realm, but to grow in wisdom. His sovereignty was constrained only by his need for external fellowship and guidance. Man could be immortal, but not his own master.

The book of Genesis, which serves as the basis for our examination of Adam's original endowments, offers four interesting categories for consideration: his physical stature and potential for immortality; his ability to converse with God directly; his ability to communicate with other species; and his maximized brain potential.[17]

---

* As the renowned Princeton University physicist John Wheeler has put it, "The quantum principle . . . destroys the concept of the world as 'sitting out there.'"

Physical Stature and Immortality

While Scripture is not explicit about Adam's size, it does offer several indirect clues that point toward great physical stature. The first of these is God's expectation that Adam would "take care of" and "work" a vast garden (Genesis 2:15). Given the data provided in verses 9–11, we may assume that this mandate would have required extraordinary strength and stamina.

Another indicator of Adam's stature is found in the reference to the mysterious Nephilim, or giants, that resulted from the union of the "sons of God" with "the daughters of men" (Genesis 6:1–2).[18] In these direct descendants of Adam, also described as "heroes of old" and "men of renown" (verse 4), it is likely that we are glimpsing characteristics possessed by their progenitor.

We must also remember that immortality was an integral part of Adam's original blueprint—a fact that should not be shrugged off as relating to his spirit alone. Adam was created with a body, and if sin had not entered the world, his body would not have known death. Given this fact, we may be forgiven our curiosity over just what kind of body it was.

The proposition that Eden's abundant fruit (Genesis 2:9, 16–17; 3:1–6, 11–12) provided Adam and Eve with resistance to disease and aging receives support from at least two Bible passages. In one of them, the Godhead reasons that fallen man "must not be allowed to reach out his hand and take also from the tree of life and eat, and live forever" (Genesis 3:22). In the other passage, the apostle John refers to a heavenly tree bearing life-giving fruit and healing leaves (see Revelation 22:2).

Capacity to Converse with God Face to Face

Another of Adam's remarkable endowments was his capacity to dialogue with God face to face (see Genesis 3:9–10). While later biblical figures also encountered the manifest presence of the Almighty, they did so either through dreams and visions (Jacob, Ezekiel, Paul and John) or in carefully controlled circumstances (Moses on Sinai and Jewish high priests in the Holy of Holies). None of these parties, so far as we know, had the ability to hear the "sound of the LORD God" in the manner described in Genesis 3:8.

Further evidence of Adam's direct dealings with God is provided in the apparent absence of angelic messengers prior to the Fall.[19] Since the first man and his Maker were still on intimate terms, these intermediaries were frankly redundant, becoming necessary only when man's act of rebellion altered his system so that he could no longer tolerate the direct presence of God. With the advent of sin, the divine presence that once delighted Adam and Eve suddenly threatened to consume them. What once meant fellowship now elicited fear.[20]

Interspecies Communication

In his twelfth-century apologetic work *Guide for the Perplexed,* Jewish theologian Maimonides makes an interesting comment. "In the time of Adam," he writes, "there coexisted animals that appeared as humans in shape and also in intelligence." Their design lacked only "the image of God."[21]

Although Maimonides' assertion that animals appeared in human form is suspect, the idea that humans and animals may once have possessed the faculties necessary to sustain an intelligent relationship is plausible. Passages like Genesis 3:1 and Genesis 3:13–15 strongly imply that at least some animals had the ability to make rational judgments.[22] In addition, the first five verses of Genesis 3 reveal Eve carrying on a sophisticated dialogue with the serpent. At no point does she indicate that this inter-species communication is anything but routine.

Even today millions of people experience what might be called "the Disney effect"—the enveloping comfort and joy that comes from exposure to talking animals.[23] So strong and universal is this phenomenon that it makes one wonder if the creative magic of Walt Disney, Beatrix Potter and Jim Henson is not conjuring latent longings for a world that once existed.[24]

Maximized Brain Potential

Although Scripture does not elaborate on Adam's ability to communicate with animals, there can be no doubting the fact that his mental prowess prior to the Fall was formidable. The mere act of naming the creatures must have required him to remember millions, perhaps billions, of appellations so as not to duplicate them.

We can deduce other of his cerebral powers through careful examination of his posterity. Even as we acknowledge that the capabilities of the modern mind reflect only dimly the fires that once burned (an estimated 96–99 percent of all mental potential lies fallow),[25] these lingering traces are impressive nonetheless.

Researchers often contend that the human brain is an underutilized supercomputer, an organ that appears overendowed. When Dr. Kenneth Boulding declares that the capacity of the human brain is "inconceivably large," he means that the 3.5 pounds of gray matter sealed in the skull of a typical adult human contains between fifteen and one hundred billion neurons—neurons that collectively fire ten million billion times per second![26]

Other glimpses into the deep well of the mind have been provided by savants—mentally diminished individuals who demonstrate flashes of brilliance in a given area. In the 1988 film *Rain Man,* Dustin Hoffman portrayed a savant whose ability to perform complex calculations rapidly was temporarily exploited by his brother in casino games. In real life, American savant twins "Charles and George" manifested a similar ability to calculate calendar dates. They could answer in an instant if asked when April 21 fell on a Sunday as far back as the year 1700. When the British neurologist Oliver Sacks accidentally spilled a box of matches in front of the twins, they cried out in unison, "One hundred and eleven." On retrieving the matches, Sacks confirmed that exactly 111 matches had fallen from the box. Asked how they had counted the matches so quickly, the twins replied: "We didn't count . . . we *saw* 111."[27]

This ability to "see" numbers is closely related to another cerebral anomaly known as *synesthesia.* In this rare syndrome, memories generated in one sense are routinely expressed in terms of another. The senses are commingled. According to experts like Richard Cytowic and Harry Gilbert, colored hearing is the most prevalent form of synesthesia. "One of the things I love about my husband," wrote one female synesthete, "are the colors of his voice and his laugh. It's a wonderful golden brown, with a flavor of crisp buttery toast."[28]

Other synesthetes perceive shapes, weight or texture when they taste something with an intense flavor. In the case of North Carolina teacher Michael Watson, mint flavoring produces rows of invisible columns whose smooth, cool surfaces can be caressed and embraced. The late Soloman Shereshevsky, an extraordinary synesthete studied by Russian psychologists for more than thirty years, connected sound with three senses: sight, taste and touch. When exposed to a tone with a pitch of two thousand cycles per second, Shereshevsky commented:

> It looks something like fireworks with a pink-red hue. The strip of color feels rough and unpleasant, and it has an ugly taste—rather like that of a briny pickle. You could hurt your hand on it.[29]

Although clinical research is ongoing, Dr. Cytowic believes that synesthesia is probably a *normal* process in the brain, perhaps centered in the limbic system, that is suppressed in most people.[30]

Similar hypotheses have been proposed in relation to human psychic abilities. One of the most complex and controversial of these "gifts" is what parapsychologists call extrasensory perception, or ESP. Long viewed by the scientific community as untestable and by the Christian community as either superstition or demonic activity, the field has been attracting second looks lately from both camps. While trickery and genuine demonic manifestations are still seen as responsible for most of today's so-called paranormal phenomena, a select number of cases seemingly defy both explanations.

In an effort to learn more about these cases, researchers at various prestigious institutions have launched a spate of experiments designed to take an objective and controlled look at *clairvoyance* (the ability to see distant or hidden objects), *telepathy* (the ability to transfer thoughts), *precognition* (the ability to see future events) and *psychokinesis* (the ability to manipulate objects mentally).[31]

In one battery of controlled experiments to study clairvoyance, Stanford Research Institute physicists Harold Puthoff and Russell Targ supplied a New York artist named Ingo Swann with map coordinates for various locations around the world, then asked him to describe the actual location. In one test, Swann deliberated over a set of latitude and longitude coordinates mailed to the lab by a highly skeptical East Coast scientist, then ventured some initial impressions:

> There seems to be some sort of mounds or rolling hills. There is also a city to the north—I can see taller buildings and some smog.

> This seems to be a strange place, somewhat like . . . a military base. I
> get the impression of something underground, but I'm not sure.

After Swann had sketched a picture of what he had seen, the drawing and a transcript of his description were mailed across the country to the waiting cynic. The shaken scientist reported in his subsequent analysis that Swann's vision was accurate in every detail, right
down to the dimensions and distances on the sketch. The target
turned out to be a little-known, restricted-access missile site.[32]

In the early 1970s, documentary filmmaker Douchan Gersi
(whose observations of Haitian voodoo appear in chapter 1) spent
nearly eighteen months living with Tuareg nomads in Mali and
southern Algeria. Gersi was able to record numerous examples of
telepathy and precognition that were later woven into his *Explore*
series on the Discovery Channel.

Once in the remote Sahara, Gersi and several companions in a
Land Rover came across a solitary Tuareg sitting in the shadow of
his camel. Since the man was far from any well or nomadic trade
route, the group stopped to offer tea and inquire about his circumstances. The Tuareg said he was waiting for a friend, and that the
appointment had been set seven months earlier in Gao, a city in Mali
some six hundred miles away. Since the day was nearly exhausted,
Gersi's party pitched camp with the stranger.

The following morning, as they were packing up the Land Rover,
Gersi offered the Tuareg some of the team's extra water. The man
expressed gratitude but refused on the grounds that they would need
it more than he. Gersi looked at him quizzically. "Last night," the Tuareg
explained, "my friend told me that he was two days away. He had to
make a detour in order to fill up his *guerbas* [goatskins used to carry
water]." Still perplexed, Gersi asked how his friend had communicated
this information. "He told me in my mind," the Tuareg replied. "And
in the same way I let him know that I would be waiting. . . . I just thought
about him deeply, and repeated what I wanted him to know."

Turning to his companions, Gersi proposed that they wait two
days to see what happened. When everyone agreed, the party
removed their gear from the Land Rover and set up a vigil. At the end
of the second day, a silhouette suddenly appeared from beyond the
rocky hills. As the figure moved closer to the isolated campsite, Gersi

and his colleagues were astonished to learn that it was indeed the friend for whom the Tuareg had been waiting.[33]

While psychic activity remains mysterious and, in many quarters, suspect, it is generally considered less controversial than so-called "mind-over-matter" feats. Officially known as psychokinesis, this field also has its star performers. At the top of most lists is Nina Kulagina, an unassuming Russian woman who was the subject of rigorous experiments in the 1950s and '60s. Conducted by Soviet physicists at the A. A. Utomsky Institute in what was then Leningrad, these tests saw Kulagina's extraordinary mental powers not only move and break a variety of objects, but even separate the white of an egg from its yolk.

Similar research has been conducted at the Princeton Engineering Anomalies Research Laboratory (PEAR) in New Jersey. Fifteen years and several million trials into their program, Dr. Robert Jahn and University of Chicago psychologist Brenda Dunne have concluded that "scientific evidence [suggests] that human consciousness plays an active, albeit small, role in the creation of physical reality."[34]

With this we have returned full circle to the notion that God equipped Adam to operate as a genuine creative force in the physical universe, and that He did this, at least in part, by opening up for the man a vast array of natural sensory channels to facilitate a high level of consciousness. On the basis of scriptural inference and/or contemporary scientific observation, we can speculate that Adam, in his original glory, may have been able to:

- command a virtually unlimited and flawless memory;
- communicate with other species;
- perform instant and accurate analyses;
- process external stimuli through all or most of his senses simultaneously;
- "see" remote places and events mentally;
- transfer his thoughts into other minds without verbalizing them;
- manipulate external objects with his mind;
- instantly teleport himself to other locations.

Even with these superman-like endowments, however, Adam was not invulnerable to failure. This magnificently engineered man soon turned to treachery against his Maker, as history sadly confirms. To contain the damage that this moral meltdown wrought upon the world, God was forced to place severe limitations on Adam's original design. Debate continues over the extent of this action, but at least one fact is sure: No human in post-Edenic history has ever manifested Adam's full suite of capabilities.

This observation raises two possibilities: either that these gifts were removed from human beings, in which case apparent lingering manifestations are attributable to demonic counterfeiting; or that man's original endowments lapsed into subconscious dormancy, in which case we need to ascertain whether it is wise or lawful to try to rekindle them.

Noted researchers Willis Harman and Howard Rheingold seem to favor the latter hypothesis. In a review of psychical studies conducted at the prestigious Stanford Research Institute (SRI), they conclude that "the ability to know what is happening at a place one has never visited is not a rare talent but a trainable skill, latent within all of us."[35]

The late Christian author Watchman Nee adopted a similar position. He suggests in his book *The Latent Power of the Soul* that many of Adam's original capabilities, rather than being removed after the Fall, were buried deep within his subconscious mind. As generation succeeded generation, "this primordial ability of Adam became a 'latent' force in his descendants."[36] According to Nee, "The work of the devil nowadays is to stir up man's soul [in order] to release this latent power within it as a deception for spiritual power."[37]

A Pair of Lies in Paradise

God's original intentions for His well-endowed human friends were as easy to remember as they were profound in their implications. As Adam and Eve assumed dominion over physical creation and multiplied their own species, they had but one additional obligation: to depend on their Creator for wisdom and sustenance.

In terms of exercising dominion, the first couple's descendants have done well. Since the dawn of history, fully half the earth's ice-free ecosystems have been modified, managed or utilized by human beings.[38] According to a scientific report released in 1990, the flows of materials and energy that are removed from their natural settings (or synthesized) now rival the flows of such materials within nature itself.[39]

Mankind has also been exceedingly fruitful. Despite the severe setback inflicted by the great Flood, the human family has managed to grow to nearly six billion members. Moreover, many researchers predict confidently that this number will double or even triple before growth rates level off. Even now the human population is expanding by about ten thousand people per hour![40]

One glaring disappointment has been humankind's failure to find wisdom. One generation after another, separated from her watchful companionship, has found itself hopelessly entangled in the sticky-sweet web of sin. In their determination to explore life's mysteries independent of their Creator, the intended masters of the earth have become "vain in their imaginations," their foolish hearts darkened to the true source of wisdom.[41]

It is a tragedy that need never have been written. From the moment Adam took his first breath, he stood distinct from creation in his ability to become wise. This capacity for wisdom was rooted in his spirit—a deep core essence that the Hebrews called *ruach*. Synonymous with "breath," the term reminds us that humanity's conscious life force was spawned by nothing less than the exhalation of God. With divine air in his lungs, man was forever and uniquely equipped with the ability to commune with his Maker.

God's intent in establishing this special channel was to ensure that man could always find his place, whether he was exploring the mysteries of the physical universe or wandering the confusing pathways of the heart. So long as the human creature reached out to his heavenly Father for wisdom, it would be to him as "a tree of life" (Proverbs 3:18).[42]

As spiritual creatures, Adam and Eve possessed not only the capacity for wisdom, but a hunger for it as well—a fact evidenced in Eve's observation that the forbidden fruit was "desirable for gaining wisdom" (Genesis 3:6). Each day their finely tuned senses absorbed information from the world around them, then processed this data into questions. Most of the time the answers came easily. Those that did not—often relating to the "why" of things—were resolved (we may surmise) in their daily spiritual communion with God.

This arrangement, unhappily, did not preclude trouble in paradise. Wherever and whatever Lucifer was at the creation of the first man and woman, his observations of God's obvious affection for these dust-fashioned creatures ignited an unquenchable jealousy within his heart. Thereafter, his only thoughts focused on darkening the Creator's dream.

Setting out on his bitter mission, Lucifer knew the only sure way to destroy the humans was to sever their dependence on God. The question was, How? Possessing souls, the man and woman were self-aware; but being sinless, they were not self-absorbed. If he was to lure Adam and Eve from God-consciousness to self-consciousness, he had to find an enticement.

Eventually Lucifer settled on an ingenious plan. Rather than deny man's intuitive pursuit of wisdom, he would promote the idea of an expanded quest. By appealing to a legitimate hunger, he could emphasize possibilities rather than prohibitions. All he needed to make his risky proposition work was an alternative source of knowledge—and a creative argument to get Adam and Eve to pursue it.

Scripture does not tell us who, if anyone, lured Eve to Eden's center, but it does speak of her encounter with an enchanted tree and a silk-tongued serpent. By partaking of the appealing fruit, he assured Eve, the old regimen of regulated mentoring could be replaced by instant wisdom. The decision was hers alone; but if she made the "right" one, it would make her more, not less, like God.

Eve entertained the serpent's rhetoric a moment too long, and his carefully conceived trap sprang shut with a cosmic shudder. Although Eve's consciousness was indeed flooded with carnal knowledge, the promise of instant wisdom proved as hollow as the devil's own heart. The sad and lingering consequence of the matter was later recorded as a moral epitaph by Solomon:

> God made mankind upright, but men have gone in search of many schemes.
>
> Ecclesiastes 7:29

There are several reasons the serpent's words were so persuasive. First, the creature was part of the original, friendly order Adam had named. Because sin had not yet entered into the world, Eve had little reason, at least initially, to be suspicious.[43] Also, as we have seen, the serpent appealed to a legitimate hunger. Since humans were designed to seek knowledge and wisdom, it was easy for the devil to encourage them in this direction. At the same time, he made shrewd use of Adam and Eve's undiminished sensory endowments. Recognizing their ability to savor environmental perfection, he simply highlighted the natural enticements of the forbidden fruit.[44] Eve partook of the fruit, according to Genesis 3:6, "when [she] saw that [it] was good for food and pleasing to the eye, and also desirable for gaining wisdom."

At its core, the devil's deception was based on a pair of potent lies. The first of these was the serpent's reassurance to Eve: "*You will not surely die . . .*" (Genesis 3:4, emphasis added).

With these five simple words, he managed to conceal not only the physical pain and emotional bereavement of generations to come, but the devastating reality of spiritual death. Having thus dealt with Eve's concerns, the serpent followed up quickly with a second lie aimed at the heart of her ambitions. "*You will be like God,*" he told her, "knowing good and evil" (verse 5, emphasis added).

As Eve allowed this powerful deception to enter into her mind, the poison spread quickly. Within a matter of moments, her will was engaged in an act of open rebellion against the God of heaven.[45]

In reality the serpent's cloak was threadbare. If Eve had not been so impulsive, she would have realized this. She had only to consider the simple fact, as Francis Schaeffer pointed out, that "experiential knowledge of evil is not what makes God God." Sadly, Eve did not bother with such considerations, and in the end her "fall [was] not a fall upward but a fall downward in every conceivable way. . . ."[46]

The Sacred Tree: Disconnecting from the Divine

The moment Eve allowed pride and independence to enter her heart, she triggered a process that would invert the very design of God. Her offspring, instead of experiencing fruitfulness of soul, would reap spiritual barrenness. Rather than exercise dominion, they would now be dominated by the fear of death.

The roots of this disaster did not lie in the knowledge of good and evil *per se*, but in the manner in which Adam and Eve had acquired this knowledge.[47] As the wisdom-giver, God intended His children to be well informed about evil—it lurked close at hand, after all—but only *after* they had attained a state of healthy and practiced dependence.

When Adam and Eve ate the forbidden fruit, their eyes were opened to their own nakedness. Realizing they had changed, they assumed God had changed, too. Though butterflies still danced along Eden's familiar trails, the masters of the Garden were gripped by a discomfiting sensation that more experienced generations would recognize as the pangs of primal fear. Endeavoring to hide from their Maker, they were confronted instead with the question of the ages: *"Who told you that you were naked?"* (Genesis 3:11, emphasis added).

For the first time in their lives, Adam and Eve were concerned with how they looked. Self-awareness had metamorphosed into self-consciousness. The premature knowledge of evil had become an internal strobe light, distracting them from the divine agenda.

Adam and Eve's descendants became even more preoccupied with self-aggrandizement and death—a condition that heightened their vulnerability to the devil's original lies. From the ancient civilizations of Mesopotamia to the contemporary ranks of the New Age, history sadly records the accounts of men and women willing to pay almost any price for the promise of immortality and inner divinity.[48]

In more recent times, the primary Edenic motifs—the serpent, the woman and the center tree—have resurfaced in connection with efforts to resacralize the feminine aspects of nature. One of the more articulate proponents of this movement is Dr. Elinor Gadon, the art historian who has taught at Tufts University and Harvard Divinity School.[49]

In the spring of 1992, I had the opportunity to meet Dr. Gadon at a small French restaurant in a southern suburb of Berkeley, California. I found her both pleasant and consumed with her mission. Adorned with a ring of intertwined serpents and arriving in a car with a bumper sticker that read *The Goddess Is Alive and Magic Is Afoot,* I expected, and got, an engaging interview.

Dr. Gadon's present interests were quickened, she told me, during a 1967 visit to India. Her comments on this experience (which she also offers in her 1989 book *The Once and Future Goddess*) were particularly revealing.

"What happened in India," she explained, "was that I experienced myself as sexual, sacred and powerful in a way no woman in the West can. When I later returned to the United States, there was a radical rupture in the fabric of my being. My erotic self, the deep life force within, had been activated, and there was no way to put the genie back in the bottle."[50]

Elsewhere in her widely circulated book, Gadon introduces the ideas of "erotic feminist" Deena Metzger. As Metzger sees it, the only way to revamp today's dysfunctional culture is to adopt fundamentally new beliefs, and the best way to do this is to reinvoke the Goddess.[51] As part of this new spiritual order, Metzger insists, "we must engage in two heresies." The first task is "to return to the very early, neolithic, pagan, matriarchal perception of the sacred universe itself," and the second is to "re-sanctify the body." At the same time, Metzger seems to sense the awkwardness that inevitably accompanies the unnatural act of circumventing the Creator in pursuit of wisdom. "We often feel as though we are defying God in the act of seeking the divine," she says. It is a "state of torment" in which we feel "alone, ashamed, bewildered. . . ."[52]

Unfortunately Metzger, like Eve before her, fails to acknowledge that this inner conflict is a product of her own rebellion. It is precisely this rebellion (and deception) that the apostle Paul addressed in the first chapter of Romans. Although mankind "knew God," he wrote, "they neither glorified him as God nor gave thanks to him." As a consequence, "their thinking became futile and their foolish hearts were darkened" (verse 21). Because they exchanged divine glory for mortal images, the Almighty "gave them over in the sinful desires of their hearts" (verse 24), permitting them to degrade their minds and bodies through sexual impurity.

Tearing a page from early Mesopotamian and Canaanite religious practices, Metzger declares to her female readers, "We must allow ourselves whatever time it takes to re-establish the consciousness of the Sacred Prostitute. . . ."[53] In her rush to embrace this alternative imagery, Metzger reports being confronted during a season of guided meditation "by a large, luminous woman" whose hair was "light itself." Finding herself face to face with what was "clearly an image of a goddess," Metzger mused: "If I were to take her into me, I knew my life would be altered. The woman was powerful . . . she drew me to her."[54]

Standing enticingly behind the woman was a tree, sometimes appearing as a branch, pillar or notched pole. With its deep and primal roots, it too has become a universal symbol of wisdom and immortality. From Dyak villages in Malaysia to the weathered highlands of Ethiopia, the belief persists that the first human ancestors were born from the tree of life.[55]

In other settings the tree has become synonymous with dimensional gateways and cosmic centers.[56] Of particular interest are early Babylonian inscriptions that declare: "Near Eridu was a garden, in which [could be found] a Tree of Life." Planted by the gods and protected by guardian spirits, the tree had roots that were said to run deep, while its branches reached to heaven. Related myths reveal not only that this tree had limbs of lapis lazuli and bore wonderful fruit, but also that the whole universe revolved around it.[57]

Always lurking in the vicinity of the woman and the tree is the serpent. In the mythical realm, the Greeks spoke of the golden apples of the Hesperides that hung on a paradisaical tree guarded by a fearsome snake coiled around its trunk.[58] In the real world archaeologists have discovered at least two Mesopotamian seals depicting scenes even more suggestive of the Genesis account. One of these, an ancient Babylonian tablet now residing in the British Museum, depicts a man and woman plucking fruit from a central tree. Behind the woman a serpent stands erect, as though offering encouragement. On the other seal, discovered in the Tepe Gawra Mound just north of Nineveh and dated to 3500 B.C., a serpent follows a naked and dejected couple.[59]

Days of the Giants: Life in Eden's Fading Glow

Unlike the hard sciences, which are built on theories and formulae, history is essentially a fascinating collection of stories. The majority of these are accounts of things that really happened. Given their antiquity, however, they must be conveyed into the present via a transgenerational chain of storytellers.

In 1872 George Smith of the British Museum encountered some of the early links in this chain while conducting research in what is now northern Iraq. He was studying tablets from the library of Assurbanipal at Nineveh that had been copied from similar records dating back to the first dynasty of Ur. Intriguingly, these earthen messengers contained references not only to "the Flood," but to "the age before the Flood."[60]

Although most storytellers from the antediluvian epoch were destroyed in the Flood, this does not mean their stories perished with them. Illustrated pages from this mysterious chapter of human history have been preserved at a wide variety of sites in the form of rock art and fossilized remains. Each of these records offers its own explanation of the world that was—a kind of documentary account of everyday life in prehistoric times.[61]

What do these accounts tell us? For one thing, it appears that, from an environmental standpoint, Eden's fading glow was still sufficient to sustain remarkably luxuriant life. Paleontological snapshots of this era reveal that swaying palms, grapevines and ninety-foot fruit trees covered regions that are now polar and desert landscapes. They further disclose that man was joined on the earth by enormous animals, including seventeen-foot-high rhinos and fifty-foot crocodiles. Oversize camels shuffled across the Alaskan wilderness, while mammoths, panthers and hyenas roamed the misty vales of continental Europe.[62]

Game was also plentiful and man became a relentless hunter.[63] One of the more interesting references to this is found in the Genesis 10 account of Nimrod. Although he does not appear on the scene until after the Flood, his physical prowess and legendary reputation as "a mighty hunter" (verses 8–9) make it difficult to avoid associating him with the Nephilim spoken of in Genesis 6:4.[64]

In addition to their imposing stature, early men and women were also blessed with remarkable longevity. The Jewish historian Josephus cites agreement among Egyptian, Chaldean, Phoenician and Greek historians that "the ancients lived a thousand years."[65] Genesis 5 not only concurs, but ends with the astonishing note that Noah fathered three sons after the age of five hundred![66]

There is also a dark side to the antediluvian story, a sinister sub-plot that winds through secret initiation caves, urban shrines and hallucinogenic landscapes. Nestled at the heart of this plot is a conscious, if unfathomable, decision by Adam's progeny to abandon the divine order for a world in which fertility is the province of bulls, and wisdom is dispensed from the mouths of birds and reptiles.

It remained for the ancients, once they embraced such a worldview, to instill their tribal myths into the minds of succeeding generations. To overcome any natural skepticism, young initiates were taken into limestone caves where they confronted what paleontologist John Pfeiffer calls "deep art"—sacred and suggestive images of bison, bears, owls and lions. Not only was this art located in utter darkness, far from familiar places, but it was often "anamorphic"—painted on natural protuberances and depressions so as to give the rendering a three-dimensional appearance. The effect was especially powerful when viewed unexpectedly from the proper light and angle.

Shamans and clan leaders knew precisely when and where to light their animal-fat torches. They also knew their primitive virtual reality displays could be enhanced by anticipation (whispered myths), sound effects (drums and chanting) and disorientation (dark, labyrinthine passages and mind-altering substances). With these elements in place, Paleolithic caves were transformed into subterranean sanctuaries where novices could be initiated into the alternative realities of their elders.[67]

Evidence suggests the practice was widespread. More than two hundred of these ceremonial chambers have been discovered in southwestern Europe alone, including Lascaux, Altamira and Chauvet Cave (see map 1). They have also been found in southern Anatolia (Kara'In), Libya (Tadrart Acacus) and the Czech Republic (Pekarna Cave).[68] Aboveground ritual sites also exist. The most impressive examples: the aboriginal galleries of northern Australia and the so-called "Round Head" murals in the western Sahara.

The Round Head murals are located on southern Algeria's Tassili-n-Ajjer Plateau, a remote badlands described by one visitor as "a landscape hallucinated by inner fevers." Here in a labyrinth of eroding stone escarpments are some of the earliest known depictions of shamans in ritual trance. In one set of pictures, masked figures dance with fists full of hallucinogenic mushrooms. In another, a stylized

MAP 1

The Antediluvian World

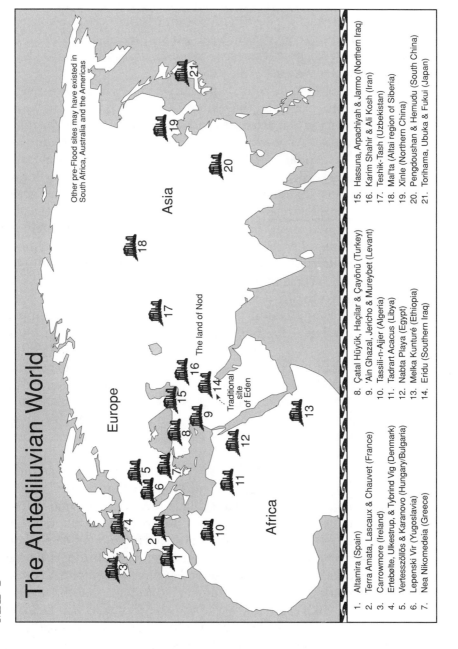

Other pre-Flood sites may have existed in
South Africa, Australia and the Americas

Europe

Asia

Africa

The land of Nod

Traditional
site
of Eden

1. Altamira (Spain)
2. Terra Amata, Lascaux & Chauvet (France)
3. Carrowmore (Ireland)
4. Ertebølle, Ulkestrup, & Tybrind Vig (Denmark)
5. Vértesszőlős & Karanovo (Hungary/Bulgaria)
6. Lepenski Vir (Yugoslavia)
7. Nea Nikomedeia (Greece)
8. Çatal Hüyük, Hacilar & Çayönü (Turkey)
9. 'Ain Ghazal, Jericho & Mureybet (Levant)
10. Tassili-n-Ajjer (Algeria)
11. Tadrart Acacus (Libya)
12. Nabta Playa (Egypt)
13. Melka Kunturé (Ethiopia)
14. Eridu (Southern Iraq)
15. Hassuna, Arpachiyah & Jarmo (Northern Iraq)
16. Karim Shahir & Ali Kosh (Iran)
17. Teshik-Tash (Uzbekistan)
18. Mal'ta (Altai region of Siberia)
19. Xinle (Northern China)
20. Pengdoushan & Hemudu (South China)
21. Torihama, Ubuka & Fukui (Japan)

priest-magician has the charmed plants sprouting out of his body. Though the exact purpose of these exotic frescoes is open for speculation, several scholars who have studied the Tassili rock paintings believe their placement and style suggest a role similar to that played by European cave art.[69]

As to whose hands actually produced these entrancing images, scholars have ventured the names of several prehistoric bands, among them the Magdalenians and the so-called Caspian people.[70] Another intriguing possibility is that these pagan hunter-gatherers were the descendants of Cain. According to Genesis 4, "Cain went out from the Lord's presence" because the ground would "no longer yield its crops" for him (verses 16, 12). Condemned to live as "a restless wanderer on the earth" (verse 12), he traveled first to the land of Nod. Located somewhere east of Eden, it may well have included cave dwellings like Karim Shahir in the north Zagros Mountains. In time, the nomadic Cainites presumably spread westward, migrating through various Balkan and Anatolian caves en route to destinations in North Africa and southwestern Europe.[71]

As wandering Neolithic clans continued to expand in numbers and knowledge, they gravitated toward more permanent settlements.[72] In the process of this social evolution, the ritual art that had been confined to caves and gullies was brought into communal shrines. At Lepenski Vir, an ancient fishing center in the Danube River basin, archaeologists have uncovered the foundations of more than fifty such shrines. Similar discoveries have been recorded at the eight-thousand-year-old settlement of Çatal Hüyük in central Turkey.[73]

Çatal Hüyük's shrines, like its private residences, were adjoined vertically in pueblo-style architecture. Entry to the doorless and windowless chambers was provided via ladders that descended from roof openings. Inside, the walls were adorned with painted images and clay friezes in low relief. Most portrayed totemic animals—leopards, vultures and especially bulls. In the center of the rooms, horned altar seats known as *bucrania* served as receptacles for ritual grain and blood offerings. And while archaeologists are doubtful that any of Çatal Hüyük's estimated seven thousand citizens was included among the sacrifices, they have yet to explain the significance of human skulls found in nearby baskets.

An element of mystery also surrounds the presence of special "recliners" built into some of the shrine rooms. At least one scholar has speculated that they may have facilitated the ritual use of psychoactive substances.[74] If this conjecture is correct, it is possible that these early visionary trances fed the emerging cult of the Earth Goddess, whose symbolic presence, like that of the virile bull, was felt in every corner of the community.

As in Lepenski Vir, where she appeared with half-human, half-fish features, the Goddess at Çatal Hüyük was chimerical, or of mixed species. In one shrine her face and body are feline; in another her features appear both human and birdlike. Many of the images are portrayed with their legs spread far apart, some giving birth to bulls, rams or leopards, others bringing forth human children.[75]

Whether the Goddess precipitated or merely reflected the moral collapse referred to in Genesis 6:5 and Romans 1:21–32, there is no doubt she was used skillfully by her demonic patrons to erode the uniqueness and nobility of man. Having rejected God's injunction to assume dominion over the animal kingdom, the people of Çatal Hüyük—and indeed the whole world—soon found themselves bowing before the "Mistress of the Animals."[76] As the influence of the Goddess expanded throughout the Neolithic period (between 8000 and 3500 B.C.), tens of thousands of Goddess figurines flooded Europe and the Near East. Many featured the elongated heads and serpentine eyes of their spiritual father.[77]

These developments led not to an era of spiritual bliss, as many contemporary Goddess advocates would have us believe, but to a season of unprecedented violence and sexual perversion.[78] Men and women, persuaded they were possessed of an animal nature, began to act accordingly. Pursuing what Terence McKenna calls an "orgiastic and psychedelic" religion, Goddess cults in Africa and at Çatal Hüyük used hallucinogens "to promote open and unstructured sexuality."[79] In the sacred caves of southwestern Europe, early artists included images of human decapitation and women being mounted by bulls.[80]

Scripture hints at two primary catalysts in the spread of this wickedness: the proliferation of urban communities[81] and the unhealthy marriages between the "sons of God" (the Sethite line) and "the daughters of men" (the wayward Cainite line). The city, with its dual capacity to sustain life and offer a marketplace of ideas, became the new Eden. It was here that the Sethites first heard their well-traveled cousins relate captivating tales of magic mushrooms, subterranean temples and even a great Goddess. It was here that they came in contact with the seductive beauty of "liberated" Cainite women, and eventually ignored their spiritual instincts, embracing these women and their gods. It was also here that, like their cousins before them, they left the presence of the Lord.[82]

The scope of this exodus was so comprehensive that, according to Genesis 6:6, God's "heart was filled with pain." Everywhere He looked, the earth was corrupt and full of violence. People no longer wanted to keep Him in their thoughts. The inclination of their hearts was now "only evil all the time" (verse 5). It was a catastrophe of epic proportions, and to contain it God had no choice but to visit the earth with judgment. When the time finally came, His tears coursed through the heavens for forty days and forty nights.[83]

The environmental changes wrought by the Flood were enormous, but the full effects were not felt for many centuries. Having spared only one family from the waters of judgment, God realized that a temporary continuation of antediluvian longevity was necessary to repopulate the earth. Accordingly, the last restraints on the natural course of the environment were not removed until history pulled up at Babel's doorstep.[84]

The timing of this pivotal event is marked in Scripture by the mention of two brothers—siblings remembered not for their exploits but for the global events associated with their times. Genesis 10:25 informs us that Peleg, whose name means "division," was so named "because in his time the earth was divided." According to the Jewish Talmud, his brother Joktan, whose name means "little," derived his identity from the fact that "the duration of the life of man was shortened in his time."

These brief but extraordinary historical epitaphs remind us not only of God's ability to integrate His sovereign purposes into the processes of nature, but of His deep concern over the circumstances that led up to, and were likely to result from, man's initiatives at Babel. If the Flood represented a great dividing gulf in human history, so, too, did the strange and infamous Tower on the plain of Shinar.

The Tower across the Gulf

While little is known of the so-called recovery years between Ararat and Babel, the book of Genesis hints at two important developments during this period. The first of these, which can also be inferred from archaeology, is that humanity expanded from a single family to a full-fledged civilization. Population growth, with no external enemies, was both rapid and socially coherent. At the same time, man's knowledge and fear of God were decreasing. Men who once had built altars to the Lord began instead to erect monuments for themselves.[85]

This unhealthy trend was doubtless facilitated by mankind's linguistic unity (see Genesis 11:1). Communication, after all, allowed for conspiracy. Whether or not this early monolingualism was a carry-over from the pre-Flood world, its subsequent presence in the Near East has been attested to by various Sumerian sources,[86] as well as by several credentialed linguistic scholars. One of the most articulate and forceful of these scholars, Stanford University's Dr. Merritt Ruhlen, argues that comparative evidence alone leads us to the "inescapable conclusion that all extant languages share a common origin."[87]

If common speech facilitated the infamy at Babel, however, it was hardly the only factor. A venture of this magnitude also required leadership, a role apparently filled by the enigmatic Nimrod. A great-grandson of Noah, he was arguably the most dominant figure on earth during the Babel era. Given his elevated stature, it is surprising how little has been written about him. In fact, were it not for the remarkable résumé of Genesis 10—in which the "mighty hunter" is said to have established no fewer than eight urban centers, including the great city-states of Babylon and Nineveh—it is unlikely that Nimrod's fame would have lingered into modern times. Although his legacy is strongest in Assyria (northern Iraq),[88] the Jewish Zohar reveals that in Babylonia Nimrod "commenced to attach himself to other powers."[89]

If the construction of Babel's dark Tower was simply a large-scale reenactment of the Fall, then rebellion was its foundation stone. As the sweat-drenched descendants of Noah hoisted their bricks under the unrelenting Middle Eastern sun, their goal was as obvious as their architecture: If God would not manifest Himself on terms more to their liking, then they would pave their own route to wisdom and stability.

In what Francis Schaeffer calls the "first public declaration of humanism," we hear them cry, *"Let us make a name for ourselves"* (Genesis 11:4, RSV, emphasis added). The pride of self-sufficiency is unmistakable, but that is not the only motive at work. They also express their concern that they will "be scattered . . . over the face of the whole earth" (verse 4).

There may be no greater fear than that of being lost, of losing one's identity. It is an emotion with roots in self-consciousness—and self-consciousness, as we have seen, is a trail that leads back to Eden. As Os Guinness observed in *The Dust of Death,*

> . . . The very drive to transcend implies a degree of alienation. Man is the only known species who experiences the urge to escape his ordinary range of consciousness which is obviously unsatisfying to him; this urge gives him a sense of being at odds with himself; feeling other than he is.[90]

Man is also the only creature possessed with the capacity to conceptualize death—the ultimate in lost identity. Unless he has made peace with God, angst will be the natural partner to his alienation.[91] In such a condition, two things become especially important: *traveling companions* (safety in numbers) and *a method of divining the future* (safety in foreknowledge). In the collective paranoia that ruled southern Mesopotamia, people addressed these needs in the form of an immense, baked-brick ziggurat that spiraled up to the very habitation of the gods.[92]

With memories of Eden's golden age still fresh on their minds, the people of Babel were apparently trying to reopen a dimensional gateway to the divine. Like the paradisiacal center tree, the sacred ziggurat represented an axis around which the rest of the world revolved. It was the *dimgal,* or "binding post," where, according to Geoffrey Ashe, spiritual lines of force converged—the opening "by which passage from one cosmic region to another was made possible."[93]

Equally suggestive were the names applied to the sanctuaries at the base of this cosmic ladder—names like the "House of the Base of Heaven and Earth" and the "Link between Heaven and Earth."[94]

(Babel itself meant "The Gate of the Gods.") The temple at the top of the Tower was considered an important way station for the gods as they descended from heaven to earth.[95]

Although this duality of divine presence was almost certainly patterned after the Edenic archetype, in which God descended from His holy mount to walk with Adam and Eve, there was one important distinction: In Babylonia the gods did not descend in order to walk with humans, but to lie with them. This practice involved both men and women and took place inside the ziggurat-crowning temple.[96] In addition to ritual intercourse between a deified human king and the goddess Innana (an annual rite undertaken to ensure fertility for the coming year),[97] there were also high priestesses known as *Entu* who made themselves available to male deities.[98]

Whatever else may have taken place atop the Tower of Babel, or any of its many clones,[99] the cosmic mountain to which it led was the principal domain of *Enlil,* popularly known as "Lord Air." It was Enlil's potent winds that charged the atmosphere over Sumer.

Northern Lights and Swarming Darkness

To conclude that something serious was unfolding at Babel, we have only to note God's extraordinary interest in the situation. According to Genesis 11:5, "The Lord *came down*" for the purpose of conducting a personal, on-site inspection of the emerging city and Tower.

Although the Babylonians' idolatry and base ambition were deeply troubling, the focus of divine concern was apparently their unity of purpose. "If as one people speaking the same language they have begun to do this," God reasoned, "then nothing they plan to do will be impossible for them" (Genesis 11:6).

This telling observation reminds us of the awesome power of synergy. Sin is never tame, but when it is pursued as part of a common cause, its effects are magnified exponentially. In the case of Babel, the people's moral and physical unity had attracted great attention in the spirit world. The plain of Shinar, which means "strange power,"[100] was being covered with a swarming darkness. God was distressed not over architectural designs but over the emerging nexus between unified men and gathering demonic hosts.

Put simply, demons congregate where people are. There is no reason for them to be anywhere else. Their ugly mandate is to "steal and kill and destroy" (John 10:10) what is precious to God; and, as Psalm 8:5–6 and Matthew 6:26 tell us, human beings are securely ensconced at the top of heaven's list of valuables.

Cities, with their concentrations of humanity, are especially potent magnets for demonic powers, which helps to explain why they are so often dark and oppressive places.[101] Babel was no exception, except that her citizenry represented the entire population of the earth. Given these unique demographics, it is easy to hypothesize that the city and her infamous Tower were at the center of the greatest demonic ingathering in human history.

The Hebrew Scriptures, in support of this notion, make repeated idiomatic use of the term *Tsaphon* for north (including as a synonym for Babylon).[102] Used strictly of the north as a quarter, *Tsaphon* means "hidden, dark or gloomy." Derived from the word *tsaphan,* meaning "unknown, to hide (by covering over) or to lurk," the general idea is that the north is an envelope of darkness—a concentration of the greatest evil powers.[103]

Although there is considerable Zoroastrian and Jewish apocalyptic literature on the subject, the notion of a dark spiritual north is by no means confined to the ancient Near East. The Aztecs believed that each cardinal direction has a personality manifesting particular aspects of the human journey. The north, suggestively called "the land of the cloud serpents," was the direction of death and decay. To face or travel north carried grave implications, for it was there that a soul could lose itself forever.[104] To the Chinese, the north has long symbolized fear, winter and primordial chaos; while New Mexico's Zuni Indians avoid it as the "Swept or Barren Place."[105]

The prophet Jeremiah wrote not only that "evil looks down from the north," but that this is the direction from which "a destroyer of nations has set out" (Jeremiah 6:1; 4:7, NASB).[106] As to who this evil destroyer might be, the book of Daniel presents us with the demonically inspired Antiochus IV Epiphanes, while Zoroastrian literature offers Ahriman, or the devil himself (the upper hemisphere being the site of his infernal kingdom).[107] St. Augustine also saw the devil—

but symbolically—in the stormy northern winds of Ezekiel 1:4: "Who is that north wind save him who said: 'I will set up my seat in the north, I will be like the Most High'?"[108]

If the north is a realm of power, however, it is also perceived as a locus of revelation. Examples include the belief that the Greek god Apollo absorbed his wisdom from a mysterious northern people known as the Hyperboreans; and the Qumran community's expectation that the messianic "Interpreter of the Torah" would appear in Damascus, a city regarded not only as "the Land of the North" but also as the gateway of hidden knowledge passing from the Near East to Israel and Europe.[109] It is also noteworthy that the Persian philosopher Manes received his calling from the "King of the Gardens of Light" while living in the Babylonian city of Tesiphon.

This and other evidence linking the hosts of darkness to the northern hemisphere[110] helps us understand why God was so distressed by the developments at Babel. Had He not intervened when He did, it is possible that the power of collective visualization would have allowed coalescing demonic forces to imperil the human race. As it was, the Tower had already become an alternative source of knowledge—an Edenic *déjà vu*. The Lord God, who had already pledged Himself to refrain from any more mass destruction of life, elected to deal with mankind's unholy alliance through geographic and linguistic separation. Men and women would be confounded rather than consumed.

Attesting to the success of the divine plan, one ancient Mesopotamian tablet declared:

> The building of this illustrious tower offended the gods. In one night they threw down what [men] had built. They scattered them abroad, and made strange their speech.[111]

With the outward explosion of humanity, our quest to discover why spiritual darkness lingers where it does takes on added momentum. We have now been given several valuable clues, including mankind's preoccupation with dimensional gateways and the special attraction human communities hold for demonic powers. To learn how these can help us solve one of the labyrinth's most important mysteries—the origins of territorial strongholds—our next step will be to follow Babel's aboriginal peoples as they migrate out from the Plain of Shinar.

CHAPTER FIVE

OUT FROM BABEL

People were on the move long before the Romans' Appian Way or the Incas' awesome Royal Road were even conceived. From weary tribal clans who trudged along on foot to horse-borne armies that consumed real estate at a gallop, their goal was to probe the world's outer limits in search of greener grass.

The record of these early explorations is often an exotic mix of fact and fancy. Europe was buzzing as late as the 1700s over the travelogue of Lemuel Gulliver—an account purporting to describe the people of hitherto unknown lands such as Brobdingnag and Lilliput. Even when it became known that *Gulliver's Travels* was actually the imaginary invention of Jonathan Swift, many refused to let go of the fantasy.

Nor was Swift the first purveyor of such visions. The third-century geographer Julius Solinus (surnamed *Polyhistor,* or "Teller of Varied Tales") routinely embellished his pages with the likes of four-eyed men and a tribe of monopeds who used their large single feet as parasols to protect them from the sun. Once again, leading thinkers of the day, including St. Augustine, preferred to suspend credulity rather than dismiss a potential source of knowledge.[1]

Even today the movements of ancient humans remain a tangle of truth and legend. Those who try to document the faint trails often find themselves sidetracked by the contrived narratives of false religions (the Hindu Mahabharata and the Book of Mormon spring to mind) or the theoretical decoys of evolutionary anthropology. The few who maintain their bearings in the thicket of disinformation do so by taking frequent readings from the compass of Scripture.

But the biblical record, while reliable, is also disturbing, especially as it relates to the centuries following man's dispersion from Babel.[2] Not only does this era feature humans reaching the planet's outer extremities, but it has them reconnecting with the dark spiritual forces that once hovered over Shinar. Just how they accomplished these feats is one of history's great puzzles.

Reconstructing the Past

The task of gathering prehistoric information is not easy. With eons of time and a full complement of natural erasers at its disposal, the deep past is proficient at maintaining its secrets. Not wishing to become lost in this "dark backwash and abysm of time,"[3] many historians have elected to confine their investigations to the boundaries of literate civilization.

Indeed, the word *prehistory* did not enter European vocabularies until the mid-nineteenth century. Taken literally, it means "prior to the use of writing," and implies that there are stringent limitations on what it is possible for us to know today. As acclaimed British archaeologist Colin Renfrew reminds us, however, "This does not mean that we have to assume complete ignorance."[4] In fact, Renfrew's own field of archaeology represents one of the best means of peering into the deep past. People are messy animals, and the debris our ancestors left strewn about the terrestrial landscape can offer valuable insights into their movements, habits and aspirations.

Many prehistoric peoples, recognizing the retentive properties of certain inorganic materials, sought to preserve their thoughts and feelings by impressing them into matter.[5] In time these etched and sculpted records were discovered and brought back to Europe by missionaries, merchants and explorers. After years of languishing in private "cabinets of curiosities" owned by the rich and powerful, they eventually became the star attractions of public museums.[6]

In the years since, new technologies have allowed scholars to recover thousands of artifacts from around the world.[7] In the presence of these ancient objects and places, the past has become more than a warehouse of myths.[8] Each new discovery reminds us that real people manufactured these intimate records. And although their calling cards may be worn with time, the brittle and often faint messages they convey can tell us plenty about life in earlier ages.[9]

Bones and artifacts are not the only messengers from the past. According to linguists like Aron Dogopolsky, much can also be learned from man's use of words.[10] Claiming to have identified or reconstructed more than one thousand prehistoric terms—most relating to such things as hunting, animal anatomy, magical forces and spell-casting—the Russian-born Dogopolsky likes to talk about "looking through the telescope of vocabulary" to capture an understanding of ancient lifestyles.[11]

Reconstructing prehistoric events through linguistic analysis involves many of the same detecting skills employed in archaeology. Foremost among these is drawing inferences—logical hypotheses based on known facts.[12] If developed correctly, inferences can reveal significant details about a people's movements, actions and relationships. If a community in an area devoid of tigers, for example, speaks a language that includes a term for this animal, we may surmise either that they once lived in or passed through a tiger habitat, or else they came in contact with a people group that knew tigers.[13]

Language nuggets may also be retained through oral traditions. As Renfrew writes, "It is now generally agreed that this is precisely how the epics of Homer . . . and the Irish epics were preserved."[14] The epics were passed on through the chanting of Druid priests in much the same way that Indian holy men conveyed the Vedic hymns over many centuries.[15]

In fact, most oral transmission of literature has taken the form of songs sung by specialist bards or priests. In Celtic lands, bards or files were epic poets who often accompanied themselves on the harp. Highly trained in their art, they were held in unusual esteem.[16] In fact, only in ancient Africa, where the storytellers were called *domas* (masters of knowledge), do we find similar reverence.[17] As a local proverb puts it, "The mouth of an old man smells bad, but good and salutary things come out of it."[18]

Scattered Clans and Drifting Shores

Although smartly painted aircraft today convey hundreds of thousands of passengers over the earth's great seas, ancient men would have found such a proposition unthinkable. In their minds, the oceans were as impassable as the heavens, not simply because of their immeasurable girth, but because they emptied into the vault of oblivion.[19]

Eventually, of course, curiosity, bravery and technology combined to overcome these primal fears. There is evidence that as early as 1200 B.C., the Egyptians were employing sturdy sailing vessels to move thousands of men across the Indian Ocean to work the gold mines of South Africa and Sumatra. By the eighth century B.C., Phoenician seamen were crossing the open Mediterranean to establish the trading colony of Tarshish in southern Spain, a route they maintained with the largest ships in the Semitic world (one of which carried the reluctant prophet Jonah).[20] Six hundred years later, on the opposite side of the globe, the Chinese emperor Wu led a large part of his court on an epic transoceanic trading expedition from north China to the east coast of India.[21]

As impressive as these early voyages are, however, they offer no solution to the conundrum of indigenous peoples. Virtually every time nautical explorers waded onto the shores of a new land, they discovered people already in residence. The question is, How did they get there?

To resolve this dilemma, scientists and theologians have suggested two possibilities. The first contends that the primeval earth was a single land mass—the continent of Pangaea. This theory, once considered no more credible than that of the lost continent of Atlantis, has picked up much support in recent years.[22] From a creationist viewpoint, the breakup of the supercontinent began with the Flood[23] and climaxed in Peleg's day when "the earth was divided" (or, in Hebrew, "canaled"—see Genesis 10:25).

It is not easy to map out the geography of an ancient epoch on a dynamic planet, but there is little doubt such a breakup occurred.[24] In addition to the geological harmony between several mountain ranges on either side of the Atlantic Ocean, magnetic data and satellite images of the ocean floor reveal deep fractures along which the continents slid apart.[25]

An alternative theory holds that the continents had already divided at the time of the great Dispersion and that early peoples were able to reach these far-flung habitats via low-lying land bridges.[26] Later, when global warming melted vast polar ice sheets, these busy intercontinental footpaths were swallowed up by rising seas.

Whether ancient men dispersed via these short-lived causeways or by rafting tectonic plates across reservoirs of molten magma, we may never know.[27] We can state with relative certainty, however, that Babel's emigrants found this geological upheaval every bit as disorienting as their scrambled tongues. To explore new worlds is one thing; to see your only connection with the past sinking under the waves is quite another.[28]

Among those who encountered this trauma were the forebears of the Hopi and Navajo Indians who presently inhabit the American Southwest. The creation myths of both tribes speak of ancient migrations through four worlds. Navajos write poems about walking the "Long Walk," while Hopis assert that the polar center of the earth shifted from the now-vanished third world to the Hopi homeland on this present fourth world.[29]

Before we dismiss these assertions as imaginary inventions, it is important to remember that myths are often based on facts, events that really happened. In the case of the Hopi and Navajo, it is conceivable that the myths reference a long and arduous journey their ancestors took from Mesopotamia to the American Southwest. It is also plausible that their "four worlds" correspond to sequential homelands in Shinar, the Siberio-Altai region (where they adopted shamanic motifs), the Alaska-Western Canada corridor (where they have linguistic and genetic relatives to this day) and the sacred buttes of Arizona and New Mexico.

Other cultural myths contain similar references to ancient migrations that originated in settings consistent with the Near East. As William Howells states in his well-known textbook *Mankind So Far:* "If we look . . . for that part of the world which was the hothouse of the races, we can make only one choice. All the visible footsteps lead away from Asia."[30]

It is also clear that whoever left these footprints was moving fast. According to anthropologist Randall White, one of the most common forms of body adornment in prehistoric Europe was the canine teeth necklace. Intriguingly, the same fashion was in vogue in ancient Australia. An unremarkable coincidence? Anthropologists have learned that such coincidences are rare. As *Time* magazine's Michael Lemonick observes, "If [this] art did move around the world, it moved with astonishing speed."[31]

Such observations, obviously not conclusive, lend added support to the idea that the earth was still a solitary land mass at the time of humanity's dispersion from Babel. With neither oceans nor land bridges to cross, early men could have fanned out much more rapidly. If there was only one land mass, the discovery of "coincidental" ideas and fashions at opposite ends of the earth is not so surprising.

Nor is the task of determining actual migration routes as daunting as we might expect. This is because movements of men, like those of fluids, tend to take the line of least resistance. Whereas mountains, seas and swamps typically constrain the flow of humanity, plains and valleys provide ready thoroughfares.

Language studies are also helpful in reconstructing the circumstances that led to the present distribution of the world's peoples. Starting from the theory (called *monogenesis*) that humanity initially spoke a single tongue, linguists like Joseph Greenberg and Aron Dogolpolsky have mapped distinct genealogies that point to original and secondary homelands.[32] What's more, these linguistically inspired maps have recently been correlated dramatically with Luca Cavalli-Sforza's census of worldwide blood types[33] and Colin Renfrew's newest dating of the spread of agriculture.

This development is exciting for scientists and Bible scholars alike. It means that for the first time, data from three separate disciplines—linguistics, genetics and archaeology—are all telling more or less the same story about early homelands and migrations.[34] Armed with this new evidence, we are able to construct a far more accurate and complete scenario of man's exodus from Babel.

As we begin our investigation into the great exile, an interesting fact presents itself. Man's departure from Shinar, it seems, was not as fluid or fragmented as we have been led to believe. Rather than fanning out immediately across the face of the earth, Babylonia's refugees apparently regrouped in several secondary staging areas, most notably Arabia, Anatolia (eastern Turkey) and the Siberian Altai (see map 2). In addition to serving as linguistic homelands and spiritual seedbeds, these destinations became leading transit hubs.

Scripture is tight-lipped about the size of these early pilgrim bands, but almost loquacious on the subject of who they were and where they went. Much of this information is contained in the Table of Nations found in Genesis 10. Here we are told unequivocally that "the clans of Noah's sons," namely the Semites, Hamites and Japhethites, were responsible for the nations that "spread out over the earth after the flood"—mostly via Babel.

The Semites

The first arterial out of Babel led southward into Arabia, a land that bore little resemblance at the time to the arid landscape we know today. This was Job's country, and his memoirs, considered by many scholars to be the oldest record in Scripture, speak of snow-capped mountains, vineyards and shade trees. Abundant waters (mentioned more than 25 times) nourished golden fields of grain and a diversity of pastoral animals.

This desirable place was known as Uz, and according to Jeremiah 25:20, it eventually attracted a sizable population.[35] Uz was named after a descendant of Shem,[36] and evidence suggests that the region served as an early Semitic homeland from which colonizing tentacles later extended into North Africa, the Levant and even back into Mesopotamia.[37] Other descendants of Shem apparently remained behind in Shinar (where they presumably spoke Sumerian) and southwest Persia (where they developed a distinct, non-Semitic language known as Elamite).

The Hamites

Other southbound exiles ignored this Arabian off-ramp in favor of a lush region that stretched from modern-day Yemen (biblical Sheba) to the mountain heartland of Ethiopia (biblical Cush).[38] For the most part these travelers were Hamites,[39] a robust and darker-

MAP 2

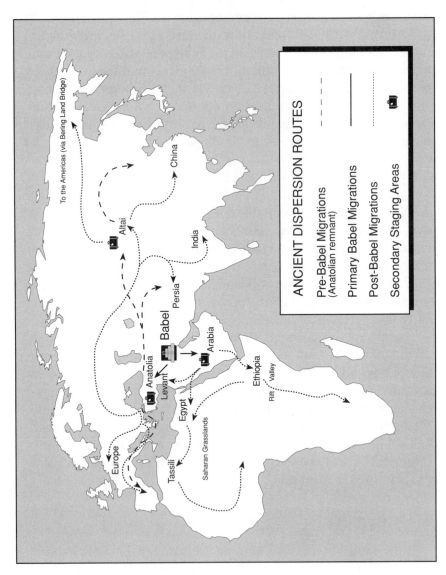

ANCIENT DISPERSION ROUTES

Pre-Babel Migrations
(Anatolian remnant)

Primary Babel Migrations

Post-Babel Migrations

Secondary Staging Areas

To the Americas (via Bering Land Bridge)

China

Altai

India

Persia

Babel

Anatolia

Arabia

Levant

Egypt

Ethiopia

Rift Valley

Tassili

Saharan Grasslands

Europe

skinned conglomeration of peoples that would eventually spread out across the entire African continent.[40]

Early branch migrations apparently included at least two west-bound groups—northern pastoralists who drove their herds through the vast Saharan grasslands around Lake Chad, and hunter-gatherer bands who harvested the bounty of the dense forests around the Futa Jallon range (Guinea) and the Atakora hills (Togo). Although early rainfall levels were enough to prompt the pastoralists to build their homes on mounds as a protection against flash floods, encroaching drought eventually forced them to reassemble farther south.

While some groups, like the Kintampo culture in Ghana, continued to raise dwarf goats and shorthorn cattle, many others turned to agriculture.[41] In time the domestication of millet, rice and yams became sufficient not only to support the ancient kingdoms of Ghana, Mali, Songhay, Benin and Asante, but to spur the expansion of the so-called Bantu peoples who presently dominate much of southern and eastern Africa. The birthplace of this expansion, according to most scholars, was the Benue Valley, located on the Nigeria-Cameroon border just north of the imposing equatorial rain forest. From here, archaeological evidence suggests, the proto-Bantu headed south along the Atlantic coastline and, more circuitously, via the Great Lakes region of East Africa.[42]

Africa's most heavily trafficked thoroughfare may have been the Rift Valley, a fifty-mile-wide cleavage that spills across the equator into Kenya, Uganda and Tanzania. Part of the larger Afro-Arabian rift system that extends four thousand miles from Israel to Mozambique, this winding depression has channeled the footsteps of literally millions of men and beasts over the centuries.

Sometime around 2500 B.C., at the end of a wet phase known as the Makalian, ancient Hamitic clans poured out of Ethiopia and into the highlands fringing the Rift Valley. They were the first humans, so far as we know, to pass this way in the post-Flood era. Their journey, which preceded the Bantu migrations by nearly two millennia, is at least partially documented by tools and bones left behind in various caves.[43]

The Japhethites

Several centuries earlier, a third major group was leaving Babel—the Japhethites. From their cozy quarters on the plain of Shinar, these clans spread northward into Anatolia, where they established a linguistic homeland,[44] and from there to the farthest reaches of the Northern Hemisphere. Their pace, by most reckonings, was swift. Within the span of a single millennium, they managed to establish a presence in settings as far-flung as Italy, Armenia and western China.[45]

From Anatolia, the Japhethites' departure routes led in two directions: westward through the Balkans into Europe, and eastward across the Russian steppes into Asia. Those who pursued the former course were, in Renfrew's words, "immigrant farmers" who brought their domesticated cereal grains and animals across the Aegean into Greece. Arriving as early as 4000–3000 B.C. (not Renfrew's date), they represent the linguistic ancestors of both the Anatolian Hittites and the Mycenaean Greeks. The evidence shows that these farmers moved from the rich farmlands of mainland Greece westward across the Adriatic to Italy, whence they continued on into France and Spain, and northward into the Balkans. The latter path, apparently the more well-trodden of the two, also forked. The western branch led into Central Europe, where the Celtic and Germanic languages would eventually emerge, and the eastern branch led into the Slavic lands of Eastern Europe.[46]

The easterners are worth following a bit farther because, as recent archaeological evidence confirms, not all of them lingered to exploit the fertile black soil of the southern Ukraine. Instead, many of these early Indo-European speakers continued eastward until they reached the steppes of southern Siberia and the Altai. Here they flourished for several centuries, perhaps millennia, as the so-called Andronovo culture.[47]

Meanwhile, however, they were differentiating.[48] One large group headed south into Persia to become the Indo-Iranians. Another group, the Aryans, advanced into the Indus Valley, where they superseded an older, darker-skinned civilization at Mohenjo-daro and Harappa. Using a language that evolved into Sanskrit, the Aryans went on to produce a sacred book, the Rig-Veda—presently the oldest surviving Indo-European literature. All the while their descendants expanded deep into the South Asian subcontinent to create the India of Hindu history and tradition.

Evidence also appears to link Indo-Europeans with western China—specifically the territory of Xinjiang (Sinkiang) Province. For many centuries this arid expanse situated between Tibet and Mongolia had only one claim to fame: that it was host to some of the final stations of the Silk Road. At one time these oases, most notably Kucha, Khotan, Turfan and Tun-huang, supported thriving towns—towns that today are quite literally obscured by the sands of time.

It was into this region, which Colin Renfrew describes as "one of the least investigated areas of the earth," that the Hungarian-born Aurel Stein ventured in 1907. One day while exploring the now famous "Caves of the Thousand Buddhas," Stein gleaned an extraordinary piece of information from the site's Taoist caretaker, Wang Tao-shih. Seven years earlier, while cleaning religious artwork on the wall of one of the caves, Wang had discovered a crack in the plaster. He was astonished to find, on further examination, that it was actually the entrance to a secret chamber containing a substantial collection of ancient documents.

Stein, recognizing the magnitude of the caretaker's find, persuaded the priest to reopen the chamber and sell him part of the library.[49] Later, when these and other documents were taken back to Europe for analysis, scholars were surprised to find that several were written in a previously unknown language, albeit one that employed a north Indian alphabet.[50] The language was called Tocharian and later associated with an Indo-European people the Chinese called the Yü-chi.[51]

More recently, researchers have unearthed hundreds of Caucasian mummies from sites in Xinjiang, some dating back as far as 2000 B.C. Early evidence suggests that they are the horse-riding Yü-chi (or Andronovo people) referred to in early Chinese records.[52] If so, modern scholars have been presented with a truly extraordinary window on the past, an opportunity to gaze into the face of an ancient, extinct culture.[53]

Whoever these people turn out to be, they serve to remind us, for the moment at least, of yet another unresolved Asian mystery. On the basis of evidence we will look at in a moment, it is clear that the Andronovo culture came into active contact with shamanic tribes that had preceded them to the Siberian Altai. It is equally clear that none of these tribes spoke Indo-European tongues.

Questions abound. If aboriginal peoples indeed roamed the Altai, who were they? How did they get there? When did they arrive? If the identity and history of an obscure band of animists were all that was at stake, we might be tempted to dismiss such questions as academic trivia. But the issue is considerably larger, for it is in these Altaic peoples, some suggest, that we find the linguistic and spiritual roots of the great cultures of China, Mongolia, Korea, Japan and Tibet.[54]

Happily, an explanation for the origins of these North Asian peoples may be at hand. And if our theory is correct, the breakthrough clues lie not in some grand archaeological discovery but in an obscure language family and a reassessment of the first eight verses of Genesis 11.

First discovered by linguists in the 1980s, the Dene-Caucasian language family presents some interesting challenges. Besides the fact that its member families are scattered in widely isolated pockets (see map 3), Dene-Caucasian also manifests weaker cognates (words related to words in other languages) than most language groups. In addition, as Ruhlen points out in *The Origin of Language,* "The family as a whole fails to appear as a cohesive unit in [Cavalli-Sforza's] genetic tree of the world's populations."[55] In short, Dene-Caucasian, unlike every other language family, seems to be a contrived patchwork of linguistic remnants.

This assessment, however, is premature. Not only are there reasonable explanations for the apparent shortcomings of Dene-Caucasian, but these explanations go a long way toward resolving the mystery surrounding the origins of the people groups with which it is associated. Ruhlen contends, for example, that the discontiguous locations of the Dene-Caucasian families "suggest we are dealing with two separate migrations." In the first of these, proto-Dene-Caucasian speakers spilled out of an ancient Middle Eastern homeland to establish enclaves in Europe, the Near East and northern Asia. At some later date, this initial migratory wave was overwhelmed by a more powerful expansion that included people who spoke various Uralic, Altaic and Indo-European languages.[56]

As to why Cavalli-Sforza's census of worldwide blood types failed to turn up a unique Dene-Caucasian classification, Ruhlen points

MAP 3

DENE-CAUCASIAN LANGUAGES

1 – Na-Dene family (including Navajo)
2 – Basque
3 – Caucasian
4 – Yeniseian
5 – Burushaski
6 – Sino-Tibetan

to the likelihood of genetic admixture.[57] Given time and proximity, people of differing languages inevitably develop closer genetic affinities with their neighbors than they do with their ancestral cousins elsewhere in the world. When this occurs, languages, not genes, preserve a clearer picture of the earliest state. Ruhlen, asked why languages do not mix the way people do, responds, "I think the answer is obvious. Languages don't have sex."[58]

We are still left, however, with one final question: How did Dene-Caucasian-speaking peoples make their way into Europe and northern Asia *before* the great explosion at Babel? One promising theory points to an ancient remnant that may have remained in Anatolia at a time when, according to Genesis 11:2, the bulk of Noah's descendants "moved eastward" to Shinar "and settled there."

Although most of us assume that the entire human race was present at Babel, Genesis 11:1–9 does not say so. The only certainties in this passage are, first, that the whole world spoke a common language; second, that the Babelites' actions prompted God to confuse this language; and third, that people were scattered widely from Babel. If we equate this Anatolian remnant with the proto-Dene-Caucasians, we can hypothesize that, sometime prior to 3500 B.C., they set out on migratory journeys that took them into northern Asia, the Caucasus and Europe (as the forebears of the Basques).

Backward Glances: Longing for the Golden Age

Although God's judgment on the people of Babel involved a profound rewiring of their cerebral cortices, their perception of the confounding of language was limited to its social consequences. Their instant absorption of new tongues circumvented the conventional learning process, which stimulates an awareness of internal change. Perceiving their own speech to be what it had always been, they could only assume that the sudden breakdown in communication was somehow the fault of their newly bewitched neighbors.

In virtually every neighborhood throughout Babel, the unity and military-style precision that had facilitated the city's architectural achievements evaporated. Orders were shouted but not understood. Fear and chaos danced in the streets like maniacal jesters.

The city's gridlock, however, was not without end. Like ants scurrying from a disturbed nest, the departing Babelites eventually fell in line with their kind. As far as the eye could see, their undulating caravans fanned out across the rich grasslands of Shinar. Destined for an uncertain future and still attached to their dream of a heavenly stairway, many broke down and wept. Others, prefiguring the action of Lot's wife, cast backward glances until the retreating horizon gobbled up what remained of their illustrious Tower.

In the centuries that followed, the descendants of these early emigrants spread out to the extremities of the earth. And while memories of Shinar and even Eden traveled with them, these tended to fade the farther they traveled from the land of their origin. To preserve their connection to the past, many aboriginal peoples developed a collection of core myths that could be passed conveniently to succeeding generations. A mixture of factual history and human imagination,[59] these myths were bound by two closely related themes: the golden age and Ancient Wisdom.

To the primitive peoples of the earth, the golden age spoke of a lost paradise, or at least a time when life was better and more enlightened. The vivid and recurring elements of this world included sacred heights, life-giving trees, sentient animals and companionship with benevolent and wisdom-dispensing deities.[60] Ancient Wisdom was merely a variant with a shift of emphasis: the "what" rather than the "when" of the matter. In the words of Geoffrey Ashe, "Benign deities or sages, knowing much that ordinary humans did not, once illuminated and aided them." Unfortunately, "the illumination faded with the departure of Ancient Wisdom's teachers."

Recovering the power, wisdom and bliss of this extraordinary age soon became the consuming passion of an elite group of priest-magicians known as shamans. Not content with merely making (or keeping) myths, these spiritual intermediaries began to take active—and dangerous—measures to reestablish contact with gods and spirits.[61]

While shamanic activity flourished throughout most of northern Eurasia, there is evidence that a particularly important center existed in the Altai-Baikal region of southwestern Siberia. At Mal'ta, a small settlement located some 55 miles west of Lake Baikal, Russian archaeologists have uncovered an impressive collection of Goddess figurines, snake images and seven-circuited spirals. Here shamanic animism was not only practiced, but defined and exported. Here, as Ashe emphatically insists, "something began."[62]

A Common Pain: From Traumas to Pacts

The experiences of Babel's outbound tribes were as varied as their tongues and destinations. But a careful examination of history reveals at least one important common denominator: At one point or another along their long march, each of these ancient peoples encountered some form of *collective trauma*.

Regardless of whether Satan caused these circumstances or simply took advantage of them, their effect was to provide him a direct entrée into the psyches of otherwise distracted people. It was a perfect setup. Not only did the trauma provoke open discussion of supernatural powers; it also prompted distraught souls to call on these powers.

By posing as golden age deities capable of delivering the community from their present ordeal, demonic agents lured a desperate general populace into long-term *quid pro quo* pacts. The deal was simple. In return for allegiance pledged to these masquerading demons, the community would receive immediate trauma relief as well as restored access to the power, wisdom and deities of their forefathers.

As to the nature or source of the traumas that precipitated these pacts, history records at least five notable phenomena:

1. Intimidating natural barriers;
2. Climatic and natural disasters;
3. Disease and pestilence;
4. Famine and environmental ruin;
5. Wars and raids.[63]

Intimidating Natural Barriers

In the years following the violent upheaval of the great Flood, significant geological activity continued on the earth as the planet sought to regain equilibrium.[64] A major part of this activity (as I have suggested) was the likely breakup of the Pangaea supercontinent, an indescribably forceful process that created new mountains, islands and continents. Wide-eyed travelers journeying through this terrestrial turbulence assuaged their fear by binding themselves to the spirits they believed to be in control of these vast and powerful forces.

Oral traditions tell of numerous instances, even after the great Dispersion, in which tribal elders sought passage for their weary people at the boundaries of forbidding mountains, scorching deserts or deep forests. Disorientation and death, particularly among the young and the elderly, was common. On a few occasions—such as when the Hebrew children stood before the Red Sea—distress was heightened by the fact that these physical obstacles blocked the only means of escape from imminent human threats.

Climatic and Natural Disasters

Natural disasters have scarred humans and their habitat with agonizing regularity.[65] Diverse and deadly, their legacy includes everything from rivers of boiling salt that once flowed through ancient Iran, to a sixteenth-century earthquake that took an estimated 830,000 lives in China's Shensi Province.[66]

Nature's most fearsome features have more often been perceived in the face of storms. (At least eighteen hundred rumble over the earth's surface at any given moment!)[67] Human beings, having encountered the dark, brooding brow of the thunderhead, the bone-chilling breath of the winter blizzard and the primitive, overwhelming sounds of the typhoon or tornado, have learned to fear and personify the powers of the air.

But despite the drama and immediacy of the tempest, most weather-related traumas derive historically from long-term climatic changes affecting agriculture.[68] Whenever the cultivation of staple crops has been disrupted or eliminated, dislocation and death follow quickly.

Not long ago University of Tokyo geographer Hideo Suzuki began wondering if changing climate patterns had anything to do with the fact that, five thousand years ago, major civilizations developed, and quite rapidly, in the Tigris-Euphrates, Nile, Indus and Yellow River valleys. Why, he asked himself, did they develop at that particular time, and why in those particular places? Upon investigation, Suzuki noticed that it was at that very moment in history that the Hypsithermal Period—in which higher temperatures prevailed, along with a more northerly track for the equatorial westerlies—began to wane. The practical impact of this development: The green area extending from the Sahara through Arabia to northwestern India began to dry up. Cultivated lands were gradually lost to desertification, and cultivators were forced to take refuge in the big river valleys.[69]

As the refugees flooded into these valleys, the original inhabitants used them as cheap labor or outright slaves. Suddenly tools, dwellings and crops were produced in greater size and quantity than ever before. Civilization appears to have been "born." But while history has celebrated this period as a milestone of human achievement, it must also be marked as a time of profound hardship. For many people living in squalid slave quarters or immigrant ghettos, the nights were filled with weeping over lost land, lives and freedom.[70]

Disease and Pestilence

Another source of trauma in human experience has been the rotting hand of pestilence. This mass murderer made its first appearance in history when people settled down for prolonged stays at single sites. Initial problems stemmed from parasitic invasions associated with increased contact with human waste and contaminated water supplies. Later the clustering of people made communities vulnerable to infectious diseases spread by such means as sneezing and sexual activity.[71]

The Babylonians, Aryas, Greeks and Egyptians all feared gods of pestilence—and understandably so. In addition to the divine afflictions mentioned in Exodus 7–11, Egypt faced a two-year assault of the bubonic plague in the fourteenth century, which took the lives of one out of every three Egyptians.[72] Roman epidemics, which rolled in like waves from about 387 B.C., were equally devastating. Two particularly vicious plagues, each lasting fifteen years, were recorded in A.D. 165 and 251. The first of these consumed a third of the population in afflicted areas; the second at its height claimed five thousand lives *per day*.[73]

The infamous Black Plague that visited Europe for four years in the mid–fourteenth century resulted in 75 million deaths, making it the largest human catastrophe (short of the Flood) in human history. In one attempt to describe the horrors of a secondary epidemic in early seventeenth-century London, English playwright and poet Thomas Dekker wrote of "the loud groans of raving sick men, [and] the struggling pangs of souls departing." The scale of death was massive: "A hundred graves stand gaping and every one of them hath swallowed down ten or eleven lifeless carcasses." At day's end, the number of bodies in each grave might reach sixty.[74]

In the years between A.D. 1200 and 1393, the population of China was cut virtually in half, declining from 123 million to about 65 million.[75] Once again plague, along with warfare, was suspected as a major factor. Chinese records, offering a revealing peek into this traumatic period, reveal that a single epidemic in the province of Hopei killed a staggering ninety percent of the population.[76]

Famine and Environmental Ruin

One of the earliest examples of a civilization decimated by environmental ruin[77] is found in the Indus River valley, where hydrologist Robert Raikes suggests that Harappan culture "was terminated by destruction of their fields and settlements through floods"—floods that were themselves "brought on by major shifts of the earth's crust near the mouth of the Indus River."[78]

The Ur III dynasty that flourished in southern Mesopotamia around 2100 B.C. was brought low by an equally traumatic problem. As the soil became more saline, agriculture shifted from wheat to the more salt-tolerant barley. When there was no more barley, the society depended on imported grain before collapsing under the burden of overpopulation (and assaults from neighboring Elamites). One of the last written records from Ur is a plaintive message from King Ibbi-sin to one of his functionaries in northern Babylonia: "Where is my shipment of grain?"[79]

Although salinization also spelled the doom of the Hohokam Indians who lived in the area now occupied by the city of Phoenix, most early American cultures were done in by other environmental crises. In nearby Chaco Canyon, the great Anasazi civilization apparently met its demise when an overharvesting of trees led to the loss of fertile topsoil.[80] The same problem may have been true of the Maya and other Central American cultures, including the "People with No Name," who for some six hundred years lived along the south coast of Guatemala. Contemporaries of the Maya and Teotihuacan, they seemingly came out of nowhere, then, just as suddenly, disappeared.[81]

Wars and Raids

Perhaps the most devastating traumas are those that men and women bring upon their fellows with malice aforethought. Unlike the perils of nature and the gods, human-wrought violence is both imminent and cannibalistic—an evil perpetrated against us by our own kind.

Societies over the years have developed a marked tendency to measure similitude and filter out "impurities" (people not "of us")—a practice that first surfaced with the confusion of tongues at Babel. Neighbors finding themselves unable to communicate with one another suddenly became strangers, the nuances of their lives reduced to clumsy gesturing. In time, and inevitably, this awkwardness gave way to alienation; and when it did, Babel became the staging area for all wars that would ever be waged.

From the early Gutian, Elamite and Amorite raids on Sumeria's city-states, to the fierce Mongol attacks of the thirteenth century, bloody military invasions have precipitated many desperate bargains with the spirit world. The ruthless warlord Genghis Khan once boasted, "The greatest joy is to vanquish your enemies and chase them before you, to rob them of their wealth and see those dear to them bathed in tears." The rest of the world trembled at such words because the Khan's deeds gave them credence. When his hordes sacked Peking, looting and raping continued unchecked for a month. Many girls threw themselves from the city walls. "The soil," wrote one eyewitness, "was greasy with human fat, and at the city gate lay a pile of human bones."[82]

According to well-known trauma expert Kai Erikson, the traumatic experience is both alien and vicious:

> It invades you, possesses you, takes you over. . . . It becomes a dominating feature of your interior landscape, and in the process threatens to drain you and leave you empty.

As to where this debilitating force comes from, Erikson replies:

> It can issue from a sustained exposure to battle as well as from a moment of numbing shock, from a continuing pattern of abuse as well as from a single searing assault, from a period of severe attenuation and erosion as well as from a sudden flash of fear. The effects are the same.[83]

Erikson also accents trauma's social dimension. "The fabric of community," he insists, "can be injured in much the same way as the tissues of mind and body." The sudden loss of familiar and nurturing institutions, for example, can destroy a community's sense of identity. At the same time, "traumatic wounds inflicted on individuals can . . . combine to create a mood, an ethos—a group culture, almost— that is different from (and more than) the sum of the private wounds that make it up."[84] Either way, trauma changes the collective.

There is also evidence suggesting that the severity and complexity of psychological dysfunction is related directly to the frequency and length of an individual's or community's exposure to trauma.[85] Whereas individuals, particularly abused children, tend to cope with their pain through sexual promiscuity or multiple personality disorder, communities are more inclined to turn to some form of idolatry.[86] In both cases the rule is the same: *The more traumatic the circumstance, the greater the number of "saviors" solicited.*

Nowhere is this rule more in evidence than in India, a land where gods and their shrines are the only commodity in greater supply than suffering. On any given day in this heavily burdened nation, millions of pilgrims make it their primary goal to secure the intercession of a vast mélange of superhuman beings. So deep is their despair, they do not seem to mind that these deities appear with spiderlike arms or the heads of elephants or monkeys. Having learned the "purchase price" of their prospective champions, they approach their shrines fully prepared to offer whatever reciprocal sacrifices or vows are necessary to obtain relief.[87]

Ancient Welcome Mats

We cannot reconstruct the details of every pact that has welcomed demonic forces into the human community, but this does not mean these contracts are speculative. In many instances, quality documentation does exist—and when the evidence is examined, a compelling and consistent pattern emerges.

What we see is this: After an initial bargain is struck, almost always under circumstantial duress, demons proceed to prove themselves by providing the community or individual with a measure of trauma relief. In some situations the relief is real; in others it is simply a cleverly administered placebo. Whether real or imagined, however, the onset of recovery signals that it is time to pay the piper.

Most commonly, debt servicing on such pacts is accomplished through some form of ritual tribute or public allegiance—and the "interest" can be brutal. Those who fail to read the contractual fine print up-front are often distressed to learn that they have obligated themselves to long-term and radically one-sided arrangements. When this reality sinks in, they become prisoners of fear and despair. If they default on their part of the bargain, they risk inviting a recurrence of the original trauma. If they honor the pact, they remain subject to the power and capricious temperament of their new master.

In the pages that follow, we will take a brief look at several real-life examples of mankind's budding relationship with territorial spirits. Drawn from settings that span four hemispheres and five millennia, their common testimony offers clear evidence of the linkage between trauma and spiritual pact-making.

The Great Saharan Drought

When an ancient shift in the equatorial westerlies began to dry up the lush Sahara, distressed inhabitants turned first to various fertility gods and goddesses, then to solar cults. At Acacus in Libya and

Wadi Djerat in the Tassili, ancient rock paintings show masked men with giant, erect phalluses about to copulate with women. It was believed that ritual intercourse, along with dancing, could forge a link between the community and whatever invisible forces were responsible for sustaining life.[88]

Eventually, however, the Saharan tribes were forced into full-scale retreat. Many headed southward into the Sahel, while others staked a course for the Nile River valley. As the relentless drought gobbled up lakes, vegetation and animals, the gods associated with these life-sustaining elements disappeared as well. In the end, the sun was the only thing visible—a blazing ball that patrolled continually from one horizon to the other.[89]

To the aboriginal tribes of eastern Egypt, and to the Saharan refugees who joined them there, this awesome and primeval power became known as Aten. From his early center at Heliopolis,[90] the sun god's cult spread far and wide, reaching its zenith under the reign of Amunhotep IV, husband of renowned Queen Nefertiti.[91] Although Aten ultimately fragmented into various personas—doing stints as Atum, Ra, Khepri and Amon-Ra—some aspect of the solar deity was always present at the pinnacle of the Egyptian pantheon.

In Egypt's dynastic era, the pharaohs themselves were taken to be incarnations of and partners with the sun god.[92] In the following passage from one of the Pyramid Texts, the sun god Atum-Khepri is first extolled and then petitioned:

> O Atum-Khepri, you became high on the "Height," you rose up as the Benben stone in the temple of the Phoenix in On [Heliopolis]....[93]
> O Atum, set your protection over this king, over this pyramid of his, and over this construction of the king, prevent anything from happening evilly against it for ever....[94]

Courting Mother Smallpox

If drought prepared the way for Aten's success in Egypt, it was smallpox that ushered in one of India's most popular aboriginal goddesses—Sítala, or "She that Makes Cool." While the origins of smallpox have never been established conclusively, experts like William McNeill acknowledge that there is "a perfectly sound basis" for the

modern tradition that the disease was indigenous to India. Whatever the truth may be, the debut of smallpox on the subcontinent
was clearly early.

In the years that followed, the disease became a familiar, if unwel-
come, resident in many of South Asia's burgeoning cities. Many came
to call smallpox *Mata,* or "the Mother."[95] Oral traditions from across
the country tell of horrendous epidemics in which thousands perished with symptoms that included fever and skin boils. During
these times of trouble, dangerously ill patients were placed in front
of Sítala's image, along with vessels of sanctified water, often drawn
from the holy Ganges. When these measures failed to stem the
advancing tide of death, some communities entreated the goddess
with an additional delicacy: human blood.[96]

The traumatic effect of these episodes on the national psyche was
(and still is) considerable. To this day Hindu temples dedicated to
Sítala attract thousands of worshipers from the farthest reaches of
the subcontinent—a remarkable phenomenon considering that the
disease has since been eradicated.

Crossing the Hindu Kush

In his outstanding book *Eternity in Their Hearts,* veteran missionary and author Don Richardson recounts the circumstances of
another ancient pact-making crisis, this one involving the ancestors of India's Santal people. After a long eastward migration, these
early wayfarers suddenly found their way blocked by the imposing
Hindu Kush Mountains (which bisect modern Afghanistan). Trapped
in this treacherous terrain, the weaker members began to grow faint.
Lack of sustenance and unpredictable weather conditions became
serious concerns. Concluding that their progress was being impeded
by powerful mountain spirits known as Maran Buru, the tribal elders
decided to proffer a *quid pro quo* pact. "O Maran Buru," they
covenanted, "if you release a pathway for us, we will bind ourselves
to you when we reach the other side."

Centuries later, in 1867, two Scandinavian missionaries encountered the Santal people living in a region north of Calcutta, India.[97]
They puzzled as to why the Santal word for *demons* translated as

"spirits of the mountains," since there were no mountains in the immediate vicinity. The mystery was solved when an esteemed Santal elder named Kolean filled in the final details of his ancestors' journey through the Hindu Kush.

"After covenanting with the Maran Buru," he explained, "they came upon a passage in the direction of the rising sun." This opening, which may have been the famed Khyber Pass, they named *Bain,* or "Day Gate." Emerging onto the plains of the Indian subcontinent, the relieved tribe fulfilled their oath by practicing spirit appeasement.[98]

Chak Lords and Ocean Gods

The ancient Maya Indians were addicted to pilgrimages, especially in times of great stress. Whenever their lands were threatened by drought, disease or military invasion, royal runners were dispatched to announce pilgrimages and gather up offerings of precious gold, ceramics and jade. Often these messengers were also instructed to secure beautiful virgins who could be sacrificed to the Chak Lords (or rain deities) at the sacred well in Chichén Itzá. By extending to their gods the best the land had to offer, they hoped to persuade them to release life-giving rain on their parched land.[99]

Further south, Chile's Mapuche Indians still hold their own annual rain ceremony. The event, known as the *guillatún,* culminates with the blood of animals being poured out to Lafquén Ullmén (a deity known as "The Rich Man of the Sea") and to Manquián, the ocean god.[100] While drought is the main concern, it is not the only one. Mapuche history is a deep well storing hundreds of other traumas, gods, and offerings, including an early account of a child sacrificed in the aftermath of a terrible earthquake in 1575.

As traumatic as this temblor was, its power pales in comparison to another quake that struck southern Chile in 1960. This one, measuring an astonishing 9.5 on the Richter scale, is easily the most potent earthquake recorded in the twentieth century. In addition to collapsing buildings as if they were sand castles, the quake redirected rivers, dropped hundreds of square miles of land below sea level and triggered dozens of volcanic eruptions. Worst of all were the massive tidal waves. Patrick Tierney, who spent months in southern Chile investigating the incident, describes the scene:

> First the ocean pulled back, stranding boats like toys, exposing miles of seabed and the refuse of centuries. Then, after an ominous silence, the ocean began boiling like an angry pot as it roared inland swallowing trees, houses, and people, all of which tumbled head over heels into the tidal wave's wake.[101]

Led by a powerful local shamaness named Machi Juana, the surviving community clambered up to Cerro Mesa, a sacred, flat-topped hill overlooking the South Pacific. There, according to neighbors Senovio and Rosario Opazo, they danced until a third tidal wave almost washed them all away. "It must have been sixty-five feet high!" exclaimed the neighbors. "We thought that the world was going to end."

At that point, according to several eyewitnesses, Machi Juana insisted that a child be sacrificed to the sea so the community could survive. The victim turned out to be a five-year-old shepherd boy named José Luis Painecur. "The little boy was frightened," recalls family friend María Trangol. "Before he died he said, 'I'll be good, Papa. Please don't kill me.'" But it was too late.

Even while he was begging his grandfather's forgiveness, Rosario Opazo remembers, "they cut off the boy's arms and legs. . . ." Partly to drown out his screams, the people beat on drums and blew reed-like whistles called *trutrucas*. When the *machi* received the severed appendages, she "passed them on to old Trafinado" (the chief of the community), who then "danced with the boy's arms, waving them about as he went." Others cut out Luis' heart and intestines and threw them into the sea.[102] Finally they took what remained of his torso and placed it into the ground, like a defensive stake or talisman, facing the ocean.[103]

As the ritual drew to a close, another eyewitness, María Nahuelcoy, recalls that the shamaness dipped a maqui branch into the boy's blood and started to sprinkle it into the swirling waters. "Then," María said, "the *machi* sang like this:

> We are paying you with this boy . . .
> We give him to you as a gift,
> So that the tidal waves are calmed,
> So that there are no more disasters."[104]

The Pact at Chang Ganka

A final example of early pact-making with the spirit world is taken from the Himalayan hermit kingdom of Bhutan, a nation I was privileged to visit twice in the early 1990s.

My expert guide for the first of these expeditions was Kunzang Delek, a research and program officer with the Special Commission for Cultural Affairs. He and two other young functionaries had been assigned by the government to aid my research into the origins of the ancient temples, shrines and monasteries that decorate Bhutan's central valleys.

A particularly interesting stop on this exotic itinerary was Chang Ganka Lhakhang, a whitewashed temple compound that crowns a knoll above the national capital of Thimphu. Strolling around an exterior catwalk designed for ritual circumambulation, I found it easy to understand why this site had been chosen for spiritual meditation. With its superb view of the valley below and surrounded by a forest of rippling prayer flags, the place manifested a serene, almost surreal atmosphere.

But there was something else. I knew virtually nothing about Chang Ganka's history, yet from the moment we stepped onto the compound, my spiritual antennae began to pick up powerful signals—signals that suggested there was more to this hilltop temple than met the eye. My initial suspicions were heightened when I discovered that no sound would record on my microcassette player beyond the threshold of the inner sanctuary.[105]

The idols that occupy Chang Ganka's interior spaces are hideous and perverse. Among the worst: fanged guardians standing watch over the temple's spirit-summoning drum, and a ghoulish mask that hangs menacingly above the entrance to the main idol room. The mask, reminiscent of artist Edvard Munch's famous work *The Scream,* appears to have emerged from a demonic nightmare. Even more disturbing is the image of Palden Lhamo. A counterpart to the Hindu Kali-Ma, she is depicted with a human infant being torn asunder in her razor-sharp teeth. It is hard to shake the feeling, walking through this repellent menagerie, that one's every move is being observed by malevolent spirits whose bloodshot eyes and slobbering hatred are barely concealed behind the craftsman's work.

At least three ruling deities are attached to Chang Ganka and the community of Thimphu. The first of these is a blue, horse-borne figure named Domtshab. His throne is situated to the left of Avalokitesvara (the eleven-headed Buddha of compassion) in the main sanctuary. The images of two other special deities, Palden Lhamo and Yeshey Guempo, are housed in a detached structure on the opposite side of an inner courtyard. Both are considered powerful protectors, not only in Thimphu but throughout the Buddhist Himalayas.

According to Delek, my government-appointed guide, the account of how this trio of deities assumed their responsibilities in the Thimphu valley goes back at least 550 years, and possibly much further.[106] Shortly after settling on the banks of the Wang Chu River, early immigrants from Tibet began to solicit supernatural help to cope with severe weather conditions, virulent diseases and bloody tribal conflicts.[107] Discerning no local protector in the area, a high lama named Nima decided to establish a covenant with *mi-ma-yan*[108] spirits that had accompanied him over the mountains from Tibet.[109] To seal the arrangement, he constructed the Chang Ganka Lhakhang.

Pausing near a row of prayer wheels in the compound's inner courtyard, Delek took a moment to elaborate on the reciprocal nature of this covenant. "As the consecrator of this place," he explained, "Nima gave full authority to these *mi-ma-yin*, officially confirming them as local deities. From that day forward, however, the roles were reversed. In return for looking after this temple and the surrounding community, the deities required daily *pujas*—ritual prayers and appeasement. Even today," he continued, "if people want to make a road, construct a house, cut down a tree or remove a deceased person from his home, they must first perform a puja in order to please the local deity."

To ensure that I had not misunderstood, I released the pause button on my microcassette recorder and lifted it toward Delek. "Are you saying it was the people themselves who authorized Domtshab, Yeshey Guempo and Palden Lhamo to assume control over this area?" Nodding vigorously, Delek replied: "Yes, that's exactly right."

To keep the community and its needs before these deities, Chang Ganka's monks often carry a large mirror out onto the temple catwalk and position it so an image of the city is reflected into the main idol room. This done, an elaborate offering of butter, incense, food and money is heaped onto the altar by a phalanx of temple attendants. Since these local gods do not generally manifest a corporeal presence, specially trained lamas must be brought in to determine if and when the puja has been received by the *mi-ma-yin*.[110]

Although trauma has visited human communities in many forms and in countless settings over the years, it is a mistake to view these painful episodes as simply the outworking of a divine curse. God is not ultimately a punisher[111] but a rescuer. Despite their outward ferocity, the vast majority of these circumstances have arrived on the scene laden with grace. Disguised as moral alarm clocks, they have rung in fresh opportunities for wayward men and women to return to God in repentance and to establish Him as their rightful ruler and sole deliverer.

Unfortunately, the sackcloth prostrations of Nineveh have proven a rare exception to the historical rule. The overwhelming majority of people down through the centuries have elected to exchange the revelations of God for a lie. Heeding the entreaties of demons, they have chosen in their desperation to enter into intimate compacts with the spirit world. In return for the consent of a particular deity to resolve their immediate traumas, they have collectively sold their proverbial souls.[112]

Through just such agreements, demonic forces were authorized to establish territorial strongholds during the long sojourn out from Babel. The basis of these transactions was (and is) entirely moral. People made conscious choices to suppress the truth and believe a falsehood. In the end, as Romans 1:18–25 reminds us, the people were deceived because they chose to be.

Knowing how deceptions take root, however, does not make them any less real. In the vast majority of cases in which humans and demons have chosen to live together, the former are genuinely convinced that their partners are who they say they are—which can be anything from elemental rulers to enlightened masters. Only on the rarest of occasions do people come to recognize the true nature of their ostensible protectors.

So how does Satan enchant, or animate, this great lie? Keen observers offer a dual explanation: first, human wills and minds are enlisted in the suppression of truth; and second, demonic features are transformed to blend with prevailing cultural perceptions. Not as apparent are the physical and social mechanisms that allow the enemy to weave these elements into a seamless deception. For this reason, and because understanding their role is crucial to successful spiritual warfare, their discovery will be our next order of business in the labyrinth.

CHAPTER SIX

ENCHANTING THE LIE

In the mid-1950s British novelist Nigel Dennis wrote a humorous yet penetrating book entitled *Cards of Identity.*[1] At the heart of the story, which is set in a bucolic English village, a dreary brother and sister are taken in by the kind and silver-tongued owners of a nearby manor house. Soon after a hearty welcome, the two are drawn into conversations that raise serious questions about what is going on. As the talks progress, the children are given to understand that they are not the people they thought they were. Eventually the pair forget their past altogether and embrace the new identities that are woven around them skillfully by their psychological kidnapers.

As the mysterious manor owners proceed to lure still more purposeless locals into the household, we learn that they are members of the Identity Club, an organization whose purpose, as one reviewer puts it, is "to compensate for the psychological uncertainty of modern life by creating entirely new structures of reality." They are, quite simply, "manufacturers and entrepreneurs of reality."[2]

A darker version of this story has been unfolding in the real world for at least eight millennia. In this long-running serial, the manor owners are felicitous demons who appeal to the empty, fearful and fallen sons and daughters of Adam. These posturing spirits, like the members of the Identity Club, are highly skilled at exploiting human vulnerability while concealing their own identities and intentions.[3] After all, asked Tertullian, "What is daintier food to the spirit of evil, than turning men's minds away from the true God by the illusions of a false divination?"[4]

Turkish Delight and the Trail of Beans

The biblical observation that each sinner is dragged away and enticed "by his own evil desire" (James 1:14) suggests that the primary threat to our well-being lies not in external enticement but in the disposition of the heart (see also Matthew 15:19). And although it has become increasingly popular to attribute inappropriate choices to ignorance of what is right, Romans 1:18–32 makes it clear that men and women become prey for the enemy when they "suppress the truth" (verse 18) and determine that it is no longer "worthwhile to retain the knowledge of God" (verse 28). It all starts, in other words, with an act of will. As God advised Cain, "If you do not do what is right, sin is crouching at your door; it desires to have you, but you must master it" (Genesis 4:7).

The relationship between evil desires, self-control and enchantment is one of the primary themes of C. S. Lewis' hugely popular novel *The Lion, the Witch and the Wardrobe.* Of particular interest is Edmund's encounter with the White Witch, a dissembling queen who uses magic to create and then feed the boy's craving for her own special Turkish Delight. Once having tasted her wares, Edmund is hooked. "He was thinking all the time about Turkish Delight," we read, "and there's nothing that spoils the taste of good ordinary food half so much as the memory of bad magic food." Soon the lad's judgment is dulled to the most imminent of threats. While it made him uncomfortable to hear that the lady who had befriended him was actually a dangerous witch, "he still wanted to taste that Turkish Delight again more than he wanted anything else."[5]

In a similar vein, Michael Green relates the story of the celebrated eighteenth-century preacher Rowland Hill. While walking down the street one day, the good Reverend was surprised to see a drove of pigs trundling behind a gentleman as if he were the Pied Piper of Hamelin.

> "This," said Hill, "excited my curiosity so much that I determined to follow. I did so, and to my great surprise I saw them follow him to the slaughterhouse. I said to the man, 'My friend, how did you induce the pigs to follow you here?' He replied, 'I had a basket of beans under my arm, and I dropped a few as I came along, and so they followed me.'"

This, says Green, "is precisely Satan's strategy."[6]

There is a difference, of course, between pigs and humans. While people like Edmund will take the enemy's bait, they often do so with a nagging sense of unease. This is because our consciences are set, by factory default, to alert us whenever we are venturing into dangerous or self-destructive territory. Like most alarms, however, the conscience can be defeated (and often is) by a will intent on pursuing its own evil desire.

Tinkering in the Wetware: The Latent Power of the Mind

If the will is ultimately responsible for deception and alienation, the mind must be seen as a crucial ally. As Romans 1 informs us, men who worship created things are given over to sexual impurity (a degrading of the body) and a depraved mind (that not only abandons but hates God and invents ways of doing evil).[7]

This reference to our ability to "invent" evil is important. It reminds us that, by design, the human brain is a reality engine. Besides being able to turn the contents of external stimuli (such as words and images) into metaphors that make sense to us, our imaginations can also *create* reality[8]—a capability the enemy has found particularly useful.

This process is not as rare as you might assume. During nightly dream episodes, for example, the imagination routinely uses fragments of memories to fashion realities (including landscapes, personalities, relationships and adventures) that exist apart from any external stimuli. This phenomenon has also been widely documented among individuals forced to endure conditions of social isolation (such as mountain climbers, abused children, religious ascetics and prisoners in solitary confinement). Medical researcher Richard Cytowic notes, "A brain deprived of external input will start projecting an external reality of its own, readily perceiving things that are 'not really there.'"[9]

Some individuals, wanting to experience these alternative realities at will, have set about to create the conditions necessary to trigger the magic of the imagination. For shamans and tantrics, this involves commitment to elaborate visualization disciplines.[10] After years of training, Buddhist lamas are said to have the capacity to generate, then inhabit, entire worlds within their psychic spaces.

Better-equipped Western scientists have found that a soundproof flotation tank[11] can serve the same purpose. After leaving the National Institute of Mental Health in 1958, neurophysiologist John Lilly underwent a near-death experience in which he encountered two radiant entities who claimed to be his guardians. When they informed him that he could perceive them only in a state close to death, Lilly decided to try to restore contact with the beings by using a flotation tank in combination with LSD. During subsequent "out-of-body" experiences, Lilly tethered himself to a single point of consciousness in an otherwise black, silent void. From this reference point, he launched out on numerous journeys through vivid psychic realms. Along the way he claimed to encounter "a wide range of beings, some composed of liquids or glowing gases, and some of which [suggestively] resembled Tibetan deities."[12]

Our thoughts, ephemeral as they may seem, possess real substance in the dimension of the psyche. While some vanish like sparks from a smith's hammer, others linger about us for a time, appearing as complexes, neuroses or, in extreme cases, quasi-autonomous personalities.[13] In a sense, the Westerner concentrating on a lust-filled fantasy is engaging in precisely the same activity as the Tibetan lama visualizing his demons. Both are creating environments and populating them with presences and activities they have called into being.

One recent account should urge us to keep our psychic spaces clean. Dion Fortune, an occult author who in 1922 cofounded the Fraternity of the Inner Light, claims to have created a werewolf unintentionally by projecting her will and imagination against an individual who had victimized her. As she lay in bed one night, half asleep and brooding over her resentment, Fortune was seized with "the thought of casting off all restraint and going berserk." At almost the same moment, she found herself contemplating the image of Fenrir, the malevolent and terrifying wolf of Norse mythology. "Immediately," recalls Fortune, "I felt a curious drawing-out sensation from my solar plexus, and there materialized beside me on the bed a large wolf." When she moved, it snarled at her, and she had to muster all her courage to speak sharply to it and push it off the bed. Although it eventually vanished through the wall in the northern corner of her room, the next morning someone else in the house reported "dreaming of wolves and waking in the night to see the eyes of a wild animal glowing in the dark."[14]

Throughout much of the Christian world, experiences like Fortune's are viewed as clear-cut instances of overt demonic manifestation, which they often are. Filmmaker Douchan Gersi, however, offers another intriguing possibility:

> The mysterious powers that I have witnessed many times ... might represent old abilities and knowledge that all mankind used to have—whether to contact forces outside of us, or to make use of powers (psychic and otherwise) that are still within us.[15]

This is the position (as we saw in chapter 4) taken by the late Chinese writer Watchman Nee. When Adam and Eve fell, according to Nee, their original powers were not lost but buried within them as a latent force. The reason Scripture does not promote these potentially latent capabilities seems simple enough: Heaven does not need supermen. Given the long-standing (and lethal) propensity of men and women for independence, the last thing God wants to do is reinforce our notions of self-sufficiency. Instead He works with our spirits (for this is the seat of the regenerated life)[16] and invites us to call on the resources of His Holy Spirit whenever we find ourselves in need.

The enemy's objective is different. He desires, in Nee's view, to use the old creation—namely, man's "soul force"—to create a convenient and deceptive alternative to spiritual power. By hijacking our psychic machinery, he hopes to generate substitute realities that will effectively steer people away from relying on the Holy Spirit.[17]

Unfortunately, a steady stream of evidence suggests that the enemy's strategy is succeeding. Using provocative slogans like *Your Inner Doctor Is Always "In"* and *Healing Yourself with Your Own Voice,*[18] New Age catalogs find thousands of anxious customers willing to pay handsomely for unconventional medical advice. While many of these new programs are larded with pseudo-science and religious quackery, others seem to be producing impressive results. According to Arizona State University anthropologist Michael Winkelman,

> A wide range of experimental laboratory studies demonstrate [sic] that humans do have the ability to affect and heal a variety of biological systems through psychokinesis. . . .[19]

One of these apparent success stories involves a psychic healer who for several years worked alongside a conventional doctor in the southern United States. During the course of their partnership, the doctor performed blood tests on the patients both prior to and immediately following the psychic healing sessions. The samples were then forwarded to an independent laboratory for testing. In the monitored cases, patient DHEA[20] levels rose between 23 and 100 percent, providing biochemical evidence, according to the doctor, that psychic healing works.[21]

In an effort to resolve these and other cerebral mysteries, scientists have begun to plumb the brain's inner workings, affectionately known as the "wetware." Using an impressive tool chest of patch clamps, oscilloscopes and electron microscopes, they are capturing glimpses of a barely visible yet breathtakingly complex world.[22]

It is here, in what one writer has dubbed "the palaces of memory," that we find the archives holding the essential record of who we are. While scientists used to believe that memories were stored in discrete areas of the brain, they now know that individual thoughts or recollections are actually patterned neural interactions that span the entire cerebral cortex. In this sense our memories resemble twinkling stellar constellations or the flashing messages on an electronic scoreboard.[23]

Exposed to a new event—which can be anything from the image of a face to the taste of kiwi fruit—the brain immediately dispatches electrochemical signals along a tangle of neural wires known as axons and dendrites. Within our vast web of brain cells, a unique constellation suddenly lights up. According to memory expert George Johnson, this new circuit "acts as a symbol [or] representation of something in the outside world." Recognition occurs whenever we encounter external stimuli that evoke a neural pattern similar to one we already have in storage. By reactivating this pattern or circuit, the brain can retrieve a memory "as complex as an evening in Santa Fe, or the trajectory through a maze."[24]

Although most memories are retrieved voluntarily, some may appear as bolts out of the blue. There is a startling, even eerie, aspect to these events. The mind, which we have always assumed is under our control, has seemingly moved at its own impulse—and to a certain extent it *has*.

As Japanese researcher Gen Matsumoto points out, memories act at a subconscious level. And in this vast and mysterious dimension of the human mind, associative connections are established in accordance with a complex set of rules. While some associations are obvious and expected (such as appetite and the smell of a barbecue, or fear and the sight of a syringe), others appear to have no immediate connection. The sight of a rising harvest moon, for example, might conjure remembrances of bedtime stories heard in childhood. A whiff of burning hay might flood the mind with memories of a long-ago trip through the country. Despite their apparent randomness, these unexpected associations are actually the product of neural connections forged subconsciously on earlier occasions.

Other associations may not be so pleasant—or wholesome. Depending on one's habits and experiences, mental flashbacks can also resurrect significant pain or temptation. A military veteran, for instance, may find a severe thunderstorm transporting him back to the battlefield. His pornographically inclined neighbor may find the movie theater of his mind clogged with sexual reruns, each image triggered by nothing more graphic than a flowing hairstyle or a satin bedspread.

Although the *process* of carving distinct circuitry out of a chaos of potential connections is common to humanity, the resulting *collection* of memory patterns is unique to the individual. As Australian physicist Paul Davies puts it, "It is the patterns inside the brain, not the brain itself, that makes us what we are."[25]

Not surprisingly, this collection interests the devil greatly. If the human mind serves as his workshop, then our memories are his building blocks. Given an ample supply of the right kind of neural patterns, he can control both our inner reality and often the people and circumstances that surround us. If he cannot find enough memories to work with, he will often aid in the creation of new ones. A favorite tactic is to expose his subject to images or circumstances brimming with violent or sexual content. This works for two reasons: First, our deepest memories are of highly stimulating events; and second, memory storage is connected strongly with emotions.[26]

Whenever we read a good book, tour a foreign country, comfort a distraught friend or engage in a stimulating conversation, the experience prompts physical changes in our brain.[27] This remarkable process, which scientists call *sprouting,* involves the rapid growth of new neural connections—dendrites, axons and the synapses between them.[28] Experiments conducted by Dr. Gary Lynch, senior professor at the Center for the Neurobiology of Learning and Memory at the University of California at Irvine, revealed that stimulated neurons produce new synapses in as little as *ten minutes!*[29]

The enemy's strategy is simple. He wants to influence the kinds of thoughts that enter our minds so he can alter the neural structure of our brains. This process, as we have seen, does not require much time. An event lasting all of a few seconds can cause long-lasting neurological change. If we allow ourselves to be enticed by the devil's fare, we grant him a psychic platform, or "head nest," from which to manipulate our inner world. The apostle Paul, recognizing this danger, warned, "Do not give the devil a foothold" (Ephesians 4:27). Instead he urged that we submit our psychic machinery to the Lordship of Jesus Christ by focusing on things that are true, noble, right, pure, lovely, admirable, excellent or praiseworthy (see Philippians 4:8). Whatever thoughts or philosophies the enemy might offer up, we are to "take captive" and "make . . . obedient" to Christ (2 Corinthians 10:5).[30]

The Kindling of Cultural Mythology

Armed with a better understanding of how new memories can forever change the way we think about the world, our task is to discover the manner by which these internal images are transferred from the individual to the larger community. This, in turn, will help us discern how the enemy promotes the collective deceptions (cultural myths, philosophies and traditions) that have come to define the world's spiritually oppressed peoples.

Although the value of the subjective experience has grown increasingly suspect in recent years, at least in the Western world, it does not necessarily follow that a public (or objective) reality is more real than a private one. Nor, as Asian religious scholar Stephan Beyer warns, is it safe "to presume *a priori* that there is a boundary between the two." As history reveals, "Public reality is as amenable to magical control as private reality."[31]

To unlock the mysteries surrounding the development of early public realities, we must familiarize ourselves with three thematic keys: mushrooms, memes and myths. The first of these addresses the likelihood that at least some cultural mythologies originated in the hallucinogenic visions of tribal holy men. The second explains how these revelations became a self-replicating cluster of ideas. And the third illustrates how collective imagination can serve as a lasting habitat for supernatural powers.

Magic Mushrooms and Spiritual Vision

In many traditional societies, the experts who confront the supernatural directly are shamans—a term derived from the language of the Tungus people of Siberia. According to anthropologist Michael Harner, the shaman is a respected figure who typically makes contact with the Otherworld through a trance state and "has one or more spirits at his command. . . ."[32] His spiritual journeys, undertaken to gain knowledge, are facilitated by animal guides that have retained connections to the pre-Fall world.

Early shamans, as we noted in chapter 5, were deeply nostalgic for the golden age. They wanted nothing more than to revisit the paradisaical conditions and divine beings that could easily be perceived before mankind fell. In order to realize this dream, many of these ancient "world walkers" consumed hallucinogenic mushrooms—an action that all but invited demonic agents to seize control of their psychic machinery.[33] Affected by the powerful intoxicants, and stimulated by the steady beat of magical drums, their cerebral computers conjured the images they longed to see. It was the ultimate in virtual reality.

Harner suspects these visions not only reinforced the shamans' notions about the supernatural world, but they "may have also played a role in the *innovation* of such beliefs."[34]

Mircea Eliade agrees, and concludes his classic study on archaic shamanism with the proposition that a culture's mythology (including epic themes, images, motifs and literary clichés) is derived largely from the journeys of historical shamans into the Otherworld:

> The lands that the shaman sees and the personages that he meets during his ecstatic journeys in the beyond are minutely described by the shaman himself, during or after his trance. The unknown and terrifying world of death assumes form . . . and, in course of time, becomes familiar and acceptable. In turn, the supernatural inhabitants of the world of death become *visible;* they show a form, display a personality, even a biography.[35]

Other scholars dispute the notion that ecstatic experiences are the source of cultural motifs or traditions. They contend instead that the entranced mind merely reflects or builds on imagery imprinted on the brain already. "The [vision] is personally enkindled by the shaman," explains Celtic scholar Tom Cowan, "but the kindling is collected, in part, from the beliefs and values of the culture."[36] Hallucinogens are important to the visionary process because of their ability to help retrieve and reassemble stored visual images, especially intense or disturbing ones.[37]

The problem with this argument, other than its failure to acknowledge the capabilities of a real devil, is that it loses sight of the fact that we are talking about the *origins* of cultural mythology, about an archaic period in which many tribal beliefs and values remained largely undefined. It is unlikely that visionary shamans, operating in such a context, would have found the community a ready source of psychic kindling.

In Siberia, *Amanita muscaria* (a hallucinogenic mushroom sometimes known as fly agaric) was used widely and early on by shamans.[38] Although this practice was intended to facilitate the visionary journeys of local psychonauts, there are intriguing hints that it may also have provided the inspiration for one of the Western world's most celebrated cultural traditions.

Careful research reveals that, prior to 1823, the legend of Santa Claus gave him neither a team of reindeer nor the ability to fly or descend chimneys. These elements arrived with the publication of Clement Moore's classic poem "A Visit from Saint Nicholas" (or "The Night Before Christmas"). Some have speculated that Moore, a professor of Oriental languages, drew his inspiration from the rituals of Siberia's Koryak, Kamchandal and Chukchi peoples—rituals that, to this day, include worship of the "great reindeer spirit." The only person who can communicate with the reindeer spirit, according to these traditional societies, is the tribal shaman, who does so by eating the fly agaric mushroom. Once entranced, he "flies" to the spirit world, where he collects messages and "gifts" in the shape of new songs, dances and stories for the tribe. Interestingly, the shaman enters the realm of the spirits through the smoke hole on the roof of his *yurt,* or hide tent.[39]

Ancient literature also speaks of a mysterious plant called *soma* that played a big role in the pre-Zoroastrian religion of Iran and stimulated the visions on which Hindu myths and doctrine were based.[40] While some scholars have hypothesized that this intoxicating "pillar of the world" was none other than the fly agaric mushroom, New Age ethnobotanist Terence McKenna dissents on the grounds that *Amanita muscaria* is not potent enough. Offering a clue as to what he thinks it might be, McKenna declares, "Again and again, and in various ways, we find Soma intimately connected with the symbolism and rituals related to cattle and pastoralism."[41] This linkage suggests to McKenna that the ancient mystery plant is more likely the dung-loving mushroom *Stropharia cubensis,* a fungi containing a powerful, tryptamine-type hallucinogen known as psilocybin.

It is possible the Indo-Europeans first came into contact with *Stropharia cubensis* while tending their cattle on the Konya Plain of Anatolia. (Evidence for this comes in the form of a distinctive double mushroom idol found among the remains of these ancient pastoralists.)[42] From Anatolia the magic plant simply followed tribal clans and their livestock as they migrated eastward into Russia, Persia and India.

The main difficulty with this theory is that scientific field work so far has been unable to confirm the presence of *Stropharia cubensis* in India. McKenna claims, by way of explanation, that "desertification of the entire area from North Africa to the region around Delhi has distorted our conception of what occurred when ancient civilizations were in their infancy and the area received higher rainfall."[43] As we saw in the last chapter, mushroom cults existed among early cattle-raising societies in the Sahara (Tassili-n-Ajjer) until drought conditions gave solar deities the upper hand.

McKenna still expects to find *Stropharia cubensis* hiding among the flora of modern India. In support of his optimism, he cites the work of the late ethnomycologist Gordon Wasson. After several years of botanical study in India, Wasson determined that psychoactive mushrooms were present not only on the subcontinent, but were common "in lower regions" wherever there was a steady supply of cattle dung. He also raised the intriguing possibility that one of these potent fungi, *Stropharia cubensis,* might be "responsible for the elevation of the cow to a sacred status. . . ."[44]

If the chemically induced trance was the ancients' preferred means of receiving and transferring spiritual revelation, it was not the only option available. The famous oracular center at Epidaurus, Greece, included both a dream incubation temple and an amphitheater for ritual drama. According to Mara Lynn Keller, a specialist on the Eleusinian mysteries, pilgrims

> would await a vision that would come during sleep, [usually] in the form of a visit by a god or goddess. After receiving a divine visitation or vision, it was customary to enact the details for the benefit of the whole community.

In many cases this ritual enactment would take place immediately in the adjacent theater. Similar arrangements existed at Asclepius' shrine in Pergamum where, according to Revelation 2:13, "Satan has his throne." Here dream incubation was aided by the presence of long snakes that glided through the underground chambers and "licked" sleepers in their beds. Those with a phobia for reptiles had the option of Amphiaraus' temple in Attica, where priests required worshipers to sleep on the skins of sacrificial sheep; or various Egyptian temples, where sweet dreams were brought on by inhaling a compound of sixteen spices.[45]

The Nature and Role of Memes

In *The Lucifer Principle,* a book that has been called "a new perspective on world history," author Howard Bloom asks the question, "What propels the cultural tides of human beings?" In response, Bloom introduces the concept of the *meme*—"a cluster of ideas that leaps from mind to mind changing the way entire societies think and act."

Memes, like all ideas, start off small. Occupying nothing more than the private mental spaces of individual artists, philosophers or politicians, they jump and shout until they finally manage to seize the imaginations of their hosts. From this point on, their fate depends on catching a favorable wave of circumstance. If they can surf the prevailing Zeitgeist, their potential is virtually limitless. If not, they will eventually decompose, along with their mortal hosts. What sets the transforming meme apart from the ordinary idea is its ability to transcend the confines of the single mind and infect the consciousness of millions.

To illustrate the explosive potential of the meme, Bloom offers the example of Karl Marx, the angry young socialist who, for twelve frustrating years, incubated his theories of class struggle alone in the British Museum.

> By the mid–1980s, the ideas brought together [in a single] brain in the corner of a lonely library . . . had gone from controlling one 150-pound man to mastering millions of tons of this planet's matter. These memes were alive in the minds and the social mechanisms of over 1.8 billion human beings, spreading their influence over the lands, the minerals, the machines, and the domesticated animals that those human beings controlled.[46]

Bloom explains:

> As genes are to the organism, so memes are to the superorganism, pulling together millions of individuals into a collective creature of awesome size. Memes stretch their tendrils through the fabric of each human brain, driving us to coagulate in the cooperative masses of family, tribe, and nation.[47]

In earth's earliest ages, the primary incubators of memes were shamans who relayed their visions of the Otherworld by way of paintings, dreams and epic stories. At other times and in other places, equally influential memes burst forth from the minds of Buddha, Confucius, Plato, St. Paul, Mohammed, Martin Luther, Thomas Jefferson, Charles Darwin, Albert Einstein, Walt Disney and the Beatles. In each of these cases, nations and cultures were transformed by visions (implanted by heaven or hell) that took up "even less space and mass than the tangle of atoms required for a single strand of DNA."[48]

Spiritual powers, in their efforts to release these transforming visions, have focused historically on two critical variables: the original vessel and propitious timing.

The incubator of the meme does not have to be brilliant, only yielded. In fact, from God's perspective, weakness is often a virtue (see 1 Corinthians 1:27; 2 Corinthians 12:9–10). Many of Scripture's greatest triumphs were brought about by individuals whose initial selection was as unlikely as their ultimate success. The enemy's chosen vessels have been no less improbable. It has been said that Karl Marx "was not a promising person in which an idea would wish to start its life." Not only was Marx poor and without influence, but his foul temper tended to drive off what few friends he had. Bloom quotes one of Marx's old college professors as saying that he was always waving his fists in the air "as if a thousand devils gripped his hair."[49] No doubt they did. From their vantage point, visceral anger was what made Marx so useful.

If memes are to take root and spread, however, they must also be planted in fertile contextual soil—the second critical variable. Prevailing attitudes and circumstances can affect the fortunes of a meme just as readily as the initial host can. For this reason, spiritual rulers have long sought to create or capitalize on conditions likely to foster change. The Greeks went so far as to coin a word to describe the arrival of these conditions: *kairos*. The term, connoting a fullness or ripening of time, is used in Scripture to convey the unique sense of God's timing.[50] Examples of such *kairos* occasions include the rebuilding of Jerusalem under Cyrus, Artaxerxes and Darius; the spread of Christianity under Constantine; and the demise of Communism under Mikhail Gorbachev.[51] On the flip side of the historical coin, demonic agents have often advanced memes through the skillful exploitation of traumatic events like war (the Russian Revolution), pestilence (smallpox in India) and natural disaster (Pele worship in Hawaii).

In ultimate terms, cultures represent our collective fantasies about the divine, the profane and whatever lies across the threshold of death. As studies have shown, these "tapestries of memes" (or world-views) begin to form in the mind at childhood and take a lifetime to build. Their essence, as we noted earlier, comprises distinct collections of neural patterns that represent our experiential database of reality. It is impossible, apart from this vast grid of metaphors, to recognize or interpret the thousands of events that parade past our senses every day. So it should not surprise us that societies will do almost anything to defend the memes that constitute their belief systems. As Bloom observes, "To allow a faith or ideology to be overthrown [is] to abandon a massive neural fabric into which you have invested an entire life. . . ."[52]

This also explains why true conversion is (and must be) such a radical process. As our minds are renewed by the Holy Spirit, old mental patterns are actually replaced with new, undistorted metaphors. If these memes go on to become part of the larger societal imagination—as occurred in Nineveh, Judah and Antioch (see Jonah 3; 2 Kings 22–23; Acts 11)—the glory of God is released in public revival.

Myths as Psychic Habitats

Imaginary memes that become part of the public psyche are called myths. Among archaic peoples, the origins of these myths are generally traceable to shamanic visions (which we have already explored) or to the explanations affixed to collective traumas. The latter are important not only because they represent shared solutions to common pain, but also because intense experiences, especially fearful ones, tend to forge lasting memories.[53]

Myths also provide a dwelling place, a psychic habitat of sorts, for personified supernatural forces. Since these fantasy realms are not confined to a single mind, they can exist over many generations, or until such time as they are replaced by competing memes (such as the Gospel). The very longevity of these myths is often enough to endow them, like esteemed societal elders, with an illusory aura of truth.

With the passage of time, these mythological worlds often extend their borders into the real world. The monstrous gods of the Phoenicians, Aztecs and Tibetans are nothing less than external projections of internal images. In the tradition of Pygmalion, Pinocchio and Frankenstein, these demonically inspired deities are first given corporeal "bodies," in the form of graven images, then animated by evil spirits who are themselves empowered by the collective will and imagination of human communities.[54]

In the absence of genuine spiritual awakening, the mental strongholds formed by deceptive memes can (and often do) prepare a society for collective possession by demonic spirits. A frequent hallmark of this condition, which can last for brief or extended periods, is extraordinary violence—a fact that should come as no surprise since one of the devil's titles is Apollyon, or "Destroyer" (see Revelation 9:11). Our spiritual adversary, as Michael Green reminds us, "is a killer by instinct and appetite."[55]

Time and again, as we survey the tortured landscape of human history, we find evidence of this collective possession—men and women succumbing to the savage spell of Apollyon. This was true of the Aztecs, who ran what author Ptolemy Tompkins calls "the most death-obsessed civilization that the world has ever produced." At festival after festival, sacrificial victims would line up in queues that stretched for more than a mile. These "parades from being into nonbeing," as Tompkins calls them, "gave daily life in the Aztec cities a surreal and nightmarish flavor that left its mark on every member of society."[56]

In his book *Paris in the Terror,* Stanley Loomis provides a similar description of the period in the late eighteenth century when the French Revolution spun frighteningly out of control:

> A spell of horror seems temporarily to have fallen over the city of Paris,[57] a nightmare in which all communication with reality was suspended. It is impossible to read of this period without the impression that one is here confronted with forces more powerful than those controlled by men.[58]

Employing nearly identical language in response to the horrors of the second World War, Green asks:

> Who can look back at those years of phenomenal destruction, the deaths of more than fifty million people, the genocide of the Jews, and

the unbridled reign of evil in Germany, and *not* believe that there was something more at work than mere human beings?[59]

That question might be posed with equal passion in relation to the Mayan institutionalization of torture, the Ugandan terror under Idi Amin Dada[60] and the infamous killing fields of the Khmer Rouge (including their penchant for decapitating babies). China's Cultural Revolution, which left an estimated ten million people dead, is another candidate. During this bloodfest, Communist Party leaders in the Guangxi region of southern China reportedly incited followers not only to kill "class enemies" but to eat their flesh in public ceremonies. One suppressed government report refers to cadres "eating people as an after dinner snack [and] barbecuing people's livers...."[61]

More recently, in the territories of the former Yugoslavia, 200,000 civilians were killed and 20,000 women raped in a vicious campaign of "ethnic cleansing." Nedzida Sadikovic, a Muslim escapee from the town of Srebrenica, testified that when Bosnian Serb commander Ratko Mladic saw the men and boys in a crowd of several thousand refugees, he exclaimed to his troops, "It is going to be a *meze* [a long, delectable feast]. There will be blood up to your knees!"[62]

Nineteen-year-old Tarja Krehic from Bosnia, at a 1995 Venice youth conference called by Holocaust survivor Elie Wiesel, told her peers about the mysterious onset of evil in her neighborhood: "Hate came, I don't know from where." In Rwanda, where an outbreak of tribal warfare in April 1994 claimed more than 500,000 lives, missionary Per Houmann expressed equal astonishment:

> To be in the middle of all this, to watch them turn from the most wonderful, the most smiling, the most gentle of people to such treacherous murderers is almost beyond comprehension. It is almost as if someone flipped a switch.[63]

As successful as the devil is at manipulating man's psychic machinery, he does not confine himself to the realm of human imagination. The risk of exposure is too great. By lingering in one place or becoming too predictable in his methodology, he will eventually trigger divinely engineered safety alarms like reason and conscience.

So the devil's challenge is to keep these endowments inactive; and to do this, he must vary his deceptive repertoire.

The enemy also knows that subjective illusions, if they are to remain effective, must be set up or given credibility by objective realities. Spirits (or ancestors) must occasionally be observable; idols must hear and deliver; astrological predictions must sometimes come to pass. To help him meet these objective expectations, he relies on a vast army of demonic agents capable of oscillating between the spiritual and material dimensions.

Although the devil is practiced at disguising the nature, size and movements of his fallen army, God's people have not been left defenseless. Scripture has plenty to say about these creatures that manipulate the external world in order to maintain strongholds in the mind. Learning more about them, and in particular their penchant for shadow ruling, is a critical step in our quest to understand why spiritual darkness lingers where it does. In chapter 7 we will take the closest look yet at the malevolent powers that lurk in the shadows of the labyrinth.

Chapter Seven

The Art of Shadow-Ruling

From ancient times, the inhabitants of the Indonesian islands of Bali and Java have been mesmerized by elaborately choreographed shadow plays known as *wayang kulit*.[1] Thought to have originated in the region of Jogjakarta, the performances combine Hindu epics with Buddhist philosophy and local folklore, including the *Calonarang,* or "call to witches."

The animating force behind the *wayang kulit* is the *dalang,* or shadow artist. Crouching behind a linen screen backlighted by a flickering oil lamp or electric light, the *dalang* manipulates carved leather figures between the lamp and the screen. As he works his magic, lacy silhouettes begin to dance and flutter, their graceful gestures awakening the essence of ancient kingdoms and other worlds.

A master of many talents, the *dalang* is often a carver, painter, dancer, musician, impressionist and priest. Besides fashioning the original rawhide characters and providing their voices (sometimes in multiple languages), he is also responsible for blessing each *wayang kulit* performance and the surrounding area with a sacred mantra. Whenever possible, the shadow artist chooses stories appropriate to the village or venue sponsoring his performance. To provide this additional level of relevance, visiting *dalangs* often make it their first order of business to glean information on current local events from village elders.

The role of the Indonesian *dalang* is analogous in many respects to the spiritually bewitching performances put on by the prince of darkness himself. By relying on his considerable knowledge of physics and psychology, he, too, has been able to make people believe in shadows, inducing them to overlook his deft manipulations behind the screen of everyday circumstance. Like the *dalang*, our spiritual enemy has a repertoire of stories, both deep and rich, and a capacity to customize each performance for maximum impact.

Behind the impressive collection of characters and settings, however, satanic deceptions are essentially variations on one of two primary themes: the personification of natural forces (animism) and the elevation of manmade kingdoms (humanism). Both currents flow out of the earliest seasons of human history, and it is likely that the apostle Paul had them in mind when he warned the Ephesians about "world rulers of . . . darkness" and "principalities and powers" (see Ephesians 6:12, RSV). Whereas the former apparently represent evil spirits that stand behind the fallen systems of nature, the latter are intended to designate co-conspiring human authorities and national archons.[2] Both warrant a closer look.

World Rulers of Darkness:
Exploiting the Forces of Nature

> "As the thief is shamed when he is discovered, so the house of Israel is shamed; they, their kings, their princes, and their priests, and their prophets, who say to a tree, 'You are my father,' and to a stone, 'You gave me birth.'"
>
> Jeremiah 2:26–27, NASB

The souls of our distant ancestors yearned for answers. Like us, they had a passion to understand the mysteries of the universe. Recognizing this tendency, and noting the fact that human brains are designed to detect patterns, special demonic agents known as world rulers (*kosmokratores,* or "cosmic powers") set out to influence, distract or otherwise manipulate their explorations.[3]

Some of the earliest examples of these "guided observations" are contained in the sacred Hindu writings known as the Upanishads. As part of the so-called "Forest Books," the Upanishads describe how, in the magic of the deep woods, the senses can lead to profound revelations. In the stillness of the forest, for example, the sound of breathing becomes a focal point for meditation.[4] In wooded lushness the meditator can readily observe the cycles of life—leaves, seeds and cocoons falling to the ground, only to stimulate the next round of rebirth. Enchanted by an ancient, silver-tongued serpent, most do not notice that the conceptual heart of these "revelations"— the transmigration of the soul, or reincarnation—is nothing less than an old Garden-variety lie.[5]

Animism as a Worldview

Most people of tradition are persuaded that everything in nature is alive (although specifics differ from culture to culture). Each natural element, from stars and mountains to trees and animals, has a personal identity and emotions subject to influence. Anthropologists and theologians call this belief *animism* (from the Latin word *anima*, meaning "soul," or "that which animates"). While some cultures believe all matter is alive, others believe that life force is found only in forms inhabited by, or which embody, particular deities or ancestors.

As British historian Stuart Piggot notes in *The Druids,* the ancient Celts endeavored to depict the intelligence behind and within creation by personifying it. One of the ways they accomplished this was by carving grim-faced gods in rotting tree trunks situated in woods near natural springs. Even today people in Celtic lands "dress" wells with flowers and make vow pilgrimages to ancient oaks and special stones.[6]

Along the volcanic spine of South America, many windswept peaks belong to a category of supergods called *tius* (or uncles).[7] Piles of centuries-old wood found in these highlands testify to former bonfires that once lit up Andean nights in honor of these tius. Tierney has noted that the Incas were committed to the notion that "every *huaca*, or sacred place, had to be fed every year." If they were, they would in turn feed human beings.[8] Mount Kaata, which helps define the frontier between Peru and Bolivia, is particularly rich in huacas. Represented symbolically as a human body, this sacred landscape is fed a steady diet of ritual *chicha* (a corn-based alcohol), as well as animal (and occasionally human) blood, fat and fetuses.[9]

Animists also contend that the ensouled universe communicates with humanity consciously, transferring everything from information to counsel and wisdom. According to Eskimo shaman Najag-neq, the divine power speaks not only through "the forces of nature that men fear," but also "by sunlight and calm of the sea." The voice of the universe can be "soft and gentle" so that "even children cannot be afraid."[10] Similar claims are conveyed through the lyrics of popular children's recording artist Raffi[11] and in the hit song "All the Colors of the Wind" from Disney's *Pocahontas.*

"Once we become aware that we are one with all natural phenomena," says Goddess lecturer Marcia Starck, "we begin to acquire our lessons from the plant world, the realm of the winged ones, and the celestial sphere."[12] New Age guru Terence McKenna speculates that nature's various members may communicate with one another through the release of chemical signals into the environment. The interspecies translators in this theory are natural hallucinogens like ibogaine, harmaline and psilocybin. Through their assistance, human beings can pursue a deeply bonded relationship with plants, animals and the earth itself.[13]

Astrology, Destiny and the Heavens

Not long ago, the Griffith Park Observatory near Los Angeles was flooded with anxious phone calls in the aftermath of a local earthquake. Nearly all the callers wanted to know what was "different" about the sky. Baffled astronomers spent hours searching the heavens before the explanation finally dawned on them. The quake had knocked out a large grid of power transformers, and many city-dwellers were seeing the stars for the first time in years!

For the ancients, whose nighttime vision was unhindered by the lights and pollution that accompany modern civilization, such spectacles were commonplace, but no less mysterious or awe-inspiring. If they did not yet understand the cosmic complexities that would later be expounded by the likes of Copernicus, Einstein and Hawking, they did record bona fide patterns.[14] Unfortunately, the interpretations they affixed to these patterns were heavily influenced by demonic world rulers. Viewing the heavens through these faulty lenses, the ancients arrived at four spurious conclusions:

1. Since the starry canopy revolved around a fixed point, the polestar and its attendant constellation, Ursa Major or the Big Dipper, were thought be the center of, and possibly the entrance to, the heavenly dimension.[15]
2. Many heavenly bodies, exalted and bright, were considered deities or spiritual figures. Indo-Aryans and Babylonians offered devotion to the seven *rishis* (or sages) embodied in the constellation of Ursa Major,[16] while the Greco-Roman world accorded divine status to the five nearest planets (whose names have remained to the present day). Virtually everyone personified and worshiped the sun and moon.[17]
3. In many societies, the orbits of celestial bodies were "conceived of as gods moving through the night sky en route to rebirth each sunup"; and as author John Carlson has pointed out, "To observe and predict the recurrent paths of divine lights was to know the fates of kings and empires, to discern the proper day for rituals, and to forecast . . . the season of life-giving rain."[18] Even more prophetic were exceptional phenomena such as planetary conjunctions, eclipses or comets. Observations of these signs, which date to at least to 2400 B.C., became known as "omen astrology."[19]
4. The motions and positions of the heavenly bodies were also assumed to control individual destinies, although to decipher one's fortune required a complex form of divination called "horoscopic astrology." In this system, the planetary forces that influenced a person's character were modified by the signs of the zodiac, in the same way that rays of light are modified when they pass through colored panes of stained glass.[20]

Whatever we may think about such conclusions, there is no doubt that our ancestors' relationship to the sky and its countless glittering orbs was a fundamental component of their primordial religion. Nor can we doubt that their perceptions were influenced profoundly by cunning demon powers. According to Clinton Arnold, professor of New Testament at Talbot School of Theology, the very word Paul uses for "powers" *(dynameis)* in his letter to the Ephesians is also "found in astrological contexts for star spirits." So, too, are his terms for "world rulers" *(kosmokratores)* and "elemental spirits" *(sto-*

icheia).[21] These terms, as Arnold points out, would have been "especially relevant to people who believed the luminaries populating the heavenlies were gods and spirits."[22]

It is also interesting to note the special attention the astrological community gave to the atmosphere of the earth. In the minds of many early priests and diviners, the region known as the "lower heavens" harbored mysteries and forces of extraordinary import. One of the first to write extensively on the subject was the Greek astronomer Ptolemy. In treatises composed in the Egyptian coastal city of Alexandria, he claimed that the earth's atmosphere was pervaded by an ethereal power called the "Ambient." Through this power, he believed, planetary and stellar forces were relayed to people on the earth's surface.[23] At the very least, Ptolemy's ideas provide an intriguing parallel to "the ruler of the kingdom of the air" whom Paul describes as being "at work in those who are disobedient" (Ephesians 2:2). They may also offer an explanation as to why, at the final judgment of the earth, the seventh angel will pour his bowl of wrath into the air (see Revelation 16:17).

Those who insist there is nothing in the "silent signs of the heavens" to warrant such concern would do well to consider the Sabians of Harran. In *The Golden Bough,* J. G. Frazer relates that this heathen population "offered to the sun, moon and planets human victims who were chosen on the ground of their supposed resemblance to the heavenly bodies to which they were sacrificed." An example is given of blood-smeared priests offering a red-haired victim to "the red planet Mars" in a temple duly decorated in vermilion.[24]

Unfortunately, as Dr. Arnold reminds us, "astrology was widely practiced" by the Israelites as well.[25] The prophet Amos mentions the names of several of their Assyrian star gods, while Jeremiah describes how incense was burned before the "Queen of Heaven," who was the Babylonian goddess Ishtar (see Jeremiah 7:18; 44:17–19, 25).[26] This practice, which biblical writers described as "[bowing] down . . . to worship the starry host," so angered God that He said He "will cut off" those who do such things.[27]

The New Testament scene was not much better. Astrological beliefs hung over the first-century world like ivy. As Cavendish and others have pointed out, even the Lord's Day had become "the day of the Sun."[28] Nearly all the early communities of faith, including those at Ephesus, Colosse, Rome and Galatia, struggled with syncretism, many rationalizing that the astrological art was the study of God's "signs," not His "causes."[29] Among the most influential of the early syncretists were figures like Julius Firmicus Maternus and Synesius of Cyrene, individuals whose legacy would later be built on by the likes of Thomas Aquinas and Dante.[30]

Animal Imagery (Wisdom and Power)

While demonic world rulers have enjoyed great success with astrology, their deceptive repertoire is by no means limited to illusions involving the starry hosts. Equally powerful performances continue to be delivered in the terrestrial theater, most often in the role of divine beasts and animal spirit guides.[31]

Recognizing man's nostalgia for paradise lost, the devil has sown the enticing proposition that animals have somehow retained a connection with the golden age and can be counted on as sources of wisdom and power. John Lame Deer, a Lakota Sioux medicine man, relates how in the course of his vision quest, he heard a voice speaking for the birds. "We are the fowl people," said the voice, "the winged ones, the eagles and the owls. We are a nation and you shall be our brother."

While perceptions of interspecies relationships are common and welcome among Native Americans, they often obscure a dark and telltale presence. A testimony by Dick Mahwee, a Paviotso shaman from Nevada, suggests that the eagle and owl are actually "messengers that bring instructions from the spirit of the night." This spirit, which according to Mahwee "is everywhere" and "has no name," represents the ultimate source of the healer's power.[32]

To the Druids, this spirit was none other than Cernunnos, the Animal Master. Viewed by some as a shaman, by others as a god, his image appears throughout Celtic lands in the presence of various forest animals. In his hand he holds the mysterious horned serpent, "a beast respected for its ability to travel quickly and silently between the worlds."[33] The Maya would have known this reptilian deputy as the vision serpent—the embodiment of the path to and from the Otherworld. In imagery of the Classic Period, "ancestral figures were often shown leaning out of its open jaws to communicate with their descendants." Earlier tribes referred to this awesome portal as the "Black Transformer" and the "Mouth of the White-Bone-Snake."[34]

For many, this otherworldly serpent is still a reality. In 1980 a young woman by the name of Margaret Umlazi shared a recurring dream she had while attending a Christian missionary school in South Africa:

> I was taken to a large pool of water by spiritual beings who I could not see. A python came out of the water, wrapped itself around me, and pulled me into the pool. My father brought a goat to the water so that I could be delivered from the python. I found myself coming out of the pool and heard a whistle from the snake. As I looked back, I saw the python turning into my dead grandfather. I felt the wind blowing on me as I awakened.[35]

Another woman, a recovering alcoholic and student of shamanic *tonal* dance (ritual visualization with power animals), dreamed that a large serpent entered her bedroom and slithered across her legs and stomach onto her chest. From this position the serpent struck, fastening itself onto her face with its fangs and powerful jaws. No matter how she struggled, the snake would not be dislodged. Even after she woke from her dream, she felt that the serpent was still attached to her. Her spiritual mentor encouraged her "to dance and sing her experience and to make a mask of what the serpent's energy felt like." After constructing a hideous death mask, she was guided to put it on and speak with its voice. Instead, the woman "broke into sobs, gasping that she wanted alcohol, poison, *anything* that would take her out of the painfulness of human existence and into nothingness."[36]

In yet another dream, a patient of Swiss psychologist Carl Jung described a disturbing perversion of the heavenly scene recorded in Revelation 8:3–4:

> We go through a door into a tower-like room, where we climb a long flight of steps. On one of the topmost steps I read an inscription: *"Vis ut sis."* The steps end in a temple situated on the crest of a wooded mountain, and there is no other approach. It is the shrine of Ursanna, the bear-goddess and Mother of God in one. The temple is of red stone. Bloody sacrifices are offered there. Animals are standing about

the altar. In order to enter the temple precincts one has to be transformed into an animal—a beast of the forest.

The central chamber of that temple, according to the subject, was unroofed, and worshipers could look directly up at the constellation of the Great Bear, Ursa Major.

> On the altar in the middle of the open space there stands the moon-bowl, from which smoke or vapour continually rises. There is also a huge image of the goddess, but it cannot be seen clearly. The worshippers, who have been changed into animals and to whom I belong, have to touch the goddess's foot . . . whereupon the image gives them a sign or oracular utterance like *"Vis ut sis."* [37]

This strange Latin phrase might best be rendered, "You will that you may be."[38] Jung called the goddess in the dream "Cybele-Artemis." This powerful deity, honored by the Romans and Ephesians as Diana, was known as the Mistress of Wild Animals, whose astral form was the constellation of Ursa Major.[39] Moreover, as ancient goddess figurines attest, the Mistress, like Cernunnos, maintained "a special companionship with serpents."[40]

Goddess Imagery (Fertility and Nurture)

If animals are looked on as purveyors of power and wisdom, their Mistress, the great Goddess, is seen as the primary fount and sustainer of life. Closely linked with the earth itself, she is sometimes referred to as Mother Earth or Gaia (a name borrowed from the Greeks).[41] In what may be the ultimate statement of her independence, a 1963 painting by Judy Chicago depicts the Earth Mother giving birth to herself, extruding primal matter in a great wave spouting from her mouth.[42]

As Elinor Gadon informs us,

> Archaeological evidence affirms overwhelmingly that prehistoric peoples worshipped a female deity. The religious quest was above all for renewal, for the regeneration of life—and the Goddess was the life force.[43]

In time this quest took on the form of a ritual, now revived, known as "Drawing Down the Moon." The twofold intent of the rite, as described by former pagan priest Aidan Kelly, was to "draw down" (or take on) the persona of the Goddess, and to symbolize her "gift of immortality through reincarnation."[44] By inspiring such ritual imagery, the enemy hoped to extend the original Edenic deceptions to successive generations.

By 2500 B.C. the Goddess culture had reached its apogee. On the windswept islands of Malta, more than thirty temples were built in honor of the Great Lady, many designed in such a way that to enter them was to enter her sacred body. An underground ceremonial center known as the Hypogeum (located in the Tarxien complex we discussed in chapter 2) was considered both a womb, where revelations were conceived through dream incubation and serpent venom, and a place of burial, where the dead returned to the Mother. In Minoan Crete, there is evidence that Goddess devotees contacted their Mistress by pouring out offerings of blood and other sacred liquids. Cave sanctuaries were numerous, and serpents and opium poppies appear to have played a major role in Minoan rituals. Other images reveal the Goddess "pulling down the bough from the sacred tree" and dancing in an orgiastic fashion.[45]

While her influence continued to be felt through the Greco-Roman period, by the seventh century A.D. the Goddess' ideological "market share" was being lost to the so-called patriarchal religions—notably Judaism, Christianity and Islam. Faced with this threat, her demonic patrons settled on a clever ploy. They would contextualize their star performer, casting her as "the Mother of God."[46] Although this had little impact on Islam, which the enemy was controlling in other ways, it transformed Christianity. Early adopters included Gnostic sects such as the Nicolaitans (whose syncretistic practices, including ritual prostitution, infiltrated the church at Pergamum) and the Collyridians, who offered cakes to Mary as the Queen of Heaven.[47] "The power of the Goddess was not denied in Christianity," Gadon explains, "she was [merely] given a new name."[48]

But while this adaptation provided the Goddess with extended life, it was not enough to restore the flower of her youth. As history progressed into the modern age, the once-dominant Lady became increasingly marginalized, sidelined by a new breed of deceptive heavyweights, including rationalism, materialism and Communism. Some speculated that her career was over.

This obituary proved premature. After centuries of declining influence, the Goddess staged an impressive comeback starting in 1979. This revival can be traced, to a large extent, to the release of two huge-selling books, Starhawk's *Spiral Dance* and Margot Adler's *Drawing Down the Moon;* and two groundbreaking events, the Great Goddess Re-Emerging Conference in Santa Cruz, California, and the launch of the Radical Faerie Movement ("gay pagans") at a desert conference near Tucson, Arizona. Together these developments gave impetus to hundreds of new Goddess-related festivals, courses and publications.

By September 1995 the influence of this pagan renewal was being felt at the U.N.–sponsored Conference on Women in Beijing. Delegates to that conference, besides being presented with an array of seminars celebrating Goddess theology, were given an opportunity to bring ritual fruit offerings to Mother Earth. While some women openly dedicated their workshops to various goddesses, others constructed actual shrines and idols, at least one of which was later sent on a celebratory tour around the world.[49]

Not everyone views this current revival as authentic. Aidan Kelly points to the fact that many ancient goddesses, including Artemis, Orthia, Kali, Cybele and the Morrigan, "were often fierce and uncompassionate"—ladies whose demonic slips were showing. Kelly calls the female divinities described in current feminist and neo-pagan literature, by contrast, "saccharine." He refuses to accept that these modern goddesses, sanitized of their dark and bloody features, are figures that "have been restored from history."[50]

Nature Worship and Gender-Bending

We have already seen that, according to Romans 1:21–27, there is a direct connection between nature-based idolatry and sexual perversion. By substituting the glory of God for images of humans, birds, animals and reptiles, the ancients were given over to sexual impurity and homosexual behavior. "Women," says Paul, "exchanged natural relations for unnatural ones," while men "committed indecent acts with other men . . ." (verses 26–27). By placing themselves under the influence of evil world rulers, they found their imaginations darkened to the implications of violence and sexual defilement—a blindness that eventually led to a devastation of their bodies, minds and cultures.

Anthropological and archaeological findings over the last several years have lent credence to the apostle's claims. Not only are Celtic priests known to have been open homosexuals or of ambiguous sexual identity,[51] but scholars have noted a similar penchant among Siberian and Amazonian shamans. Offering the Siberian Chukchi as a case in point, Eliade relates that even when they are heterosexual, *"their spirit guides oblige them to dress as women"* (emphasis added).[52] This is not unusual, according to Cowan, since the beings encountered by shamans on their spiritual journeys are themselves bisexual. This androgyny allows them to "play a key role in the drastic reorganization of categories that shatters the shaman's old perception of reality and opens him or her to the multiple dimensions of existence."[53]

Shamans are not the only idolaters to be troubled by these spirits. In ancient Babylon the masculinity of temple personnel known as *kurgarru* and *assinnu* was alleged to have been changed by the goddess Ishtar into femininity. Saggs, inclined to view these cult servants as homosexuals, also notes that they took part in masked ritual dances, possibly as transvestites. If they did, their performance would no doubt have inspired the notorious cross-dressing that attended later folk festivals honoring Diana.[54]

More recently, gay men searching for spiritual role models have begun to rediscover figures such as the shaman and the *berdeche*.[55] In articles contained in the gay country journal known as RFD *(Radical Faerie Dust)*, there is much discussion about the role of androgyny, cross-dressing, role-changing and homosexuality in shamanic cultures. Summarizing this interest in an interview at the 1985 Pagan Spirit Gathering, Peter Soderberg declared:

> We feel there is a power in our sexuality . . . [a] queer energy that most cultures consider magical. It's practically a requirement for certain kinds of medicine and magic.

At a forest celebration in the Berkshires, another gay pagan told Margot Adler, "It is simply easier to blend with a nature spirit, or the spirit of a plant or animal, if you are not concerned with a gender-specific role."[56]

Demonic Manipulation of Natural Forces

One of the reasons nature-based religions have garnered so many converts over the years is that world rulers of darkness have done a masterful job presenting the cosmos as conscious and interactive. Their effectiveness in this task is apparently linked to a profound understanding of the physical universe and to an ability to manipulate matter, energy and other invisible forces. When these capabilities are mobilized in response to the actions of shamans and astrologers, the deception is often seamless.[57]

Accounts of supernatural phenomena are as numerous as they are old.[58] Although some have proven to be hoaxes or frauds perpetrated by clever magicians, not all incidents are so easily explained away. A case in point is a 1944 power encounter between Chile's Mapuche Indians and local Catholics. Betting on whose deity could produce rain to end a severe drought, the parties gathered on a hill near a sacred pool known as The Cat's Water. According to an account provided by Felipe Painén, the skies were unresponsive to the first petitioner, a priest named Father Luis. But when an old *machi* named Juan Cheuquecoy came out and prayed, "The sky turned black [and] it rained very hard."[59] Similar examples have been recorded by credible witnesses in Soroti, Uganda; Thimpu, Bhutan; and various Indian reservations in the American Southwest.

In his book *Healing the Land,* Winkie Pratney reminds us that God created not only life but life systems—that is, systems that are themselves capable of reproducing life.[60] But animists, with the encouragement of demonic world rulers, have determined to deify these creative processes rather than seek out their ultimate Designer. By making nature the story rather than the setting, as C. S. Lewis once observed, they have forgotten that "nature is a creature, a created thing." And although nature "comes with her own particular tang or flavor . . . it is not in *her,* but in Something far beyond her, that all lines meet and all contrasts are explained."[61]

Principalities and Powers: Governmental Co-Conspirators

While Paul referred to Satan as the ruler of the kingdom of the air, Jesus called him the prince of this world—an appellation that, in the

Greek, means "ruler over kingdoms or structures."[62] Whereas the former title suggests the enemy's mastery over the natural realm, the latter is a straightforward acknowledgment that, for the moment at least, he also maintains dominion over human systems—political, economic and religious.

In general, Satan secures his authority over these systems by forging explicit links with human governments and by encouraging the spread of potent humanistic memes. Either way, as Michael Green points out, demons "interpenetrate the climate of a country, the *Tendenz* of its politics and the *nuances* of its culture."[63]

The demons in this case are not nature-manipulating world rulers but territorially oriented principalities and powers.[64] The Bible does not concern itself with the precise hierarchy of these powers (presumably because this information is immaterial to successful spiritual warfare), but it does appear to link them to specific nations, cities and institutions (see pages 192–198).[65]

There is also evidence that these demonic princes (archons) are linked to human counterparts—evil (or at least pliable) kings, priests and governors who serve as their earthly representatives.[66] The powers manipulate these terrestrial rulers, like Machiavellian viziers, by keeping them refreshed with the enchanted wine of pride. The prophet Isaiah, acknowledging God's displeasure with this collusion, declared: "In that day the LORD will punish the powers in the heavens above and the kings on the earth below" (Isaiah 24:21).[67] We find examples of these loathsome alliances in the Old Testament accounts involving the kings of Tyre and Babylon (see Ezekiel 28 and Isaiah 14). Several other passages make reference to the Roman imperial system. One of them, Revelation 2:13, speaks of Pergamum, the locus of political power in Roman Asia, as the spot "where Satan has his throne." In Daniel 11, the wicked king Antiochus IV Epiphanes, whose name means the Manifest (god), is identified indirectly as the blaspheming monarch from the north.[68]

A more recent example of this power axis was evident in Ethiopia during the brutal reign of Communist dictator Mengistu Haile Mariam. After attending an exorcism performed in the late 1970s, one credible witness reported the boast of the reluctantly departing spirits: "We are ruling the country through him [Mengistu], and we are going to destroy it." Ten years later a government defector with access to the ruling *Dergue** recalled a telling comment made to him by fearful party officials. "When we sit in cabinet sessions," they confided, "nobody looks up at Mengistu's eyes. They are always darting back and forth, while his serpent tongue speaks of harsh measures involving killing and death."[69]

God, knowing the dangers inherent in human kingdoms, labored to persuade the Israelites to forgo an earthly king in favor of His direct supernatural leadership. At the heart of His concern was the knowledge that man-inspired initiatives turn quickly into manmade substitutes—idolatrous doorways through which demonic agents gain access to societies and inflict spiritual bondage. God also knew that control of the king means control of his kingdom.[70]

In earlier days, Babylonian kings, Egyptian pharaohs and Roman emperors validated this concern by standing in the threshold between the heavenly powers and human society. Like exalted shamans, they represented the people before the gods, and served as the pipeline through which heavenly deities regulated the affairs of state. Reveling in their grandeur (see Ezekiel 31:10; Daniel 4:30) and persuaded of their divinity (see Isaiah 14:13–14; Ezekiel 28:2; 29:3), these god-kings set their hands to the unending task of conquering rivals and building glorious cities and temples.[71]

Further evidence of the linkage between fallen angels and earthly monarchs is found in ancient Mesopotamian artwork. One famous, if enigmatic, illustration depicts kings flanking a stylized fruit-bearing tree surrounded by what appear to be serpents. Floating overhead is the sun god Samas in a "winged disk."[72] Whatever the inspiration of the original artist, the similarity of the image to both the Edenic center tree and Ezekiel's wheeled creatures is striking.[73] The stele of Ur-Nammur, a ten-by-five-foot limestone slab found on the floor of the Hall of Justice in Ur, describes the building of a ziggurat. Called the "Stele of the Flying Angels," it, too, reveals winged creatures hovering above the head of the king.[74]

Variations on this theme have been observed in a variety of other settings as well. During Egypt's 26th dynasty, for example, a statue was carved showing the goddess Hathor, in the form of a fire-

---

* The name given to the nation's Marxist military clique.

crowned beast, protectively covering the pharaoh Psammetichus. In the Nepalese city of Patan (which early Tibetan traders called *Ye Rang,* or "Eternity Itself"), a statue of the seventeenth-century King Narenda sits atop a free-standing pillar. Over his head an upright cobra flares a protective, and threatening, hood. Similar images are found at Cambodia's Angkor Wat complex, where intricately carved serpent deities *(nagas)* bolster early Khmer god kings;[75] and at Yax-chilan, where glyphs depict the great Maya king Yat-Balam emerging from the mouth of an enormous vision serpent. (According to Linda Schele and other Mesoamerican scholars, the notion of powerful humans having special soul bonds with gods is well documented in classic Maya thought. In many instances these spirit companions, or *wayob,* are portrayed floating in the air above the bodies of their earthly partners.[76])

Although it is tempting to dismiss such partnerships as belonging to a bygone era, this temptation should be resisted. If demonic powers exist at all, they can hardly be expected to content themselves with artistic reminiscences of their past exploits. What they have done, as the following vignettes illustrate, they are doing still.

Africa and Asia

It is well known that most African heads of state consult regularly with traditional spiritual leaders and make periodic forays into the sacred bush or forest. Some, like the former Ugandan dictator Idi Amin Dada, visit sorcerers as well. Although these contacts are generally viewed as innocent, and even healthy, cultural form, in reality they are the breeding grounds for deadly conspiracies.

Amin, after receiving what he called a "prophetic dream" in 1952, was seized with an insatiable lust for power. When a successful military coup later thrust him into national leadership, the ruthless nature of his demonic allies was soon put on public display. In addition to manifesting a sudden and virulent anti-Semitism, including a televised boast that he would become "a second Hitler," Amin launched a massive extermination campaign against Christians. Some were buried up to their necks in cesspools, while others were shot in the knees, doused with gasoline and set ablaze. In certain camps women had their eyelids sewn open so they could not avert their eyes when their children were fed to crocodiles. At one point so many bodies had been thrown into the Nile River that divers had to be dispatched to clear the intake duct at the Owens Falls Hydroelectric Plant.[77]

One survivor of these horrors, Hassanain Hirji-Walji, told me that when he first arrived at a death camp outside Kampala, trucks were dumping hundreds of decaying human corpses into open pits. The stench was so overwhelming that Hirji-Walji was struck by a wave of nausea. Looking for a place to vomit, he slipped into an adjacent building. It was empty—and very cold. When his eyes adjusted to the dim light, he noticed a frosted glass display case containing racks of dark objects. Creeping over for a closer look, Hassanain suddenly realized they were severed human heads. As he recoiled in horror, an amused soldier appeared in the doorway. "These are Amin's trophies," he chuckled. "He keeps them as reminders of what happens to his enemies—and he does the work himself!"[78]

The rulers of the Dark Continent, despite their frequent dealings with demonic principalities, hold no monopoly on the unseen realm. Equally robust and dangerous alliances with the spirit world can be documented throughout much of Asia. As the "divine mandates" of imperial Japan and revolutionary Iran demonstrate, these partnerships are often the driving force behind unpleasant social upheavals. At the same time, however, Asia's archons are sophisticated enough to adapt to situations in which violence is neither possible nor desirable. They know that when it comes to the realization of their objectives, the wand of deception is often just as effective as the club of destruction.

The nation of Indonesia has been particularly susceptible to magical control. While gods and enchanters can be found on almost every island in this emerald armada, most knowledgeable observers agree that the primary haunt of the powers is the Javanese city of Jogjakarta. One local intercessor reports that "a majority of the powerful witches whom the government leaders rely on and consult" come from this community. A 1993 *Asiaweek* article, sustaining this claim, describes the Jogjakarta *kraton* as "a palace world governed by tradition and a firm belief in mysticism." It also notes that the chief of Indonesia's Department of Education and Culture, Dr.

Suradi, is a devotee of a spirit known as Nyai Roro Kidul—the "Queen of the Southern Ocean."[79]

In other parts of Asia, Singaporean and Taiwanese government officials routinely acknowledge invisible spirits in their public speeches,[80] while the Dalai Lama takes advice from a national oracle, a practice dating back more than thirteen hundred years. Japan's Emperor Akihito, during his 1989 coronation, performed elaborate rituals to reaffirm his country's allegiance to the sun goddess Amaterasu Omikami. To many Japanese, these ceremonial rites symbolized Akihito's final transformation into a divine being—a process that involved receiving the soul of Amaterasu as he joined with her in symbolic sexual union.[81] In Nepal, Bhutan, Thailand and Cambodia, divine monarchs provide similar links to the spirit world.

Middle East and North Africa

The Middle East, a region in which God has been particularly interested over the years, has always attracted the attention of demonic powers and principalities. This present age is no exception. The enemy's influence over human authority structures, from Marrakech to Baghdad, ranges from heavy to astonishing. In Libya, for instance, strongman Muammar Gaddafi is said to retire periodically to a desert tent where he solicits revelation through *velatio*—the practice of covering one's head with a garment in order to encourage spiritual inspiration. Taking a different route to the same end, several Israeli Knesset members—most prominently Shas Party leader Aryeh Deri—call regularly on Moroccan-born kabbalist Yitzhak Kaduri at his home in Jerusalem's Nahla-ot quarter.[82]

Many Saudi princes are also known to have personal witches or wizards, although this is forbidden by Islam. A number of these soothsayers (often Ethiopians or Moroccans) actually reside in the royal household. It is an open secret in the kingdom that one of King Fahd's nephews has a special room in his palace dedicated to the black arts. Another royal employs a witch full-time to promote his favorite soccer team (by casting spells on rival players); while several Saudi princesses have used their private jets to visit top Moroccan wizards (whose talents they hope will help them find suitable lovers or husbands).[83]

Latin America

Latin America's political leaders manifest a similar fascination with the spirit world. Unlike their Middle Eastern counterparts, however, they have not been shy about discussing their practices or hesitant to factor their "revelations" into public policy. At a recent news conference, Peruvian president Alberto Fujimori told reporters: "I consult a seer. Without telling her specifically what my question is about, she gives me a reading. Then I make my decisions." In a subsequent cover story documenting Fujimori's reliance on witches, Peru's weekly news magazine *Caretas* named Fujimori's principal seer as Carmela Pol Loayza.

Fujimori's story is not unique. In Argentina, charismatic president Carlos Menem boasts openly about his visits to psychics and has often ordered his political life around the recommendations of astrologer Evelia Romanelli.[84] He has also asked several shamans to visit his home and cleanse it of evil spirits. In Brazil the recently ousted president Fernando Collor de Mello not only consulted psychics, often flying Mae Cecilia Arapiraca to Brasilia aboard his private jet, but (according to his brother and former chauffeur) participated in regular sorcery rituals, complete with goat sacrifices and drums, in the basement of his home. When the Brazilian congress began debating Collor's impeachment in 1992, the president and his wife reportedly drove pins into the pictures of people they wished to silence.[85]

Similar measures were employed by the former Panamanian strongman Manuel Noriega. When U.S. troops invaded Panama several years ago, they discovered a "witch house" on the grounds of Fort Amador in which Noriega had prepared curses (called *workings*) against former U.S. Presidents George Bush and Ronald Reagan. Extensive documentation was gathered by the military under the direction of officer James Dibble. Among the items found: a split cow's tongue with nails in it, several sacrificial altars, and workings encased in gelatin and banana leaves.[86]

The Western World

Despite the countervailing influence of Judeo-Christian values, dark powers have also managed to secure a foothold in the palaces of Europe, America and Australia. This infiltration, which dates back to the very origins of colonial expansion, has been attended historically by high-level fascination with esoteric and occult philosophies, including Rosicrucianism, neo-Paganism and Freemasonry.[87] By the end of the nineteenth century, two of Europe's most powerful men, Germany's Kaiser Wilhelm and Russia's Nicholas II, were routinely attending séances and heeding occult advisors.[88]

Four decades later, dark powers scored an even bigger coup with the rise of Adolf Hitler's Third Reich. While the Führer's personal involvement in occult rituals has been vigorously debated, there is no doubt he was surrounded by true believers. The more notable of these include Munich University professor Karl Haushofer, whose organization, the "Luminous Lodge," was later incorporated into the Nazi Occult Bureau; Dietrich Eckart, a die-hard occultist and spiritual founder of the Nazi Party; Rudolf Hess, the deputy Führer, whose devotion to astrology bordered on fanaticism; and Joseph Goebbels, Hitler's chief propagandist, whose beliefs included omens and reincarnation.[89]

The most avowed Nazi occultist, however, was Heinrich Himmler, leader of the Nazi elite forces, the dreaded SS.* Several times a year Himmler gathered with his senior officers at a special mountaintop retreat known as Wewelsberg Castle, located near Paderborn. Here black-shirted mystics assembled around a great oak dining table, where they participated in solemn rites known as "the ceremonies of the stifling air." Led by Himmler himself, who was secretly dubbed the Grand Master of German occultism, these rituals allegedly included divination, spell-casting and meditative contacts with the "racial soul." Guided by the powers they conjured at Wewelsberg, Himmler's SS Death's Head division went out to torture and kill fourteen million human beings.[90]

Although nothing of such magnitude has been recorded in American history, this does not mean that the powers associated with the world's leading democracy have been without influence. In fact, all but six of the original 56 signers of the Declaration of Independence were members of the Masonic order, including such political luminaries as John Adams and Benjamin Franklin. George Washington

---

* SS is an abbreviation of *Schutzstaffel*, the German term for *Elite Security Force*.

was himself a high-level Mason, and Abraham Lincoln reportedly became involved in the practice of spiritualism after the death of his son.[91] Even during the Reagan administration, which many American Christians continue to hold up as a symbol of spiritual renaissance, the First Lady was deeply involved with an astrological consultant who actually influenced national policy.[92] The occult conduit was reopened a few years later when Hillary Clinton invited New Age guru Jean Houston to preside over guided visualization sessions in the White House solarium.[93]

While the prince of this world seeks continually to seduce key political leaders, this is not his only strategy for gaining dominion over human systems. Acquiring control over the apparatus of state does not, as he well knows, automatically give him sway over the hearts and minds of the people. To achieve that, he must find a way to promote the spread of humanistic memes.

Once again, the solution lies in finding and seducing the right kind of people. While the list can include politicians, it is just as likely to feature television producers, screenplay writers, performing artists, university professors, pastors, journalists and economic policymakers. Such individuals, properly controlled, can be of immense value to demonic powers who wish to inject their poison deep into the cultural bloodstream.[94]

The enemy's ultimate intention is to gain control over the prevailing societal mindset and the institutions that fashion and sustain it. The apostle Paul, recognizing this dark ambition, refers to Satan as "the god of this age" who "has blinded the minds of unbelievers, so that they cannot see the light of the gospel" (2 Corinthians 4:4).[95] Using more contemporary speech, Clinton Arnold simply calls him "the god of many of the structures that order our existence."[96] Both descriptions help us understand how the powers can be equally at home in the ancient, temple-infested cities of Asia, or in the budding shrines of Western culture, which often take the form of shopping malls, sports complexes and universities.

In Babylon the Great we find the first, and perhaps the most vivid, example of a society whose basic structures and values became utterly polluted by demonic powers. In addition to becoming "a home for demons and a haunt for every evil spirit" (Revelation 18:2), the city is portrayed in Jeremiah 51:7 and Revelation 17:4–5 as an international anti-hero—a seducer of the nations. Revelation 18:3 says:

> "All the nations have drunk the maddening wine of her adulteries [polluted philosophies and structures]. The kings of the earth committed adultery with her, and the merchants of the earth grew rich from her excessive luxuries."

Although the themes of seduction and unfaithfulness play strongly here, there is more going on than meets the eye. Babylon is not merely a spiritual prostitute; she is the archetypal "Mother of Harlots."[97] Her corrupt offspring, the fruit of a passionate union with the prince of darkness, include renowned temptresses like materialism, Freemasonry,[98] astrology and divine kingship. With the magic of the powers flowing through their veins, these daughters of the great mistress have cast a powerful spell over the earth's kings and merchants.[99]

If Babylon's legacy is obvious in the great empires of Egypt, Greece and Rome, her features can also be seen in the exalted intentions of the British Raj, imperial Japan and the Third Reich. Even the stateless United Nations exhibits her swagger, as do the European Union, OPEC and the World Council of Churches. Despite their bloodlines, however, these and other examples of institutionalized conceit are mere warm-up acts for the real star of the show: the Antichrist. Under the reign of this powerful figure,[100] economic, religious and governmental forces will unite in a kind of super-Babylon. Revelation 13:2–8 indicates that the Antichrist's power and authority will derive from the dragon[101] and extend over "every tribe, people, language and nation" (verse 7). It also reveals that these governmental co-conspirators will be worshiped by "all inhabitants of the earth" (verse 8). "Proud humanism," in Schaeffer's words, will be "joined to the acme of the occult."[102]

As they did at Babel millennia before, the powers will coalesce like a dark cloud over a unified humanity. This time, however, their conspiratorial plans will be allowed to proceed as a prelude to the final judgment.

Idols and Role-Playing

During the many years I have spent investigating demonic activity around the world, one observation has always caught my attention: The enemy is hopelessly addicted to power and adulation, yet he will go to great lengths to keep from being recognized. Although he delights in controlling the affairs of nations, cities and households, he seems to understand that role-playing is an important part of maintaining that control.

In some quarters the devil's talent for shadow-ruling has been so effective that he is routinely dismissed as a serious explanation for social and political bondage. As we noted in chapters 2 and 3, even Christians seem to have their doubts. Characterizing demonic agency as "simplistic" and "superstitious," a growing number of Western churchmen (including some evangelicals) have taken to seeking their answers in the social sciences.

This tendency to search out "rational" explanations has placed many modern Christians in open conflict with the early Church fathers. In case after case, the fathers reminded their readers that while pagan gods have no life of their own,[103] they are still dangerous as fronts for lurking demons.[104] This was how John Chrysostom viewed the Greek god Apollo. It is also why early Christian apologists like Origen, Justin and Tatian were so concerned about the mythological foundations of Greco-Roman paganism.[105]

Although the first Christians saw demons as the animus of the gods, the pagan world viewed these deities as the life force inhabiting their idols. In ancient Babylon, priests performed an elaborate ritual known as the "Opening of the Mouth" that served as a kind of housewarming for their transcendent gods. The rites began when a freshly crafted idol was carried by torchlight to the banks of the Tigris and Euphrates Rivers. There, after the statue was loaded onto a reed mat, its mouth was washed repeatedly with holy water. When this task was completed, usually by the next morning, cult priests sacrificed a ram to the accompaniment of chanted invocations. Finally, as the ritual reached its climax, the high priest proceeded to "open the eyes" of the image by touching them with the twig of a magical tamarisk. At this point the idol became a sentient thing. With the deity now immanent within the sculpted form, it was left to enthrone the image ceremonially in a temple dedicated to his or her honor.[106]

The story, as Winkie Pratney points out, has often been repeated. Humans begin by making up their own gods, and end when their creations, invested with demonic power, begin to rule them instead.[107] As to why people tend to experience only their own cultural spirits, I can answer only that the devil knows to stay in character. He inhabits the script he has been given (or has inspired). He assumes the characteristics we expect. His sole intent, achieved through deceptive, behind-the-scenes manipulation, is to make the fantasy credible.[108]

Regional Deities

A popular notion in the Middle Ages suggested that the world was haunted by precisely 133,306,668 fallen angels. Alphonsus de Spina divided the majority of these demons into ten categories (such as poltergeists and incubi) and asserted that each town and castle had its own attendant demon.[109] While this specificity impressed medieval audiences, especially those eager to understand the structure of the invisible world, the thrill was soon tempered by a healthy skepticism. Many people seeking scriptural support for these claims came to find the Bible strangely silent on the issue of infernal populations and hierarchies.

What it does seem to offer is evidence of evil spirits being linked, at least temporarily, to specific peoples or territories. This evidence (as we noted earlier) includes Daniel's mention of the angel princes linked to Persia and Greece; Ezekiel's reference to the guardian cherub associated with the king of Tyre; and John's revelation of Babylon as "a home for demons and a haunt for every evil spirit" (Revelation 18:2). We also have the demonic Legion of the Gerasenes begging Jesus "not to send them out of the area" (Mark 5:10) and the correct rendering of Deuteronomy 32:8, which, according to F. F. Bruce, "implies that the administration of various nations has been parceled out among a corresponding number of angelic powers."[110]

The concept of territorial spirits is also observable in cultural traditions. Early Mesopotamian city-states like Babylon, Ur and Nippur were considered the property of particular deities who ruled them as they saw fit. The same was true in Egypt, where every town, village and district had its god that bore the title *Lord of the City*.[111] In Syria and Palestine, these local gods were called Baals, an appellation that signified their mastery over specific territories and communities.[112] In the New World, the Aztec city of Tenochtitlan was divided into 21 corporate areas *(calpollis)*, each with its own pertinent gods.[113] Harmonizing these examples was a dual understanding that (1) The activity, power and dominion of the gods were bounded by certain limits; and (2) The divine residences were maintained at certain fixed sanctuaries.[114]

In Roman times the subject of divine borders got complicated. The Romans, being superb administrators, had a god for every place. Although Terminus stood unchallenged as the god of boundaries, one also had to acknowledge Janus, who presided over the gates. Entrances to homes were congested by the presence of three deities: Limentius, the god of the threshold; Cardea, the goddess of the hinge; and Forculus, who ruled over the door itself. There were also guardians of the storeroom, the hearth and the home in general.

In some places this situation has not simplified with time. The Himalayan nation of Bhutan still boasts more than 8,400 deities, all of whom are profiled in texts maintained in the National Library and in some monasteries. Specific categories include regional deities (affirmed through area traditions), house and altar deities (determined through family traditions), door and foundation deities (recognized as preexisting) and personal deities (obtained through individual choice or selection by lamas).[115]

In rural India, village deities known as *dihs* are installed at the moment a community is founded. As local guardians, they help define the identity of the villages by controlling the coming and going of all supernatural forces and influences across village boundaries. According to one South Asian scholar, "Any human act that attempts to propitiate, exorcise, or otherwise control the supernatural must begin with the Dih's permission and blessing."[116] A similar arrangement exists in the Buddhist-dominated Gyasumdo region of Nepal. But here the village god and Buddhist doctrine are believed to be supported by an army comprising guardian deities drawn from individual households.[117]

Among the Hausa people of rural Niger, *alijanu,* or "close" spirits, are numerous, equipped with wings and distinctly territorial.[118] In their malevolent form, they are similar to "shadow spirits" recognized by Native American tribes like the Karuk of Northern California. According to shaman healer Medicine Grizzlybear Lake, "These shadow-spirits are very territorial" and will sometimes "attack humans because [they] are in their territory."[119]

In the early 1970s, evangelist Herman Williams discovered just how nasty these spirits can be. The encounter took place shortly after he and his wife, Fern, had settled in Fort Thompson, a small town on South Dakota's Crow Creek Indian Reservation. From their first day in the area, the couple attracted unusual attention, not only as the new blood in a small town, but as ethnic Navajos in the midst of traditional Sioux territory.

This much was to be expected. What the Williams did not anticipate was the level of hostility their Christian faith would provoke among local demonic powers. The trouble began, according to Williams, when a middle-aged man dropped by their home to welcome them into the community. The visit was not the courtesy it seemed. Although Herman and Fern had no way of knowing it, their ostensible goodwill ambassador was actually a traditional Sioux sorcerer. Recalls Williams:

> At one point in our conversation, this man says to me, "Although you're a Navajo, I'm glad to have you here. I also want you to know that I'm a barber, and if you ever need a haircut, I won't charge you anything." I thought it was a great offer, and a few weeks later I took him up on it. He did a good job. After he finished trimming me, however, he had Fern sweep up my hair and put it in a bag that he brought with him. At the time I thought it odd that he would want to keep my clippings. I should have known better.
>
> About two days later I began to get sick. It was so bad that I went to see a doctor about sixty miles away, over the reservation line. My wife was driving because I was so ill. Oddly, as soon as we crossed the reservation boundary, I started feeling better; and by the time we pulled into the hospital parking lot, I was completely normal. I told my wife I felt silly going to the doctor with no symptoms, but she insisted that since we had come this far, I should go in anyway. After examining me, the doctor just shrugged and suggested I probably had

an allergic reaction to something. So we just shopped a little and then headed back home.

Once again, however, something happened when we passed the reservation border. We were no more than a few miles into Crow Creek when I began to get sick again. When we reached our home, I was really bad off. So my wife called the doctor that evening and made arrangements to bring me in again the next day. When the same thing happened at the reservation boundary line, we began to suspect that we were dealing with territorial spirits.[120]

About a month later I was so sick I could hardly get out of bed. One particular night—it was quite late—I began to hear Indian chanting. Strangely, it seemed to be coming from an interior wall located next to the kitchen. As I listened for a while, my wife suddenly woke up and said, "Honey, do you hear something?" I replied, "Do you?" She said, "Yes, I hear singing. It sounds like a peyote chant." So I got out of bed real slow and walked toward the sound. As I stood there, it became apparent that the singing was somehow coming from between the walls. It was frightening. Right at that moment, however, I felt a voice rising up from deep within me. I just repeated, "Lord Jesus! In Jesus' name!" Immediately the singing stopped and I began to feel better. For the first time in a month and a half, I was able to get a good night's sleep.

Early the next morning I was up making coffee when a lady knocked at the door. She said, "Mr. Williams, would you please come quickly? We have a situation that needs prayer." So I got ready and followed her to a little tarpaper shack. Upon entering the shack, I found a man curled up on a cot. His eyes were rolled back up into his head so that you could only see the white portion of his eyeballs. The rest of his face was grotesquely deformed, and his hands and fingers were twisted like a rope. I looked at the lady and asked, "Who is he?" She replied, "It's the medicine man, Joshua Turtle Bull. Last night around 1:30 A.M. he let out a terrible scream. When I came to investigate, I found him in this condition." Sadly, even as we talked that morning, Joshua Turtle Bull died a terrible death.

Three days after the funeral, another medicine man invited me to his house for dinner. After some small talk, he suddenly blurted out, "Did you know that Joshua Turtle Bull was trying to kill you? He had taken your hair and used it in a sorcery. Unfortunately for him, your power was too strong and his witchcraft backfired. That's what killed him."

I was stunned. Never before had I encountered such graphic evidence of the hatred—and the very real power—of territorial spirits. Never had I been so grateful for the protective mantle of the Holy Spirit.[121]

As I have documented numerous accounts like this one, it has become apparent to me that territorial forces are every bit as prevalent today as they were in the heyday of the ancient Baals and city lords. In certain areas they even seem to have proliferated—or at least to have consolidated their authority over local peoples and social structures.

Asia's Tibetan community offers a sobering case in point. As those who have walked these high-altitude neighborhoods will tell you, territorial spirits are honored not as guests but as "the lords of the soil of this continent." These unseen rulers, according to sacred tantric texts, are teeming in number and represent a complex spiritual hierarchy. Their haunt is the stark terrain of the Tibetan national psyche, where they venture forth in the form of "demonic breeds" (such as *tsen, damsi, klu* and *geg*) or as specific deities (like the Lady of the Turquoise Lamp and the God of the Great Northern Plain).[122]

In the Caribbean nation of Haiti, which by some accounts is 85 percent Catholic and 110 percent Voudon, the invisible order is dominated (as we saw in chapter 1) by powerful spiritual entities known as *loas*. Among the ranks of these animating spirits of Voudon are several well-known personalities, including *Legba* ("Protector of the Entries"), *Calfou* ("Ruler of the Crossroads") and the top-hatted *Baron Samedi* ("Keeper of the Dead"). The influence of loas, as one Port-au-Prince *houngan* has said, should not be underestimated. For while "Haiti may appear to be like any other forlorn child of the Third World . . . this is just a veneer. In the belly of the nation there is something else going on."[123]

Most Christians would offer no argument. Even if the average believer has not trekked personally through the spiritual underbrush of Haiti or Tibet, he or she has little difficulty believing that demonic powers are actively engaged in such places. Less clear is the nature and mechanics of their evil assignments.

In the current debate over territorial spirits, some Christians are persuaded that national archons are preassigned and permanently stationed; others are convinced the process is more random and spontaneous. Rather than follow some kind of scripted strategy, these believers claim, evil spirits simply gravitate to the most immediate opportunity to animate the imaginative inventions of men. In actuality, these alternatives are probably not as contrary—or important—as their proponents would have us believe.[124] The question of whether demons are on permanent assignment in certain areas or whether they, like actors in a long-running Broadway play, are rotated in and out of the same role begs the point. They are there, and their deft impersonations of local deities have placed them in firm control of the prevailing worldview.

Other Christians get sidetracked over names, some going so far as to dismiss the demonic credentials of a deity simply because it cannot be linked to a specific Scripture reference. But God does not distinguish between biblically identified fallen angels (Lucifer, Beelzebub, Apollyon) and deities whose appellations have been whispered into the vain imaginations of men (Artemis, Moloch, Kali). His promise to "punish Bel in Babylon" (Jeremiah 51:44) is comprehensible only if Bel is viewed as a demonic power.[125]

In the final analysis, the current theological critique of territorial spirits must be seen as a uniquely Western indulgence—a kind of academic polo for tenured (and mostly Anglo) professors. Even if the doctrine of territorial spirits stood on shaky ground biblically, the concept so dominates the lives of non-Western peoples that it takes on a practical validity that cannot be ignored by those who want to minister effectively among them. As anyone knows who has visited Bali, Peru, Bhutan or New Guinea, elaborate territorial pantheons are as much a part of the daily experience as sunshine and commerce. They are real because millions of people over the centuries have believed them to be real. They thrive because entire communities have shaped their spiritual and material environment to accommodate this reality.[126]

If the influence of regional, demonically controlled deities is readily seen, however, the question of what determines the extent of their authority, geographically speaking, is more challenging. While God, demons and politicians have all been suggested as solutions to this puzzle, the answer seems to involve none of these—at least not directly. Rather, as William Robertson Smith has noted, "The land of a god corresponds with the land of his worshippers."[127] If Calcutta-based devotees of Kali move to Houston and bring their idols and devotion with them, then the borders of Kali's influence have clearly been extended. The same applies to the gods of Chinese Buddhists moving from Hong Kong to Vancouver, or African Voudon deities traveling with their followers to Haiti, Brazil or New Orleans.[128]

     ▣   ▣   ▣

Over the last several chapters, we have learned much about the nature and denizens of the labyrinth. These discoveries have allowed us to draw useful conclusions about the manner in which spiritual strongholds are established in the human mind, in societies and in various geographical regions. Along the way we have developed a new appreciation for the roles played by trauma, memories, memes and myths. We have also seen that shadowy demons manipulate the forces of nature and conspire with human leaders, all in an effort to distract people's attention from the tender overtures of their heavenly Father.

Despite this progress, however, our journey is not yet over. Knowing how the enemy enters human communities does not fully explain how he is able to linger in them. Insight into this matter is vital, especially since a high percentage of our evangelistic search-and-rescue missions are conducted in areas where the kingdom of darkness has become dynastic. If we can discern how the enemy has managed to perpetuate his presence in these vicinities, our efforts to evict him will be enhanced.

Chapter Eight

Territorial Dynasties

If pristine scenery is what you are after, few areas on earth can match the stunning landscapes of British Columbia's Sunshine Coast. At virtually every turn in this Pacific wonderland, rugged mountains, off-shore islands and fjord-like inlets offer a true feast for the eyes. Unfortunately, nature is shy in these parts, and more often than not she conceals her beauty in a misty veil. The Sunshine Coast, with more than two hundred days of annual overcast, may bear the most misleading of all Canadian place names!

The climate in Alaska's southern panhandle is even worse. Beset by moisture-laden storms that roll in off the Gulf of Alaska, cities like Juneau and Ketchikan average an astounding 280–300 cloudy days a year. Not surprisingly, many people find it difficult to live in this perpetual shadow. This is because natural light is vital to human life. Deprivation can lead not only to sleep and appetite disorders but to severe depression. Norwegians refer to their dark winters as *morketiden,* the "murky times"—referring to both the weather and the dismal mood it produces. Others speak of winter blues or cabin fever.[1]

In many respects, spiritual strongholds resemble these stationary weather fronts. Anchored by an absence of godly repentance, their thick overcast blots out the spiritual light and warmth that make life worth living and exposes underlying communities to a steady downdraft of confusion, violence and despair. Sometimes this overcast blankets individual cities (like Marrakech, San Francisco and Jogjakarta), while at other times it mushrooms out across entire regions (like Tibet, North Africa and the Arabian Peninsula).

The evolution of spiritual darkness, like adverse weather patterns, is governed by rules that are at once intelligible and predictable. Although these rules focus primarily on moral actions, as opposed to physical elements like topography, air currents and water temperature, their effects are equally discernible.[2]

In determining the relative strength of a given stronghold, we must consider at least three factors:

1. The explicitness of the original pact or welcome;
2. The nature of the evil spirits involved;
3. The amount of time a particular pact has been in force.[3]

The first factor relates to the truth that, when it comes to the onset of spiritual bondage, intention counts (see Numbers 15:30; 1 Kings 11:1–10). The second factor reminds us that some spirits are more powerful than others (see Daniel 10:13; Luke 11:24–26). And the third warns us that the enemy will erect formidable deceptive bulwarks whenever he is unhindered by corporate repentance (see Exodus 32:1–25; Matthew 23:27–39; 2 Corinthians 4:4; 11:2–4).

The last of this trio of factors is particularly relevant to the theme of this chapter: the longevity of spiritual strongholds. If the topic sounds familiar, it is because we have now come full-circle in our quest to answer the opening question of this book: *Why does spiritual darkness linger where it does?*

On the basis of evidence we have reviewed thus far, we may make two assertions with confidence: First, strongholds are born whenever cultures welcome evil powers into their midst through unambiguous pacts; and second, strongholds are extended when the provisions of these pacts are honored by successive generations.

What we do not yet know is how the enemy manages to stay in fashion for such considerable periods of time. Even if we agree that demonic forces attain their initial entrée into communities through the misplaced choices of earlier generations, we need to discover how these powers manage to secure "lease extensions" centuries after their original business partners are dead and buried.

As we proceed to investigate this matter, at least four possible explanations present themselves:

1. Religious festivals and pilgrimages;
2. Cultural traditions (especially initiation rites and ancestor worship);
3. Adaptive deceptions (or syncretism);
4. Unresolved social injustices.

History has shown that any one of these practices is capable of maintaining a climate of spiritual oppression and despair, and their combined potency is nearly irresistible. To better understand why, we will take a closer look at each of these practices in turn.

Renewing Allegiances: The Role of Festivals and Pilgrimages

Viewed as opportunities to contact higher powers and the rhythms of nature, religious festivals and pilgrimages have been part of the human agenda since the dawn of civilization. The Babylonians welcomed the full moon—which they regarded as a symbol of spiritual power and danger—with kettle drums and sacrifices. The Hittites honored sun and storm deities with a month-long festival known as An Tah Sum. Festivals were also common among the Egyptians, Chinese, Persians and Phoenicians—cultures whose celebrations routinely encompassed demons as well as divinities.

Ancient Athens, a city well known for its idolatry and superstition, devoted more than 120 days a year to religious festivals.[4] But this level of public commitment to the Otherworld was only a shadow of the astonishing dedication that would emerge in Nepal (where not a day goes by without at least one collective overture to the supernatural) and Japan (which holds about sixty thousand festivals a year).[5]

Although times have changed, some ancient (and bizarre) rituals remain largely intact. The Persian community, for example, still marks the three-thousand-year-old festival of Nowruz by watching eggs quiver on a flat mirror and leaping over bonfires.[6] In the Japanese city of Yokaichi, naked young men follow an age-old tradition by jumping for "cocoons" (actually rice cakes) that hang from a crossbeam in the temple. Each year in the Indian state of Kashmir, seventy thousand Hindu pilgrims follow the footprints of their ancestors to Amarnath Cave, where they venerate an icy, twelve-foot stalagmite believed to be the phallus of Lord Shiva.[7]

A newer, equally eccentric festival takes place each year in the village of Lopburi, Thailand. Here villagers honor the spiritual guardian of the community's thirteenth-century shrine by inviting the six hundred or so long-tailed macaque monkeys that live in its ruins to an elegant banquet. The feast, accented by red tablecloths and napkins, consists of fruit, nuts, rice—and Pepsi.

It is easy to dismiss such behavior as silly superstition. But many frontline Christian workers argue that something more sinister is at work during these religious festivals and pilgrimages. Offering a hint as to what this something might be, the late mythographer Joseph Campbell noted that

> the whole purpose of participating in a festival is that one should be overtaken by that state known . . . as "the other mind"—[a state in which] one is "beside oneself," spellbound, set apart from one's logic of self-possession. . . .[8]

There is little doubt that such surrender, especially when expressed corporately, often leads to the release of significant spiritual power. Nearly all the national believers and missionaries I have interviewed associate religious festivals with a heightened sense of oppression, increased persecution and manifestations of demonic signs and wonders. One believer living in the holy city of Mecca requested special prayer covering for the upcoming *hajj*.* "At the time of the pilgrimage," he explained, "it is as if devils are walking through the streets. One can almost see and feel the presence of Satan."[9] Others have noted that prayer traffic during these intense seasons seems to move more slowly, and they speculate that responses to intercessory petitions are delayed by spiritual strongmen like the one that delayed God's response to Daniel.

Religious festivals, ceremonies and pilgrimages are not the benign cultural spectacles they are made out to be. There is nothing inno-

---

* An Islamic pilgrimage that attracts some two million Muslims each year from throughout the world.

cent or "natural" about them. When their colorful veneer is stripped away, they are conscious transactions with the spirit world, occasions for successive generations to reaffirm choices and pacts made by their ancestors. In this sense festivals are a kind of generational passing of the baton, a chance to dust off ancient welcome mats and extend the devil's right to rule over specific peoples and places. Their significance should not be underestimated.

Festivals: Renewing Community Pacts

A precise tally of contemporary religious festivals and pilgrimages is hard to come by. But most experts estimate their number in the hundreds of thousands, easily enough to establish spiritual pact-making as a 365-day-a-year business.

Examples of these events range from the annual Balinese ceremony called "The Gods Descend All Together," an elaborate Hindu ritual involving idol pageantry and animal sacrifices,[10] to the nine-day Festival of Mevlana, during which Turkish Sufi dancers endeavor to commune with the divine through hypnotic whirling. In mid-summer the town of Beselare, Belgium (nicknamed "the Parish of the Sorceress"), holds a public Procession of the Witches;[11] while the Lakota Sioux of North America pierce their chests at Sun Dance ceremonies in order to renew their allegiance to various nature spirits.

For many participants, these powerful and sublime occasions also represent an opportunity to brush against Ancient Wisdom and identify with cultural points of origin.[12] During India's Maha Kumbh Mela, a festival that Nehru once described as being "lost in an unknown antiquity," fifteen million Hindus gather to bathe in the confluence of the sacred Yamuna and Ganges Rivers. In this auspicious spot, according to legend, a drop of *amrit* (the nectar of immortality) fell during a primordial conflict between Hindu gods and demons. As a consequence, the waters are said to convey an invisible river of enlightenment. During its long reign, according to Indian scholar D. P. Dubey, the popular festival "has had immeasurable influence in strengthening the religious and cultural foundations of Hinduism."[13]

Other festivals aim to entertain (or placate) spirits believed to inhabit the ghostly realm of the dead. Because these spirits often appear in the form of ancestors (a demonic guise), rituals that emphasize their care and feeding have become particularly effective in furthering transgenerational deception. A good example is Japan's midsummer O-bon festival. At the beginning of this widely observed ritual, families journey to mountain graveyards with lighted lanterns in order to guide ancestral ghosts back to their homes. The invisible guests, upon arriving at the doors of the houses, are greeted by kimono-clad hostesses, who bow respectfully and lead them over to a vase of feathery flowers. For the next three weeks, this bouquet will serve as their temporary accommodation. When the time comes for the esteemed visitors to return to their own world, they are placed aboard small, candlelit boats and gently nudged toward the "other shore."[14]

Halloween, rooted in the Druid festival of Samhain (pronounced *sow-en*),[15] is perhaps the ripest time for making connections with the spirit world. According to Celtic scholar Tom Cowan, this is because Halloween is a "time outside of time," a season

> when the veils between the worlds are lifted and much trafficking takes place between spirits and mortals. In Scotland it is called a "night of mischief and confusion." Modern celebrants, especially children, keenly sense that the normal laws are suspended. Tricksters seek admittance to others' homes, even as spirits from the Otherworld seek entry into this world. On Samhain we are reminded that doorways are open, thresholds are bridgeable, and the ordinary and nonordinary intermingle.[16]

The characterization of religious festivals as portals to the supernatural realm is also found in the classic Maya pageants. As University of Texas professor Linda Schele has noted, these mystic spectacles were "more than just acts of civic pride and piety." The Maya, motivated by fear, faith and fascination, designed their festivals to facilitate collective access to the Otherworld. "[When] the paths across the abyss opened on the grand stairways and plazas of their cities," Schele explains, "participants were transformed into supernaturals."[17]

As these accounts illustrate, men and women have never abandoned their age-old attempt to reopen Eden's primordial gateway. This persistence is due in part to our unquenchable longing for the eternal (see Ecclesiastes 3:11). Put simply, human beings need to make contact with the Otherworld. But apart from God this task remains difficult at best. As critical links in the spiritual continuum, religious festivals and pilgrimages must be executed properly. If they are bungled or neglected, the benefits they are meant to sustain (such as divine access and protection) may disappear—or so the enemy would have us believe.[18]

In an effort to amplify this fearful prospect, and thereby maintain his control over a particular culture, Satan often resorts to the selective use of magic. On the morning of May 3, 1996, two elderly Navajo men visited Irene Yazzie's home near Big Mountain, Arizona. Presenting themselves as Navajo deities, they instructed Irene and her daughter not to be afraid and inquired why they were no longer receiving prayers from the people. When the women failed to answer, the visitors warned that if the Navajo continued to forsake tribal traditions, they would face grave danger, and the spirits would no longer be able to render assistance. With this sobering admonition, the men literally vanished, leaving only footprints and a sprinkling of corn pollen.[19]

In the ensuing months, word of the incident reached Navajos living as far away as San Diego and Albuquerque. Sobered by what they heard, thousands took time off work to make the long pilgrimage out to the remote visitation site. Many brought sacred objects as tribute and spent long hours in prayer. In an open memo, tribal president Albert Hale declared: "This is a significant event to Navajo people everywhere." Ruth Roessel, a teacher of Navajo culture, expressed the hope that the visitation would inspire a return to abandoned traditions. "This may just wake some people up," she said.[20]

Another bid to reestablish lapsed ties with the spirit world took place in 1982, when residents of the depressed Japanese mountain town of Oe (near Kyoto) determined to renew a six-hundred-year-old pact with the demon Shutendoji. In addition to launching an annual festival in Shutendoji's honor, the town also consecrated a special park and museum to display ornamental devil masks. The town's deal with the devil, according to Masaichi Murakami, director of the International Oni *(devil)* Association, has thus far been successful. As evidence, he cites a significant upswing in tourist traffic—some two hundred thousand visitors per year. States Murakami:

"I think that this town where demons dwell can become a home-town for city people."[21]

Appeasement rituals, which can range from full blood sacrifices to the smearing of malt candy on the mouths of idols, represent an important component of most religious festivals. In typical settings, these actions are perceived as installment payments on insurance policies, the *quid pro quo* of pacts negotiated by previous genera-tions. A good example is found in Japan's Aoi Matsuri, an annual fes-tival celebrated by the residents of Kyoto to honor a sixth-century pact in which the gods agreed to end a season of destructive flood-ing.[22] In another centuries-old festival, inhabitants of Hong Kong's Cheung Chau Island bake buns to satisfy spirits angered when their ancestral graves were disturbed.

On Indonesia's Sumba Island (nicknamed "Spirit Island"), the local Merapu people hold an annual festival known as the Pasola. The ritual begins at midnight when village priests *(ratos)* call out to the sea goddess Nyale in a low howl: *"Hoo-hoo-huaa."* Soon, and ever so faintly, the sound is echoed back. This is the sign that Nyale has come ashore in the form of worms that will make the land fer-tile. In an effort to honor the goddess for her provision, hundreds of villagers gather on horseback to offer her blood—human blood. Fac-ing off on a long beach near the coastal village of Wanokaka, the men suddenly charge. Many are upended by long, blunted spears used as jousting instruments. When the first blood is spilled, the onlook-ers rejoice: "The harvest will be good!"[23]

Pilgrimages: Individual Quests for Revelation

While religious festivals engage entire communities, pilgrimages are more personal in nature.[24] The objective is still to secure spiri-tual revelation and protection, but only insofar as these relate to the individual supplicant. Like cities and cultures, individuals often experience crises that require the intervention of a higher power. If the crisis is new, a pilgrimage may be taken in order to summon help; if it is related to a chronic or past condition, the pilgrimage is more likely to be a means of servicing a pact to which earlier entreaties have led.

Examples of such pilgrimages are numerous. Some have as their destination a particular shrine or power point. Others offer the journey as its own reward. Most combine both elements. The arduous pilgrimage around Tibet's 22,000-foot Mount Kailas is said to wash away the sins of a lifetime. Before undertaking the three-week journey, which becomes possible only after one has managed to reach this exceedingly remote site, pilgrims symbolically shed their old lives by removing their clothes and pricking their fingers at a nearby lake. Those hardy enough to complete 108 circuits around this sacred peak—which Hindus and Buddhists alike consider the center of the universe—achieve *nirvana* (ultimate bliss) in this life.[25]

A similar, if less spontaneous, event is the Islamic hajj. Each year in the twelfth lunar month, millions of Islamic pilgrims descend on holy Mecca and the nearby plain of Arafat. They come, as the Qur'an has it, "from each distant point"[26]—a coordinate just as likely to be London or Paris as Senegal, Samarkand or Mindanao. As in the sacred Himalaya, arriving pilgrims disassociate themselves from the world by casting aside their garments. Then, after donning the white cloth *ihram,* they proceed to fulfill a week-long series of rites that includes, among other things, orbiting the sacred Ka'aba and stoning devils at the pillars of Mina. Proper performance of the hajj, the so-called Fifth Pillar of the Islamic faith, is said to wash away all past sins.[27]

If Mecca is the ultimate terminus for Muslim pilgrims, the Indian city of Varanasi is the destination of choice for Hindus. Regarded as the earthly abode of Lord Shiva, the city is host to no fewer than 140 recognized pilgrimages. Among the better known of these is the Pancakrosi Yatra, a 55-mile route that encircles Varanasi's most sacred terrain. Those who traverse this pathway of 108 shrines are said to move through "a tunnel of sanctified space."

Dr. Rana Singh, a noted expert on Hindu religious rites, identifies three stages of the pilgrimage experience. The first of these, the *separation* stage, is particularly important. Besides being the time when pilgrims unhook from worldly affairs—a process facilitated by a purifying bath in the Ganges—it is an occasion for spiritual pact-making. Dr. Singh told me in 1992 that most supplicants follow up their cleansing dip with a visit to the shrine of Dhundhiraja, where they make a solemn vow to the gods: "If you help me in my hour of need, I will make the journey to your shrine again and perform devotion."

Having put this promise on the table, pilgrims move on to the second, or *liminal,* stage of the journey. During this five-day period, most of the hard work of the pilgrimage is performed. By walking long distances, abstaining from food and sex, and prostrating themselves before ubiquitous shrines, participants hope to impress the gods with the seriousness of their intentions. In this sense the exacting journey becomes a down payment on freshly drafted pacts, although many also report a mystical bonding with ancestors and fellow pilgrims.

During a final *reaggregation* phase, pilgrims return to their normal lifestyle by offering *prasada* (sweets) to the gods and sprinkling Ganges water in every room of their homes.[28]

The rigors of the Pancakrosi Yatra, although considerable, are a far cry from those experienced by Malaysian Hindus on Thaipusam, the birthday of Lord Subramaniam. On this occasion more than a half-million Tamil celebrants flock to sacred sites in Kuala Lumpur and Penang in order to transact business with their patron deity. For many it is a time to recompense Lord Subramaniam for answers to prayer, a solemn responsibility that leads some pilgrims to perform acts of self-mutilation.

The process typically begins as crowds begin to chant a refrain of *Vel, vel* (in reference to the leaf-shaped lance that is a symbol for Subramaniam). As the chanting is joined by rhythmic drumming, the devotee is suddenly possessed by the "deity," a moment often attended by a chilling scream. Fully entranced, he or she is then anointed with camphor ash and pierced with one or more steel lances. In most instances these skewers are inserted horizontally through the cheeks or vertically through the tongue. Other devotees fulfill their vows by carrying the *kavadi,* an elaborate wooden harness supporting an image of Subramaniam. The enormous structure, attached to the pilgrim's body by dozens of hooks and wires, is borne up 272 dizzying steps to the Batu Cave Temple. Upon entering this sacred precinct, the perspiring devotee presents himself before a priest, who breaks the trance by spewing coconut juice down his throat and extracting each ritual device.[29]

Although such high drama has its uses, it is nearly always employed as part of a larger deceptive strategy. The reason is simple. If the devil is to maintain control over human communities, he must persuade men and women of his power not only to protect and provide, but also to reveal secret knowledge. Few things are more important to humans (as the enemy well knows) than finding a way to probe the mysteries of tomorrow. While death is the biggest of these riddles, and the central focus of most religions, a useful deity must also be prepared to field questions relating to love, business and health.

For many people, the promise of special revelation shines like the proverbial pot of gold at the end of the rainbow. Every day its powerful (and largely ephemeral) lure prompts millions of men and women to spread their wings in sacred quest. For some, the pilgrimage leads to sanctuaries chiseled by human hands; for many others, the trail ends in hallowed forests, ancient caves or seaside shrines.

While the sacred landscapes of Egypt, India and Peru have commanded much international attention, it is the pilgrimage-crazed nation of Japan that offers the most explicit linkage between spiritual journeys and divine revelation. In the "Land of the Rising Sun," pilgrimages are of two kinds: pilgrimages to lowland shrines (such as Izumo, Ise and Shikoku Island) and those to sacred summits (like Mounts Omine, Fuji and Haguro). Both of these are the popular pursuits of pilgrimage clubs known as *kosha* or *ko*. Membership in these traveling bands has declined since the 1800s, when they were estimated to involve eighty percent of the population; but their overall numbers remain high.

Of the two kinds of spiritual journeys, mountain pilgrimages are more serious. This is because Japanese peaks, like many high places around the world, are deemed the habitation of the gods. Here it is possible not only to summon deities but to cause them to speak—a prime objective of the various ko.

And of the divine habitats, none is more revered than Mount Ontake. Sometimes called the Great Original *(Hon Moto)*, this ten-thousand-foot volcano in the Hida-Shinshiu range has long been viewed as Japan's premier gateway to the divine. The Ontake ko, unique among pilgrimage clubs, are known as divine possession societies. As nineteenth-century astronomer Percival Lowell once observed: "Ontake is the mountain of trance. To its summit pilgrims ascend, not simply to adore, but to be there actually incarnate of the gods."[30]

In early August 1992, I made my own visit to Mount Ontake. The purpose of this expedition, which included Dr. Mamoru Ogata and my son Brook, was to assess the current strength of the Ontake cult. (According to some, the phenomena had been waning in the face of public secularization and alternative religions.)

Catching an early morning bus out of the tiny village of Kiso Fukushima, we chugged up a series of steep switchbacks to the modest lodge that serves as a staging area for the final ascent.[31] As we gazed up at the peak through the filtered light of early morning, we gained our first insight into the current state of Ontake's continuing popularity. What we saw was both remarkable and sobering. Although it was not yet five A.M., literally thousands of white-clad pilgrims were already ascending and descending the mountain's sacred flanks. Drawing nearer to these undulating ribbons of humanity, we asked several ko members why they had come. Although they hailed from distant cities and varied walks of life, their answers were remarkably similar. Most informed us that the gods had ordained their pilgrimages, often prescribing the precise date of departure. One solemn pilgrim, summing up the prevailing sentiment, declared, "I wouldn't dream of making any important decision in my life without first consulting the divinities of Ontake."

Irresistible Forces: The Black Hole of Cultural Tradition

Half a world away from Japan's sacred heights, the hills of Galilee attract their own stream of spiritual supplicants. These pilgrims, primarily Muslim and Druze, can be seen making their way to the tombs of long-deceased holy men. Each of these sites is widely believed to be infused with special power, or *baraka*. "Whether it's true or not doesn't matter," observes one historian. "Once a tradition is believed, it becomes real."[32]

The web of belief spun by Haiti's Voudon society generates a similar illusion of total comprehension. "No matter how an outsider might view it," Wade Davis explains in *The Serpent and the Rainbow,* "for the individual member of that society the illusion holds, not because of coercive force, but simply because for him there is no other way."[33]

The point of these examples is that reality is dictated by belief. Myths govern history and are, at the same time, responsible for justifying it. Once a people group has given in to vain imaginations, demonic powers, operating like the Wizard of Oz, are quick to animate resulting mythologies. So long as these powers continue to absorb allegiance from their credulous subjects, the lie will remain enchanted.

Unfortunately, hundreds of thousands of children are born every day into these enchanted systems. From the very moment their tiny bodies grace the cradle, the lie surrounds them. The first tugs are gentle: the gift of a tiny amulet, a whispered myth, the beat of a ceremonial drum. Soon, however, the intensity increases. Along with daily prayers and annual festivals, there is suddenly talk of initiations. Beyond this stage, barring divine intervention, their spiritual prospects are bleak—for, as history shows, children who embrace the lie into adulthood generally carry it as the truth.

The gravitational forces associated with tradition, like the vortices of celestial black holes, often appear irresistible. Sociologists attempting to explain this phenomenon point to the strong linkage between tradition and identity. Like it or not, we are all part of a tribal continuum, and this continuum largely dictates what we think about ourselves and our world. Because this imagery includes events and perceptions that exceed the borders of our own life spans, and because we all need a positive sense of self-worth, reality and myth are inevitably intertwined.[34] In the course of this subconscious revisionism, notorious regimes are routinely airbrushed into a glorious heritage. No other explanation fits Saddam Hussein's obsession with ancient Babylon, or the fascination many modern Mongolians have with Genghis Khan. As Bern Williams once observed: "The average man will bristle if you say his father was dishonest, but he will brag a little if he discovers that his great-grandfather was a pirate."[35]

Initiation: Gateway to an Alternate World

Most children have their first encounter with the intense gravitational suction of tradition during puberty rites and initiations. In primordial societies these rituals took place in deep limestone caves (refer to chapter 4). Here, according to paleontologist John Pfeiffer, the youngsters' deliberately sensitized psyches were reframed by carefully orchestrated sequences of sights and sounds. The novices, confronting the alternative realities of their elders, were reborn from the subterranean womb into a newly enlivened world.

Initiatory rites, given their capacity to forge relational identities and imprint memories (an important engine of tradition), represent a particularly potent means of instilling the tribal encyclopedia into the minds of succeeding generations. Recognizing this, the enemy has worked tirelessly to promote their observance in a wide range of cultural settings.

Every society has its own unique recipe for conducting effective initiations, with at least two ingredients in common: physical separation and retreat, and symbolic death and rebirth. The former is designed to introduce the neophyte to the world of the gods and ancestors, typically manifest in the bush or wilderness. The latter is intended to highlight the means of entering this world. Novices among Australia's aboriginal Karadjeri are carried off into the forest at night.[36] As family and clan members mourn their "deaths," the boys hear the sacred songs for the first time. Stripped of their clothes, they are seated near a fire where they are required to drink a large quantity of human blood. At the end of their ordeals, which continue over several years, they are considered newborn—a status that places them "in the know" about the spirit world, human origins and the meaning of rituals.[37]

A similar process, although shorter, is found among some of Africa's Bantu peoples. In a ceremony known as "being born anew," male initiates are ritually enfolded into the skin and stomach membrane of sacrificed rams. When they are unwrapped from this simulated womb three days later, the boys proceed to climb into bed beside their mothers and cry like newborn infants.[38]

In his remarkable book *Of Water and Spirit,* Malidoma Patrice Somé describes in unprecedented detail the role that supernaturally charged initiations play in preserving the ancestral past.

Somé, a Dagara[39] shaman with doctoral degrees from the Sorbonne and Brandeis University, was given up by his parents at age four to be trained in a rigid French Jesuit seminary. After fifteen troubled years at the institution, he returned to his village of Dano in the mid-1970s. According to traditional Dagara belief, a person who stays away from his home for a long time leaves a large portion of his soul abroad when he returns.[40] So the Dano elders, in an effort to "cure" Malidoma, asked him to submit to Baor, a grueling, six-week initiation generally reserved for pubescent boys.

The ordeal would not be easy because Malidoma knew things the spirits would rather he did not know. "There is a ghost in you," his father explained, "and this thing will be on the defensive each time you try to come alive. For you to live as one of us, that one is going to have to die." With that, Malidoma and 63 other young initiates from five villages were sent into the belly of the bush.

On the first night of Baor, one of the instructors lit a bonfire from a bundle of dry millet stems and burning grass. Instantly, as if compelled by an invisible force, the boys began to sing to the dancing fire. Then one of the elders, after circling the fire pit three times, pulled something out of his pouch—a pouch that seemed strangely alive. Bringing the thing to his mouth, he uttered something in primal language.[41] Suddenly the fire became a violet ghost rising nearly eighteen feet in the air. The elder, standing before his awestruck charges, explained that fire is a link to the spiritual dimension. "When we know without being told that we must perform a certain sacrifice or ritual," he said, "we know because the fire tells us this."

That night Malidoma glimpsed a pair of eyes staring at him out of the darkness. The two luminous oval lenses had a magnetic effect. Initially seductive and cajoling, they were also capable of generating panic. How long this staring match continued, Malidoma could not say. But one thing was clear: Whatever ideas he had cherished about the world were going to change.[42]

The reality shift took another sharp turn during the fire ceremony the following evening.

"As the elder spoke," Malidoma recalls, "the fire grew bigger and . . . hotter; yet suddenly a wave of cold enveloped all of us. First, I began shivering and [then] noticed that everyone around me was too. I wanted to try and figure out how something that was so hot could be so cold, but I had no time for analysis. The elder was now inside the fire, walking in circles and speaking. In his hand he held a hyena skull, all alight and burning with an unearthly fire."

As light streamed out of the luminescent skull, voices seemed to emanate from all around. They belonged to entities gathered "in a place that had no equivalent to anything I had seen before. The place where they stood seemed groundless. It appeared as a dark carpet surrounded by a multiplicity of stars."[43]

Then the elder spoke again: "Our ancestors used to say that unless you return to the other world, you will not know the difference between there and here." The next stage of the initiation experience, he explained, would involve traveling, soul *and* body, into this strange and awesome realm.

In preparation for the voyage, the other elders held up a buffalo skin dripping with a green, gelatinlike material. The substance reminded Malidoma of the "fermentation produced by algae in the middle of the rainy season." Watching the swamplike material ooze out of the round skin, he realized he was gazing on a light hole—the gateway that would transport him and his fellow initiates to an alternate world. Accessing this realm would require converting the body's cellular structure into a form of light energy.

As the boys lined up to jump one by one into the light hole, the elder offered a final instruction: "Once in the hole, do not let yourself fall indefinitely. You will go too far and we will lose you. Instead, as soon as you are in, notice the countless lines of light. They have many colors. You can see them if you have your eyes open, but it takes an effort to open your eyes. No one can do that for you. The lines are there for you to use. Grab them and hold onto them. When you have grasped a wire of light, you will float. Do you understand me?"

"Meanwhile," recounts Malidoma, "the elders had begun chanting and swinging the skin back and forth. It appeared to me that the amount of green gelatin oozing out of it was increasing. The elders intensified their formula in primal language while the drum intoned a breathless rhythm. Around us an energy field of immense magnitude was developing. My first sensation was that of coolness that soon developed into an icy cold all around us. Our bodies reacted to the change of temperature by shivering violently. The green gelatin became violet and danced like burning methane."

The light hole, when it opened, was no more than three feet in diameter. After the first boy jumped in, they heard something that sounded like sustained thunder. Several anxious moments later, the elder ordered the light hole attendants to pull. Lifting the skin, they made a tossing motion with it, as if it contained something they wanted to pour out. At that moment a violet blob of light detached itself and sailed nearly thirty feet through the air. Landing noisily on the ground nearby, the human projectile feverishly brushed the remaining tongues of fire off his body.

The next initiate had trouble. After being regurgitated from the light hole with a roar, he screamed as if he were caught between two worlds, as if his molecular structure was still struggling to reconstitute itself. Lying motionless in a pool of greenish slippery fluid, he appeared unable to quench the part of his body that was still burning. Finally, after five more boys had entered and exited the light hole successfully, the young man fell silent. The pool of greenish fluid coagulated and formed a crust. Then, as Malidoma looked on in horror, he realized the boy himself had coagulated, becoming hard as a rock. His appearance was more like a grotesque statue than a human being.[44]

Soon it was Malidoma's turn to enter the light hole. As he approached the volcanic gate, its ominous roar produced an almost intolerable tension. The moment of reckoning was at hand. Ordered to run, he inhaled deeply and dove into the hissing orifice.

"At first my body felt extremely cold," he writes, "[almost] as if I had fallen into a freezer." Descending with furious speed, Malidoma exercised his last ounce of willpower to open his eyes. Slowly he began to see the light like a breaking dawn—an aurora borealis of color and majesty. He grabbed hold of a wire, as he had been instructed, and his plunge came to an abrupt and silent stop.[45]

In this fairyland of light, Malidoma was particularly drawn to a "living mountain crowned with gold and luminescent sapphires and all kinds of precious metals." So compelling was its attraction that the only way Malidoma could avoid succumbing was to take his eyes from it. In addition to the visual enticement, the mountain produced music so enchanting that it made him want to weep.

As he drew closer, a living figure suddenly appeared out of its side. "His eyes were especially disconcerting," Malidoma remembers, "like fiery globes that protruded unaesthetically out of their sockets. As I looked at them, I felt an immense magnetic force overwhelm me and pull me toward the mountain."

Instead of slamming against it, however, Malidoma suddenly found himself swatting out small violet flames that were still alight on his trembling body. His interdimensional journey had come to an abrupt halt on the earthward side of the thundering gate.

When the initiates returned to the village six weeks later, Malidoma's father was waiting for him, holding out the young man's first traditional suit. "This suit," he said proudly, "will be a tribute to the continuity of our ways. . . ."[46]

That night the initiates gathered in the village circle to sing the song of return:

> I had a date in the bush
> With all the gods,
> So I went.
> I went and knocked at doors
> Locked in front of me.
> I craved to enter.
> Oh, little did I know
> The doors did not lead outside.
> It was all in me.
> I was the room and the door.
> It was all in me.
> I just had to remember. . . .

Lineages and Ancestors: Spiritual Tethers to the Past

The succession of generations represents the moving biological ground over which the past is transferred into the present. To ensure that his interests are preserved along this continuum, the enemy cultivates elaborate deceptions involving lineages and ancestors. Using these powerful elements of tradition, he is able to recycle ancient enchantments. As we noted in chapter 7, this is what happened to Margaret Umlazi, the South African schoolgirl who dreamed that her grandfather, in the form of a serpent, was pulling her back into the pool of cultural tradition.

The Quiché area of Guatemala's Mayan highlands blends ancestor worship and reincarnation. This is manifest in the practice of presenting pregnant women before "lineage shrines" so that shamans can "sow" or "plant" the soul of the new family member into her womb from the pool of ancestral souls. Because these shrines, or "sleeping houses," are gathering points for the spirits of deceased shaman-priests, they are considered particularly auspicious sites for these ritual plantings.[47]

Another manifestation of dynastic darkness is found among the neighboring Aguacatec Maya and the distant Hausa of rural Niger. Both of these peoples believe that certain kinds of spirits are inheritable, and that annual sacrifices must be offered to appease the same spirits their fathers appeased before them. Wycliffe scholar Harry McArthur, elaborating on the practice of the Aguacatec, notes that religious duties received from one's parents must be performed without deviation:

> If one's father had a certain responsibility to a household or family god to perform certain rites at certain times, then the son must assume the responsibility; if he fails in the slightest way he may lose his *banl* (good fortune).[48]

In many areas of the world, the carrot-and-stick approach is a common feature of the relationship between "ancestors" and the living. On the island of Madagascar, for example, ancestors who want to speak do so through wise men known as *ombiasa*. From time to time these ancestral mediums instruct the living to host a *famadihana,* or "bone-turning celebration," in which the ancestors' remains are taken out of their tombs and reinterred in stiffly woven cloth. Compliance with this request is rewarded with health and prosperity, while indifference may bring on misfortune or even death.[49] In Hindu Nepal, families are expected to feed lineage gods and two kinds of ancestral ghosts. The diet of these otherworldly beings is unusual—bananas, rice and lighted wicks—but those who provide regular meals are promised freedom from harm and special fortune-telling powers.[50]

Another way the devil makes it difficult for people to break with the past is by linking it with "social time"—history experienced by the group. In parts of Africa, collective history is believed to amass power, which is often symbolized by a sacred object held by the king or clan leader. The Soninke people, for instance, fashion chains, the individual links of which represent members of an ancestral dynasty going back to Sunni the Great. When the tribal patriarch is ready to die, he disgorges the chain from his mouth while his successor swallows it from the other end.[51]

This bizarre act, besides symbolizing continuity, is a reminder that the most important spiritual traditions are transferred orally. This, as any elder or guru will tell you, is because traditions are empowered less by their content than by the manner in which they are delivered—and few forms of communication are more intimate (or potent) than speech.[52]

In the Tibetan Buddhist world, initiatory secrets associated with the worship of particular deities are passed from teacher to student *nyin guyd,* or ear to ear. These initiations, accumulated over a lifetime from a multitude of teachers, are recorded in a special "book of acquisitions," or "book of what was heard."[53] (Since the efficacy of Tibetan rituals depends on their direct linkage to proven masters, each entry must include the lineage of the master who bestowed it.)[54]

One disturbing account of oral transmission was recorded in the 1930s by ethnographer Eric Thompson. The report, detailing shamanic initiation among the Q'eqchi Maya of Belize, includes a remarkable description of the climactic encounter between novices and the vision serpent called Och-Kan. During this encounter, Thompson explained, "the initiate and the [serpent] meet face to face." When this occurs, "the latter rears up on his tail and, approaching the initiate till their faces are almost touching, puts his tongue in the initiate's mouth. In this manner, he communicates the final mysteries of sorcery."[55]

Adaptive Deceptions: The Blender of Syncretism

The third approach to maintaining territorial dynasties employs what we might call "adaptive deceptions." These deceptions, which can be defined either as necessary course corrections or as upgrades to the devil's product line, are introduced into situations in which traditional structures are in danger of losing their deceptive potency.

The enemy, pragmatic to the core, does not care how people are deceived, only that they are. If this means he must occasionally adapt his message to changing times and circumstances, he is perfectly willing to do so. By maintaining flexibility, he can exploit our human propensity to try new things—a tactic that, in turn, allows him to transform ancient deceptions into modern attractions.

Adaptive deceptions do not replace preexisting ideological bondages; they build on them. In this sense they resemble the exorcised demon who returns with seven other spirits more wicked than himself (see Matthew 12:43–45). The aim is not simply to advance spiritual darkness chronologically, but to thicken it. The common term for this blending of beliefs and practices is *syncretism*. Its emergence can often be traced to dissatisfaction with the ideological status quo (a prime motivator of New Age thinking) or to the subjugation of one society by another.[56]

Satan prizes syncretism not only for its ability to introduce deceptive agents into the cultural bloodstream, but for its capacity to absorb and disarm Gospel incursions. Rather than deny Christians access to the societies he controls, the enemy simply uses the blender of syncretism to dilute their message. The resulting product is often a culture in which Christian symbolism is cleverly commingled with indigenous history and alternative doctrines. While some scholars and theologians tout such cultures as examples of contextualized faith, in reality they are nothing less than idolatry with an acceptable face. The old ways and gods, as any informed observer will tell you, are still very much alive.

Syncretism is energized by two powerful arguments: tolerance and tradition. In the first instance the devil reasons, with feigned fair-mindedness, that any belief may be added to the cultural mix so long as it does not exclude other objects of affection. And at first glance this appears to be an expansive argument, affording Christianity a place in the community worldview. But the enemy is well aware that genuine relationship with the Almighty is possible only in the absence of rival gods. If he can keep at least one other deity on the public agenda, relational faith and power will wither into an anemic form of godliness.

Finding an alternative deity is easy, thanks to the pervasive influence of tradition. Even when a people tire of a particular god or practice, they are generally reluctant to sever all links with the past. Motivated by guilt, fear or even plain habit, they prefer to maintain their old spiritual mistresses (sometimes quite lavishly) at the same time that they are courting new flames.

Some researchers, observing this dynamic at work in early Greece, are convinced that Hellenistic Christianity was advanced not through repentance but by adapting the religion to the prevailing pagan culture. Rather than renounce their ubiquitous gods, many Greeks simply replaced them with the saints.[57] (In this regard their behavior was similar to that of medieval Christians in southern France who erected their churches on ancient pagan ritual sites and maintained decorated idols in their crypts.)[58]

The accommodation of paganism has also left its mark on the British Isles. On the last Sunday of July, for example, thousands of pilgrims make the arduous climb up Croagh Patrick, a 2,500-foot mountain that rises above Ireland's Clew Bay. Although a majority of the pilgrims claim to be Christians, their reverence for the site is rooted in Celtic rituals established centuries earlier by pagan Druid priests.[59] Few see any contradiction since the histories of the two faiths, Christianity and paganism, have been intertwined here from the beginning of the first millennium. As William Irwin Thompson wrote in 1976, "The Irish Church was no outpost of an imperial ecclesiastical Roman legion, but the continuation of archaic religious forms derived from pagan Ireland. . . ."[60]

In the Americas this deceptive continuity is seen in pilgrimages honoring the Virgin of Guadalupe, whose image is located on the very hill where the Aztecs once worshiped the goddess *Cihuacóatl*,[61] and in Mexico's darkly festive Day of the Dead. The latter, according to writer Homer Aridjis,

> is a tradition predating the 16th century Spanish conquest, when the Aztecs honored their ancestors with feasting and their gods with human sacrifices. The sacrifices stopped after the Spaniards arrived, but the feast days were moved to coincide with Christian observances.[62]

Peru's well-attended Qoyllur Rit'i (Star Snow) festival has evolved along similar lines. Whereas in earlier times human blood was offered routinely to deified peaks and stars, modern participants have replaced these oblations with a fetishism that calls on the miraculous powers of Jesus Christ to assure material success. Some insist that the Catholic elements of the festival are "merely ornaments pasted on an indigenous religion that hasn't appreciably changed since the conquest," but eight-time pilgrim Robert Randall believes they play an important role. "In order to maintain their vital significance for a people," he explains, "rituals must change in accordance with [the] changes in a society."[63]

A good example can be observed in the religious history of Cuba's black community. For much of the past two centuries, Cubans of African descent were enmeshed in a Catholic folk culture rooted in ethnic clubs known as *cabildos* or *reglas*. When tribal drumbeats announced the great festivals of Epiphany, Carnival, Holy Week and Corpus Christi, members poured onto the streets of Havana wearing masks of Yoruba tribal gods and hoisting icons of Catholic patron saints. In time, however, a new tradition emerged: Santería, or "the Way of the Saints." Its adherents saw Catholic saints and African *orishas* simply as different manifestations of the same spirit.[64]

Despite the prominence of Christianity in syncretistic societies, many adaptive deceptions find their roots and symbolism elsewhere. Freemasonry, for example, derives from Egyptian mythology,[65] while Tibetan Buddhism may be an outgrowth of an ancient, demon-infested religion called Bön.[66] In the fifteenth century the Incas added sun worship to long-established rites honoring mountain deities. When solar temples were built at Cuzco, Pachacamac and the Island of the Sun at Lake Titicaca, the Incas were merely claiming pilgrimage sites that had been well-trodden for centuries.[67]

Within the Islamic world, adaptive deceptions have left their imprint on the annual hajj pilgrimage, the Shi'ite festival of Ashura and the daily routines of folk Islam. To appreciate how this could happen, it is important to remember that Islam, like the other great monotheistic religions, emerged in a profoundly pagan context. In early years the city of Mecca not only sanctioned worship of multiple gods and goddesses, but incorporated this idolatry into ceremonies associated with a great city feast.[68] Muhammad, rather than dispense with these potent symbols, incorporated them into his new religion, giving birth to (among other things) the hajj.[69] Similarly, when Shi'ite Muslims flagellate themselves on the Day of Ashura, ostensibly to identify with the sufferings of the martyr Hussein, they are emulating rituals perfected centuries earlier by the priests of the Cappadocian goddess Ma.[70] Known as *fanatici,* these ecstatic worshipers would often gash themselves with a variety of sharp weapons in order to arouse a warlike spirit and become invincible.

If the rites of traditional Islam are seen as instruments of reinforcement, the practices of folk Islam are often rooted in crisis. In the face of visceral concerns like hunger, barrenness or war, a majority of Muslims[71] resort to remedies that combine elements of Islamic orthodoxy and animist mysticism. Whereas mornings may be devoted to performance of the *sujud* (formal prayers) and listening to Qur'anic readings in the mosque, the afternoon is a time for calling upon amulet-makers, folk apothecaries and the spirits of deceased saints.[72] By maintaining these dual channels to the spirit world, folk Muslims aim to expand their options. What they often get is a life constricted by the double cords of legalism and superstition.[73]

Another set of adaptive deceptions is at work in Japan's New Religions.[74] Unlike folk Islam, which weaves religious orthodoxy around animistic beliefs and practices, these burgeoning cults offer a creative synthesis of Buddhist ritual and materialistic ideology. With this brilliant, if eclectic, architecture, the enemy has managed to sustain his presence in a country that values both tradition and the entrepreneurial spirit.

In terms of numbers of adherents, these new religions are hugely successful. Soka Gakkai boasts over sixteen million members, while the Rissho Koseikai sect numbers six million. A third group, Kofuku-no-Kagaku (or "Science of Happiness"), skyrocketed from 25,000 members in 1991 to more than nine million in 1995. This rapid growth is explainable in part by the ability of the sect to address social needs, and in part by urbanization trends that have loosened the hold of the rural-based traditional religions, Buddhism and Shintoism.[75] In the words of 35-year-old investment counselor Yuko Higuchi: "Buddhism and Shintoism are spiritually exhausted. Buddhist temples are for sightseeing. They have no commitment to the modern world, and their teachings are outdated."[76]

To upgrade their aging arsenal of deception, demonic powers in Japan have turned to the New Religions. Young people put off by musty temples and ascetic ordeals are drawn in by seductive self-help sermons, often delivered in the style of Western television evangelists, while stressed-out urban businessmen are welcomed into high-tech meditation rooms. If the enemy can no longer encourage his charges to forsake worldly attachments through the Buddhist doctrine of emptiness, he is content to entangle them in the corporate ladder.

Another aspect of adaptive deceptions is seen in the current stir over UFOs and alien abductions. As David Fetcho, former editor of the *SCP Journal,* noted back in 1977: "Each succeeding age changes the context in which fallen speculations operate, but the essential pattern of these speculations remains the same." Whereas former worldviews were colored by magic and conjured "spiritual realms replete with gods and goddesses," modern expectations, at least in the West, are more likely to be the product of what Fetcho calls "speculative materialism." Having been fed a steady diet of science fiction *(Star Trek, Close Encounters, Alien Nation, Star Gate, E.T., Independence Day* and *The X-Files)* and quasi-scientific television *(Sightings, Mysterious Universe, Terra X, Encounters, The Extraordinary),* we are now prepared to welcome an entirely different set of cosmic visitors.

These expectations, Fetcho believes, "determine both the *form* of transcendent encounters and the *content* of whatever message is received from 'beyond.'" By modifying human expectations and then conforming himself to them, Satan can perpetuate his deceptive control over hundreds of generations and a myriad of cultures. It is this principle, according to Fetcho, that conditions the experiences of the Hindu polytheist visited by Saraswati, the Sioux medicine man in his vision of the White Buffalo Calf Woman, and the modern UFO contactee. The basic pattern of fallen human speculation, working within culturally defined boundaries, has in each case "set men up to receive the message in just the form it has come."[77]

History's Open Doors: Unresolved Social Injustices

Now that we have examined how the enemy uses religious festivals, cultural tradition and adaptive deceptions to maintain dynasties of spiritual darkness, it remains for us to consider the role of unresolved social injustices. No longer the hidden factor it once was, thanks to voices like John Dawson's, the issue has lately been shown to be a powerful catalyst for both revival (through reconciliation) and spiritual bondage.

The latter is most likely to emerge in situations in which moral injuries have been left untreated by repentance and restitution. In such an unhealthy environment, bitterness moves like a raging virus, invading the inner sanctuaries of human identity and reason. If unchecked, it will go on to shrivel the souls of individuals, communities and even entire generations.

A vivid illustration of this process is found in the unremitting sectarian strife of Northern Ireland. "The Troubles," as the locals call their bloody conflict, began in the late eighteenth century when, burdened by rising rents and unbearable working conditions, secret Presbyterian bands began riding the nights to intimidate Catholic landlords and their agents. Within a decade the anti-Catholic vigilantes set their sights on burning their perceived oppressors out of Ulster. After emerging victorious from a showdown fight near Armagh Township in 1795, the Protestants named their organization after an earlier champion, William of Orange.[78]

Organized as pseudo-Masonic lodges replete with secret oaths and handshakes, today's Orange Societies (or Orders) come into public view during the so-called "marching season." Tattooing massive Lambeg drums, ancient Scottish weapons of psychological warfare, marchers pass frenzied crowds en route to the sites of ancient battles and sieges. As bonfires blaze, revelers kick the Pope in effigy and belt out partisan songs with venomous gusto:

> A rope, a rope
> Tae hang the Pope!
> A pennyworth o' cheese
> Tae choke him!
> A pint o' lamp oil
> Tae wrench it down
> And a big hot give
> Tae roast him!

As one pilot preparing to land at Belfast Airport said over the intercom, "We are about to land in Ulster. Set your watches back three hundred years." Ulster's Orangemen, like their IRA counterparts, use the memory of past injustices—and bloody retributions—as a bellows to stoke their inner rage.[79] In the process, laments acclaimed author Leon Uris, the people of Northern Ireland have found themselves on "a dark, narrow path of spiritual slavery."[80]

Demonic exploitation of unresolved social injustices can also be seen in the Crusades. Widely perceived in the Middle East to have been a genocidal jihad against Muslim peoples, not to mention the beginning of European colonialism, these religious-political expeditions may be rivaled, in terms of harm done to the cause of Christ, only by the Holocaust and slavery.[81] As Islamic scholar George Braswell Jr., has observed:

> Muslims through the centuries have used the Crusades as illustrations of the worst that is within Christianity. In their schools, from the sermons in their mosques, and from their various writings, Muslims remember the Crusades as a Christian blight upon Islam.[82]

The one thing Crusaders were not particularly concerned about was evangelism. In the late thirteenth century, Franciscan martyr Raymond Lull declared: "I see many knights going to the Holy Land beyond the seas thinking they can acquire it by force of arms, but in the end all are destroyed before they attain that which they think to have." Lull believed that the only appropriate "conquest" of the Holy Land was one attempted "by love and prayers, and the pouring out of tears and [one's own] blood."[83] Decades earlier, an equally troubled Francis of Assisi urged that love rather than the crusading spirit be demonstrated toward Muslims.

Not all Christians have been so enlightened. Dante depicted a mutilated Muhammad languishing in the depths of hell, while Martin Luther castigated the Qur'an as a "foul and shameful book" and described Turks as devils following their devil god.[84] Not surprisingly, such attitudes, combined with shameful acts of violence and greed, have led many Muslims to brand Christians as hypocrites no longer worthy to be called "peoples of the Book." The Gospel, having been fouled by its messengers, is avoided in Islamic lands as the polluted effluence of "the Great Satan."

In reality, historical injustices represent open doors into the psychic habitats of affected communities and cultures. Unless these doors are slammed shut through repentance and reconciliation, they lead to infestation by demonic manipulators. The danger here is considerable. The singular goal of these pernicious spirits, once they have penetrated the societal mindset, is to enslave their "hosts"—an end they achieve typically by converting bitter memories into shackles of rejection and revenge.

Scripture hints that social injustice has a voice that resonates to the farthest reaches of the spiritual realm, and possibly through our more familiar space-time dimensions as well. Addressing the murderous Cain, God says: "What have you done? Listen! Your brother's blood cries out to me from the ground" (Genesis 4:10). Several chapters later, the Lord declares to His servant Abraham: "The outcry against Sodom and Gomorrah is so great and their sin so grievous that I will go down and see if what they have done is as bad as the outcry that has reached me" (Genesis 18:20–21).[85]

Note that the outcries in these examples emanate not from godly intercessors but from victims of violence and social debauchery (see Genesis 19:4–9). Abel's case takes us even further, suggesting that the voice is not that of a living petitioner, but of his spilled lifeblood. When this observation is coupled with the lament of Revelation 6:9–11, we are led to the conclusion that violence and injustice continue to speak long after their victims are dead.

Such musings may also cast light on the growing mystery of hauntings. In nearly all credible cases in which occult activity can be ruled out as an explanation, the conspicuous common denominator is violent death.[86] One theory posits that the lingering memories of human and divine pain at such sites attract demons, in much the same way that blood in the water draws sharks. Whether the lingering residue of life is measurable in the material dimension (a possibility suggested by the hypothesis of morphic resonance)[87] remains to be seen.

Topsoil and Bedrock

Demonic manipulations, problematic enough in themselves, are often made worse by the human tendency to classify people and situations according to their immediate appearance. No matter how hard we try to avoid these quick, superficial appraisals, the practice is habit-forming. Most of us, whether we admit it or not, do judge a book by its cover.

Unfortunately, these facile tendencies have been put on prominent display recently by certain zealots within the spiritual warfare movement. In their haste to identify and assault territorial strongholds, these well-meaning but ill-informed prayer activists have embraced conclusions that, in another field of life, even they would consider wild speculation. The consequences of this parade of folly—which include dampening the enthusiasm of potential intercessors, squandering valuable supplies of time and money and granting the enemy additional cover for his work—have been severe.

More disciplined prayer warriors have made an ally out of patience. By taking time to educate themselves about areas of concern, then waiting on the Holy Spirit for understanding, they have learned to make accurate distinctions between *prevailing bondages* and *root bondages.*

This distinction is not always easy to make. Prevailing bondages, while visible and active, can be thin and transitory. Like agricultural topsoil, they tend to ride the fickle winds of change—a characteristic that makes them unreliable indicators of the true nature of a stronghold. While these bondages cannot be ignored, neither should they be mistaken for the spiritual bedrock that must be broken up if territorial strongholds are to succumb to the Gospel. Only by plowing beneath the surface of a given society are we able to confront the root bondages that control it.

In a recently published essay, Elinor Gadon draws attention to what she calls "the inherent power" of many sacred sites in India. Associating the influence of this primal (or root) power with a long continuity of associated religious practice, Gadon notes that archeological evidence recovered from these sites "often reveals *multiple layers* of ritual use" (emphasis added). At Sankisa, a site near the Nepalese border, two millennia of prevailing bondages are documented in sequential layers that include a third-century B.C. Buddhist monument, a Hindu temple, an Islamic mosque, the tomb of an Islamic saint, and a second Hindu temple.[88]

Vasudeva Agrawala, an expert in ancient Indian folk cults, writes: "In the religious tradition of our country we find that older gods and goddesses . . . are sometimes put into [the] background by new ones." At the same time, states Agrawala, "It is with difficulty that two things ever disappear: firstly, the spot of the shrine of a godling or deity, and secondly, the fair or public festival held to honor it."[89]

Another example of how spiritual topsoil is easily mistaken for bedrock is found in Albania, a nation whose repressive, anti-religious policies were once interpreted as sure evidence of a controlling stronghold of Communism. At the time, many of us overlooked the fact that Communism was an imposed experiment with little popular appeal. With less than five decades of influence,[90] it represented at best a thin veneer on a history dating back thousands of years to biblical Illyria. Virtually ignored were the far more important contributions of Rome, Byzantium and the Ottoman Turks; and Christians distracted by the regime's public espousal of atheism saw little reason to worry about animist symbolism, Islamic allegiances or the bitter blood feuds that had dominated Albanian history prior to the twentieth century. When the ancient vendetta system reemerged after the downfall of Communism in the early 1990s, Roman Catholic priest Injac Dema lamented that he could not stop "this primitive force." Few intercessors heard him; they were too busy celebrating the demise of Albania's "true" spiritual stronghold.[91]

Similar mistakes are being made with regard to China, the Andean countries and the Near East, to cite but a few examples. By fixating on Johnny-come-lately bondages like Communism, drug cartels and Islamic fundamentalism, spiritual warriors are missing deeper, more profound connections:

- In Communist China, party officials admit openly that trust in ancient local gods "far outweighs any allegiance to the ideology of Mao, Marx, and Lenin."[92]
- In South America, researchers have revealed recently that many so-called drug hits are actually religiously motivated human sacrifices linked to mountain and serpent cults. The sorcerers who perform these acts are seen as preserving "an ancient legacy."[93]

- In Iraq, Saddam Hussein has linked his nation's spiritual roots and destiny publicly to Nebuchadnezzar's Babylon.[94]

Appearances, as these examples remind us, can be deceiving. Those who attempt to interpret the world solely through the lens of geopolitics, sociology or spiritual imagination tread on risky and often unrewarding ground.

Even hardened journalists sense there is more to the story than meets the eye. After touring the ancient Khmer temples at Angkor Wat, one Asian reporter could not help wondering what had "turned a once great civilization into the poverty-ridden, war-torn country that Cambodia is today."[95] Lawrence Harrison, writing about Haiti in *The Atlantic Monthly,* felt compelled to ask, "Why has this benighted country experienced since independence a virtually unbroken chain of brutal and corrupt leaders?" And, "Why is the country that was once the richest in the Caribbean now the poorest?"[96]

And so it goes. If the questions seem endless—and hopelessly complex—this, too, is an illusion. In reality they are adaptations of a single inquiry: Why does spiritual darkness linger where it does? Although our labyrinthine journey so far has not allowed us to uncover the root bondages of every local stronghold, it has given us the principled understanding we need to conduct these investigations successfully. What we do with what we know is the subject of the remaining three chapters.

PART TWO
OVER THE UNDERWORLD

Defeating the Powers of Darkness

Chapter Nine

Rising Stakes

As human beings most of us want to know where we are at any given time. If we have not yet reached our destination, we need to be assured that we are on the right path. Our ancestors gained this confidence by consulting natural reference points like mountains and stars. We are more likely, however, to rely on the ubiquitous "You-are-here" displays that adorn large airports, shopping malls and theme parks.

There is also a temporal aspect to our innate need to fix our bearings. As creatures of destiny, we long to know our position in time as well as in space. The difficulty in charting the fourth dimension is that hard reference points are visible in only one direction: the past. These historical markers, useful in measuring how far we have come, are inadequate for determining how far we have yet to go. The sole solution is to identify a finish line, and the only way to do that is to journey into the future.

Despite our obvious limitations in this respect, most of us cannot help but wonder where we fit on the continuum of human and Church history. The fact that world affairs have suddenly become kaleidoscopic, fracturing and changing at every turn of the earth's axis, only adds to our curiosity. Are the days in which we live a passing phase, or have we finally reached the threshold of the "end times"?

It can be argued that every generation of believers has expected to witness the climax of history, but until now there has been a lack of objective evidence to support such expectations. In defining what has changed, contemporary Christians point to three developments:

1. A quantum leap in human knowledge that is unbridled by wisdom
2. A rising tide of spiritual interest and supernatural activity
3. The onset of "critical mass" in global evangelization

While much can be said about each of these important developments, the prospect of completing the Great Commission is undoubtedly the most compelling. Powerful new technologies have not only allowed Christian evangelists to track our progress against Matthew 24:14, something no other generation of believers has been able to do; they have opened the door for long-reach mass evangelism.[1]

Employing these tools, and backed by a growing army of committed prayer warriors, contemporary missions has begun to realize an unprecedented level of success. In the mid-1990s, Justin Long of the Global Evangelization Movement estimated that 114 people were coming to Christ every minute—an evangelistic torrent that translates into a net gain of 44,000 new churches a year! During this same period, the Lausanne Statistics Task Force reported that, for the first time in history, the ratio of nonbelievers to biblical Christians had fallen to less than seven to one (compared to 220 to one in A.D. 100).[2]

The Challenge of the Latter Rounds

In the midst of all this good news, however, comes what radio commentator Paul Harvey would call "the rest of the story."

In most escalating ventures (business negotiations, political campaigns, athletic tournaments), the stakes tend to rise in proportion to our position. The closer we are to the end of the process, the higher the stakes. And since no stakes are higher than those associated with completing the Great Commission—an accomplishment Jesus prophesied would usher in the end of the age—today's Christian warriors can expect to face challenges on the spiritual battlefield that are unique in both type and magnitude. It is the challenge of the latter rounds, and desperate times, as they say, call for desperate measures.

Accordingly, while the remaining task of world evangelization is getting smaller, insofar as the number of unreached people groups is concerned, it is also becoming more difficult. In strategic areas like the 10/40 Window, intercessors and evangelists are finding themselves locked in the fight of their lives. Standing eyeball to eyeball with some of the most formidable spiritual forces on earth, these heroic ministers are reporting two substantial challenges to the continued expansion of God's Kingdom: *demonic entrenchment,* an obstacle resulting from an excess of time, and *demonic desperation,* an obstacle linked to a lack of time.

Demonic entrenchment is hardly unique; the Hebrews encountered it in Egypt and Babylon, and the apostle Paul found it in Ephesus. But now we are centuries deeper into history. There are places on earth, notably in Asia, where demonic pacts have been serviced continually since the great Dispersion. In these ancient strongholds, spiritual light is extinguished routinely by powers wielding the four candle-snuffers we examined in the previous chapter.

Consider, too, the proposition that darkness now has a wider human base. As *Time* essayist Lance Morrow noted in June 1991, "If evil is a constant presence in the human soul, it is also true that there are more souls now than ever." Using this logic, Morrow reasoned that evil is rising on a Malthusian curve—or at least at the same rate as the population, 1.7 percent per annum.[3]

Demonic desperation, as we noted, is a problem associated with the lateness of the hour. In the book of Revelation, God warns the inhabitants of the earth that "the devil has come down to you, having great wrath, because he knows that he has a short time" (Revelation 12:12, NKJV). As much as these days distress us, they are even more disturbing for the powers of darkness. Confronted with growing incursions into their prayer-eroded strongholds, Satan's hordes are beginning to taste the same salty panic they have long induced in human beings.

Facing the prospect of eternal ruin, the prince of this world has infected his domain with what Michael Green calls "an increasing tempo of chaos."[4] Under the shadow of Satan's presence, earthly kingdoms have begun to shake like a terminal patient casting off the final vestiges of life, thereby validating Jesus' two-thousand-year-old prophecy that "the love of most will grow cold" (Matthew 24:12). The enemy, determined to fill every seat in his hell-bound bus, has ordered a dramatic escalation of counterfeit signs and wonders. To protect against those who would probe or escape his lair,[5] he has initiated a series of violent counterattacks.

These counterattacks are generally aimed at two kinds of targets: territories that have recently experienced a unique move of God, and individuals instrumental in conveying the Gospel to unreached peoples. Territorial counterattacks are usually accompanied by political persecution,[6] while assaults on individuals include everything from relational breakdowns to physical illness and injury.

Territorial Counterattacks

Noteworthy territorial counterattacks have taken place recently in countries like Saudi Arabia, China, Algeria, Pakistan, Egypt, Iraqi Kurdistan, Vietnam, Mongolia and the Sudan. While space does not permit me to review all of these cases, the following examples illustrate the severity of the problem.

Saudi Arabia

Most people are familiar with the military juggernaut that rolled through the Middle East in the aftermath of Saddam Hussein's invasion of Kuwait. But a second, more consequential desert storm was blowing across the Arabian Peninsula about the same time. Stirred up by the prayers of passionate intercessors and quickened by the redemptive breath of God, this divine tempest precipitated what may have been the most significant ingathering of souls the Islamic heartland has seen in modern times.[7]

The breach of an elite stronghold yielded stern demonic countermeasures. Raids were orchestrated through the Saudi religious police, or Muttawa, on several of the home fellowships that had proliferated throughout the kingdom. Amnesty International and other human rights groups documented more than 350 arrests of Christians in the first four years after the war. (In May 1992 the New York–based Middle East Watch blasted new judicial reforms as even more inflexible than those they replaced.)

While the death sentence of one church leader, Filipino pastor Oswaldo Magdangal, was commuted at the last minute to deportation, at least one presumed national believer has been beheaded.[8]

China

The Church in China has also found herself subject to severe persecution following a season of unprecedented harvest, particularly in Sichuan, Henan and the coastal provinces. A 1996 campaign to force Christian house churches to register with the government was described by one knowledgeable mission executive[9] as the "biggest crackdown against Christians since 1979."

In a special news report for *Christianity Today*, Kim Lawton revealed that the city of Shanghai and the provinces of Anhui and Xinjiang bore the brunt of the campaign, "with hundreds of unregistered churches being raided, and dozens of Christians being arrested, detained, and fined."[10] Authorities in Zhejiang province have destroyed fifteen thousand churches and religious sites, with much of the destruction coming in response to a June 1996 Ministry of Public Security document urging a renewed struggle against religion, particularly Christianity.[11] Other distressing accounts have cited the expulsion of foreign evangelists and the fatal beatings of several national believers.

Algeria

Another territorial counterattack has rocked the North African nation of Algeria, this one in reaction to a dramatic move of God that swept through the country in the 1980s. During that extraordinary season, hundreds and perhaps thousands of Arabs and Kabyle Berbers came to Christ, their lives touched by a wave of divine healings and dreams.

The enemy, undoubtedly stung by these losses, stirred up the fundamentalist Armed Islamic Group (GIA) to carry out a "policy of liquidation" against resident Jews and Christians. In the process of this "religious cleansing," disguised gunmen murdered four priests of the Catholic White Fathers order, shot two nuns in the head as they walked home from vespers, and slit the throats of seven Trappist monks. Although most missionary personnel have now left the country, nearly one hundred Christians, mostly French Catholics, have lost their lives. Another report from inside the country reveals that national believers are also receiving death threats and several house churches are "weak and struggling to survive."[12]

Iraqi Kurdistan

A final example of the enemy's campaign to regain control over spiritually contested territory is found in Iraqi Kurdistan. Having dominated this strategic area for several millennia, demonic forces were put on the defensive in the early 1990s when Christian relief workers began packing food, shelter and the Gospel north of the 36th parallel. According to Douglas Layton of Servant Group International, these benevolent efforts led to startling openings for witness and church-planting.

At an annual feast near Lalish, for example, the supreme prince of the Yezidi sect, an ancient community of devil worshipers, told Layton, "The thread between our people and Christianity is so thin, we wait only for someone to come and break it." Other Yezidi leaders, after attending a subsequent meeting in nearby Dohuk, not only applauded the Gospel but extended an open invitation for further ministry in their unreached community. In March 1996, the governor of Dohuk, Abdul-Aziz Tayeb, granted official church building rights in his governorship.

Nor surprisingly, the enemy has reacted against these and other developments with a full-scale counterattack. In addition to putting contracts out on Christian personnel (a tactic favored by local Iranians), he has endeavored to neutralize the influence of evangelical relief projects by promoting the construction of mosques (with Saudi money) in target neighborhoods. When the Iraqi military moved in to support the Kurdish Democratic Party in the summer of 1996, many Christian workers promptly fled the country, some petitioning the U.S. Department of State to help evacuate their converts as well.

Assaults on Individuals

In several areas of the world, notably China, the Middle East and the Himalayas, formal networks have been set up to gather intelligence on Christian workers and their plans.[13] This information is being used increasingly to fuel direct attacks against a variety of frontline ministries. Former Reagan administration official Michael Horowitz, noting this ominous trend, declared recently:

As a Jew, I find what is going on with the persecution of Christians throughout the rest of the world eerily parallel to what happened to the Jewish community in Europe during the late nineteenth century.[14]

The rising tide of persecution is an integral part of the enemy's strategy to protect his turf. But more is at work here than a possessive spirit. A careful analysis of the crime scenes also reveals a perpetrator driven by anger and desperation. The violence is not just strategic; it is personal. This explains why, in addition to the public rampages I have just mentioned, we hear increasing reports of demonic "micro-rages" against individual servants of the Lord. As I have tracked these devastating assaults over several years, it has become painfully obvious to me that the enemy reserves particular venom for Christians working with Scripture translation, media ministries (especially the *Jesus* film) and unreached peoples.

I have drawn the following excerpted accounts from my files.

Edmund Fabian

For twenty years, Wycliffe translator Edmund Fabian and his national co-worker had labored diligently to put the New Testament into the Nabak language of Papua New Guinea. In the spring of 1993, however, Edmund became concerned about his colleague, who had begun to hear voices and act strangely. His concern proved well-founded. On the afternoon of April 29, while they were translating 1 Corinthians 13, the helper grabbed a nearby ax and plunged it into the back of Edmund's head. Edmund died four hours later.

The helper, after turning himself into authorities, explained that his actions were prompted by inner voices that caused his mind to "go dark."

Himalayan Translators

During a recent visit to Kathmandu, I was told by a veteran missionary, "The spiritual warfare surrounding trans-Himalayan ministry, particularly efforts aimed at reaching Tibetan Buddhists, has been fierce."

Over a span of several years, a small army of Bible translators has been forced off the field by illness, discouragement or death. In the 1980s, a female translator from Australia was struck suddenly with epileptic seizures—symptoms that did not recur after she left the field. Another translator working on the Solukhumbu Sherpa language was replacing corrugated metal roofing in Kathmandu when a sudden gust of wind sent him crashing three stories to the ground. Transported by Medivac to Norway with a broken spine, he underwent a year of physical therapy before returning to Nepal in a wheelchair to resume his work. Less than six months later, in the early fall of 1988, he was diagnosed with terminal cancer and died quickly.

Other recent losses include a 42-year-old translator who succumbed to ovarian cancer and a talented Bhutanese helper who died of leukemia. A key Tibetan translator has lost two sons to drug-resistant tuberculosis, while other national workers have simply disappeared.[15]

Tibetan missionary Stephen Hishey told me in 1993: "We need to face the fact that Satan's power is very explicit. He declares that anyone who comes to disturb his territory will be stopped. We really have to stay on our knees."

Rodney Vaughn

This ordained Assembly of God minister decided to combine his love of teaching and evangelism by joining University Language Services, a Tulsa-based agency that places English teachers in China. From the outset, Rodney Vaughn proved a skilled classroom teacher. His students loved him, and hundreds came to know Christ as their Savior during his two years in the country. Alongside his wife, he spent extended periods in prayer for his young flock.

During his third term he was assigned to Siping, a modest-sized city located in the northeastern province of Liaoning. In the spring of 1989, one week after Easter, Rodney came down with flu-like symptoms. He felt miserable but there was no indication of serious illness. After several days, however, he took a dramatic turn for the worse with Ebola-like hemorrhaging. In 24 hours he was dead. No autopsy was performed, but the Chinese diagnosis was meningococcal septicemia. Rodney had encountered the wrong microorganism at the wrong time.

There is no proof of demonic agency but, in the words of mission director Hallett Hullinger, "Neither can we ignore [Rodney's] great effectiveness in evangelism, and the impact he clearly had on the forces of darkness in China."[16]

Native America

Serious illness, especially cancer, has also ravaged the ranks of believers ministering among Native Americans. While some of these cases are clearly linked to witchcraft activity, others appear to be the overflow of demonic hatred. The Navajo reservation has been particularly hard-hit, with a list of victims that includes Tom Dologhan, the former director of the Navajo Gospel Mission (brain cancer); Rudy Yazzie, a powerful, influential young Navajo pastor (colon cancer); and Genevieve Chiquito, a strategic intercessor from Lybrook (bone cancer).

Sheryl McLaughlin, a Northern Arapaho, drove out to Wyoming's Wind River Reservation recently to witness to family members. Arriving at the boundary of the reservation, she parked her car, opened her Bible and began to read aloud from Isaiah 43. As she did so, a gale force wind roiled up out of nowhere, tattering her Bible and disrupting her concentration. No sooner had this occurred than her nose started to bleed uncontrollably. Sensing a malevolent presence enveloping her, Sheryl started the car and headed back toward her home in Casper. During the return trip and throughout the following night, a trio of demonic apparitions proceeded to chastise her for what she had intended to do.

Pakistan/Afghanistan

In October 1989, God warned the mission community in a conservative Islamic city to prepare for an impending season of intense spiritual warfare. The storm hit several months later in the form of violent attacks by militant fundamentalists. On Eid, the last day of Ramadan in 1990, a frenzied mob attacked and demolished a Christian relief warehouse in a looting spree that lasted three days and inflicted $1.5 million in damage. The director of the agency and his six-year-old son miraculously survived an assassination attempt when their Jeep was riddled with bullets. Badly shaken by this experience, he bundled up his family and fled the country. On the very day of his departure, the deputy director of the organization was seized by a serious illness that led to a similar evacuation several weeks later.

As the spiritual assault on Christians continued, two other workers were kidnapped. One was imprisoned briefly in an isolated cave[17] while the other, a young Canadian with a pregnant wife, was brutally murdered. A third worker left the country after his wife's skull was fatally crushed by a freak rock fall at a popular hill station. (At the time of this "accident," he had been carrying on a successful correspondence ministry among Muslims.) Several Christian marriages were also caught in the crossfire. In one case, the wife of a highly respected team leader deserted him for a national associate. In another, a gifted intercessor suffered a nervous breakdown, left her husband and backslid into virtual prostitution.

Elusive Targets: Enhancing Battlefield Protection

While some Christians (including a few whose stories I have told) are content to explain these incidents as the natural, if unfortunate, consequences of gravity, politics and sociology, I find this attitude a form of denial. By minimizing the influence that spiritual powers have over human lives and habitats, these individuals hope to limit their vulnerability. If their view does not make them any safer, it at least makes them feel more modern.

The Scriptures, however, offer no such harbor. From Genesis to Revelation, we are reminded that activist Christian living is inextricably bound up with the spirit world—a world that consists not of abstract forces or laws but of powerful and interested personalities. And because we are the focus of their interest, few happenings in ministry can truly be called coincidence.

Demonic powers have never been shy about getting in the way of God's servants. Satan, who stood as accuser at the right hand of Joshua (see Zechariah 3:1), is also on record as having afflicted Job with painful sores (see Job 2:7), tampered with Daniel's intercessory mail (see Daniel 10:12–13) and tried repeatedly to distract Jesus from His mission (see Matthew 16:21–23; Luke 4:1–13). The apostle Paul lamented to the Thessalonians, "We wanted to come to you—certainly I, Paul, did, again and again—but Satan stopped [hindered] us" (1 Thessalonians 2:18).

Despite these examples, many Christians today hold the view that the enemy is best ignored. I can still remember the indignity of one Pentecostal man who approached me after I had concluded a teaching on spiritual warfare. Calling my accounts of demonic assaults on Christian workers "lurid," he asserted that Satan can only be empowered by such attention. The best approach to dealing with the enemy, he insisted, is to dismiss him.

But the apostle Peter seems to commend a different approach. "Be self-controlled and alert," he urges. "Your enemy the devil prowls around like a roaring lion looking for someone to devour. *Resist him...*" (1 Peter 5:8–9, emphasis added). James offers similar advice. After instructing believers in his brief epistle to submit themselves to God, he adds the proactive charge, "*Resist the devil, and he will flee from you*" (James 4:7, emphasis added). Passive neglect, as these biblical writers well understood, is a poor tactic against an adversary who blatantly—and frequently—refuses to be ignored.

Surviving the enemy's gauntlet of snares, however, is not a task to be taken lightly. As many well-meaning believers have learned (often too late), Satan is a cunning and relentless adversary, a devious wizard whose mastery of the dark arts enables him to fashion salacious temptations or fling fiery darts with equal ease. Nor are these devices directed solely at the weak and wayward. If the experiences of Job, Daniel and Paul tell us anything, it is that men and women are not invulnerable to trouble simply because their intentions and ministries please heaven. If Satan is audacious enough to tempt the Son of God and impede an angelic messenger dispatched by the Almighty, we can hardly expect him to steer clear of us!

Where, then, does this leave us? If spiritual invulnerability is an unattainable goal, can we not at least make ourselves more elusive targets? The answer is yes. While we cannot put on a magic suit or claim an exemption from battle, God's Word does present us with six tried-and-true steps that, if followed, promise added protection. Latter-day warriors should review them carefully.

1. Cultivate Humility

Scripture presents humility as a divine requirement (see Micah 6:8) and an endearing characteristic (see 2 Chronicles 33:12–13; Isaiah 57:15; 1 Peter 5:5–6). It is also a potent moral weapon in the battle against pride—a deceptive power that Francis Frangipane calls "the armor of darkness itself."[18]

If God is drawn to humility, He abhors pride. From the moment this lethal and unholy poison bubbled out of the secret recesses of Lucifer's heart, it has brought nothing but pain to the heart of God. Of all the forces at work in the universe, none is more destructive or antithetical to heavenly principles. For this reason we are told that "God opposes [or resists] the proud but gives grace to the humble." This proverb, quoted twice in the New Testament,[19] is linked contextually in both instances to spiritual warfare. And for good reason! If we want to resist the devil, we had better make sure God is not resisting us.[20]

Humility comes, as successful spiritual warriors have learned, from seeing God—and the devil—for who they really are. One such warrior, the great reformer Martin Luther, preserved his insights on the subject in the words of the classic hymn "A Mighty Fortress Is Our God." Speaking first of our adversary, Luther penned (in the original):

> The old, evil Enemy
> Is determined to get us;
> He makes his vicious plans
> With great might and cruel cunning;
> Nothing on earth is like him. . . .

In this last line (later translated as "On earth is not his equal"), Luther rightly acknowledged Satan as a higher-dimensional being whose power and cunning on human terms are unmatched.

After giving the devil his due, however, Luther moved quickly to the other side of the equation:

> But if the right man [Christ] is on our side
> One little word shall fell him.

In this magnificently balanced theology, Luther acknowledged two important truths. First, Satan's power is such that we cannot defeat him in our own strength—*ever*. Second, Christ's power is such that Satan cannot defeat Him in his own strength—*ever*. While there is an obvious strategy in these profound mismatches, it is visible only to the humble. Underestimating either of these supernatural combatants will lead to certain defeat.

Although some critics have accused the contemporary spiritual warfare movement of ignoring divine sovereignty, I have not observed this to be a serious problem. What I *have* found, at least among Western Christians, is a tendency toward unqualified triumphalism, a kind of swaggering religious play-acting that belittles the capabilities of the enemy and incites believers into battle without first ensuring that "the right man" is indeed on their side. To these believers, the devil is little more than an abstract punching bag, an ethereal bogey man at whom they can hurl epithets and chant clichés.

Such bravado before the enemy, far from being a badge of experience, is a sure sign that these believers have never seen their reflection in his malignant, bloodshot eyes. Like a naïve child toying with a cobra, they have no idea what (or whom) they are dealing with.

As the sons of Sceva discovered, cockiness has no place in spiritual warfare (see Acts 19:13–16). The devil's power is real and he is not afraid to use it. Fuller Seminary student Wilson Awasu relates that, in the West African country of Ghana, a pastor ignored the warnings of local villagers and ordered them to cut down a tree that had been enshrined by animist priests. When the last branch was lopped off, the minister collapsed and died. In a similar case, another well-meaning pastor commanded that a fetish shrine be demolished. When parishioners proceeded to carry out his wishes, he was struck down by a debilitating stroke.[21]

One evening in Papua New Guinea, missionaries Jim and Jaki Parlier listened as a group of Managalasi boys fearfully described the consequences of violating the taboo against speaking the names of the deceased. "Sometimes," the boys explained, "the [ancestral] spirit will just climb on your body. It feels heavy, like a huge log on your chest, and it's hard to breathe."

Hearing this, Jaki determined to teach the boys a lesson about superstition. Facing a grove of banana trees that concerned them, she yelled out the name of a powerful warrior spirit: "Ekileta, can you hear me? If you can, come and bite me. I'm waiting for you!"

The lads huddled together and covered their ears with their hands. Jaki, however, was just getting started. Feeling smug, she began calling out the name of every dead person she could think of, including an old sorceress named Avami. At this, the terrified boys started to cry. Jaki recalls:

> A few hours later, an eerie presence entered [our] room and woke me. Suddenly I felt a heaviness on my chest, like the weight of a huge log, pinning my body to the bed. I tried to wake Jim, but the weight was squeezing every ounce of breath from my body. I couldn't move or speak. Finally, in one desperate attempt, I forced the words *the blood of Jesus.* The weight lifted immediately.

Recoiling from her trauma, Jaki sat straight up in bed. Two red lights, like butterflies, were dancing in the middle of the room. After she rebuked them in the name of Jesus, the orbs flitted toward the window, slipped through gaps in the bamboo and danced into the night.[22]

When it was over, two of God's people had learned a hard lesson on the risks of spiritual bravado.

2. Walk in Obedience

The second ingredient for spiritual protection is obedience. Some may consider this requirement too general or simplistic to include in a list of practical advice. But the hard fact is, human presumption is among the most common attractors to the demonic.[23] In the arena of spiritual warfare, the devil is concerned less about the words cast in his direction than about who is doing the talking (see Acts 19:15). When it comes time to size up an adversary, he has one primary question: Does this person have an active relational link with God?

In Scripture, this link involves not only hearing but hearkening to the voice of the Lord. Whereas the former affords us knowledge of God's will, the latter indicates that we intend to do it. The prophet Samuel declared that "to obey is better than sacrifice" (1 Samuel 15:22), for one simple reason: With sacrifice, we decide what God will get; with obedience, we give God what He asks for. Spiritual obedience allows God to defend His own purposes.

Walking in obedience not only makes us safer by limiting enemy inroads into our lives; it also allows God to defend His own purposes. While this support does not prevent the devil from taking his best shot (witness Elijah, Mordecai and Paul), it does make us more difficult targets. God can also intervene on our behalf without our even knowing about it.[24] When the Moabite king Balak endeavored to curse the Israelites through the sorcerer Balaam, God's Spirit caused the well-known oracle to pronounce a blessing instead (see Numbers 23–24). In a contemporary episode, a young Nepali girl died in her sleep after eating food offered to idols (or demons; see 1 Corinthians 10:20–21) at a Hindu temple in Kathmandu. At that moment the Lord awakened her mother, a godly woman, with a warning that the girl's life was in imminent danger. Walking over to her daughter's bed, she found the little body ice-cold and lifeless. Embracing the child like Elijah (see 1 Kings 17:21–22), she resisted the powers of darkness until the soul of her beloved was returned.[25]

Another remarkable case of God defending His own was related to me almost casually by Bhutanese pastor Dawa Sandrup.[26] I had been visiting this high-perched Buddhist nation, officially known as Druk Yul (Land of the Thunder Dragon), for less than a week when we met at his modest apartment in Thimphu.

Having spent the previous four days in the company of a Buddhist astrologer, a "reincarnated" lama, and a *chöd* master (whose daily practice was to visualize his dismembered body being fed to hungry demons),[27] I was under a weight of oppression. Now, ushered into what Dawa called his prayer room, I took a seat on one of two facing cots. Despite the cold concrete floor, it was the first place I had visited in the country where the spiritual atmosphere felt clean. Looking into Dawa's kind face, I asked him how he managed to cope with this intense spiritual pressure year in and year out.

"Actually," he replied, "the devil has come to take my life many times. The pattern is almost always the same. I awake in the middle of the night with an overwhelming demonic presence in the room. It remains even when I turn on the light. The first stage is physical; I feel a strong binding or weight on my chest. Sometimes I can't breathe. This is often followed by a psychological attack. The walls of my mind start closing in and thoughts become difficult to form. It's like mental claustrophobia. The final phase of the attack—and I am usually on my knees at this point—is spiritual. Even though I pray through until dawn, it seems no one is there to listen. The heavens are like brass.

"The Lord is so kind, however," Dawa continued. "He always sends a breakthrough. Sometimes as I pray in the Spirit, the room is suddenly flooded with divine peace and power. At other times He sends believers to minister to me. They knock on my door in the morning, saying, 'The Lord has sent us to help you.'"

Then Dawa pointed at something over my shoulder. "Do you see that?"

Craning my neck around, I spied a walking cane hanging on a solitary nail in the wall.

"The elderly man who came to my door with that stick traveled all the way from Himachal Pradesh in northern India. He walked over a thousand kilometers! His name is Sadhu Subhas. Prior to that moment, we had never met or corresponded. But he told me that two years earlier, in 1988, God had shown him a vision of Thimphu and instructed him to come here. Shortly afterward, as he prepared to leave, the Lord supernaturally revealed all the roads and mountain passes he was to take. He arrived at my house on the morning after one of the enemy's attacks. As I opened the front door, he said, 'The Lord sent me to pray for you.'

"The day before he came here, there was a heavy snowfall. The day he arrived it was calm. The evening before his departure, it snowed heavily again. On Monday morning, however, it once again cleared up. When I asked the Sadhu about this, he replied quietly, 'The Lord honors His people.'"*

At this point in our conversation, Dawa reached under the mattress on his cot and pulled out a well-worn black leather prayer journal. For the next several minutes, with tears coursing down his cheeks, he read aloud from entries recorded during the visits of other "ministering angels." The messages, which included words of prayer, encouragement and prophecy, were powerful. As they permeated the air around us, I realized that this tiny, nondescript room was no ordinary place. What had looked like a cold concrete floor now appeared as hallowed ground. I found the urge to kneel overwhelming.

---

* "Let all who take refuge in you be glad; let them ever sing for joy. Spread your protection over them, that those who love your name may rejoice in you. For surely, O LORD, you bless the righteous; you surround them with your favor as with a shield" (Psalm 5:11–12).

Dawa's prayer room was a heavenly outpost on the edge of a vast supernatural battleground. That this Bhutanese pastor had held firm in the face of withering demonic attack was testimony to his steadfast obedience.

When finally I stood to leave, a faded wall-hanging caught my eye. Entitled "The Beacon Light of Faith," it bore words that could not have been more appropriate:

> Faith is like a beacon light across a troubled sea,
> A glow of hope that casts its rays wherever we may be;
> And sometimes through the darkest night our hearts will
>   find the way,
> Following that light of faith into a brighter day.

3. Put On Spiritual Armor

Given the amount of enemy flak in the air these days, it is astonishing to find so many Christians going about without spiritual armor. When it comes to risky behavior, one can offer better odds to three-pack-a-day smokers, promiscuous fornicators or drivers who shun seatbelts.

The most common reason seems to be simple carelessness. People just do not think about putting on their spiritual armor. While the subject may have been fun in Sunday school, where it was presented in coloring papers and on flannel graph boards, the task of relating helmets, shields and breastplates to the modern world has caused many adults, at least in practical terms, to abandon Paul's ancient metaphor.

Other Christians decline to don spiritual armor out of a misguided assumption that divine protection is a guaranteed byproduct of godly service. The problem here is not a lack of information but a display of machismo. Like the football player who shuns pads or the police officer who refuses a bulletproof vest, these individuals see themselves as indestructible warriors. The otherworldly nature of this battle is of little concern. As "King's kids" they believe they automatically command all the power and protection heaven has to offer. In any case, the devil smirks at their macho spirit.

In one graphic example in the early 1990s, a young, well-traveled missionary decided to engage the powers over the city of Kathmandu. Clambering up to a high point above the sacred Pashupatinath Temple complex, he proceeded to do battle with these potent spirits. Upon returning to his accomodations, however, he suddenly fell to the ground and lost control of his senses—an acute condition that lasted for three days. A week later, after being examined by a local psychologist, he limped out of town like one of the sons of Sceva. Friends who fetched him at the airport in Singapore report that he was a basket case—broken physically, psychologically and spiritually. It took months to nurse him back to health.[28]

Sometimes it is not carelessness or machismo but a narrow theological worldview that relegates our spiritual armor to the closet. When Dr. Linda Williams signed on for short-term missionary work with World Medical Missions in 1984, she was assigned to The Evangelical Alliance Mission hospital in Taitung, Taiwan. Several days before a scheduled return flight to the United States, Williams and a colleague attended an idol parade associated with the local Lantern Festival. The idol-bearers wore exotic face paint and carried feathered fans. Celebrants, drunk and empowered by evil, swarmed the streets exploding firecrackers.

"Suddenly," Williams recalls, "one of the temple leaders stepped from the parade line, waved his feathered fan in front of me and chanted angrily." Confused, she turned to her colleague for an explanation. His eyes were popping.

"He pronounced a curse on you," he stammered. "He asked the devils to demonstrate their power to you within 48 hours."

Two days later, having dismissed this bizarre event from her mind, Dr. Williams headed off on a farewell beach trip with several friends, including a dear missionary couple, Art and Leona Dickinson. As their vehicle approached a curve, a dog darted onto the road, causing their Chinese-American driver to swerve instinctively. The vehicle careened into two large trees and flipped.

Coming to her senses, Dr. Williams found herself covered in broken glass. A warm, oily substance was dripping onto the back of her neck. "Suddenly," she recalls, "I could hear Art calling, 'Linda, Leona's dying!' It was then I realized the warm substance on the back of my neck was actually Leona's blood."

For the next several days, Leona's life hung in the balance. She was comatose and fighting for every breath as surgeons worked to repair her lacerated organs and broken bones. When one of her pupils dilated suddenly, it became apparent that her brain stem was herniating. The head surgeon, unable to transport Leona to neurosurgical care in Taipei, assembled the missionaries to announce that she was probably going to die that night.

Even in the face of this pessimistic report, Dr. Williams recalls,

> The non-medical missionaries, teachers and pastors remained appallingly hopeful.... They seemed to have identified, before I did, that the accident was the result of the curse placed on me. But they also believed 1 John 4:4 and claimed it for Leona: "Greater is He who is in you than he who is in the world" (NASB).

Despite sustaining a C4 vertebral fracture, a condition that should have resulted in quadriplegia, Leona recovered fully. Says Dr. Williams:

> Today I no longer dismiss the reality of spiritual warfare. I have quit trying to fit [demonic power] into a philosophically neat compartment that will not disturb my Christian comfort zone or scientific rationale.[29]

As these testimonies remind us, spiritual armor is no optional accessory. Those who dismiss it do so at their peril. As to the question of what this armor is and how it is put on, Paul summed up the matter in four simple words: "I die every day" (1 Corinthians 15:31). It is Christ, he told the Galatians, who "lives in me" (Galatians 2:20).

In practice, then, putting on the armor of God is synonymous with daily surrender to the Lordship of Jesus Christ. Rather than visualize ancient and imaginary clothing, we simply dedicate our first conscious thoughts each morning to the will of our Master. Spiritual armor becomes lifestyle when, for the balance of the day, we choose to walk in the consciousness of His presence and purposes.[30]

4. Maintain Spiritual Accountability

Author Carol Shields once said, "There are chapters in every life which are seldom read and certainly not aloud."[31] Although these secret chapters are sometimes journalized memories of past failures, they are more likely to concern ongoing difficulties we would prefer to handle on our own. This tendency, as Charles Kraft noted in *Christianity with Power,* is most common among Westerners who cherish individualism and independence. It is not a healthy habit. Kraft points out that, besides engendering and legitimizing self-centeredness, a go-it-alone mentality makes us "vulnerable to Satan in the deepest recesses of our being."[32]

It is worth remembering that a viewpoint—*our* viewpoint—is only a view from a point. While we are entitled to our perspective on things, we must also be willing to admit that our view is limited. By habitually rejecting the counsel and insight of others, we become easy marks for the master deceiver.

Christian intercessors are also vulnerable to brief lapses of awareness known as *microsleeps.* These episodes, triggered by extreme fatigue, can occur in prayer meetings, in the middle of conversations, even while we are driving. Although microsleeps are brief, usually lasting no more than a few seconds, they are rich in hypnagogic imagery—fleeting, undefined forms that serve as the building blocks for hallucinations. The danger in these episodes, as UCLA Professor Ronald Siegel points out, is that "the fatigued brain can embroider these ambiguous forms with specific features."[33] Without adequate rest or a grounding support system (wise leaders and loving friends), long-haul intercessors can fall prey to false, even demonically inspired impressions.

As the pace of life and ministry continues to quicken around us, accountable relationships become increasingly important to our spiritual well-being. In a reference to this hour, the biblical writer said:[34]

> Let us not give up meeting together, as some are in the habit of doing, but let us encourage [or exhort] one another—and all the more as you see the Day approaching.
>
> Hebrews 10:25

In the end, the purpose of spiritual accountability is to establish guardrails to keep us out of trouble, and a safety tether in case we stumble into it. It is like hiking in a wilderness area at a national park. Maps and trail markers are provided, but recreationalists are also asked to sign in at a ranger station or trailhead. Hikers are asked to indicate the number and names of people in their parties, a proposed itinerary and projected entry and exit dates.

Some outdoorsmen see this as an example of overbearing authority, just as certain believers chafe at the disciplines of spiritual accountability. But there are good reasons for requiring such information. Every year adventurers are incapacitated in the wilderness by broken bones, animal attacks and capricious weather. When these things happen—and who ever plans for them?—it is nice to know you are tethered for "deep rescues." After all, wasn't this why a priest entering the Holy of Holies wore bells on his garment and a cord around his ankle?

5. Establish Faithful Prayer Support

One thing that has amazed me in counseling spiritual assault victims over the years is how few believers bother to establish any form of personal prayer support. With the exception of a few pastors and frontline missionaries, most of these individuals never even consider themselves eligible for such an arrangement. While understanding on this subject has improved in recent years, thanks in large part to books like C. Peter Wagner's *Prayer Shield,* there are still far too many Christians flying solo.

A practice I have found of immense benefit is giving my intercessors advance details about each sensitive mission or project I plan to pursue. If my agenda calls for research work, be it in the highlands of Tibet or the streets of New Orleans, I try to provide each member of my support team with a daily schedule of events, including travel, interviews and observational activities. Once the mission gets under way, the intercessors agree to keep a daily prayer journal, detailing how God led them to pray, while I maintain a daily trip report, detailing what actually happened. When I return from the field, we swap documents.

Invariably this post-trip review proves mutually rewarding. The intercessors discover why they were prompted to pray in a certain fashion or at a certain time, while I am grateful for their sensitivity and God's watchcare over my every move.

A few years ago a woman from the Seattle area began to pray for me after the Lord gave her an impression of a stranger standing over my bed as I slept. This prayer entry, cross-checked later with my trip report, matched the precise date and time that I had been awakened in Tsering Dorje's idol room in Dharamsala (the story I recounted in chapter 1). Another time, an intercessor from Atlanta sensed an urgent need to pray for my travel safety on the very day the car I was traveling in blew a tire on a treacherous mountain road in Bhutan. Had the tire given out two minutes earlier or later, we would have careened off the cliff to our deaths.

My most vivid reminder of the power of prayer occurred in July 1995. Having just completed a rigorous season of ministry, I was vacationing for a few days with my wife, Lisa, and our four children at my parents' home in Southern California. On a warm Monday morning, our two-year-old daughter, Jenna, trundled off unnoticed in pursuit of adventure.

My mother, following an inner prompting, headed into the backyard to check on Jenna's whereabouts. When an initial scan proved unfruitful, she moved in the direction of her worst fears. Peering over the concrete lip of the swimming pool, she spied Jenna's yellow-clad body lying motionless near the deep end drain. Rushing into the house, she screamed, "George, the baby's in the pool!"

By the time I bounded into the backyard, Lisa was already retrieving Jenna's body from the pool. Breaking the surface with a vengeance, she cried, "Take her!"

As I grasped Jenna's limp frame in my arms, she seemed utterly lifeless—a grim reminder of the meaning of dead weight. I had no idea how long my baby had been submerged. Looking down on her wet little face, I saw every fine feature just as it had always been. Inside, however, I knew the serious business of life was rapidly shutting down.

Caught inside our own slow-motion universe, Lisa and I became increasingly aware that a fierce spiritual battle was being waged over Jenna. The adversary, having stalked our daughter from conception, was closing in to *devour* his sweetmeat—an action that, in the Greek *(katapino)*, means literally "to swallow up" or "to drown" (see 1 Peter 5:8).

If these intentions were to be contested, we knew it would take more than CPR. It was now painfully obvious that Jenna was lost in a place we could not reach and could understand only dimly. Her destiny was being decided not on a soggy lawn in my parents' backyard, but in the boundless corridors of eternity. Only God could navigate those mysterious interstices between mind and spirit; only He could lead Jenna back to the threshold of life.

With time evaporating like drops of expensive fragrance, our minds struggled to fight off dark images of death: the unspeakable agony of being pulled off of Jenna's unresponsive body; the rigors of arranging and attending a premature funeral; the lingering torment brought on by the sight of lonely teddy bears and unfilled slippers. These are the primal fears of every loving parent, and they rolled through our minds like unrelenting swells on open seas. Our one glimmer of hope was that none of these imaginary waves had yet crashed on the shores of reality.

We were soon joined by a trio of Ventura County paramedics. The interrogation was rapid-fire: "Is she breathing? Is there a pulse? How long was she under? Is your pool heated?"

Jenna, locked in her silent world, seemed blissfully unaware of the cacophony above her. To the rest of us, however, the clanking gear and squawking radios meant that our private vigil was turning into a public war. Placing an oxygen mask over Jenna's face, the paramedics rushed her into the back of an idling emergency aid vehicle and flipped on the siren. Seconds later we were off to the hospital.

When we finally tiptoed up to Jenna's bedside some six hours later, the sight nearly broke our hearts. Instead of the talkative bundle of joy we had known only that morning, we found an unconscious stranger whose vital functions were being controlled or monitored by machines. Not even at birth had she looked so vulnerable, so tiny. Leaning through an impossible tangle of tubes and wires, we brushed a few stray locks off her forehead.

"Hello, sweetheart. Mommy and Daddy are here."

The Great Physician was there, too. Unknown to us, word of Jenna's accident had already traveled around the world. Alerted by a variety of electronic trumpets—including The 700 Club, the Voice of Hope radio network and the Internet—a massive army of intercessors had joined the battle for Jenna's life. Another prayer mobilization effort orchestrated by Peter and Doris Wagner prompted calls and faxes from as far away as Perth, Australia. Each one assured us that thousands of intercessory allies were rushing to the cause.

As a consequence of faithful prayer and God's grace, Jenna not only survived her ordeal, but suffered none of the adverse effects—cerebral edema, pneumonia and brain damage—that the doctors had warned about. Calling her a little "miracle girl," the ICU charge nurse proceeded to tell us that in twenty years, she had seen only one other child with Jenna's profile recover so rapidly and so completely.[35]

6. *Take Godly Risks*

The final step in our spiritual protection program involves an activity many Christians overlook: taking godly risks. Although we generally assume risk is something we need to protect ourselves against, the real danger is often found lurking in the status quo. In Jesus' Parable of the Talents, for example, the servant who buried his master's capital in a napkin for safekeeping was sternly rebuked for his actions. Why? He neglected to advance the master's interests. To his self-centered mind, the potential for loss was of far greater concern than the failure to gain.[36] In the end, the steps this servant took to alleviate loss actually promoted it.

Things today are not much different. Parents who worry about their children's safety or "proper" education respond by holding them back from frontline Christian ministry. (All too often this decision backfires when the youngster is lost to some addiction or compromised by the cares of this life.) Missionaries concerned about persecution or deportation take conscious steps to muzzle their witness on the field, leading to the very result the enemy had in mind all along: the effective silencing of Jesus Christ's primary voice on earth.[37]

Prayer warriors can also be impaired by excess caution. A good example surfaced during an extended prayer journey I led in the early 1990s. As our team neared the end of a three-week mission to the Himalayas, which included on-site intercession at multiple Hindu and Buddhist strongholds, several participants reported feeling oppressed and asked to remain in their hotel rooms. Of those who proceeded into the temples and monasteries, many spent considerable time looking over their shoulders. In the midst of this spiritual malaise, God reminded us of the time His presence had been conveyed into the Philistine temple at Ashdod. As the Ark of the Covenant was set next to the image of Dagon, the idol promptly collapsed and shattered (see 1 Samuel 5:1–5).

Although the presence of God no longer resides in a gilded ark, it *is* contained in our earthen vessels. Wherever it is conveyed, we may be sure that it will have a greater impact on its environment than its surroundings have on it.

As I pointed out in *The Last of the Giants,* God seldom calls His people to a fair fight. The recurring theme of Scripture is one of giants and multitudes. Time and again Christian warriors are asked to face foes whose natural resources exceed their own.[38] If we are to succeed on such battlefields, we must learn to walk in faith; and faith, it has been said, is spelled *R-I-S-K.* If something is not risky, it does not require faith.[39] And "without faith it is impossible to please God" (Hebrews 11:6).

"The risk-free life," as the late Jamie Buckingham once said, "is a victory-free life. It means lifelong surrender to the mediocre. And that is the worst of all possible defeats."[40] Going out on a limb not only takes us to where the fruit is, but it prevents us from being picked off by the enemy. As any marksman knows, there is nothing easier to hit than a stationary target.

Reckoning Force:
Acquiring and Using Spiritual Power

There is more to Christianity than becoming an elusive spiritual target. Our mission to extend the borders of Christ's Kingdom on earth also requires us to be practiced in the art of *offensive* warfare. And while the truth of God's Word is our ultimate weapon, it is often more effective when accompanied by demonstrations of divine power.

In Acts 8 we read that "when the [Samaritan] crowds heard Philip and saw the miraculous signs he did, *they all paid close attention to what he said"* (verse 6, emphasis added). Elaborating on this point, Bible scholar Jack Deere draws attention to Paul's statement that "the kingdom of God is not in word but in power" (1 Corinthians 4:20, NKJV). This miraculous power, according to Deere, "is more than temporary evidence of God's kingdom—it is actually a characteristic of His kingdom."[41]

People are nearly always attracted more to indigenous power than to foreign dogma. Indeed, until Philip arrived in Samaria with great signs and miracles, "all the people, both high and low" (Acts 8:10) gave their attention to a powerful sorcerer named Simon. Christian success in the Roman world was also largely attributable to the ability of the believers to offer convincing evidence of the power of the faith over demons.

The modern appetite for spiritual power, whatever its source, is no less ravenous. We have only to look at the unprecedented popularity of paranormal television programming, the proliferation of New Age teaching and the revitalization of various indigenous religions. People want power, and the enemy is only too willing to oblige.

Since demonic signs and wonders will increase as we edge closer to the Second Coming of Christ, we face some critical questions: Are we prepared? Do we have the necessary battlefield experience to stand up to this expanding competition? For many believers, including some in positions of ministry leadership, the answer is a resounding *no*.

Examples of this dearth of experience are not hard to find. A recent episode of the popular television program *Unsolved Mysteries* featured a Midwestern family traumatized by a demonic infestation of their home. Unable to cope with a daily routine that included flickering lights, levitating dishes and appliances that switched on without warning, the distraught couple turned to a local pastor for comfort and advice. After observing the unsettling phenomena firsthand, the dismayed clergyman could only conclude, "There are just some things we are unable to understand."

The problem, as one Native American believer told me in 1992, is that "many Christians are afraid to venture into situations more powerful than they are." Having little firsthand experience with the supernatural, they are inclined to shy away from its mysteries.

Those who admit their lack, however, can improve their performance on the spiritual battlefield by following six basic steps:

1. *We must expose ourselves to real battlefields.* Many of us are committed to notions about spiritual warfare that we have never proven personally. Having confined ourselves to artificial worlds like academia (where spiritual "war games" are waged on paper) or charismania (where battles are fought in rallies), we are often left unprepared for the real thing. The only sure corrective is to venture out beyond our established comfort zones.

2. *We must find a qualified mentor.* The best way to learn how to wield spiritual power effectively is to grab onto the coattails of someone who has gone to battle before.

3. *We must remain clean, humble vessels.* Only the righteous can lay claim to the promise of divine power. According to Psalm 66:18, Isaiah 1:15 and John 9:31, God will not even listen to the entreaties of sinners.

4. *We must remember the purpose of divine signs and wonders.* Although spiritual gifts are often associated with the personal welfare of Christians, the Bible teaches that divine power is manifest primarily to glorify God and to facilitate evangelism (see Mark 16:20; Acts 2:43; 1 Corinthians 14:22; Hebrews 2:3–4).

5. *We must release ourselves to God's sovereignty.* If we are truly yielded to the Lordship of Christ, we must allow Him to regain His voice in each circumstance that confronts us. This will require more patient listening on our part and fewer demanding formulas.

6. *We must develop a sense of expectation.* This is especially relevant for those of us who live in (or with) the rationalist ghettos of Western society. Although we may find it difficult to picture ourselves in the role of exorcist, seer or healer, this is how God has chosen to minister to our bound and broken world. If we do not expect the Holy Spirit to manifest His power through us, He probably won't.

Whatever posture we decide to adopt on the issue of spiritual power, it is important to note that our competition has already cast their lot. Almost anywhere you care to look, men and women are paying desperate prices to acquire and employ spiritual power. For thousands of Tibetan monks, the cost involves years of solitary meditation and mental discipline. In other parts of the world, power-seekers use a variety of techniques that includes ordeals (Australia and Native America), initiations (West Africa and Melanesia), fasts (India and Java) and trances (Haiti and Turkey). In northern India, a Hindu disciple has been standing before his guru's grave for more than four years in order to fulfill a vow. Sleeping in an upright sling, he refuses to leave until his mentor releases him through a sign in his dreams.[42]

In many instances, the spiritual power derived from these actions is used to defend existing spiritual strongholds. Hearing about Christian efforts to obstruct a revival of the ancient sun dance, Sioux medicine man Ed McGaa was "moved to accept the role of the mystic warriors of the past"—a role that included a need, as he put it, for "strong spiritual armor." According to McGaa, "These mystic warriors were like knights of old. They were the spiritual helpers to the holy men and holy women, and they were fighters to protect the spiritual ways."[43]

At least one mission executive, Howard Brant of SIM USA (Society for International Ministries), has expressed open concern about these "spiritual forces of wickedness which stand opposed to the advance of the gospel and the spreading of God's kingdom on earth." In a recent position paper on the subject, Brant declared:

> We want our missionaries, our related churches, and all Christians everywhere to recognize that there are dark spiritual forces which have enormous power over entire clans, villages, towns, ethnic groups, and even over nations (Daniel 10:11–13). It is as we learn to take up the weapons of our warfare and attack these strongholds of wickedness that God's Spirit will be released to turn men and women to himself, bring salvation to the lost, and revive His church.[44]

Confronting the Powers in Soroti

In December 1983 a young Ugandan evangelist named Robert Kayanja was invited to hold an evangelistic crusade in the spiritually oppressed town of Soroti.[45] The ministry team, in an effort to break the spiritual bondage over the area, committed to fast during each day of the crusade and eat only one meal in the evening.

Nearly a thousand people showed up for the first meeting, held in an open field surrounded by mango trees, but local leaders had hoped for more. Unfortunately a prominent witch doctor, Muhamoud, had threatened to disrupt the sessions by releasing a box full of deadly snakes into the crowd. Muhamoud's real trade, despite his Muslim name, was selling magic charms and practicing witchcraft. For years he had kept the people of Soroti under his spell. Although there were several Christian churches in the area, it was rare for anyone to show any interest in joining them.

Robert, knowing nothing of Muhamoud's trade or threats, admonished the people boldly to dispense with their reliance on witchcraft and turn in faith to the living God. As the conviction of the Holy Spirit fell, people who had been hesitantly fingering their charms discarded them as if they were hot coals. The power of God swept across the crowd, dissolving tumors, opening blind eyes and restoring withered limbs. At least six cripples walked out of the meeting under their own power.

The news spread like wildfire. Recounts Kayanja:

> When I got up to preach the second day, Muhamoud was furious. He brought his box full of snakes to the meeting and threw challenges openly. The crowd by now had grown twice as large, and people were streaming in on bicycles, running and carrying their babies. With everyone looking on, Muhamoud stood up in front of me and screamed, "Get out of this town! If you bother my potions, which I have sold to the people, I'll kill you."
>
> Instead of heeding his warning, however, we carried on with our ministry. Another 111 people were saved that day, and the witchcraft charms continued to pile up.

As Robert collected the discarded fetishes for a public burning later in the week, Muhamoud blocked his path. "When the rain comes at ten o'clock tomorrow morning," he hissed, "you will see my power."

Despite this threat, Robert and his colleagues left the meeting rejoicing in everything God had done. Having fasted all day, they were very hungry. But it did not take long into their evening meal before they discovered something seriously amiss. Robert recalls:

After three bites I heard the Holy Spirit say, *Stop eating. The food is wrong.* Although I put my fork down immediately, the others had already eaten and were starting to faint. My stomach was also becoming upset, and I could not feel my tongue. I began to pray because I knew we had been bewitched. When I called the cook into the room, he confessed that Muhamoud had paid him to sprinkle a powder on the food. Not surprisingly, this man was very fearful—but we just prayed for him and extended forgiveness. As we did so, God gave us a breakthrough. Almost before we could say, "Amen," we vomited out everything we had eaten and were saved.

At exactly ten the next morning, it began to drizzle. Instead of lying dead, however, as the witch doctor had expected, the team was busy teaching a Bible seminar—a turn of events that was not lost on the people. By two o'clock the crowd had grown to about four thousand. Many individuals had climbed up into the nearby trees in order to get a better view.

Frustrated by his earlier failure, Muhamoud walked into the crowd and pulled the lid off his magic box. Looking up at me, he said, "Now we will see who has the real power." With that, Muhamoud and his two attendants pulled out a long, green snake and sent it onto the platform.

As it came slithering up, the people in the audience were leaping out of the way. Trying to ignore the whole affair, I was about to make a point when my interpreter suddenly jumped off the platform. Gesturing frantically, he yelled, "Look behind you!" Turning around, I saw the snake coiling up as if to say, "This is my turf now." It was clear that the creature had been sent to attack us.

Well, the people went wild. I've never heard such screaming in my life. People who were selling food in the nearby markets ran over to see what was happening. I vividly remember one woman standing there with a knife and potato in each hand. Attracted by the commotion, uniformed schoolchildren returning home from school also scurried over, as did the patrons of several local bars. Altogether about six thousand people were now gathered in the field.

Looking at the green snake next to me, I commanded, "You devil, go from here!" Immediately the serpent uncoiled, left the platform and returned to its box on the ground. Although Muhamoud tried to coax it out again, the snake refused to obey. In exasperation he pulled out a large cobra and yelled, "Attack!" Seconds later it came flying over the heads of the people and landed on the platform. Flaring its hood, it prepared to strike.

The crowd was now divided into two groups—those on our side and those with the witch doctor. The air was filled with the sounds of an African war chant: "Hey-ey hey! Hey-ey hey!" We were in the middle of a classic power encounter.

Even though my knees were shaking, I said to the pastors, "This thing is not a snake, as you think; it's a spirit." With that, one of our intercessors, a gray-haired, seventy-year-old lady, began to sing "There Is Power in the Blood." Soon we all joined in.

As we sang, the Holy Spirit fell upon me. I suddenly felt strong enough to kill a lion. I heard the Lord say to me, *Go to the snake.* Pointing my finger at the swaying serpent, I rebuked it in the name of Jesus. Spiritually defanged, it uncoiled and became as straight as a rod. Then I heard the Holy Spirit telling me, *Pick it up by the tail.* So I grabbed the snake up and began to walk with it.

The scene was unbelievable! Trying to see what was happening on the platform, people were pushing and stepping on one another. The heathen were chanting, "Hey-ey hey," while the Christians continued to sing worship to God. After about ten minutes, I suddenly felt a fresh surge of the Holy Spirit's power. When I looked down at the snake, it was dead.

When the astonished witch doctor saw this, he exclaimed, "You've killed my snake!" Pointing my finger at him, I said, "You're next. You are going to die like your snake if you don't give your life to Jesus." Suddenly Muhamoud fell to the ground and began to writhe like an agitated serpent.

After we had cast the demons out of this man, a process that took about 45 minutes, I asked the leaders to bring him onto the platform. He was so weak he couldn't even stand. I asked him publicly, "Do you want to believe on Jesus Christ?" When he said yes, I led him in the sinner's prayer, then instructed the people to place his snakes and charms on the witchcraft heap for burning. At this Muhamoud vomited all over the place, coughing out everything.

The people were amazed. Many had tears running down their faces. I said, looking out on the crowd, "If you also repent of your sins, then God will visit you." Thousands responded and were saved that day, including about thirty Muslims. It was the beginning of a great spiritual awakening in Soroti.

When we finally burned the witchcraft items, skin rashes that had plagued many of the pastors suddenly cleared up. Muhamoud himself was completely transformed. After preaching mightily in Zanzibar, he has since moved on to Madagascar, where he now pastors a church of about eight hundred members.[46]

The lesson in this corner of the labyrinth is that spiritual power and protection are not only available to obedient Christians; they are core components in God's strategy to liberate enchanted communities. So long as we remain focused on this purpose (as opposed to self-aggrandizement), we may call on divine gifts and power without hesitation. This will become even more important as global evangelization prompts our desperate adversary to flood the world with demonic counterfeits.

As we consider how God would have us "redeem the time" in these evil days (see Ephesians 5:15), one of the most important—and controversial—questions concerns the parameters of our warfare. What is the extent of our authority in dealing with the enemy? Does our mandate end, as some have claimed, with personal exorcism? Or is there an element of collective possession that we must also attend to? How can we ensure that our spiritual warfare initiatives are both biblically based and practically effective?

CHAPTER TEN

SPELLBENDING

I n C. S. Lewis' beloved tale *The Lion, the Witch and the Wardrobe,* four
English children stumble into an enchanted realm called Narnia.
Although their first encounters with the natives prove delightful,
they soon learn that not all is well. The kingdom, it seems, is troubled by a cruel and cunning queen. Known to her subjects as the
White Witch, she has somehow managed to keep the land in a state
of perpetual dormancy. "In Narnia," the children are told, "it is
always winter, but never Christmas." Subjects unfortunate enough
to incur the queen's wrath are summarily frozen in stone. Even worse,
the children learn, a veritable forest of these pitiable statues has been
sighted in the halls and courtyard of her dark castle.

One of the four youngsters, the self-centered Edmund, actually
witnesses the queen in action, petrifying a family of forest squirrels
in their own home. When the deed is done, Edmund finds he cannot bear the thought of those little stone figures sitting there "all the
silent days and all the dark nights, year after year, until moss grows
on them and even their faces begin to crumble away."[1]

Lewis' story is allegorical; ours is not. The enchantment and
despair are all too real. Who among us has not seen the crumbling
stone faces of human souls bewitched by the powers of darkness?
The hollow-eyed guru, the painted movie star, the abused child, the
conscience-seared businessman, the stumbling drunk—spiritual
zombies all, and in seemingly unending supply.

As citizens of a fallen world, we know what it is like to long for the
coming of Christmas, to dream of a spring thaw that will release our
race from the icy grip of sin and death. And while we may have rea-

son to believe that these happy events are not far removed, we still have much to do in the interim. Above all we must find a way to deal with "the god of this age [who] has blinded the minds of unbelievers, so that they cannot see the light of the gospel" (2 Corinthians 4:4). Like the apostles before us, we have been commissioned by Christ "to open their eyes and turn them from darkness to light, and from the power of Satan to God" (Acts 26:18).

If the purpose of hell is *spellbinding,* then the objective of heaven must be *spellbending.* Where the enemy has brought confusion, we must bring light. Where he has robbed men and women of dignity, we must bring healing. Where he has introduced despair, we must bring hope. Where he has brought disease and death, we must bring life. There is no greater role in earthly Narnia.

Pursuing Grace: Truth-Seekers and Second Chances

From the enemy's perspective, there are only three categories of human beings: prisoners (those he has already subdued), targets (those he is endeavoring to snare) and adversaries (those who are actively resisting his efforts). While Satan's hatred extends to each of these groups, his short-term objectives are governed largely by expediency. Prisoners, since they are already under his control, may be retained for the purpose of amusement (objects of torment) or doing his bidding (as destructive agents). They are likely to be disposed of once they have served their purpose. (Battlefields and overdoses do nicely.) Targets consist mainly of children and truth-seekers. Here the enemy's immediate goal is not to destroy but to deceive and entrap. To do this effectively, he must first immobilize his Christian adversaries, who can represent a serious hazard. In this arena, his weapons of choice are usually temptation, burnout and resource deprivation.

Despite his own considerable resources, Satan does not always get what he wants. The reason may be traced to God's public commitment to protect His saints (see Psalm 5:11–12; Luke 10:19), reward honest truth-seekers (see Deuteronomy 4:29; Matthew 7:7–8; Hebrews 11:6) and liberate spiritual captives (see Isaiah 61:1; Luke 19:10). While the first two of these pledges are issued in response to right choices (a fact that should make us no less grateful!), the latter is directed toward rebels whose distress is largely self-inflicted.

This pursuing grace is no aberration. As I noted in *The Last of the Giants*, "God's strategy in reclaiming His fallen creation is decidedly aggressive: Rather than wait for captive souls to petition for liberation, He dispatches His servants instead on extensive search-and-rescue missions."[2] While many prisoners are freed through passionate intercession, others are delivered by prophetic or evangelistic fire. In the end, whatever means are employed, the glorious truth is that Jesus has come to seek and to save that which is lost.

In the early winter of 1991, I encountered, quite unexpectedly, one of the most remarkable examples of pursuing grace I had ever heard.* It all started when a friend, knowing of my interest in the Himalayan region, invited me over to her Washington, D.C., townhouse to meet Sylvia, a talented young negotiator working out of the Department of State. After a pleasant dinner, we retired to the living room, where Sylvia recounted how an early quest for truth had led her to India and ultimately into the seductive web of Buddhism. Following a script that only God could write, Sylvia proceeded to describe how she was eventually led to Christ by a Bhutanese woman, the daughter of a celebrated Buddhist lama.

But there was a problem: Sylvia's mother in Christ (let's call her Choeden) had reportedly backslidden since the two had last spent time together. Although such attrition is not uncommon among Bhutanese believers, Sylvia found it difficult to accept that it had happened to Choeden. Unsure of her responsibility, she had taken her burden before the Lord in prayer.

"Almost immediately," Sylvia told me, "I was seized by a strong and persistent impression that I was to travel to Bhutan." Convinced her impression was from the Lord, she had arranged for a leave of absence. The mission of mercy was now only days away.

I wished Sylvia well, and we ended the evening in prayer.

---

* Certain names, dates and locations have been changed to protect the identities of those involved in this story.

The next time I heard from Sylvia, some two months later, she had just returned from the Himalayas. Her encounter with Choeden had not gone particularly well. "She seemed suspicious and even resentful," lamented Sylvia. "But she certainly heard the word of the Lord. At least I feel I've done my part."

For the next four months, the matter seemed to hang on this discouraging note. Then, as I prepared to make a journey of my own to Asia, there was a glimmer of light. Sylvia phoned to say that Choeden had reportedly come under conviction and was attending a weekly Bible study. Since I was going to Bhutan, would I contact her?

So it was that, shortly after arriving in Thimphu, I called Choeden, not knowing what kind of reception to expect. She sounded thrilled to hear from me, however, and made arrangements to pick me up at the hotel that evening.

An attractive woman in her mid-thirties, Choeden was dressed in a lovely *kira*, an ankle-length robe woven from colorful fabrics and fastened at the waist and shoulders with silver brooches. After driving the short distance to her tidy home, we were met at the door by her friend Dem, an elegant and well-spoken woman who spent the next half hour supplying us with an overwhelming assortment of pastries and hors d'oeuvres. When I paused to wash it all down with some local Darjeeling tea, Choeden leaned in to unfold her remarkable story.

"Most of my problems started when I returned to Bhutan after spending several years abroad," she began in fluent English. "The first thing people said was, 'You need to make a pilgrimage to your father's temple. If you don't honor your ancestral gods, you might go mad.' It sounds farfetched, but people have lost their senses here simply for changing gods. The demonic powers are very strong."

Under different circumstances these warnings would not have motivated Choeden to make the arduous journey to the family estate in the remote Sakteng Valley, especially since her parents were dead. As it was, however, the cautions stirred up feelings of curiosity and nostalgia that had been building within her for months.

"When I was traveling abroad in the early 1980s," she continued, "I picked up a copy of Alex Haley's book *Roots*. As I read his story, something stirred within me. I suddenly felt a desire to revisit my own past, to return to a family home I had not lived in for 26 years.

Unable to resist the pull on my spirit, I rounded up a servant to cook for me and headed east for three months."

Although the Sakteng Valley is a relatively short distance away as the crow flies (about 350 miles), eastern Bhutan boasts no airport and confines human travelers to a single, treacherous road. The journey, which typically takes several days, can be hair-raising. In several areas the route has literally been carved out of rock and is bordered by vertiginous drops. (It was on just such a road that the car I was traveling in had blown a tire three days earlier. Were it not for my faithful Atlanta intercessor, I would have made an unscheduled visit to the canyon depths.) The grim atmosphere is made worse by perpetual fog and the absence of any human activity. A small memorial honors 247 Indian and Nepalese workers who lost their lives while constructing the road.

After plunging down a long series of bends, the road eventually enters a semitropical zone rife with bamboo, liana and lemon grass. While most of the houses are built in traditional Bhutanese style—multi-storied wooden structures whose roofs are held down by stones—other dwellings are balanced precariously on bamboo stilts. After the provincial town of Tashigang, Bhutan's second-largest "urban center," it is still three days' walk to the high valleys (about ten thousand feet) of Merak and Sakteng. Located in the nation's isolated eastern corner, these rhododendron-covered vales are host to seminomadic yak herders, the Brokpas, whose woven black hats are famous throughout the land.

"When I arrived in Sakteng," Choeden continued, "memories of my childhood came flooding back. I had an instant and powerful sense of belonging. For the first time since my conversion, I began to question my Christian faith.

"While all this was going through my mind, the caretaker of my father's temple approached me. He made a big point of telling me that since I had been absent all these years, I needed to perform a *serkem*, a ritual peace offering, to the protective deity of our estate. Somehow this rubbed me the wrong way. Besides being a staunch Christian, I was very stubborn. I remember thinking, *This is my home. Why should I appease the local deity?* So I told the caretaker, 'I won't make the offering.'

"Not wanting to spend the night alone, I invited four other ladies to stay in the house with me. We just sprawled out on the floor of the third-floor living quarters. While the others drifted off to sleep fairly quickly, I decided to finish off the last chapters of *Roots*. Since we had no electricity, I was propped up next to a candle. It was so quiet.

"The room we were sleeping in was situated adjacent to my father's room. By tradition we were never permitted to enter this room, even while my father was alive. So I was surprised when the door to his chamber began to open. At first I thought the candle flicker was playing tricks in the corner of my eye. When I looked up, however, it was obvious that something was really happening. A moment later an enormous red dog emerged. I will never forget its eyes. They were terrifying. As it prepared to pounce on me, I screamed and tossed my book in the air. This not only startled the sleeping ladies but it blew out the candle. Enveloped by the darkness, which was horrible, we somehow managed to scramble down to the kitchen fireplace. We huddled there for the rest of the night.

"At daybreak I sent one of the ladies to get the caretaker. When he came around, I asked him if he had ever seen a red dog on the premises. I wanted to know why it would try to attack me. Looking somber, he replied that whenever my father's guardian spirit was troubled, it would attack people in this form.[3] 'I warned you,' he said. 'I told you to perform the serkem and you didn't do it.' At this point I was scared. I couldn't pray. My Christian life seemed to have gone out the window. All I wanted was to be accepted by my father. So I said to the caretaker, 'Please, let's do the serkem in my father's chapel.'"

With this act Choeden began to slide back into the dark abyss of Tantric Buddhism.[4] While her Christian lifeline still held, it was becoming badly frayed by the sharp edges of fear and tradition. Happily for Choeden, an international band of intercessors was petitioning heaven quietly on her behalf.

A year later she was asked to return to Sakteng as an escort for Dr. Julia Garrett, an associate professor at the University of California. Dr. Garrett was in Bhutan researching the social effects of leprosy. Since she was keen to observe local folk healers—herbal doctors, black magicians and lamas—Choeden arranged for several interviews. She also arranged for a *lhabab,* or Tibetan oracle ritual.

"The government has actually banned the *lhabab*," Choeden told me, "because it has been used to predict the affairs of state. You don't normally call those sessions unless you want to find out about the future of a country. But Julia wanted to see one, so I contacted a man in Merak who had previously served as a family servant. He was quite happy to perform it for us."

After riding in on horseback, the oracle prepared for the ceremony in Choeden's family temple. Short in stature, he was dressed in the traditional Brokpa *chuba* (woolen jacket) and *pishoop* (leather leggings). Under a black yak-hair hat, his strong Tibetan features were framed by a pair of dangling turquoise earrings.[5] Toward evening powerful demonic forces finally seized control of the oracle's body.

"As the spirits took over," Choeden recalled, "he started speaking in a high female voice. This was an indication that he had been possessed by Palden Lhamo, a female deity who served as my father's guardian and who is highly revered throughout Sakteng. Almost immediately the spirits in this man began to accuse me. They said, 'You have left the gods of your father and embraced another faith.'

"I was astonished! There was no way this oracle could have known that I had become a Christian. As my mouth fell open, he picked up a huge ceremonial sword and started swinging it through the air. Once again the accusatory female voice spoke to me: 'You have departed from the gods of your father. And now you will die!'

"I was absolutely terrified. As the oracle moved slowly toward us, Julia's eyes almost popped out of her head. She kept repeating, 'Translate, please! What is he saying?' All I could think of at the moment was my father. Turning around toward his idol, which had been added to the temple pantheon after his death, I begged, 'Papa, please save me. I'm so sorry for going away.'

"Suddenly the oracle stopped in his tracks. Looking directly at me, he said, 'Now we will see if you are accepted.' Taking a *kata* [white scarf] in his hand, the oracle declared, 'I'll offer this to the Jowo [an image of Buddha as an eight-year-old prince],[6] and if he accepts it, then all is well.'

"I was scared. I thought I was going to die. Amazingly, however, the scarf flew up and tied itself around the Jowo's neck. I was so relieved! But my sense of relief quickly evaporated when the oracle suddenly plunged the sword into his own stomach. Julia screamed when it went in. He just lay there motionless, and I thought, *My goodness, he's dying.*

"At that moment, however, the voice of Palden Lhamo, the female deity, called us over to the oracle's body. As I bent over him, I remember seeing a gaping wound but no blood. We were then asked to fill this hole with handfuls of sanctified grain. I can show you some photographs, if you're interested."

The impact of this experience on Choeden's mind and spirit in the months that followed was enormous. Her remaining Christian disciplines, including Bible study, prayer and fellowship with other believers, withered. By the autumn of 1990, Choeden's return to the Buddhist fold was all but complete. The only step she had failed to take was consecrating an idol room in her home.

"One day when I came home from work," she continued, "I found a good friend waiting for me. She had just returned from Calcutta, where she had been taking training as a police officer, and just wanted to say hello. So after we had chatted for a few minutes, I thought I should prepare some tea. When I called for our seventeen-year-old servant girl, however, there was no reply. After a follow-up summons went unheeded, my niece stuck her head in to inform me that the girl had gone to bed with a headache. While my first inclination was to let her rest, I became concerned when she failed to come out for dinner.

"When we knocked on her door, which was locked from the inside, we failed to get any response. Since the room has an outside window, I suggested we go out and see what we could learn. When we peered in, we could see the girl standing in what appeared to be a very awkward position. To my police friend's trained eye, the scene suggested something more. Speaking in a somber tone, she said, 'I think the girl is dead.' Sure enough, when we broke open the door, we found her dangling from my belt. She had hung herself. It was a nightmare!

"When I got over the initial shock, I went to a Nepali astrologer to find out why this girl would want to die. To my surprise and consternation, he told me that *I* was actually the target. The spirits were reportedly angry with me because I had not consecrated an altar room. 'They tried to kill you,' the astrologer told me, 'but for some reason they could not succeed, and their curse fell upon this girl.

That's why she went mad.' When I heard this I was petrified, and immediately took steps to establish an altar in our home."

But God was not ready to give up on Choeden. Unknown to her, she was caught up in a fierce spiritual tug-of-war. On one side, the forces of darkness were striving to take her peace of mind—and, if possible, her very life. On the other side, an army of intercessors was travailing before God for divine protection and second chances. Thankfully, the forces of grace were beginning to prevail.

"When Sylvia came to say she had a message from God," Choeden continued, "I must admit to being very put off. I heard her warning but gave her a rather hard time about it. But I responded like this because I was very guilty, you see. After all, here was one of my own converts coming back to exhort me! Unable to shake her warning from my mind, I finally said, 'Lord, if what Sylvia has spoken is true, please confirm it in a dream.'

"Well, what happened next is really quite amazing. That night as I dreamt, I saw an Indian lady dressed in a yellow sari walking toward me. When she reached me, she said, 'Where have you been all these years? I have been looking for you.' Then, before I could respond, she took me by the hand and led me across a bridge to a lovely cottage. Ushering me inside, she made sure I was settled, and then disappeared into a back room. At first I didn't mind being left alone. The drawing room had a window that faced a range of absolutely fantastic snow-capped mountains. It was impossible to take your eyes off them. The scene was complimented by a gorgeous river.

"But after taking my fill of the scenery, I remember wondering where this lady had disappeared to. Just as I was beginning to really worry, I heard her reciting various passages from the Psalms. It reminded me of a time long before when I had read the devotional book *Hinds' Feet on High Places*. As I meditated on this, I heard a voice saying to me, 'You are like the hind. I have longed to take you up to the heights with Me, but you have allowed your feet to become crippled.'

"When I awoke at three A.M., I knew instantly that the Lord had spoken to me. The sense of God's presence was almost overwhelming. The only thing I didn't know was where it would all lead.

"The answer, surprisingly, came a few days later when I was in Delhi, India, on job-related business. While I was there, I ran into the woman who had led me to Christ ten years earlier, a godly Indian lady named Jaymani. When I first saw her, I felt a chill go down my spine. Like the woman in my dream, she was dressed in a bright yellow sari! But before I could say anything further, Jaymani excused herself, leaving me in the company of her sister Bai, also a believer.

"Commenting that Jaymani had moved to Shillong [India] since we were last together, Bai handed me a photograph of her new home. As I stared at the picture, tears welled up in my eyes. I couldn't believe it. The cottage I had visited in my dream was identical to Jaymani's residence.

"When I told Bai I had seen this home in my dream, she seemed to understand. The back room where the yellow-clad woman had disappeared, she explained, was actually Jaymani's bedroom. This was significant, Bai said, because this was where Jaymani went to pray—and my photo was on her nightstand as a reminder. 'For the past ten years,' Bai told me, 'Jaymani has not ceased to pray that God would keep you from the evil one.'"[7]

For a moment Choeden grew quiet, the impact of her recollection stirring up barely concealed emotions. "When I returned from Delhi," she concluded, "I immediately got rid of the altar that had been set up in our home. Please inform Sylvia. She was so worried about me. Tell her that my prayer life has reawakened, along with a hunger for God's Word. I know the battle over me will continue and that the going will not be easy. But with people like Sylvia and Jaymani praying for me, I think I can make it!"*

Collective Possession and Cultural Exorcism

If our mandate as Christians calls us to perform deep rescues of enchanted individuals, it also requires us to deal with deception on a collective level. As I have pointed out, there are many areas in the world in which evil spirits are entertained warmly by the general populace. Unless and until these powers are repudiated by their host communities, they will remain firmly entrenched in the prevailing culture.

---

* The battle for Choeden's soul is not yet over. Pray that the Holy Spirit will give her grace to persevere in the face of formidable challenges.

Unfortunately, pacts between human societies and their spiritual protectors are rarely revoked. People are almost universally reluctant, whatever their education or outlook, to renounce events and systems they perceive as legitimate (if unflattering) elements of their own heritage.[8] In short, "The god of this age has blinded the minds of unbelievers, so that they cannot see the light of the gospel of the glory of Christ" (2 Corinthians 4:4).

The question is, What do we do about this blindness? Isaiah 61:4 talks about renewing cities that have been devastated for generations. Surely revival can be seen as a kind of "cultural exorcism," to use Harvey Cox's evocative term. But how do we get to that point? Are we justified in getting involved with what has come to be known as "strategic-level" spiritual warfare (addressing demonic influences over cities, cultures and nations)? Is it, as some writers have asked, our place?

For a surprising number of church leaders, the answer to this question is no. They contend that, with the exception of exorcising demonized individuals, the Church has no mandate to deal with evil spirits.

But this position presents some serious deficiencies. For example, it makes no accommodation for *location hauntings* (are we to simply live with such phenomena?) or *collective possession,* which Walter Wink has called "the most destructive and ubiquitous manifestations of the demonic in modern times."[9]

To better appreciate the nature and mechanics of collective possession, we must borrow a strange concept from the philosophy of science. The concept, known as an *entelechy,* is defined by Howard Bloom as "something complex that emerges when you put a large number of simple objects together."[10] Just as cities, towns, cultures, religions and mythologies are the results of entelechies, so, too, are collective spiritual strongholds. In the end, they are linked to, but ultimately greater than, the strongholds of deception that exist in individual minds.

As Gordon Rupp reminds us, where whole communities have entered into collective pacts with the spirit world, "there are forces at work . . . which represent [these] human solidarities." These forces are the ever-dangerous powers, principalities and world rulers that the apostle Paul takes pains to identify in his epistle to the Ephesians. The spiritual dynamics are no longer individualized. Collective action has forced the issue to a higher level. Deliverance strategies must now take into consideration a wide range of sociopolitical expressions, each of which may be linked (sometimes quite explicitly) to demonic shadow rulers. To ignore these rulers or the actions that attract them (as many do) is bad theology. As Rupp has observed, "If the Christian gospel were only concerned with the moral problems of individual men and women it would be defective indeed."[11]

In light of these arguments, the continued opposition to strategic-level spiritual warfare, particularly in academic circles, is disturbing. As Dr. Paul Thigpen noted in chapter 2:

> We . . . tend to deny the things we haven't experienced—and this lack of experience, though we think it qualifies us to make generalizations, really only reflects ignorance. In the end, we tend to measure life's possibilities by our own limited experience.[12]

In recent years, several scientific discoveries have helped us to better understand this behavior. We now know, for example, that when the human mind is presented with information that contradicts prevailing beliefs, it prefers to reject the new data rather than modify its paradigm. We call this a closed mind. And the only way to avoid this trap is to cultivate a mindset that is constantly exploring, that welcomes new facts and ideas as the best means of refining our picture of reality. When famous trial attorney Gerry Spence wrote that he would "rather have a mind opened by wonder than one closed by belief,"[13] he was acknowledging a vital truth often overlooked: *Once judgment occurs, learning ceases.*

Several scholars, set in their beliefs and convinced they have nothing more to learn about spiritual warfare, have recently taken it upon themselves to "correct" the emerging emphases on territorial spirits and strategic-level spiritual warfare. Bolstered by long lists of supportive (or inconclusive) commentaries, they have suggested that:

1. The prophet's prayers in Daniel 10 cannot be construed as strategic-level intercession against territorial forces because he is apparently unaware of the cosmic battle going on around him;

2. Paul's list of powers and principalities is directed toward individuals and has no strategic implications.[14]

If these assertions seem forced, it is because their champions have committed themselves to the difficult task of fitting supernatural evidence into an essentially rationalist paradigm. Even if Daniel were unaware of all that his intercession had triggered in the heavenlies, this would not alter the fact that he was a direct participant in a strategic-level spiritual conflict. (The assertion that the Prince of Persia is not a supernatural being lacks credibility. Could a mere mortal have resisted the angel of God for three weeks?)

Ephesians 6 (which we have already discussed at some length) describes demonic powers associated with the fallen realm of nature and with human political, economic and religious systems. How do we "wrestle" with such beings without engaging in some kind of strategic-level spiritual warfare?

Reckless Claims and Baseless Expectations

If the critics' blanket opposition to territorial spirits and strategic-level intercession is off the mark, the same cannot be said of other charges leveled against the modern spiritual warfare movement. For better or for worse, the ranks of Christian warriors have grown exponentially in recent years; and as one might expect with this rate of growth, the movement has exhibited its share of immaturity.[15]

In an article questioning the efficacy of some of today's more popular claims and practices, Dr. Barry Chant, president of Tabor College in Sydney, Australia, offers a humorous (and pointed) personal analogy:

> Years ago, as a university student, I was involved in national service training in the army. When it came to weapon training, we were not even allowed to use blanks, for fear of igniting a fire in the tinder-dry ranges of South Australia in mid-summer.
>
> Our platoon had to defend a hill from attack from the "enemy". We were to call out whenever we would normally have fired our weapons. I was in the mortar unit. So we sat on our rocky hill, four young students, repeatedly shouting at the tops of our voices, "Boom! Mortar!"

Below us were others crying, "Bang! Anti-tank gun!" or, "Bang! Rifle!" or, "Rat-atat-tat! Machine gun!" As the shadows lengthened, and our throats became parched, there was a momentary pause, and a solitary voice echoed out over the trees, through the still evening air—"Swish! Bow and arrow!"

It is hard to escape the impression that some of the spiritual warfare methodology being pursued today may be equally ineffective. There is a great deal of noise and bluster, but how much are we really achieving?[16]

What is prompting such questions? Consider the high-profile spiritual warfare rally that took place in San Francisco on Halloween night 1990. Vowing to "reverse the curse" of perversion in that city, thousands of well-intentioned Christian prayer warriors gathered in the Civic Center Auditorium (Brooks Hall) to raise a holy ruckus. Stomping their feet and chanting the name of Jesus like a mantra, the perspiration-soaked crowd commanded the prevailing powers of darkness to beat a hasty exit.

Outside, thousands of homosexuals, many costumed in what reporter Miranda Ewell called "the rags of their passion," mocked the initiative openly. Pink Jesus strutted up and down the sidewalk, clad only in delicate pink high heels and a loincloth made of stars and stripes. With a pouting lower lip and suggestive wiggle of his hips, he threw his arms around Scarlet Harlot in her tinsel wig. Others, like Max Varazslo, a local bisexual dressed as the devil, raged against the "racist, sexist, anti-gay, born-again bigots" who happened to walk by. Unfazed by it all, one prayer warrior from nearby Santa Rosa retorted with conviction, "The evil powers will be broken in San Francisco tonight!"[17]

The sentiment is laudable but the claim worthy of investigation. How, we may ask, does it stand up to the scrutiny of history? *Were* the evil powers in fact broken in San Francisco that night in October 1990? Does any objective evidence suggest that the Brooks Hall rally diminished Satan's influence in that notoriously promiscuous community?

Unfortunately, the facts paint a dismal picture. Not only has the city's militant gay community continued to leave its mark on national social politics (in 1996, the ten-member city council voted unanimously to recognize homosexual marriages), but with an estimated half-million participants, its annual Gay Pride Parade has mushroomed into the second-largest gathering in California.[18] San Francisco has also become a leading center of pornography, New Age teaching and witchcraft. (Scores of covens dot the surrounding hills.) Church growth statistics, not surprisingly, are among the weakest of any metropolitan area in the United States.

If the evil powers at work in San Francisco had been broken or banished that night in 1990, are we not justified in asking why there is no supporting evidence? To answer that the breakthrough has simply not yet been made manifest is either misguided or disingenuous. Phantom liberation is meaningless to those who remain captive to sin and death.

Despite a lack of measurable results, however, this kind of spiritual warfare methodology has become increasingly fashionable. Nearly every day, well-meaning Christians are either "claiming" spiritually oppressed cities and nations for God, or else "commanding" demonic forces to evacuate them. While there is no doubt this exercise feels good, there are two critical questions: Does it work? And is it biblical?

One obvious problem with these actions is that they are often taken in disregard of the wishes or actions of local inhabitants. At the same time visiting Christians were driving demons out of San Francisco, thousands of native residents were welcoming them with open arms. Asking God to banish demonic powers from an entire community is to suggest that He set aside the logical consequences of a people's misplaced choices. It is to assume that our role as "King's kids" gives us the authority to nullify residents' free will or the devil's ability to respond to explicit human overtures. The implications of this prospect, if true, would require drastic adjustments to our evangelistic theology and strategy. In reality, I have yet to come across a single case study in which this approach has been applied successfully.

It is simply not realistic to expect that we can facilitate the wholesale elimination of demonic powers prior to the Second Coming. As Tom White and others have pointed out, supernatural evil will continue to infiltrate our communities for as long as ungodly men and institutions make independent and self-serving choices.[19] While acknowledging Christ's ultimate victory, the New Testament reminds us that "at present we do not see everything subject to him" (Hebrews 2:8).

So where does this leave us? If strategic-level spiritual warfare does not permit us to claim converts, territory or communities, if it offers no authority to drive out culturally entrenched demons, what exactly does it accomplish? To discover the answer to this question—the final stop on our journey through the twilight labyrinth—is to make the exciting passage from imaginary to real spiritual warfare. And the good news is, our prayers really can play a role in transforming communities.

Toto and the Wizard's Curtain

When L. Frank Baum's *Wonderful Wizard of Oz* hit the big screen in 1939, it quickly became a cinema classic. In the colorful storyline, a Kansas farm girl is blown by a tornado into the land of Oz, where she is befriended by a scarecrow, a tin woodsman and a cowardly lion. Together the motley crew journeys to the Emerald City for an audience with the celebrated wizard of the realm.

In one of the film's most memorable scenes, Dorothy and her nervous friends are ushered into the vaulted sanctuary of the great and powerful Oz. As the doors close behind them, hidden altar vents belch menacing fireballs and strange puffs of orange smoke. Moments later the wizard himself appears—a disembodied holographic head whose booming voice rattles their nerves.

As the audience proceeds, Dorothy's little dog, Toto, slips from between his mistress' trembling knees to explore the shadowed corners of the sanctuary. On discovering a small, curtained booth in the back, the feisty canine sinks his teeth into the fabric and begins to tug. As the drapery finally yields, the visitors are startled to see the wizard's chief aide pulling levers furiously and speaking into an amplified microphone. And when the great Oz thunders, "Pay no attention to that man behind the curtain!", it is he who is ignored. The charade has come to an abrupt and revealing end.

As spiritual warriors, we, too, are confronted with a wizard intent on retaining his cover. Our roles, like the tenacious Toto, must be to draw back the curtain of deception that shields Satan from mortal view. For unless and until men and women can actually see the puppetmaster behind the scenes, their faith in his magic will remain undiminished.

The apostle Paul makes it clear that our spiritual weapons have "divine power to demolish [or pull down] strongholds" (2 Corinthians 10:4). It is obvious from the context of this passage that these strongholds are not demons or geographical locations* but psychic habitats. It is from these platforms, or "head nests" (as we noted in chapter 6), that Satan and his cohorts endeavor to manipulate our inner world.

In response to such deceptive efforts, we are called to "demolish [or cast down] arguments" (verse 5).[20] The word *arguments*, often translated *imaginations*, is an interesting one. Taken from the Greek word *logismos*, it is defined more precisely as "calculative reasonings over time" (as opposed to random, occasional thoughts). This definition, according to Colorado Springs pastor Dutch Sheets, makes these arguments or imaginations look more like what they almost certainly are—religious or philosophical systems.

While I have no quibble with those who contend that mental strongholds are best attacked by truth, our challenge is to gain access to the minds of enchanted people. As Paul reminds us, the Gospel is veiled to those whose minds have been blinded by the god of this age (see 2 Corinthians 4:3–4). How, then, do we "open their eyes and turn them from darkness to light, and from the power of Satan to God" (Acts 26:18)?

A potential solution to this challenge is found in another of Paul's epistles. After admonishing the church at Colosse to "devote [themselves] to prayer," the apostle goes on to add a personal request. "Pray for us, too," he pleads, "that God may *open a door for our message,* so that we may proclaim the mystery of Christ" (Colossians 4:2–3, emphasis added).

In asking intercessors to petition God for an open door, Paul is acknowledging three important truths:

* Places can be viewed as strongholds if and when they become focal points for deceptive memes (see chapter 6) or practices. Many cities fill this bill, as do various worship and pilgrimage sites—in short, any location where spiritual and cultural realities converge.

1. Unsaved people are bound in a prison of deception.
2. God must breach this stronghold if the Gospel is to enter.
3. Prayer is an important means of persuading God to do this.

If we want to practice effective spellbending—liberating enchanted minds so they can understand and respond to the Gospel—we must first neutralize the blinding influence of demonic strongmen. Jesus talks about this process in Mark 3:27: "No one can enter a strong man's house [the human mind] and carry off his possessions unless he first ties up the strong man. *Then* he can rob his house"(emphasis added).[21]

We are not asking God to "make" people Christians or to expel demonic powers that have become objects of worship. Such requests violate human free will and God will not honor them. What we *are* appealing for is a level playing field, a temporary lifting of the spiritual blindness that prevents men and women from processing truth (the Gospel) at heart level.[22]

Since our own strength is insufficient to bind higher-dimensional beings, we must rely on the resources of the Holy Spirit. While it is true that we have been given power and authority in Christ (see Luke 10:19), this authority is not for us to use at our own initiative or discretion. It is ambassadorial authority, which means it is to be exercised only at the bidding of the Sovereign (see 2 Corinthians 5:20).[23] As servants we must allow submission to reign over presumption.

The focus of warfare prayer is also important. Canadian pastor John Hutchinson, searching for a biblical model of this kind of intercession, catalogued 850 verses in the Psalms that deal directly with the enemy and warfare.[24] After analyzing these passages, Hutchinson concluded that while the psalmist is often surrounded by enemies and talks a lot about them, his words are almost always directed to God. On only nine occasions (about one percent of the time) does he speak to the enemy directly.[25]

Strategic-level spiritual warfare, as with all prevailing or breakthrough prayer, can demand prodigious amounts of time and energy. We are asking God, after all, to temporarily suspend the logical consequences (spiritual enchantment) of people's misplaced choices—an action that requires that He interpose Himself between deceived individuals and their spiritual masters. Given the nature of this undertaking, our prayers should be no less fervent or importunate than those offered by Hindu pilgrims, native shamans or Islamic fundamentalists.[26]

Once God does authorize us to act—be it to bind the influence of territorial spirits or prophesy the demise (or restoration) of social or political entities—we can expect great things. The prophet Jeremiah, describing his call to ministry, declared:

> Then the Lord . . . said to me, "Now, I have put *my words* in your mouth. See, today I appoint you over nations and kingdoms to uproot and tear down, to destroy and overthrow, to build and to plant."
> Jeremiah 1:9–10 (emphasis added)

While there is no guarantee that people will respond to the Gospel even if the strongman's enchantment is lifted (see Proverbs 1:22–33; 26:11), chances are good that many will. History has shown that these windows of opportunity—or "open doors"—are fruitful times to launch evangelistic search-and-rescue missions. Why? Because when people's hearts and minds are unfettered, truth has a chance to take root. When God makes His light shine in people's hearts, it enables them to see, often for the very first time, "the knowledge of the glory of God in the face of Christ" (2 Corinthians 4:6). It is Dante's light of creation, the brilliant ignition of God, against the satanic negation, the candle-snuffer.[27] It is the great thaw of Lewis' captive stone figures.

Drying Up the Fishing Hole

The fact that a man comes out of a drunken stupor does not mean he has been delivered from alcoholism. While outside intercession can temporarily lift the enchantment from the minds of spiritual captives, people must then repent of their sins if their freedom is to become permanent. This is true of both individuals and entire communities.

Predictably, the devil is not keen about losing access to rich "fishing holes," especially if he has caught souls there for many seasons. If there is any way to retain his interests, he will find it. For this reason it is important for liberated communities to consolidate whatever gains they may have achieved initially through prayer. In practical terms, this often means paving over the fishing hole through corporate repentance. By publicly renouncing their ties to false gods and philosophies, former captives can make it exceedingly undesirable for the enemy to remain in their communities.

An example of this occurred in January 1997 when the Ubakala Clan (Umuofai Kindred) of southern Nigeria walked away from three hundred years of idolatry. The breakthrough came after twelve months of spiritual mapping and strategic-level intercession, and saw the conversion of 61 adults, including several long-time witch doctors. Led by brothers Emeka and Chinedu Nwankpa, families living near Mgbarrakuma village then entered a season of corporate repentance (see Zechariah 12:10–13:2). After publicly renouncing the covenants their ancestors had made with the powers of darkness, the entire community proceeded to eight village shrines, where they watched the newly converted witch doctors renounce their allegiance to the ancestral spirits.

One of these animist priests, an elder named Odogwu Ogu, stood before the shrine of a particular spirit called Amadi and proclaimed:

> "Listen, Amadi, the people who own the land have arrived to tell you that they have just made a new covenant with the God of heaven. Therefore all the previous covenants you have made with our ancient fathers are now void. I have also given my life to Jesus Christ, and so it is time for you to return to wherever you came from."

Next the people brought ritual objects—including idols, totems and witchcraft poisons—for public burning. Many of these items had been handed down over ten generations. Emeka Nwankpa recalls that when it was over, "you could feel the atmosphere in the community change." Having renounced their old covenants, the clan made a collective decision that nobody would ever return to animism. Today, says Emeka, "everybody goes to church. There is also a formal Bible study going on, and the women have a prayer team which my mother conducts. Others gather to pray after completing their communal sweeping."[28]

Two other measures with proven ability to disrupt demonic strongholds are *event counterwarfare* (intercession during religious festivals) and *pilgrimages of repentance* (humble visitations of past injustices). These stratagems can be, and often are, employed by groups of local believers and outside intercessors.

Event Counterwarfare

The days surrounding religious festivals, pilgrimages and ceremonials are often charged with spiritual intensity. A primary reason for this (as we noted in chapter 8) is that powerful demonic entities are near and attentive. At the same time, however, these seasons are fragile. From the enemy's perspective, there is always a risk, however small, that people will use these occasions to deny him continued access to the community.

As concerned and knowledgeable intercessors, we want to exploit this very possibility. By rolling up our prayer sleeves during these important events, we aim to bring about conditions that will cause men and women to reconsider the pacts that have enslaved them. As Clinton Arnold reminds us, "A tradition ceases to be a tradition when people no longer pass it on."[29]

To assist intercessors in this task, my own ministry, The Sentinel Group, distributes monthly spiritual counterwarfare calendars that provide details sixty days in advance of spiritually significant events.[30] Offering an illustration of how this kind of prayer can deplete the enemy's fishing hole, Guatemalan teacher-evangelist Francisco Galli recently reported a breakdown of idolatrous pilgrimages in and around Guatemala City. This occurred when a group of concerned women with United for Prayer, an intercessory prayer consortium, posted themselves along pilgrimage routes fifteen days before the city's Holy Week processions in 1995.

According to Galli, when one of the more famous (and syncretistic) processions was pulling out of its staging area at Calvary Church, many of the people carrying the images fell down and actually broke their arms and legs. Then, when the woman in charge of the procession bent over to retrieve a fallen idol, she immediately suffered a heart attack. Equally dramatic developments were unfolding at the same time at other staging areas. In one episode, reminiscent of the scene recorded in the Philistine temple of Dagon, an idol toppled over of its own accord and was decapitated. At another location, the central idol spontaneously caught fire. In a neighboring town, the processional images were left in their crypts because the celebrants were afraid to carry them.[31]

As a consequence of these events, a number of Guatemalans have begun to question their long association with traditional gods. New evangelical congregations have been springing up from the capital to the highlands—a distressing development for demonic powers that have trolled these fishing grounds for millennia.

Pilgrimages of Repentance

Another powerful stratagem involves solemn assemblies (part of an older tradition in which believers gather in public expressions of humility and repentance) and pilgrimages of repentance (newer, reconciliation-oriented journeys to sites or victims of past injustices). Both have been employed by the identificational repentance movement.

By responding to sociocultural hostility in the opposite spirit—that is, humility—Christians in many parts of the world are slowly draining some of the enemy's best fishing holes. In August 1992, five hundred years after taking part in the bloody Spanish conquest of Central America, Guatemala's Roman Catholic Church asked the pardon of the country's indigenous people. In a publicly released pastoral letter repenting of past contradictions and injustice, the nation's bishops declared, "We, the current pastors of the church, ask for forgiveness."[32]

In an equally dramatic gesture, the U.S. Southern Baptist Convention expressed contrition in June 1995 over its past association with slavery and racism. In a public resolution supported by nearly fifteen thousand voting clergy, the denomination apologized "to all African Americans for condoning and/or perpetuating individual and systemic racism in our lifetime." A year earlier, the Evangelical Lutheran Church in America expressed remorse over the fact that its founder, Martin Luther, had engaged in anti-Jewish diatribes.[33]

Other believers are revisiting past injustices on pilgrimages of repentance. These include efforts such as the Trail of Tears Project (addressing the unjust relocation of the Cherokee Nation), the Slave Routes Project (involving activities in at least twelve African countries) and programs addressing the Balkan conflict, the Spanish

Inquisition and General William Sherman's devastating march through the American South.

In one of the most ambitious projects of all, Western Christians have embarked on an effort to retrace the routes of the Crusades. Dubbed the "Reconciliation Walk," the effort has elicited an extraordinarily positive response from Muslim leaders from England to the Middle East. Offering to write two hundred letters of support to mosques along the route, one Islamic cleric declared, "Whoever came up with this idea had a revelation—it could be revolutionary!"

While theories about spiritual warfare have proliferated like rabbits in recent years, many of these notions have failed to live up to their promises. In the real world they simply have not worked. For this reason, many Christians have become discouraged or cynical, insisting that spiritual warfare is an unbiblical pipe dream.

This is unfortunate. And while I can appreciate the frustration of these individuals, their withdrawal from the battle is not the right solution. There are lights in the labyrinth—and I hope the testimonies presented in the final chapter of this book will play a role in encouraging them back to the front lines.

Chapter Eleven

Lights in the Labyrinth

en chapters ago we looked at compelling evidence that our present workaday world is linked to a permeable shadow realm—a higher but kindred dimension whose entry points, according to writers like C. S. Lewis, are traversed routinely by human traffic.

As our investigation progressed, we learned that the decisions and actions taken in either one of these domains can, and often does, affect the other significantly. More importantly we discovered that, although we are mortals, it is possible for us to understand, and even navigate, the world next door. Having once acclimated ourselves to its unique language and order, we are in a position to do serious damage to the enemy's spiritual commerce.

A good thing, too. For a great battle is being waged—a conflict whose banners and implications have invaded the borders of at least two dimensions. From the secret places of the human heart, a complex tangle of front lines extend out through thousands of earthly cultures and communities, only to reconnect in the vast arenas, corridors and interstices of the spiritual dimension. It is here, in a place I have labeled "the twilight labyrinth," that the children of light and the forces of darkness share a common terrain. It is here that the godly in Christ are called to battle.[1]

The object of this battle, which we examined in the last chapter, is to liberate men and women from the debilitating effects of unresolved sin and demonic enchantment. On some days the results are encouraging: Prayers are answered, eyes opened, hearts turned back to God. At other times the enemy roars his defiance and the battle ebbs.

The best news comes when we look down on the battle from the lofty heights of history. From this perspective the inevitability of our victory becomes obvious. While the enemy has not yet capitulated, his grip on the remaining unreached peoples of the world is clearly weakening. Intercessory spellbending has begun to take its toll.

Many of these gains, according to recent reports, are being registered on a collective or community scale. Entire towns and neighborhoods are emerging from the thick fog of spiritual enchantment—often in dramatic fashion. Better yet, a high percentage of these initial breakthroughs are leading to collective repentance and community transformation.

Because claims of dramatic breakthroughs and transformed communities are frequently exaggerated, some ministry leaders have expressed skepticism. Others dispute the notion that spiritual warfare can have a collective impact at all. While I disagree occasionally with the theology and public attitudes of these critics, I champion their right to ask for evidence. My only request is that they remain honest seekers, willing to adjust their paradigm if and when credible evidence is presented.[2] For as the following four accounts suggest, this evidence is mounting with each passing day.

Musoke's Armies: At War in the Beirut of Kampala

In the early 1980s, before Uganda's war-weary citizens had an opportunity to recover from the nightmare of Idi Amin Dada, the nation was once again plunged into chaos. This time the conflict was between the Ugandan Army, led by Milton Obote (Amin's successor), and the National Resistance Army, led by Lieutenant General Yoweri Musevani, who in January 1986 became president of Uganda. During these civil war years, an estimated one million people were killed.[3]

For more than five years, poorly trained soldiers became a law unto themselves. Raping and killing as they pleased, they received hardly a reprimand from their military masters. Eventually the emboldened soldiers began to assault Christians openly in the streets of Kampala.

The activity in one district, a burned-out ghost town nicknamed the "Beirut of Kampala," was particularly vicious. A one-time shooting gallery for the military, the remaining husks of the community had fallen under the control of a small band of mentally unstable thieves and killers. The local kingpin was a notorious witch by the name of Musoke.

Normally this ransacked neighborhood would hardly be considered a promising location for church-planting, but Ugandan evangelist Robert Kayanja rarely thinks in normal terms. At the tender age of 22, this young firebrand followed the call of God into an urban zone that had been forsaken by all but the devil and his allies.

"When the Holy Spirit drew me to the area in 1983," Robert explained in a recent interview, "I was alone. Then Charles Lsubuga, who is now my associate pastor, joined me. Eventually we became four, and then five. Every day we covered the entire area with prayer, petitioning the Holy Spirit for a spiritual breakthrough."

Results came grudgingly. Musoke, who wanted nothing to do with God, became incensed when he learned that these Christian intruders were not only praying for his customers but burning the witchcraft charms he had given them. Barging into one of Robert's evening meetings, held in an abandoned house, he screamed, "You are not supposed to be here! This territory belongs to me. If you don't leave, I'll send my armies to evict you. Then you will die!"

"When the people in neighborhood heard these threats," Robert remembers, "they warned us to get out. Musoke's power was very real and they knew it. Everyone counseled us not to get into a confrontation."

A few days later, Robert and his fellow parishioners encountered the first of Musoke's "armies." Approaching the house for a late afternoon service, they found every door and window covered by a massive swarm of bees.

"There were thousands of them," Robert recalls. "It was like a bee factory. We couldn't get in. Everybody in the neighborhood said it was Musoke's doing. And once again they advised us just to collect our property and get out. The problem was, God was the One who had called us here, and we did not feel comfortable leaving on the basis of fear or threats. Our only alternative, however, was to cry out to God—and this is precisely what we did. It took about eight hours, but the bees finally moved away from the house."

The battle was just heating up. The very next morning the church property was enveloped by the pungent odor of burning meat.

"The smell was so strong," Robert recalls, "it gagged you. There was no getting away from it. Many of the local people told us it was a demon. We did not doubt it, because we could see Musoke staring at us from about 25 yards away.

"The next assault came on a Sunday morning—I think it was November 11 [1983]. A swarm of flies just came from nowhere. It was what you might expect if one hundred dead bodies had been rotting for a week. The flies were everywhere. You had to cover your nose and mouth so they didn't get in. For the third time, the people said to us, 'You'd better get out of here. This man is going to kill you.'

"In fact, it was this very Sunday that Musoke came to deliver an ultimatum. He said, 'I will give you three days. If you have not left by then, my snakes will come and you will die.' About twenty of us were in the midst of a worship time when he walked in to pronounce this death threat.

"People were very frightened. They had never seen anything like this before. My associate, Charles Lsubuga, said, 'This is too much.' Shortly after this, Charles was struck with a partial paralysis. It was so severe that he was unable to walk without the aid of two sticks. Since there was no accompanying fever, and the condition descended on him suddenly, we naturally suspected Musoke's witchcraft.

"To make matters worse, Obote's soldiers came looking for me. As I was not at the house on this particular night, they began to hit Charles in the back. This only compounded his physical problems. Before they left, the soldiers looted everything—our cups, saucepans, utensils. This caused many of the people who had been coming to our fellowship to run away.

"To combat the spiritual forces that were coming against us, we established a 'Wailing Wall' outside the church. We circled our property and prayed every evening for about six hours. When the soldiers came again, they found us praying. Herding us all behind the house, they placed guns to our heads and asked, 'Where is Robert Kayanja?' When I stepped forward and said, 'I am the one,' the soldiers responded, 'No, you are just a schoolboy.' God had confused their minds, you see.

"The next day we took Charles to Mulago National Hospital because he couldn't walk and was in terrible pain. He stayed there for six months. After performing a series of tests, however, the doctors could not understand the nature of his illness. Even so, they predicted that Charles would never walk again. It was very discouraging.

"When my father and mother heard about Charles and the raid on our church, they joined the chorus of voices urging me to leave. 'God wants to save these people,' they said, 'but He doesn't want you to die in the process. It's too dangerous.' While I understood their concern, it was as if the Holy Spirit had glued me to this deadly place that the devil called his territory.

"At this point there were only four of us left in the house. Charles was in the hospital, and my other associate, Godfrey, had gone to pastor a church about two hundred miles away. Still, we continued our campaign to bind the powers of darkness. One Rwandan lady came faithfully every day for nine months. She couldn't understand our language but she wanted to pray. When the Holy Spirit came on her, the tears just rolled down her cheeks.

"A month later, Musoke gave me a second ultimatum. This time I was given seven days to live. Almost immediately my body started to produce a heat that was incomprehensible. It was like my blood began to boil. The church members kept me alive by soaking a towel in a basin of water and laying it on top of me. But my temperature was so high that the towel would be completely dry in five minutes. As with Charles before me, the doctors were baffled. They could not find any disease in my blood.

"At that time an old neighbor lady came to see me. She was an alcohol vendor and we used to borrow her cups to drink tea. The purpose of her visit was to tell me that Musoke had dispatched his strongest demon against me—a *mayembe*. She added that this demon comes like an ill wind, and that if I did not have God on my side, I would already have died.

"Other people were convinced I was going to die within 24 hours. Even I was praying earnestly because I could no longer eat or drink. It was a real battle.

"A little while later I began to see snakes coming up through the concrete floor. As they entered the room, some were transformed into recognizable creatures—lions and leopards, for example—while others became monstrous and horrifying entities. One creature had multiple eyes encircling its head. Whenever it opened its mouth, something resembling miniature transport aircraft emerged. It was quite amazing. Other entities had skeletal features, fish-like scales or twisted, scarred faces.

"The behavior of these demonic creatures varied. One group of evil-looking skeletons danced and screamed at me, while various animal apparitions sat boldly on the edge of my bed. Other entities moved constantly about the room. While some have suggested this may all have been delirium brought on by my high fever, this explanation fails to account for the fact that others in the house also saw these creatures, often reacting to them with loud exclamations. No, these manifestations were all too real. The fear was so strong you could touch it.

"In the midst of this struggle, which lasted for two days, I was taken up to heaven in a dream. There I was handed a sword, which I used to fight the demons that were assaulting my mind, body and spirit.

"At one point the battle became so intense that the people around me thought I was losing my mind. A few minutes later, however, I suddenly regained full health and consciousness. At this very moment—it was one o'clock on a Sunday afternoon—the few remaining shopkeepers in the Kabusu trading center heard a loud noise. When they came running outside to investigate, they found Musoke lying dead in the intersection of Kabusu and Masaka Roads. Although his head was still connected to his torso, his face and body were split down the middle—just as if he had been struck by a thundering sword."

Two weeks after Musoke's death in mid-December 1983, Charles was discharged from Mulago Hospital with a clean bill of health. Throughout the neighborhood, and especially in the bars where Musoke had gone to drink, people were stunned that the master's witchcraft had been defeated so completely.

"After this blockage was removed," Robert recalls, "people began flocking to the church. It was like the heavens just opened. The living room filled quickly, and then the second room. Soon we were forced outside, and eventually into a temporary shelter. Within three months of Musoke's death, our fellowship had grown to about a thousand people.[4]

"By the mid-1990s, the Miracle Center, our main church, was hosting about seven thousand on Sunday morning. And the numbers continue to grow. Two hundred and thirty-six branch fellowships were planted in this same period, and at least six dead people have been raised to life."[5]

Mama Jane and the Prayer Cave

Another riveting example of godly spellbending was related to me by Kenyan pastor Thomas Muthee. In a series of interviews between August 1994 and February 1996, Thomas described how God used a handful of intercessors in a grocery store basement to bring revival to one of the most spiritually oppressed communities in East Africa. The resulting congregation, known as the Kiambu Prayer Cave, is now a model of healthy church growth.

The story began in 1988 when Thomas and his wife, Margaret, returned to Africa from post-graduate studies in Scotland. Back in their native Kenya, the couple settled in a banana-producing area called Karuri. From there Thomas launched out across Kenya as an itinerant preacher. In addition to holding crusades and teaching seminars, he also ministered in high schools and colleges.

In time the Muthees sensed God prompting them to start a church in the town of Kiambu, a notorious ministry graveyard located about fourteen kilometers (some nine miles) northwest of Nairobi. Despite years of effort, no church in this community of 65,000 had ever been able to grow beyond a hundred members. Their first step, the Muthees realized, was to ascertain why there was so much spiritual oppression in the area.

"We wanted to know what was wrong with Kiambu," Thomas explained. "We knew in our hearts that unless we could identify and deal with the underlying spiritual dynamics—the dominating spirit, if you will—we would not see things change." Accordingly, for a period of six months, the Muthees committed themselves to fervent prayer and diligent research. They continued until the community's primary symptoms, and an important root cause, were fully documented.

Despite its desirable aesthetics, including a ring of lush coffee and banana plantations, the town was in a death grip. "The newspapers were full of terrible stories about Kiambu," Thomas told me. "Even people in Nairobi were frightened by the high incidence of murder, rape and other forms of violence. Alcoholism was also prevalent, and the whole area was depressed economically. Nobody was investing in Kiambu, and the government had a very difficult time persuading people to transfer here. Most simply refused. There were so many murders in the town that people didn't dare go out after dark.

"When I told some pastors I was starting a church in Kiambu, they were shocked. They kept asking, 'How will you manage?' So many before us had come and then given up. One pastor from Gospel Outreach wanted to start a church here. It didn't work out. Then Bishop Gitanga, the man with the biggest church in Nairobi, also failed. Another attempt was made by Pastor Kuranga. He told me that when he came here, the oppression was so strong that he didn't even look for a home. Just surveying the place was enough to chase him away.

"When we arrived in Kiambu, we heard essentially the same thing. The first brother I met there told me, 'We preach, but people here don't get saved.' This was when my wife and I knew we needed some answers from the Lord.

"After several months of prayer and research, we discovered that many of the things going on in Kiambu were linked to a powerful woman named Mama Jane. As we sought the Lord for understanding, He revealed to us that Mama Jane was a witch. Although she tried to pretend she was a Christian, even going so far as to call her divination house 'Emmanuel Clinic,' her business was pure witchcraft.[6] And her business was not done in secret; it was widely known that she was visited by very senior people in both business and government. Mama Jane was feared; that was her power.

"What originally drew us to her were the accidents. In our research we had discovered that a disproportionate number of fatal automobile accidents were occurring on the dusty road in front of her clinic.[7] Not a month went by without somebody losing his life. In many of these cases, people were hit and killed but you did not see a drop of blood on the road. Naturally we wanted to know what was behind this phenomenon.

"When we began to recognize who—or *what*—Mama Jane really was, Margaret and I set ourselves to prayer. Our aim was to break the power of witchcraft over the town—a power that was preventing people from getting saved. It was a struggle that involved much groaning in our spirits. In time, however, we felt the burden lift. The dark cloud we had seen covering the town drifted away, and we felt supernatural joy inside. We knew things were going to change.

"In February 1989 we decided to start the church. My first crusade was held on a large dirt area near the petrol station. Since I'm only 5´5″ and I didn't have a pulpit, I borrowed a tire from the station. As I preached the Gospel that evening, eight people came to the Lord. One of these was a long-barren woman whose womb was miraculously opened by the Spirit of God. She showed me her baby the following year. On the second day of the crusade, fourteen people got saved.

"After this the church just took off. Throughout the next year, healings and conversions were a regular occurrence. Since the municipal hall would allow us to meet only twice a week, we decided to move our church into the basement of a nearby grocery store. Because of the darkness and the round-the-clock intercession that went on there, people began to refer to it as 'the prayer cave.'

"Not surprisingly, Mama Jane was deeply distressed over what was taking place. In fact, she began to come around our worship center at night to perform her witchcraft rituals. On Sunday mornings we would find ashes spread around with pieces of special cloth, animal horns and cock feathers. Our services became very oppressed. People would try to sing, but they just couldn't.

"Finally we decided we had had enough. The whole congregation raised its hands toward Emmanuel Clinic. We asked God to either save this woman or remove her from Kiambu.

"Do you know what happened? A few days later three children were killed outside her clinic. The people were furious because they suspected that Mama Jane's witchcraft was linked to the accident. Some were clamoring that she be stoned. When the police were called in to quell the uprising, they found a huge snake in one of the clinic rooms. Startled, the officers drew their weapons and shot it. After this Mama Jane moved to the town of Mathare, about two hours north of Nairobi. Interestingly enough, the same 'bloodless accidents' began happening there. Now rumor has it she has moved on to a place in Ngongo.

"Mama Jane has been gone about four years," Thomas told me in 1996. "We have not had a single accident during this time. In fact, since this woman moved out of Kiambu, the entire atmosphere has changed. Whereas people used to be afraid to go out at night, now we enjoy one of the lowest crime rates in the country. Rape and murder are virtually unheard of anymore. The economy has also started to grow. If you look at the town now, you will see new buildings coming up everywhere. Now that Kiambu has a good name, people from Nairobi are flocking to get houses here. The population is up by thirty percent.

"More importantly, there has been a dramatic increase in the number of conversions. Between ten and twenty-five people have been getting saved in our church every Sunday."

In February 1996 Pastor Thomas Muthee and his wife, Margaret, celebrated their seventh anniversary in Kiambu. Through research and spiritual warfare, they have seen the church grow to nearly four thousand people.

"There is no doubt," he declares, "that prayer broke the power of witchcraft over this city. Now our four hundred intercessors meet in the church 'power house' every morning at six A.M.; we call it our 'morning glory.' On Wednesdays from 4:30 to 6:30 P.M. we gather for 'Operation Prayer Storm,' while every Friday we hold an all-night prayer meeting. We also have a ministry in which, twice a month, the intercessors go into the bush about fifteen kilometers from here [a little more than nine miles] to pray. The town's pastors, formerly racked by disunity, are also getting together for regular fellowship and prayer. Everyone in the community now has a high respect for us. They know that God's power chased Mama Jane from town."[8]

The Colombian Chronicles

In today's complex global economy, few countries are associated with a single export. France may be an elite fount of fashion and fragrance, but it is also a purveyor of excellent wines and pastries. The neighboring Swiss have become a prefix not only for fine watches, but also for cheese and chocolates (to say nothing of numbered bank accounts). Even America is distinguished as much for its movies and music as for its aircraft and computers.

Besides the oil-rich kingdoms of Saudi Arabia and Kuwait, only the nation of Colombia is globally recognized by a single export. It is a reputation the country would dearly love to shake.

For years Colombia has been the world's biggest exporter of cocaine, sending between seven hundred and a thousand tons a year to the United States and Europe alone.[9] The Cali cartel, which controls up to seventy percent of this trade, has been called the largest, richest and best-organized criminal organization in history.[10] Employing a combination of bribery and threats, it wields a malignant power that has corrupted individuals and institutions alike.[11]

The good news is, the story does not end here. Recent reports provide fresh evidence that this seemingly invincible empire may finally have met its match.

Among the ranks of the encouraged are Randy and Marci MacMillan, veteran missionaries with Mission South America and the Communidad Cristiana de Fe who have worked under the shadow of the Cali drug lords for more than twenty years. Their joy over recent developments is irrepressible. The details, relayed to me through a series of late 1996 interviews,[12] are every bit as dramatic as those associated with the earlier transformations of Kampala and Kiambu.

"In May 1995," Randy explained, "the pastors association of Cali[13] hosted an all-night prayer vigil, or *vigilia,* at the Coliseo el Pueblo." This civic auditorium seats about 27,000 people and is often used for international events. "The initial hope was that we would fill up the bottom section of the auditorium. By early evening, however, the facility was so full that the police and Red Cross refused to let any more people in! It was quite amazing. This was the first time thirty thousand Christians from all denominations had come together in Cali for anything, let alone an all-night prayer meeting.

"The primary purpose of the *vigilia,*" continued Randy, "was to take a stand against the cartels and their unseen spiritual masters. Both had been ruling our city and nation for too long. After humbling ourselves before God and one another, we symbolically extended Christ's scepter of authority over Cali—including over its bondage to cocaine, violence and corruption."[14]

Results were quick in coming. Forty-eight hours after the all-night *vigilia,* the local daily, *El Pais,* reported that Cali had gone an entire day without a murder—a newsworthy occurrence in a city averaging multiple homicides a day! Corruption also took a major hit when, over the next four months, nine hundred cartel-linked officers were fired from the metropolitan police force.[15]

"When we saw these things happening," Randy told me, "we had a strong sense that the powers of darkness were headed for a significant defeat."

In the month of June, this sense of anticipation was heightened when several intercessors reported dreams in which angelic forces apprehended leaders of the Cali drug cartel. Many interpreted this as a prophetic sign that the Holy Spirit was about to respond to the most urgent aspect of the Church's united appeal.

"Within six weeks of this vision," MacMillan recalls, "the Colombian government declared all-out war against the drug lords." Sweeping military operations were launched against cartel assets in the cities of Cali and Medellín, various jungle processing centers and key transshipment points such as San Andrés Island. The 6,500 soldiers dispatched to Cali, many of whom were members of a combined special forces group known as Commando Especial Conjunto,[16] arrived with explicit orders to round up seven individuals suspected as the top leaders of the cartel.

"Cali was buzzing with helicopters," Randy remembers. "There were police roadblocks at every entry point into the city. You couldn't go anywhere without proving who you were."[17]

Among the first to be picked up in the dragnet of the *federales* was Jorge Eliecer Rodriguez. A notorious *pachanguero* (party animal) and *oveja negra* (black sheep), Rodriguez was arrested at the fortune-telling parlor of Madame Marlene Ballesteros, the famous "Pythoness of Cali."[18] By August, only three months after God's word to the intercessors, Colombian authorities had captured all seven targeted cartel leaders—Juan Carlos Armínez, Phanor Arizabalata, Julian Murcillo, Henry Loaiza, Jose Santacruz Londono and founders Gilberto and Miguel Rodriguez.

Emboldened by this early success, Cali's Christian community decided to hold a second all-night prayer rally that same month. Since the civic auditorium was too small to accommodate everyone, the organizers stepped out in faith and rented the 60,000-seat Pascual Guerrero soccer stadium. Once again demand exceeded supply. By nine P.M. intercessors were being turned away at the gate.[19]

In the months following this pivotal event, Randy worked with local pastors to map out specific political, social and spiritual strongholds in each of Cali's 22 administrative sections. The compiled results gave the Body of Christ an unprecedented picture of the powers working in the city.

"With this knowledge," Randy explained, "our unified intercession became truly focused. Praying in specific terms, we began to see a dramatic loosening of the enemy's stranglehold on our community and nation.

"In March 1996 we used our spiritual mapping intelligence to direct large prayer caravans throughout Cali. While most of the 250 cars established a prayer perimeter around the city, others paraded by government offices or the mansions of prominent cartel leaders. My own church focused on the headquarters of the billionaire drug lord, José Santacruz Londono, who had escaped from Bogota's La Picota prison in January.[20] His hacienda, located four blocks from my home, looks like the high-tech hilltop estate portrayed in the movie *Clear and Present Danger.* The day after we finished praying, we heard that Santacruz had been killed in a gunfight with national police on the streets of Medellín."[21]

About the same time, a national political shakedown launched by Colombian attorney general Alfonso Valdivieso was beginning to rattle the highest levels of government.[22] The sweeping investigation had already linked several of President Ernesto Samper's close associates—including Liberal Party campaign treasurer Santiago Medina and campaign manager Fernando Botero Zea—to drug money. Since their incarceration in the summer of 1995, both men have insisted that the president not only knew about illegal campaign donations[23] but explicitly authorized that the funds be placed in a secret New York City bank account.

In February 1996 the Colombian Commission of Accusations formally charged the president with accepting cartel money. Although

a legislative committee subsequently blocked impeachment proceedings (on Samper's insistence that any contributions were made
"behind his back"), nineteen members of Congress and five leading
administrative figures, including Botero and Medina, have been
snagged by investigators.[24]

"I've been here for twenty years," MacMillan marvels, "and I have
never seen a shakedown like this. The wheels of justice used to move
at a snail's pace. Now it's more like an avalanche!"[25]

Colombia's economy is also changing. This is especially evident
in the cities that gave the drug organizations their names. Having
become addicted to laundered money and conspicuous consumption, these cities are now suffering acute withdrawal. Porsches and
Ferraris have all but disappeared from Cali's trendy Sixth Avenue, as
have buyers for the luxury apartments lining Paso Ancho Boulevard
and retail locales at the Cosmocentro shopping center.

Many seem to accept the change with a measure of relief. "What
is important," says Fabio Rodriguez, president of the Cali Chamber
of Commerce, "is that we are back to being who we are." El Pais editor Luis Canon agrees, noting that the city has become more peace-
ful. With the demise of the cartels, he says, "the psychology of violence has decreased."[26]

Although danger still lurks in this city of 1.8 million, God is now
viewed as a viable protector. When Cali police deactivated a large,
174-kilo car bomb in the populous San Nicolás area in November
1996, many noted that the rescue came just 24 hours after 55,000
Christians held their third *vigilia* at El Pueblo stadium. Even *El Pais*
headlined, "Thanks to God, It Didn't Explode."[27]

Cali's prayer warriors were gratified but far from finished. Disturbed by the growing debauchery associated with the city's *Feria,*
a year-end festival accompanied by ten days of bullfights and
blowout partying, church officials developed plans for a healthy
alternative.

"When we approached the city about this," Marci recalls, "God
gave us great favor. The city secretary not only granted us rent-free
use of the 22,000-seat Velodromo [cycling arena], but he also threw
in free advertising and sound support for our evangelistic rallies. We
were stunned!

"An even bigger surprise came during our final rally. Our closing worship session had adopted the theme of the Holy Spirit '*reigning* over' and '*raining* down upon' the city of Cali. As the crowd sang, it began to sprinkle outside—an exceedingly rare occurrence in the month of December. Within moments the city was inundated with 24 hours of torrential tropical rain. For the first time in recent memory, *Feria* events had to be canceled."

Churches in Bogota and Medellín, hearing about these extraordinary developments, sent observers to the Cali *vigilias* to see what they could learn. As a consequence of these visits, both cities now have their own successful, citywide prayer campaigns.

Rabid Dogs and Extinguished Fires: Tales from the Sierra Madre

It is not often that one can observe two New Years in a single month. Yet that is what happened to me in January 1993. Five days after welcoming in the traditional New Year with a group of Christians in Tauranga, New Zealand, I witnessed the dawn of a second New Year in the highlands of Guatemala. While veteran travelers will immediately suspect a gimmick involving the international date line, the explanation in this case is actually linked to the ancient 260-day calendar maintained by the Maya Indians.[28]

In 1993 this unusual calendar decreed that New Year's Day would fall twice—on January 6 and again on September 23. To the Maya, this spiritually charged holiday is called Waxaqib Batz' or "Eight Monkey." Many see it as a particularly dangerous time, a season when one world is destroyed and another is created.[29]

Aware of my interest in religious festivals, Tom Hemingway, a Guatemala-based linguist, had invited me down to observe the event firsthand. The plan called for me to fly into Guatemala City on January 5. From there we would drive out to the town of Momostenango, a traditionalist stronghold in the northwestern highland province of Totonicapan.

When I exited customs, Tom seemed genuinely glad to see me. Since we had last spoken, traditionalist efforts to rehabilitate Mayan culture and religion had attracted significant news coverage in Guatemala. For this reason, and because of his own training in Mesoamerican history, Tom was eager to meet some of the movement's leaders.

By 10:30 the next morning we were winding our way up into the Sierra Madre. The vistas were spectacular. Agua volcano, with its steep, symmetrical cone, loomed on the horizon. Closer in, fertile fields awaited harvesting. Commercial crops of snow peas and cabbage were interlaced with subsistence plots of beans, squash, chilies and corn. The latter was left to dry on the stalks or rooftops, then taken in to storage. To the left of the highway, we could see the hazy silhouette of Acatenango, another volcanic behemoth whose lush flanks have served as a guerrilla stronghold throughout Guatemala's lengthy civil war.[30]

The area had never been completely sanitized by the military. A few miles later, Tom prayed divine protection on us as we entered an area that had become notorious for holdups and hijackings. For the better part of an hour, workers clearing the remains of a recent landslide left us idling like sitting ducks.

By mid-afternoon the specter of bandits and guerrillas was replaced by roadside vendors whose simple stalls displayed fruits, vegetables and woolen pouches to Pan-American travelers. Indian women wearing colorful *huipils* (cotton blouses) and wraparound *kortes* provided visual accents as they wandered down rural pathways. Many balanced clay pots atop their heads.

Hitchhikers were also ubiquitous, and at one point we offered a lift to two boys. The older lad climbed aboard with a heavy loom, while the younger one struggled to hoist an equally ponderous bag of wool. Before we could pull out into traffic again, seven others, including at least one military officer, had piled onto the back of our small Toyota pickup. Most of them were gone by the time we pulled into the provincial capital of Quetzaltenango—or Xela (pronounced "shayla"), as the Maya prefer to call it.

From here the drive to Momostenango took ninety minutes, most of it spent on a washboard dirt road that wound through fragrant pine forests before finally descending into town. A brilliant red sunset served as our welcoming committee, but it was a fleeting joy.

Within minutes the stars were out in force. The rising moon was almost full, and Venus hung in the sky like a low-slung ornament.

In the poorly lit town plaza, people were dark shadows, their faces indistinguishable. One man knelt and chanted before several small fires. Inside an adjacent Catholic church, a nativity scene replayed a scratchy recording of "O Tannenbaum," while an old woman lit votive candles and mumbled prayers to her native gods.

Back outside, we wandered past a general merchandise store, the only one still open, and found a collection of Halloween masks hanging from wires. A middle-aged customer was purchasing three hundred candles to use in the next day's New Year observances. Tom stuck his head in the door and asked if the proprietor knew where we could find the home of Rigoberto Iztep, a practicing shaman and leader in the Mayan revitalization movement. Although the proprietor was either unwilling or unable to help, another patron overheard our request and agreed to lead us to Señor Iztep's home.

Hopping onto the bed of our pickup, he directed us through eerily empty streets to the other side of town. After parking on a nondescript side street, we were escorted to the base of a narrow, inclined pathway. Marimba music beckoned from some unseen location above us. Our progress up the path was interrupted three times by suspicious Indians. Tom, who speaks fluent Spanish and the Mam Indian dialect, recognized only that the exchange was in Quiche. Afterward our guide informed us that the shaman was home but busy preparing for tomorrow's New Year observance. Who, the relatives wanted to know, had sent us? Then, apparently satisfied with our answer, the interrogators motioned us up the path.

Clambering up a final set of rough-hewn steps, we passed through a breezeway into a private courtyard. The dirt floor was strewn with long pine needles—a typical touch, I learned, on festive occasions. Although we were not the only guests, we were offered what seemed to be the seat of honor—a backless wooden bench no more than five feet in front of a three-member marimba band. The extended instrument required three players, an unlikely team consisting of a man in his mid–fifties flanked by a pre-teen boy on the lower notes and a somber-faced sixteen-year-old who seemed to be carrying the melody on the upper end. While the boys were fully occupied with just one mallet in each hand, the man's larger grip allowed him to strike the instrument with two per hand.

As the band played, the initial awkwardness of the situation subsided. A dozen or so Indians, including a shy albino girl, had taken seats along the periphery of the courtyard. Others continued to filter in through the breezeway.

In what is perhaps a universal scene at holiday time, most of the women were clustered in the adjacent kitchen, where a meat-and-potato broth simmered on an ancient-looking earthen stove. The older women were using a hollow gourd to ladle the stew out of a large clay kettle into a set of smaller bowls. Not surprisingly, we were served first.

While we ate, three men gave brief talks on the importance of observing Waxaqib Batz' and honoring the day gods. When they finished, a male dancer emerged from the shadows in a masked jaguar costume. Pantomiming the cat's movements, he rose occasionally to strike a drum tucked precariously under one arm. After ten minutes he beckoned me. When I smiled benignly, he moved closer with mock menace. As the other guests giggled nervously, the performer began to "bite" into my arm. Overwhelmed by the smell of alcohol on his breath, I was suddenly unsure where this would lead.

A few minutes later we discovered that we were being tested. The shaman had been watching us for some time. We also learned that the main New Year's activities did not start until six A.M., although a smaller preparatory ceremony would be held around midnight. We were welcome to observe.

As we headed out into the night toward the sacred gathering place, the ambiance was dreamlike, almost as if someone had slipped an ancient herb into our drinks that heightened the senses. Hearthlights flickered from mist-draped terraces while a spectacular canopy of stars added a surreal symmetry to the scene.

Xol Mumus, the original name for Momostenango, means "In the Middle of the Hills," a reference not only to the area's encircling heights, but to the sacred summit at its center. Called Paklom, this modest hill hosts the most revered site in the Momostekan world—a place known as *Waqibal*, or "Six-Place."[31] Those who worship here do so in the belief that they are standing at the very axis of the universe.[32]

Getting to Paklom entailed huffing our way up a steep, tile-covered road off the main plaza. The late-night chill left foggy evidence of our exertion all the way to the top. Cresting the summit, we encountered a grassy mound scarred by shallow offering pits and blackened by centuries of burning copal resin incense. Judging by the evidence at hand, we had found Six-Place.

The worshipers, bundled in scarves and warm *momosteco* ponchos, formed a semicircle around a concrete hearth crowned by three sooty crosses. As the shaman paused to collect an "offering" for his services (there seemed to be a premium for gringos), a young mother seized the occasion to lay her swaddled infant in a makeshift bed of straw. It was a fateful decision.

At eleven P.M. the ceremony began in earnest. Lighting a fire in the hearth, Iztep launched into a lengthy prayer designed to close out unfinished business with all 260 Mayan day deities. Despite the repetitive nature of the entreaty, the crowd stayed glued to the process. Like most Maya traditionalists, they were convinced that to carry broken vows into the new year is to invite serious economic or physical distress.

Iztep's actions, however, were not merely confessional. As an authentic shaman, he was also endeavoring to create a portal that would rejoin the human world to the Otherworld. He called this sacred, universal space *u hol gloriyah,* or "the glory hole." (This interdimensional portal is similar in many respects to the Dagara light hole described in chapter 8.) It was here that he hoped to receive and pass on a blessed substance known as *itz* (derived from the god *Itzamna*). According to archaeologist David Freidel, *itz* represents the flowing liquid of heaven and is manifest in such things as morning dew, human tears, the sap of a tree (especially copal resin) and melting candle wax. "When the village shaman opens the portal from this side," Freidel explains, "Itzamna opens it from the other and sends the precious *itz* through to nourish and sustain humanity. . . ."[33]

To keep this dimensional portal open, Iztep interrupted his prayer chant to blow mouthfuls of whiskey into the rising flames. With midnight nearly upon us, the ceremony was reaching a climax. Pivoting to the cardinal directions, Iztep and the worshipers, some of whom were fully entranced, called forth spiritual legions to receive their oblation.[34] As Paklom was transformed into a spiritual vortex, the arrival of unseen spirits became palpable.

Suddenly, as if on cue, a pack of wild, snarling dogs appeared on the opposite side of the hill. I knew instantly why they had come. Still, watching them make a beeline for the sleeping infant sparked deep indignation. Striding toward the vicious dogs, several of whom were already tugging at the little bundle in the hay, I rebuked the controlling spirits.

The effect was dramatic. In a split second the deadly spell was shattered and the snarling pack was transformed into a benign gaggle of wagging tails. Interrupted by divine power, the perverse passion play came to an abrupt halt. The child's mother, oblivious to the peril that had brushed up against her, shook off her trance and disappeared with her baby into the night.

On New Year's Day ribbons of smoke wound their way skyward from hundreds of ceremonial fires across the Mayan highlands. The ritual offerings, or *costumbre,* were addressed to a syncretistic blend of traditional deities and Catholic saints. In one ravine the heat was so intense I was reminded of Gehenna. Kneeling at the edge of this sacred inferno, a middle-aged man offered a heartfelt prayer for the nations. Nearby, an anguished mother wept for her wayward daughter. Others lit handfuls of thin, multicolored candles or corn-shuck packets of copal.

By late morning Tom and I were on the road to Zunil,[35] one of at least three highland communities that still maintained a shrine to the pagan god Maximon. Possibly descended from an ancient Maya deity called *Mam,* the unsavory deity has long wielded considerable influence in certain areas of Guatemala. Besides contriving rapes and unsanctioned elopements, he is also associated with black magic and venomous serpents.[36]

We arrived in Zunil around four P.M. The shrine, which we had difficulty finding, turned out to be a cluster of unassuming adobe houses located near a volcanic steam vent. Inside Maximon's modest quarters, we found the mustachioed, mannequin-like god surrounded by a half-dozen kneeling worshipers. Most were content to light votive candles on the dirt floor, but at least one rose to place a lit cigar and libation of whiskey into the image's hollowed-out mouth.[37]

Before the deity had time to enjoy these vices, however, he was draped with a heavy blue blanket and hoisted onto the back of a cult devotee known as a "son of Maximon."[38] With his cowboy boots sticking out from beneath the blanket, the Maximon was carried onto a dance floor, where musicians were standing at the ready with marimbas, drums and some kind of double-reed instrument.[39] As the music started, the man bearing the Maximon began to dance with mincing steps. This prompted the presiding official, or *telinel*, to raise a silver and black scepter and lead the pair across the dance floor. Soon other dancers joined the bizarre spectacle.

By the time we decided to leave, the entire enclave was reeking with venality. Most of the men were drunk and several young boys were wiggling their posteriors in a lewd fashion (a sad pass of the generational baton). An older woman lifted her dress to knee level and leaped back and forth over the embers of offering fires lit earlier in the day. Bathing in the residue of the celebration, she used her hands to wave the curling smoke over her face and body.

These images were not far removed from what Tom and I had seen all day. With their hand-carved idols and ubiquitous offering fires, the highland Maya have gone a long way toward recreating the kinds of scenes that distressed the biblical prophets. We drove out of Zunil with heavy hearts.

Ironically, just as I began to wonder on this dreary day if any community had resisted bowing the knee to Baal, I felt an immediate lifting of oppression. Anxious to link this inner sensation with an external cause, I scanned both sides of the road for evidence of ritual fires. Although we were now on the outskirts of an established agricultural community, there was no visible New Year's activity. The anomaly was glaring.

A sign informed us that we had entered the town of Almolonga. The name was familiar, but I could not remember why. Then it came to me: Fuller Seminary's C. Peter Wagner had spoken of the place during an October 1992 conference in Argentina. According to Peter, the town had experienced a genuine spiritual transformation as a consequence of focused intercessory prayer.

As we drove through the center of town, evidence of Peter's report was everywhere. Just beyond the entrance to Way of the Cross Street, we pulled up behind a truck whose mudflaps read *God Is My Guide*. Down the road we passed the Eden Cafe and another oncoming lorry whose upper windshield was emblazoned with a sticker proclaiming, *Jesus Is the Way!*

Even more impressive was the town's growing forest of churches, including a large concrete block facility being erected along the main road. It was an unusual building boom that (I found out later) had attracted mainstream press from as far away as the United States. In one interview, a *Los Angeles Times* reporter revisited the spiritual history of the area with Roque Yac, founder of the five-hundred-member Calvary Church. "Twenty-one years ago," Yac related, "God was dead for the people here. Their minds were on parties and drinking."[40] That was when the intercessors got serious. After hearing from God, they made a decision to sever the spiritual continuum linking them to centuries-old Mayan pacts.

With the extinguishing of these ancient ritual fires, Almolonga's economy began to blossom. Today the community stands in stark contrast to the depressed conditions in neighboring Zunil. And on the spiritual front, eighteen churches now service a population that is eighty percent evangelical. Some sociologists try to serve up clinical explanations for this, but local intercessors are not buying. "Our growth has not come because of fanaticism or ignorance," insists Mariano Riscaoche. "We have had supernatural experiences."[41]

Eighteen months after my visit to Guatemala, this exciting story took yet another turn when Guatemalan believers launched an unprecedented spiritual warfare campaign against deceptive territorial spirits. The 1994 initiative was led by Filiberto Lemus, an aggressive intercessor whose congregation in Quetzaltenango has battled the powers behind Maximon for years. Timing their effort to coincide with the June 25th Day to Change the World, seventy thousand evangelical Christians paraded through the streets of Guatemala City, declaring to the principalities and powers (see Ephesians 3:10–11) that Jesus, not Maximon or any other false god, is Lord over Guatemala.

On the same day, Harold Caballeros, pastor of the dynamic El Shaddai church in Guatemala City, sent out four teams of intercessors to pray at the cardinal points of the nation. One week later *Cronica*, a leading Guatemalan news magazine, hit the newsstands with the following headline:

THE DEFEAT OF MAXIMON
Protestant Fundamentalism Alters the Culture of the Altiplano and Turns the Native Religions into Tourist Attractions[42]

In the body of the article, lead writer Mario Roberto Morales asserted that "Christianity, in its Protestant form, has forced Maximon to grant his power and ideological influence over the people to Jehovah." Maximon's fraternity, which had reportedly been reduced to a mere handful of individuals, must "survive by picking up offerings from foreign tourists who want to see the idol and take pictures." In assessing these and other developments, Morales concluded that "the Evangelical Church . . . constitutes very clearly the most significant force for religious change in the highlands of Guatemala since the Spanish conquest."[43]

Lessons from the Labyrinth

As we pause to consider these closing stories, two lessons stand out immediately. The first is what I call *determined activism*. In each of the cases we have looked at in this chapter, the principal characters resolved to complete their mission in the face of strong opposition by well-meaning Christians. When things got rough for Robert Kayanja in Kampala, his own parents joined those urging him to leave. "God wants to save these people," they said, "but He doesn't want you to die in the process." Randy and Marci MacMillan, during their twenty-year tenure in the violent city of Cali, heard much the same thing.

Other warnings had to do with perceptions about spiritual oppression, unresponsive attitudes and appropriate ministry venues. When Thomas Muthee announced he was starting a church in Kiambu, his ministerial colleagues could ask only, "How will you manage?" One area pastor declared flatly, "We preach, but the people here don't get saved."

I, too, have heard such words. Over the last several years, a number of Christian friends and acquaintances have attempted to dissuade me from visiting many of the places I have written about in this book. The prevailing opinion among these people seems to be that it is unhealthy and unnecessary for Christians to expose themselves to demonic haunts like Dharamsala, Ontake and Paklom.

But if this is so, how do we explain Moses contending with the magicians in Pharaoh's court? Or Elijah challenging the prophets of Baal atop Mount Carmel? Or Jesus ministering on the home turf of Samaritans and publicans? Didn't Paul stop to reason with the Epicureans in the Athenian Areopagus? Don't we find him preaching to the devotees of Artemis in Ephesus? And when all is said and done, is there any evidence that these men were spiritually damaged, or even tainted, by their participation in these encounters?

For those who insist that I should never have attended the midnight ceremony at Paklom, I have only one question: How would this counsel have aided the infant who was to become the evening's secret sacrifice? While deep-rescue ministry is not without risk, it *is* necessary—and rewarding.

The second stand-out lesson of the cases we have looked at concerns *the power of focused and united prayer.* In all four accounts, community transformation occurred when intercessors addressed specific concerns in common cause. Details gained through patient spiritual mapping led to (and sustained) the kind of fervent prayer that produces results (see James 5:16–18). Many of these group efforts—the Kampala Wailing Wall, the Kiambu Prayer Cave and the Cali *vigilias*—took on their own unique identities.[44]

Even more encouraging is the fact that similar prayer campaigns are now unfolding, with equally dramatic results, in other areas of the world. In recent months, for example, I have collected details on intercessory breakthroughs in the nations of Nepal, Pakistan and South Africa. Although for security reasons these details cannot yet be released, they represent further evidence that God's people are taking seriously their responsibility to dismantle the enemy's encampments (see Deuteronomy 12:1–4).

While Christians are naming their prayer campaigns, it is non-believers who have taken to defining the results. In China's Henan Province, for example, church growth in recent years has been so robust that Communist authorities now refer to the region as the "Jesus Nest." In the West African nation of Burkina Faso, where eighty thousand women devote one day a week to fasting and prayer, the village of Sigli has seen so many deliverances from mental illness and demonic possession that the local fellowship has been dubbed the "Church of the Crazy People."

It has been said that history, although sometimes made up of the few acts of the great, is more often shaped by the many acts of the small. Nowhere is this truer than in the realm of spiritual intercession. Although William Carey, C. S. Lewis, Billy Graham and Mother Teresa will always be remembered for their unique contributions, even these luminaries cannot match the collective glow of countless faithful intercessors down through the ages. Unfazed by their lack of reputation, these anonymous heroes have lately approached God's throne of grace in record numbers. Some have virtually camped out on site.

Their bold persistence, according to Scripture, makes them valuable partners in the Great Deliverance. This is because God is not only stimulated by the rising fragrance of their accumulated prayers; He is changed by it. Each selfless petition He inhales becomes part of Him; and as the human and divine wills merge, power is released to dislodge enchantments from the darkest labyrinths of mind and spirit.[45]

> He [the Lamb] came and took the scroll from the right hand of him who sat on the throne. And when he had taken it, the four living creatures and the twenty-four elders fell down before the Lamb. Each one had a harp and they were holding golden bowls full of incense, which are the prayers of the saints. And they sang a new song:
>
> > "You are worthy to take the scroll and to open its seals,
> > because you were slain,
> > and with your blood you purchased men for God
> > from every tribe and language and people and nation. . . ."
>
> When he opened the seventh seal, there was silence in heaven for about half an hour. . . . Another angel, who had a golden censer, came and stood at the altar. He was given much incense to offer, with the

prayers of all the saints, on the golden altar before the throne. The smoke of the incense, together with the prayers of the saints, went up before God from the angel's hand. Then the angel took the censer, filled it with fire from the altar, and hurled it on the earth; and there came peals of thunder, rumblings, flashes of lightning and an earthquake.

Revelation 5:7–9; 8:1, 3–5

NOTES

Preface: Reflections on a Journey

1. Voters are particularly disturbed by the lack of candor, civility, creativity and clarity.

2. I was intrigued to discover not long ago that the motto on the Otis family crest reads, *He is wise who watches.*

3. Library research and more than one thousand interviews have yielded a small mountain of field notes, books, maps, photographs, transcripts and case studies.

4. Garth Henrichs, quoted in *Reader's Digest,* "Quotable Quotes," July 1994.

5. Roger C. Andersen, *The Rotarian,* quoted in *Reader's Digest,* "Quotable Quotes," June 1996.

Chapter 1: Encounters with the World Next Door

1. Douchan Gersi, *Faces in the Smoke* (Los Angeles: Jeremy Tarcher, 1991), p. 92.

2. The *orisha* may also be seen as personified natural forces such as thunder, wind and fire.

3. In the coming days Dick and I would find ourselves drawn closer to Raina—a young man who, in God's providence, played a role in our plans. Although he did not know God as we did, he was clearly a genuine seeker of truth. For the next three days this Indian would serve us in ways too numerous to recount, including a proud detour to his one-room apartment for refreshments. Inside this austere room, rented from an adjacent family, my eyes gravitated to a picture hanging on the wall above Raina's bed. Closer inspection revealed the following words superimposed on a pastoral scene: "I sought the Lord and found Him in the quiet place of my heart."

4. Later in the day the water, which the gods allegedly perceive as milk, would be removed and then reissued for "lunch."

5. For more on this topic, see chapter 5.

6. Tibetan Buddhist offerings focus on the senses and usually consist of a fine cloth scarf *(khata)* for touch, food such as rice or barley cakes *(torma)* for taste, a *mandala* or icon for sight, incense for smell, a bell for hearing and a butter lamp for consciousness.

7. A mantra is a syllable or string of syllables believed to concentrate specific energies. Uttered correctly, it can induce the presence of those energies, usually visualized as

beings in human form. The verbal repetition of mantras represents an integral part of both Buddhist and Hindu religious practice.

8. John Avedon, *In Exile from the Land of the Snows*, quoted by Ruth-Inge Heinz in *Shamans of the Twentieth Century* (New York: Irvington, 1991), p. 104.

9. Oracular service can be rigorous. In addition to preparing for each ceremony with several days of fasting and special meditation, the *kuden* is often dressed in eight layers of clothing weighing more than one hundred pounds—a curious outfit that includes red brocade trousers, knee-high white leather boots and a triangular jacket.

10. When the boy discovered we were not worshipers but simple visitors, he seemed happy to shed pretense and assume the posture and characteristics of a normal seven-year-old. His eyes were clear and showed no evidence of demonic control. Barring a miracle, however, this will surely change in time; and as Dick and I headed back down the trail, we begged God to prevent this young life from being sucked into the heart of darkness.

11. During this exciting campaign, which took place in October 1993, 25–30 million global intercessors petitioned God to erode the power and influence of demonic strongholds within the 10/40 Window, the strategic corridor of unreached souls between the tenth and fortieth latitudes north of the equator that encompasses the major Islamic, Hindu and Buddhist strongholds of North Africa and Asia.

12. A Christian since 1973, Stephen comes from a staunch Buddhist family that immigrated to India from the Kumbum region of Tibet. After his conversion, Stephen spent ten years pastoring a small church in the remote Himalayan valley of Ladakh in northern India. He is now involved with a radio ministry called Gawaylon that reaches Tibetan communities in India, Nepal, Bhutan and China.

13. In addition to conversing with Stephen Hishey in Mussoorie on October 19,1993, I conducted a follow-up interview in Lynnwood, Washington, on June 6, 1994.

14. Wade Davis, *The Serpent and the Rainbow* (New York: Warner, 1985), pp. 213–214.

15. A variation on this theme can be found in the state of Kerala on India's Malabar Coast. Here, as in Haiti, the snake is venerated as a life-giving bestower of blessings. But young adolescent girls, instead of offering themselves as mates, petition snake deities for early marriages by performing trance dances. Drenched in oil and perspiration, the girls move sensuously to the sound of round fiddles played by Hindu priests, or *pullavans*.

16. Gersi, *Faces*, pp. 147–149.

17. Shapeshifting is the demonically inspired ability to temporarily assume the form of another object or creature (most commonly birds and animals). In earlier times this practice was common among Siberian and Celtic shamans. More recently it has been documented among Tibetan lamas, African traditionalists, Native American shamans and followers of Haitian Voudon. For an interesting case study on the relationship between owls, witchcraft and shapeshifting, see Gersi, *Faces*, pp. 194-196.

18. Some of the details in this account were verified in a follow-up interview with Mrs. Gray Eyes, conducted in August 1994 by Robert Dayzie, Mike Hendricks and Betty Dologhan; and in a June 1994 phone conversation with Navajo evangelist Herman Williams.

19. It is customary in such cases for personal excreta—mainly hair, nails or feces—to be buried near "dangerous" sites like graves or trees that have been struck by lightning.

20. Richard Cavendish, *The Powers of Evil* (New York: Dorset, 1975), pp. 95, 101. See also J. C. Cooper, *An Illustrated Encyclopaedia of Traditional Symbols* (London: Thames & Hudson, 1978), p. 124.

21. Complex Navajo healing ceremonies are called Chant Ways. Some of these ceremonies can last for upwards of ten days and involve mastery of hundreds of songs (chants), herbal medicines and sand paintings.

22. Pete's wife had a dream at this time in which a bright being, probably an angel, removed some traditional jewelry from around her neck, then proceeded to heal her body.

23. Jake Page, "Return of the Kachinas," *Science* 83, Vol. 4, No. 2, March 1983.

24. Known by the Hopis as *páhos,* prayer sticks or prayer feathers (usually from eagles) are rooted in ancient mythology and used to carry Hopi prayers aloft to their Creator. Every *páho* is made with prayerful concentration and then ritually smoked over. On completion the *páho* is carried to a shrine (often a natural formation), where it is stuck into a cleft of rocks or hung on a bush. In time, Hopis believe, the invisible vibrations of the prayer it embodies will be absorbed by the forces to which it is dedicated.

25. Similar stories are told by the duty rangers at Hawaii Volcanoes National Park. Every day parcels arrive in the mail containing souvenir bits of lava that visitors have made off with. They enclose notes that recount plagues that have bedeviled their lives since taking the rocks, and they ask the rangers to return the lava pieces to their rightful owner, the fire goddess Pele. See Moana Tregaskis, "The Magic of Hawaii," *Hemispheres* magazine, May 1993, p. 67.

26. Immediately after this incident, the Goombi family took steps to cleanse their home of any objects or behavior that might make them vulnerable to demonic attack. As a consequence, none of the earlier problems has recurred. Details of this account were derived from an April 1992 interview conducted at the Albuquerque home of Wendell Tsoodle (the former medicine man I mentioned in the previous section who warned me against trip sticks) and several follow-up telephone conversations in late November 1994.

Note: Examining the role of the medicine bundle within the Beaver Indian culture of southwestern Canada, ethnographer Robin Ridington observes, "Many people my own age told me that as a child they had fooled around with a bundle of some relative and received a terrible fright because there were things in it that moved—they were alive." See Robin Ridington, "Beaver Dreaming and Singing" in "Pilot Not Commander: Essays in Memory of Diamond Jenness," Pat and Jim Lotz, eds., *Anthropologia,* Special Issue, Nos. #1 and 2 (1971), pp. 115–128.

27. In parts of West Africa, the "gizzi penny," a thin rod of iron about the length of an arm, was used as currency until the 1930s. If the penny was damaged, it was considered to have lost its soul. To restore its value, the services of a witch doctor were required to ritually "reincarnate" the money. See *Did You Know?* (New York: Reader's Digest Association, 1990), p. 271.

28. These councils take place around the winter solstice or the national New Year. See Frank Cushing, *Zuni Fetishes* (Las Vegas: KC Publications, 1883, 1990), pp. 32–33.

29. Tibor Bodrogi, "New Ireland Art in Cultural Context," in Louise Lincoln, et al., *Assemblage of Spirits: Idea and Image in New Ireland* (New York: Minneapolis Institute of Arts and George Braziller, 1987), p. 26.

30. Indonesians further believe that to maintain its potency, the knife has to be ritually cleaned at the Javanese New Year. Lime juice and a little soda are added to pure water, into which the knife is immersed for three days and nights. The blade is then wiped with scented oil, and incense is burned while a mantra invoking its maker is chanted. See Keith Loveard, "Journey through Magic," *Asiaweek,* June 9, 1993, p. 43.

31. From an August 6, 1992, interview conducted at Dr. Tanaka's home in Nagoya, Japan.

32. In a report on paranormal experiences in Mongolia, Christian anthropologist David Lewis refers to heaps of stones known as *oboo* that are traditionally associated with shamanism. One of his informants declared: "A man took some stones from an *oboo* to use for a building. He promptly died. Two or three years later, another man took some stones. He

also died." See David Lewis, "Dreams and Paranormal Experiences among Contemporary Mongolians," *Journal of the Anglo-Mongolian Society,* Vol. XIII, Nos. 1 and 2, 1991.

33. I later verified this story with Dr. Krippner during a May 1992 interview at the Saybrook Institute in San Francisco.

34. Mickey Hart, *Drumming at the Edge of Magic* (San Francisco: HarperSanFrancisco, 1990), pp. 179–181.

35. Dan Greenburg, "Confessions of a Nonbeliever," *Newsweek,* June 7, 1976, p. 13.

36. Harold Owen, *Journey from Obscurity,* Vol. I, p. 50, quoted by Richard Cavendish in *The Powers of Evil.*

37. One ethnological survey identified possession of some form in 360 of 488 cultures around the world (see Davis, *Serpent,* p. 215). Unfortunately, the conclusions of the anthropologists amount to observations, not explanations.

38. Loveard, "Journey," p. 41.

39. During location work in Haiti related to the mysterious Flying Men lodges, Gersi reports that "something influenced the operation of the batteries and interfered with the normal photographic process"—the same things that happened whenever he tried to record levitation phenomena on film (*Faces,* pp. 181–182).

Chapter 2: Navigating the Labyrinth

1. It is one thing to solve a maze from a diagram and another to solve it from within. Inside a real maze of hedges or masonry, it is difficult to form a mental map. In the geography of mazes, a node is a fork—a point where paths meet and you must make a decision. The segment of path between two nodes is called a branch. The difficulty of a maze has a lot to do with the number of branches leading from each node. When each node is allowed only one branch, the only possible arrangement is a unicursal maze—a non-puzzle labyrinth with a single unbranching path from beginning to end. You cannot make a wrong turn. Medieval mazes like Chartres Cathedral were of this type. Their convoluted but unbranching paths often led to a tree or a shrine. See William Poundstone, *Labyrinths of Reason* (New York: Doubleday, 1988), pp. 164–165.

2. This legend may have some basis in fact. Not only do ancient Cretan coins depict what seems to be an architectural maze, but the Minoan religion included a bull cult.

3. Elinor Gadon, *The Once and Future Goddess* (San Francisco: Harper & Row, 1989), pp. 62, 65.

4. Pronounced fan-*tay*-zhas, these colorful cultural shows include indigenous song and dance, local cuisine and dramatic horse and camel charges.

5. See George Otis Jr., *The Last of the Giants* (Grand Rapids: Chosen, 1991), pp. 86–87.

6. Cavendish, *Powers,* p. 39.

7. Gary Kinnaman, *Angels Dark and Light* (Ann Arbor: Vine, 1994), p. 149.

Note: In a similar incident in 1977, American missionary Brad Long and his wife, Laura, were staying in the home of some wealthy friends in Seoul, Korea. Despite the comfortable accommodations, the Longs sensed an underlying oppressiveness. In his book *The Collapse of the Brass Heaven* (Grand Rapids: Chosen, 1994), Long adds that as he and Laura endeavored to pray in this atmosphere of "mysterious hostility," they were suddenly assaulted by an "invisible wave of uncleanness."

8. Although some Christians dismiss talk of underlying spiritual explanations as overly simplistic, their argument strikes me as double-sided. If we accept that the ultimate fabric of reality is spiritual, is it not at least equally simplistic to confine our search for understanding to the realms of sociology, politics and economics?

9. Francis Schaeffer, *Genesis in Space and Time* (Downers Grove: InterVarsity, 1972), pp. 76–77.

10. C. S. Lewis, *Miracles* (New York: Macmillan, 1947), p. 42.

11. Andrew Delbanco points out in *The Death of Satan* (New York: Farrar, Straus and Giroux, 1995) that the devil lost his significance and plausibility when theologians began to "accommodate themselves to the requirements of an emerging rationalism that ultimately left no room for him." With this loss of credibility, "belief in embodied spirits was reduced to a superstition" (pp. 57–58, 68).

12. Charles H. Kraft, *Christianity with Power* (Ann Arbor: Vine, 1989), pp. 20–21.

13. The opposite of habituation is sensitization, in which a creature's nervous system becomes more receptive to a stimulus. See George Johnson, *In the Palaces of Memory* (New York: Vintage, 1992), p. 24.

14. Walter Wink, "Demons and DMins: The Church's Response to the Demonic" in *Review & Expositor*, The Faculty Journal of the Southern Baptist Theological Seminary, Vol. 89, No. 4, Fall 1992, p. 503.

15. Lewis, *Miracles*, pp. 138–139.

16. John MacArthur Jr., *Charismatic Chaos* (Grand Rapids: Zondervan, 1992), p. 132.

Note: MacArthur's blanket assertion that "those who claim miracles today are not able to substantiate their claims" is worthy of examination. Documentation has in fact been assembled in a great number of instances (including cases developed by the Christian Broadcasting Network, The Sentinel Group and several denominations) and is part of the public record. It is unfortunate that MacArthur neglected to explore these resources before going to print with his generalizations. Even more disappointing is his apparent lack of international field work. Had he elected to devote more time to a personal investigation of the front lines of world evangelization in recent years—including developments in China, Algeria, Nepal, Indonesia, Nigeria and Argentina—it is doubtful he would have reached such extreme and patently incorrect conclusions.

17. MacArthur, pp. 159, 143.

Note: In *Christianity Today* magazine, Presbyterian minister Robert Patterson described the "major flaw" of MacArthur's book as his attitude: "In claiming to see things so clearly—so black and white—MacArthur falls into a restorationist mind-set, identified by historian Mark Noll as 'intellectual overconfidence, sectarian delusion, and a stunningly naive confidence in the power of humans to extract themselves from the influences of history.'" Perhaps the most unfortunate consequence of unchecked skepticism is the fact that it leads inevitably to isolationism. Everywhere the skeptic looks, he finds that others are somehow tainted with error, so cooperative efforts are all too rare.

18. Paul Thigpen, "Did the Power of the Spirit Ever Leave the Church?" *Charisma*, September 1992, p. 22.

19. Winkie Pratney, *Healing the Land* (Grand Rapids: Chosen, 1993), p. 35.

20. Michael Green, *Exposing the Prince of Darkness* (Ann Arbor: Vine, 1991), p. 248.

21. Ibid., pp. 93–95.

22. Rene Padilla, *The New Face of Evangelicalism* (Downers Grove, Ill.: InterVarsity, 1976), p. 212.

23. Wink, "Demons and DMins," p. 504.

24. Paul G. Hiebert, "The Flaw of the Excluded Middle" (Deerfield, Ill.: Trinity Evangelical Divinity School, 1982).

25. See Jack Finegan, *Myth and Mystery* (Grand Rapids: Baker, 1989), pp. 58–59, 64.

26. See Acts 17:16–18; 13:6–8; 16:16; 19:23–34.

27. See Acts 20:9–12; 13:8–12; 14:3; 19:11.

28. See 1 Kings 18; Acts 8; Ezekiel 10.

29. Green, *Exposing*, p. 81.

30. Ibid., pp. 82–83, 13.

31. Kraft, *Christianity*, p. 32.

32. Philip Slater, *The Wayward Gate*, quoted in *Science Digest*, "Science vs. Supernatural: Bridges to a New Domain?" April 1978, pp. 83–84.

33. Ibid., p. 86. Lyle Watson points out, for example, that while the entire electromagnetic spectrum ranges in wavelength from a billionth of a centimeter to millions of miles, only a tiny slit of this—between 380 and 760 billionths of a meter—is visible to us, while many other forms of energy are not visible at all.

34. Only three and a half of these dimensions are accessible to us. As Brooks Alexander points out, "Time's arrow moves only forward: it is not reversible."

35. While hyperspace theories are becoming increasingly popular (they generated more than five thousand scientific papers and three hundred conferences between 1984 and 1994), they still cannot be tested with current instruments or defined fully by mathematics. When critics charge that science so untestable strays dangerously close to religion, Kaku admits, "We're poaching on their territory." See Bill Dietrich, "How to Travel in Hyperspace," *Seattle Times,* April 5, 1994.

36. Brooks Alexander, "Machines Made of Shadows," *SCP Journal,* 17:1–2, 1992, p. 12. (See entire article, pp. 4–15.)

37. Edwin Abbott, *Flatland* (New York: HarperCollins [1884], 1994).

38. Alexander, "Machines," p. 13. Also, conversation at Spiritual Counterfeits Project offices in Berkeley, California, on May 1, 1992.

39. If, as Alexander believes, this latter option includes viewing the interior psychology of lower-dimensional beings, the implications for Christians attempting to engage in spiritual warfare are enormous. As Acts 19:13–16 apparently suggests, demons are able to discern whether those who resist them possess a condition of heart that will attract God's attention.

40. In 1911 British physicist Ernest Rutherford discovered that the structure of the atom was not solid at all. Instead it was like an enclosed miniature solar system—a central nucleus surrounded by orbiting electrons whose speed and erratic trajectories gave the appearance of an outer shell. Between the nucleus and the electrons lay a region of nearly empty space. A few years after Rutherford's discovery, Danish physicist Niels Bohr began to scrutinize the untidy orbits of the electron. At first the broad, fuzzy swaths gave the impression they were everywhere at once. Examining them more closely, however, Bohr was startled to note that these tiny charged particles jumped from one orbit to another *without traversing the space in between.* Thus was born one of the most baffling and potent disciplines within the realm of modern physics: quantum theory. Its premise, simply stated, is that subatomic particles are capable under certain conditions of changing instantly from mass to energy.

For the Bible-believing Christian, the implications of this theory are significant. If the structure of the universe is, at its most basic level, largely hollow and exempt from the normal rules of cause and effect, then "miracles" become far more plausible. When the post-resurrection Jesus amazed His disciples by appearing suddenly in locked rooms (see John 20:19, 26), they thought they had seen a ghost (see Luke 24:36–39). In fact, in this case it was not the Master but the walls that were ethereal.

41. David Freedman, *Brainmakers* (New York: Simon & Schuster, 1994), pp. 185–186.

42. Poundstone, *Labyrinths*, p. 188.

43. Slater, *Science Digest,* pp. 86–87.

44. Abbott, *Flatland,* Introduction, p. ix.

45. William Irwin Thompson, *Evil and World Order* (New York: Harper Colophon, 1976), p. 81.

46. Cathy Johnson, *On Becoming Lost: A Naturalist's Search for Meaning,* quoted in *Reader's Digest,* "Points to Ponder," July 1994.

47. Poundstone, *Labyrinths,* p. 171.

48. Hilary Putnam, *Mind, Language and Reality* (New York: Cambridge University Press, 1975). Cited in Poundstone, *Labyrinths,* p. 51.

Note: The Talmud, for its part, offers the following instructions: "If you want to discover demons, take sifted ashes and sprinkle them around your bed, and in the morning you will see something like the footprints of a cock. If you want to see them, take the afterbirth of a black she-cat, the firstborn of a firstborn, roast it in the fire and grind it to powder, and then put some in your eye . . ." (The Talmud, Berachot 6a).

49. Poundstone, *Labyrinths,* p. 53.

50. Further investigation often turns up the truth—although not always within the most desirable time frame. In A.D. 582, for example, it rained "blood" on Paris. The terrified populace saw this as a sign from heaven and responded by casting themselves before God in repentance. The true cause of this odd event was the sirocco wind that sometimes blows from the Sahara across the Mediterranean into Europe. It is laden with a fine red dust from the desert interior, and this had dyed the rain that fell on Paris. See *Did You Know?,* p. 68.

51. Green, *Exposing,* pp. 83–84.

Chapter 3: Faces of the Dragon

1. *Did You Know?,* p. 169.

2. H. W. F. Saggs, *The Greatness that Was Babylon* (London: Sidgwick & Jackson, 1988), p. 265.

3. Jeffrey Burton Russell, *The Prince of Darkness* (Ithaca: Cornell University Press, 1988), pp. 111–112.

Note: Professor Russell also draws attention to interesting historical links between Satan and Santa Claus—a connection some Christian leaders have recently sought to minimize. From the standpoint of European folklore, Russell notes: "The Devil lives in the far north and drives reindeer; he wears a suit of red fur; he goes down chimneys in the guise of Black Jack or the Black Man covered in soot; as Black Peter he carries a large sack into which he pops sins or sinners (including naughty children); he carries a stick or cane to thrash the guilty (now he merely brings candy canes); he flies through the air with the help of strange animals; food and wine are left out for him as a bribe to secure his favors. The Devil's nickname 'Old Nick' derives directly from Saint Nicholas. Nicholas was often associated with fertility cults, hence with fruit, nuts, and fruitcake, his characteristic gifts" (p. 114). See chapter 6 for a possible connection between Siberian shamanism and Clement Moore's "A Visit from St. Nicholas."

4. Wink, "Demons and DMins," p. 503.

5. Quoted in Kenneth Woodward and David Gates, "Giving the Devil His Due," *Newsweek,* August 30, 1982, p. 72.

6. Andrew Greeley, "The Devil, You Say," *New York Times Magazine,* February 4, 1973, p. 11.

7. Woodward and Gates, "Giving the Devil," pp. 72–73.

8. Elizabeth Peer, "Speak of the Devil," *Newsweek,* February 11, 1974, p. 62.

9. Wink, "Demons and DMins," p. 504.

10. Cavendish, *Powers,* p. 194.

11. In the second appendix to his book *The Prince of Darkness,* Jeffrey Burton Russell lists 106 New Testament passages providing either the names of, or general references to, the devil.

12. Greeley, "The Devil," p. 11.

13. Cavendish, *Powers,* pp. 198–199; Russell, *Prince,* p. 172. See also *Christian History* magazine, Issue 34 (Vol. XI, No. 2), p. 50.

14. Intriguingly, firefly "lanterns" contain oxygen and a substance called luciferin. The chemical reaction between the two produces light. An enzyme called luciferase helps speed up the process, and this in turn intensifies the light. See *Did You Know?,* p. 29.

15. As Gary Kinnaman notes in *Angels Dark and Light,* when angels appear in the Bible, radiance or luminescence is their most frequently mentioned trait. See Matthew 28:2–4; Luke 24:1–4; Hebrews 1:7; Revelation 10:1; 18:1.

16. Even if Satan was intended originally as a light-bearer on earth, it is Jesus who, in the end, assumes the role of Morning Star, the bringer of light (see 2 Peter 1:19; Revelation 22:16).

17. John 12:31; 14:30; 16:11.

18. Schaeffer, *Genesis,* p. 62. "This cannot be related to anything the Bible explicitly says," Schaeffer declared, "but neither is it excluded as a possibility."

19. Cavendish reports in *The Powers of Evil* (p. 187) that many of the Jewish rabbis identified Satan with Sammael, the angel of death. It was this great angel, highest of the guardians of the divine throne, who was jealous of Adam.

20. Eden's multi-dimensional aspects, for example, are examined in chapter 4.

21. The Mandeans, as described by retired archaeology professor Jack Finegan, are "a dwindling remnant of an ancient culture that has been largely displaced in southern Mesopotamia by the Marsh Arabs." See Finegan, *Myth and Mystery,* pp. 286, 74, 259–263.

22. Tom Cowan, *Fire in the Head* (San Francisco: HarperCollins, 1993), pp. 185–186. Note: Given this real or perceived linkage between light and spirit beings, it is not surprising to find that British covens have adopted names like Servants of the Light, the Glittering Sword, and Society of the Inner Light. See T. M. Luhrman, *Persuasions of the Witch's Craft* (Cambridge, Mass.: Harvard University Press, 1991), p. 226.

23. At the same time the creatures themselves (probably cherubim) are moving, Ezekiel observes fire, or something akin to it, oscillating between them (see Ezekiel 1:4–14; 10:6–22).

24. There are almost certainly limitations here. Just as fallen man was deprived of many of his original endowments in Eden, it is likely that the rebel angels were similarly diminished upon their deportation from heaven. Even if the intrinsic changes were minor, there was still the devastating fact that they were no longer backed by the authority and resources of God.

25. See Russell, *Prince,* pp. 264–266.

26. Michael Harner, *The Way of the Shaman* (New York: Bantam, 1980), p. 9.

27. The antiquity of the image of flying serpents is attested by the Chinese primitive character for reptile—a character whose elements consist of a standing snakelike body superimposed with feathers or wings. We know that the serpent was banished at the time of the Edenic curse to a life of slithering. Prior to this he was presumably upright. See C. H. Kang and Ethel Nelson, *The Discovery of Genesis* (St. Louis: Concordia, 1979), p. 61.

28. See Stephan Beyer, *Magic and Ritual in Tibet* (Delhi: Motilal Banarsidass, 1988), p. 45, and Philip Rawson, *Sacred Tibet* (London: Thames & Hudson, 1991), p. 8.

29. The associations or characteristics of the dragon-serpent are, in fact, numerous. Among the more notable: 1) jewels and precious stones; 2) chaos and darkness; 3) the atmosphere, weather and storms; 4) the goddess, creative power and sex; 5) leadership and power; 6) mind and imagination; 7) monsters, devouring and death.

30. Francis Huxley, *The Dragon* (London: Thames & Hudson, 1979), pp. 61, 8.

31. Ibid., pp. 9, 32, 66.

32. Per Kvaerne, *Tibet Bon Religion* (Leiden: Institute of Religious Iconography, State University Groningen, 1985), p. 18.

33. Taken from "Commentary on the Hexagram ch'ien," *Book of Changes*, R. Wilhelm, trans. See Huxley, *Dragon*, p. 54.

34. Carmen Blacker, *The Catalpa Bow* (London: Unwin Hyman, 1989), pp. 169–170.

35. Huxley, *Dragon*, pp. 34–35.

36. Stephen Bertman, *Doorways through Time* (Los Angles: Jeremy Tarcher, 1986), pp. 195–203.

37. M. Oldfield Howey, "The Serpent as Amulet and Charm," *Treasury of Snake Lore*, Brandt Aymar, ed. (New York: Greenberg, 1956), p. 50.

38. Huxley, *Dragon*, p. 8.

39. Gadon, *Goddess*, pp. 62–65.

40. Elsewhere in the South Pacific, one may encounter Agunua, the primary serpent god of the Solomon Islands; Ndengei, Fiji's serpent god with stone flesh; or the Melanesian snake goddess Koevasi.

41. While some Nagas of East India also claim to have originated from snakes, the rapid spread of Christianity throughout this area has served to greatly reduce this identification.

42. The antiquity of Indian devotion to the snake is evidenced in a ten-foot serpent deity hooded by seven cobras carved into a rock at Mahabalipuram thirteen centuries ago.

43. Harry Miller, "The Cobra, India's 'Good Snake,'" *National Geographic*, Vol. 138, No. 3, September 1970, pp. 393–408.

44. E. Osborn Martin, *The Gods of India* (Delhi: Indological Book House, 1988), pp. 258–260.

45. According to Hopi legend, the snake dance began when a young man tried to find the origin of all waters by following the Colorado River to its source. Along the way, it is said, he was initiated into the Snake Clan by the Great Snake himself. See *The Spirit World* (Alexandria, Va.: Time-Life, 1992), p. 50.

46. In Hindu (and Buddhist) Tantric belief, the Kundalini is a snake of energy lying dormant at the base of the spine, which can be aroused by yogic and other practices. (Carmen Blacker recommends Gopi Krishna's *Kundalini* for a vivid and horrifying description of the arising of the "serpent power.")

47. Frank Waters, *The Book of the Hopi* (New York: Penguin, 1977), pp. 218–230. Note: Many Hopi firmly believe that their Snake Clan ancestors constructed the famous Serpent Mound near Louden, Ohio, to honor Tókchi'i, guardian snake of the East. An embankment five feet high, twenty feet wide and nearly a quarter-mile long, it represents a serpent whose body is extended in seven deep curves. Within its open jaws is a large oval mound commonly believed to be an egg that the serpent is swallowing.

48. The Ophites were a gnostic sect that thrived in the second century A.D. throughout the Roman Empire. According to their esoteric theology, the snake was not only a conduit for spiritual revelation but the revelation itself.

49. Huxley, *Dragon,* pp. 91, 94.

50. Ptolemy Tompkins, *This Tree Grows Out of Hell* (San Francisco: HarperSanFrancisco, 1990), p. 65.

51. Russell, *Prince,* p. 11; Huxley, *Dragon,* pp. 66, 6.

52. Other references to Leviathan include Job 41:1, Psalm 74:14 and Psalm 104:26.

Note: Rahab, a chaos term meaning "tumult," "violence" or "defiance," is often used in Scripture as a symbolic name for Egypt (see Psalm 87:4; 89:10; Isaiah 51:9).

53. Huxley, *Dragon,* p. 6.

54. Russell, *Prince,* p. 11.

55. William Shakespeare, *Macbeth,* Act IV, Scene I, lines 12, 16.

56. Bodrogi, "New Ireland Art," p. 16.

57. Patrick Tierney, *The Highest Altar* (New York: Viking, 1989), p. 187.

On the bright side, at least this man did not live in ancient Mesoamerica. There the Aztecs carved stone rattlesnake pendants whose jaws enclosed the entire human head.

58. Huxley, *Dragon,* p. 42.

59. Ronald Siegel, *Fire in the Brain* (New York: Plume, 1992), p. 141.

60. These kinds of spirits, thought to live at the bottoms of ravines and inside caves, are known as *Kel es Souf.* See Gersi, *Faces,* pp. 26–27.

61. Cavendish, *Powers,* p. 230.

62. See Russell, *Prince,* p. 17.

63. Divine madness is a condition of pseudo-enlightenment achieved through a kind of postmodern shamanism known as Chaos Magick. According to writer Siobhán Houston, this "form of occultism is attracting considerable attention within the American and European magical communities at present." Many practitioners cut their teeth on role-playing games like Dungeons and Dragons. Chaos is stressed repeatedly as the major prerequisite to power and enlightenment. One's personal command and values are shattered by diving into the dark void or by creating and reveling in psychological anarchy. Demons are indispensable to this process. As Crowley says, "You have only to step down to their level and fraternize with them." See Aleister Crowley, *Magick,* J. Symonds and K. Grant, eds. (London: Routledge & Kegan Paul, [1929], 1973), pp. 264n, 297; Siobhán Houston, "Magic: A Peek into the Irreverent and Anarchic Recasting of the Magical Tradition," *Gnosis Magazine,* No. 36, Summer 1995, pp. 55–59; Luhrman, *Persuasions,* pp. 92–99.

64. The very name given to the Celtic horned god Cernunnos.

65. Cavendish, *Powers,* pp. 171–174.

66. Sometimes spelled Hadad.

67. 1 Kings 15:18 and Zechariah 12:11. See Saggs, *Greatness,* pp. 282–283, 288.

68. Additional information on the devil's manipulation of natural elements is found in the chapter 6 subsection "World Rulers of Darkness."

69. From interview on Fox Network "Sightings" program broadcast on November 18, 1994.

70. A Greek word, Tartarus is essentially a reduplication of Tar, the Egyptian name for the god of the underworld.

71. The dimension mentioned in Ephesians 3:10 and 6:12 is *en tois epouranois*—a Greek phrase that Edgardo Silvoso points out means "in the realm of the spirit" or "in the spiritual realm." See also Michael Green, *Exposing,* pp. 83–84.

72. Russell, *Prince,* p. 274–276.

73. Greeley, "The Devil," p. 13.

74. See Thompson, *Evil,* p. 84.

75. Russell, *Prince,* p. 275.

76. Ibid., pp. 274, 276.

77. Peter Kreeft, *Angels and Demons* (San Francisco: Ignatius, 1995), pp. 112–113.

78. Green, *Exposing,* p. 46.

Note: In *Exposing the Prince of Darkness,* Green adds this important point: "... Despite the variety in nomenclature, the overall picture is the same throughout the Bible; a variety of evil forces under a unified head. It would be foolish and misleading to try to separate the principalities and powers of the Pauline letters from the demons of the Gospels" (p. 82).

Chapter 4: Ancient Mysteries

1. As one scholar put it, "I have no curiosity to know how awkward and clumsy men have been in the dawn of arts or in their decay." Quoted by Colin Renfrew in *Archaeology and Language* (New York: Cambridge University Press, 1987), p. 287.

2. Quoted by Daniel Boorstin in *The Discoverers* (New York: Vintage, 1983), p. 611 (see also p. 612).

3. The belief in a paradisiacal garden is shared by other traditions. Hindu literature celebrates the glorious, mountain-hugging gardens of Meru, while Islam acknowledges not one but four gardens of Paradise. See David Adams Leeming, *The World of Myth* (New York: Oxford University Press, 1990), p. 290; Cooper, *Traditional Symbols,* p. 72.

4. Citing the redemptive prophecy contained in Psalm 68:18, Paul asks: "What does 'he ascended' mean except that he also descended to the lower, earthly regions?"

5. Compare with Ezekiel 1:14.

6. Other references include Psalm 48:2, where Mount Zion is compared with "the utmost heights of Zaphon" (a sacred height in the "far north"), and Isaiah 2:2–3, where, during Christ's Millennial reign, "the mountain of the LORD" comes to earth as the New Jerusalem.

7. That Satan is allowed to participate indicates not only his previous high estate, but the fact that it is an open court—a forum where even the heavenly arch-villain is permitted to express his thoughts and launch accusations.

8. Kinnaman, *Angels,* pp. 126–127.

9. Similar beliefs surrounded the Ugaritic deity El, who presided over an assembly of the gods on a cosmic mountain in the north; and the seven divine seers led by Vasishtha, whom the *Mahabharata* places on Mount Meru. In light of the sheer frequency of these images, it is hard not to wonder if they are based on real memories of human contact with the mountain of the Lord. (These would not have been personal memories, of course, but a collective record passed on as oral tradition.) See Geoffrey Ashe, *Dawn Behind the Dawn* (New York: Henry Holt, 1992), p. 32. See also Mircea Eliade, *Shamanism: Archaic Techniques of Ecstasy* (Princeton: Princeton University Press, 1964), pp. 266–269.

10. While we cannot say with certainty what would have happened if sin had not sullied God's original intentions, there are some things about which we may reasonably speculate. One of these is the prospect that obedience to the command to multiply would quickly have filled the earth with an exponentially exploding population of immortals. Given such a scenario, we might well wonder if humankind's benevolent subjection of the planet was but the first intended step in a plan that would have eventually encom-

passed galaxies. See David Fetcho, "A Sum of Shipwrecked Stars: UFOs and the Logic of Discernment," *SCP Journal*, Vol. 1, No. 2, August 1977, pp. 25–30.

11. Andrew Murray, *The Spirit of Christ* (Fort Washington, Pa.: Christian Literature Crusade, 1964), pp. 227–228.

12. Lurking behind this issue is a more complicated question: Is the mind the brain? While early philosophers such as René Descartes insisted that the mind and brain were two distinct (though interactive) processes, later thinkers have decried this as unscientific nonsense. In Gilbert Ryle's famous 1947 critique of dualism, for example, the idea of an incorporeal soul separate from the brain is ridiculed poetically as a "ghost in the machine."

13. Richard Restak, *The Brain: The Last Frontier* (New York: Warner, 1979), pp. 18–20.

Note: According to Dr. Restak, since the brain is a process, any attempt to understand the mind by examining brain cells under a microscope is like trying to experience Beethoven's Ninth Symphony by reading a treatise on the construction of violins. Washington University philosopher David Chalmers agrees, pointing out that physical theories can describe only specific mental functions such as intention, memory, attention and introspection. What they cannot do, he insists, is address the question of why the performance of these functions is accompanied by subjective experience. See John Horgan, "Can Science Explain Consciousness?" *Scientific American*, July 1994, pp. 88–94.

14. See *The Anthropic Cosmological Principle*, J. D. Barrow and F. J. Tipler, eds. (New York: Oxford University Press, 1968).

15. *Secrets of the Inner Mind*, Robert Somerville, et al., ed. (Alexandria, Va.: Time-Life, 1993), pp. 116–118.

16. Restak, *The Brain*, pp. 271–272. See also Siegel, *Fire in the Brain*, pp. 211–228.

17. It is noteworthy that millions of people today are engaged in an aggressive pursuit to recover these very capabilities.

18. While some commentators have suggested that the "sons of God" are actually fallen angels, this explanation seems unlikely. It is more probable that they are the godly descendants of Seth who polluted their lineage by marrying the wayward, if beautiful, daughters of Cain. God's distress over this union is not related to some inexplicable human-demonic intercourse, but to the deteriorating moral trajectory of the Sethites. This interpretation is supported by the fact that the Nephilim—the descendants of this union—are literally "fallen ones."

19. The one possible exception to this is the theory presented in chapter 3 that Lucifer was engaged in Eden as the heavenly light-bearer.

20. The physical risks associated with human access to the divine presence can be seen in the serious precautions taken with Moses on Mount Sinai (see Exodus 33:19–23) and in the later maintenance of the Ark of the Covenant.

21. Cited in Gerald Schroeder, *Genesis and the Big Bang* (New York: Bantam, 1990), p. 151.

22. The serpent, for example, was "more crafty" than any beast of the field (Genesis 3:1) and was cursed above "all the wild animals" (verse 14). If these words are to be granted their standard meaning, it is difficult to avoid the conclusion that the serpent was not only morally capable, but culpable as well. (While the devil was certainly judged here, so, too, was the serpent.)

23. The mysterious and powerful bond between the species is also seen in Animal Assisted Therapy. As one successful program in Tyler, Texas, has shown, contact with animals can stimulate remarkable breakthroughs in patients recovering from strokes, spinal injuries and other serious medical challenges.

24. This hypothesis may find support in the fact that as soon as a small child has learned how to name the world and tell stories to connect its parts, one of the first things he or she will do is instruct the bedroom teddy bear.

25. Colin Rose, *Accelerated Learning* (New York: Dell, 1985), p. 4.

26. Even if we adopt a low neuron estimate (fifteen billion) and assume that each cell is capable of only two states (on and off), the brain's calculating capacity is still so staggering that it would take several years to write out this number—even at the rate of one digit per second for twelve hours a day! Working with a higher neuron estimate, the late Dr. Pyotr Anokhin of Moscow University declared that the number of neural permutations is so great that the written number would extend more than six million miles! See Restak, *Brain*, p. 183; Tony Buzan, *Using Both Sides of Your Brain* (New York: Plume, 1991), p. 20; Freedman, *Brainmakers*, p. 98.

27. *Did You Know?*, p. 152.

28. Dr. Richard Cytowic, *The Man Who Tasted Shapes* (New York: Warner, 1993), p. 118.

29. Rose, *Learning*, pp. 66–67; Somerville, *Inner Mind*, p. 105.

30. Cytowic, *Shapes*, p. 166.

Note: Not surprisingly, a number of great composers, including Sergei Rachmaninoff, Franz Liszt and Olivier Messiaen, were also synesthetes.

31. Several other universities, including Howard, Duke and Tufts, have been involved with studies linking various forms of healing with the power of the mind.

32. Somerville, *Inner Mind*, pp. 129–130.

33. Gersi, *Faces*, pp. 84–86.

Note: In a PBS documentary on psychic potential that aired in May 1994, Dr. Stanley Krippner reported on the success of experiments performed at the Maimonides Community Mental Health Center in Brooklyn during the 1960s and '70s. The tests were designed to determine whether dream content could be controlled through telepathy. The subject, a male sleeper in his late twenties, was awakened by an attendant whenever brain wave patterns indicated dream activity and asked to describe his mental imagery. On one occasion, the young man groggily described a jolly man dressed in red—"maybe a clown or Santa Claus"—who was providing some kind of public entertainment. The young man did not know that another subject seated in an adjacent room had just spent the last hour endeavoring to transfer an image telepathically that was contained in a photo magazine. The picture was of a man in a Santa suit entertaining children on a beach.

34. On the basis of the research done at PEAR and elsewhere, Cambridge University professor Brian Josephson, a 1973 Nobel Prizewinner, has called for a unified field theory that can account for mystical and even psychic experiences. See Rogier van Bakel, "Mind Over Matter," *WIRED*, Vol. 3, No. 4, April 1995; Somerville, *Inner Mind*, pp. 130–131.

35. Willis Harman and Howard Rheingold, *Higher Creativity*, quoted in Gersi, *Faces*, p. 6.

36. Dr. Robert Jahn believes these "intuitive aspects" still operate openly in animals. He cites as examples "the migration capabilities of birds and fish, and the group consciousness that is evident in swarming insects."

Further evidence for this theory is found in a series of experiments carried out at the Swiss Foundation Marcel et Monique Odier de Psycho-Physique. Here a robot called a Tychoscope was placed into an enclosed room and programmed to move about randomly. When a cage of live chicks was placed on one side of the room, however, it seemed that they repeatedly "willed" the robot to remain near the cage. Asked to explain why human subjects failed to duplicate this feat, Dr. Dean Radin, a researcher at the University of Nevada, hypothesized that "the birds were not hampered by rationalizations . . . and when you have subjects that work on an instinctual level, it presumably leads to higher motivation and more remarkable results." See "Animal Magnetism: Chick It Out," *WIRED*, Vol. 3, No. 4, April 1995, p. 84.

37. Watchman Nee, *The Latent Power of the Soul* (New York: Christian Fellowship Publishers, 1972), pp. 44, 19–20.

38. To obtain more agricultural cropland, mankind has deforested a net area the size of the continental U.S. We also divert more water each year than is contained in Lake Huron.

39. Findings of the Earth Transformed Project involving scientists from sixteen countries, quoted by Robert Kates in "Sustaining Life on the Earth," *Scientific American*, October 1994, Vol. 271, No. 4, pp. 114–122.

40. Ibid., p. 115; Denis Hayes, "It's Time for the Rich to Find New Ways to Measure Wealth," *Seattle Times*, May 15, 1994.

41. Apart from God, according to Romans 1:21, the mind of man is *futile* (or empty), while his heart, or will, is *darkened* (unable to see reality).

42. Efforts to obtain wisdom apart from God, as the writer of Ecclesiastes learned, can be deeply frustrating: "I said, 'I am determined to be wise'—but this was beyond me. . . . Wisdom . . . is far off and most profound" (Ecclesiastes 7:23–24). In a similar acknowledgment, Job noted that wisdom "is hidden from the eyes of every living thing" (Job 28:21), but he hastened to add, "God understands the way to it" (verse 23). The psalmist, having discovered this secret oasis, rejoiced, "You teach me wisdom in the inmost place" (Psalm 51:6).

43. According to the late mythographer Joseph Campbell, many cultures have held to the belief that the animals were the first teachers of humankind. Capitalizing on this misguided notion, the devil has continued to adopt this guise when dealing with "wisdom seekers" who have suppressed truth.

44. While the standard elements of deception—including the flesh, the world and the devil (see Revelation 12:9)—were all present in Eden, the first two of these elements were not yet polluted. (Although the Scriptures often define "the world" as corrupt [and corrupting] human systems, the term is also used to describe external influences in general. Similarly, "the flesh" is presented as both sin-habituated appetites and as generic human life. Although a case can be made that the flesh and the world are intrinsically neutral, they have become untrustworthy and potentially dangerous.)

45. It is interesting to note that the Chinese character, or ideograph, for *beginning* consists of three combined elements: *woman, secretly* and *mouth!* See C. H. Kang and Ethel Nelson, *The Discovery of Genesis* (St. Louis: Concordia, 1979), pp. 61–62, 64–65.

46. Schaeffer, *Genesis*, pp. 81–82.

47. If possessing a broad range of moral knowledge was intrinsically wrong, God himself would be bad (see Genesis 3:22).

48. The Egyptians were among the first to champion the idea of inner divinity. In the Egyptian Book of the Dead, for example, the deceased soul boasts: "My hair is the hair of Nut. My face is the face of the Disk. My eyes are the eyes of Hathor. . . . There is no member of my body that is not the member of some god. . . . I am Yesterday, Today, and Tomorrow, and I have the power to be born a second time. I am the divine hidden Soul who creates the gods."

49. At present Dr. Gadon spends her time lecturing at the California Institute of Integral Studies, a nontraditional graduate school that trains therapists to integrate the spir-

itual into whatever they do. Her teaching interests focus on goddess studies and, in particular, theories of prehistory.

50. One of the more interesting moments of our conversation occurred when I referred to a passage she had penned as part of an article entitled "Sacred Places of India: The Body of the Goddess." The specific passage read: "The woman-and-tree motif is long-standing in Indian culture, going back 5,000 years to the earliest Indian civilization in the Indus Valley." When I mentioned that this symbolism reminded me of the primary Edenic elements presented in the book of Genesis, Dr. Gadon looked flabbergasted. The connection, it seemed, had not occurred to her.

51. A more complete explanation of the nature and influence of the Goddess philosophy is provided in chapter 7.

52. Cited in Gadon, *Goddess*, p. 300.

53. Deena Metzger, "Revamping the World: On the Return of the Holy Prostitute," *Anima* 12/2, 1986.

54. Although she is Jewish, Metzger has jettisoned the Judeo-Christian God in favor of the goddess Asherah. Her personal icon is the tree, which as Elinor Gadon points out, "is the form in which the Goddess manifests" (Gadon, *Goddess*, p. 301). A variation on this theme is seen in a thirteenth-century B.C. Egyptian painting that presents a mother goddess distributing sustenance from the branches of a tree of life.

55. Others insist that eternal life is available by eating the peach of immortality found in the Western Paradise (Taoist tradition) or by drinking liquid extracted from the Iranian haoma tree (Zoroastrian tradition). In the Buddhist world, the pipal or bodhi tree is revered as a symbol of great awakening. See Eliade, *Shamanism*, p. 273; Cooper, *Traditional Symbols*, p. 176.

56. As Nebuchadnezzar's dream in Daniel 4:4–37 seems to indicate, the tree may also serve as a symbol of independence.

57. Henry H. Halley, *Halley's Bible Handbook* (Grand Rapids: Zondervan, 1965), p. 66; Cooper, *Traditional Symbols*, p. 179.

Note: If the Babylonian vision of a center tree with branches reaching to a heavenly realm is suggestive of Eden's dimensional gate, so is the Norse Yggdrasil, a cosmic ash tree whose branches extend to the region where the gods reportedly hold court. The mighty oak tree, in the words of an Irish shamaness, "is the doorway between the worlds." See Leeming, *Myth*, pp. 343–344; Ward Rutherford, *The Druids: Magicians of the West* (Wellingborough, England: Aquarian Press, 1983), pp. 68–69; and Cowan, *Fire*, p. 111. At least one Syro-Hittite seal features four rivers flowing from a central sacred tree. For more on the subject of cosmic centers, see Leeming, *Myth*, pp. 341–342, 432–433; Joseph Campbell, *The Masks of God: Occidental Mythology* (New York: Viking, 1959), p. 12; and Eliade, *Shamanism*, pp. 269–274.

Although from a Christian perspective many of the notions that have come to be associated with cosmic centrality are tainted and unreliable, the doctrine itself has deep biblical roots. This may be seen not only in the central trees of Eden, but in the cross of Christ. As Meinrad Craighead points out in *The Sign of the Tree:* "Origin, Hippolytus, John Chrysostom, and Augustine interpreted [the cross] as 'an immortal plant,' 'pillar of the universe,' 'bond of all things,' and 'center of the cosmos.'" During the course of his Easter sermon in the third century A.D., Hippolytus, bishop of Rome, declared, "[The cross] is the fulcrum of all things and the place where they are all at rest." See Meinrad Craighead, *The Sign of the Tree: Meditations in Images and Words* (London: Mitchell Beazley, 1979), pp. 34, 38; and Roger Cook, *The Tree of Life* (London: Thames & Hudson, 1974), p. 20.

58. Moyra Caldicott, *Myths of the Sacred Tree* (Rochester, Vt.: Destiny, 1993), p. 98. See also Cooper, *Traditional Symbols*, p. 176.

Note: In another Greek myth, which may have been based on facts established in the Garden of Eden, Persephone is tempted into the arms of Hades, the Lord of the Underworld, by the fruit of an enchanted pomegranate tree.

59. *Halley's*, p. 68.

60. Ibid., p. 76.

Note: Many Old Testament lists (i.e., Genesis 10) should be read as genealogy, not chronology. As Francis Schaeffer points out in *Genesis in Space and Time*, these genealogical lists are about "peoples bringing forth peoples rather than individuals bringing forth individuals. . . . The word *begat* in Genesis 11 does not require a first-generation father-son relationship. It can mean *fathered someone who led to*" (pp. 154–155). For this reason, dogmatic assertions about the flow of history outlined in this passage are risky. "It is not that we have to accept the concept of the long periods of time modern science postulates, but rather that there are really no clearly defined terms upon which at this time to base a final debate" (p. 156). John Whitcomb and Henry Morris in *The Genesis Flood* (Phillipsburg, N.J.: Presbyterian & Reformed Publishing Co., 1961) agree, declaring that "the strict-chronology interpretation of Genesis 11 has been shown to be unnecessary for various reasons" (p. 483).

61. To insure that these narratives were not overgrown by myth, God arranged for a handful of eyewitness reporters to cross the watery gulf intact. One of these epochal wayfarers, Noah's son Shem, was able to supply a firsthand description of the pre-Flood world for at least five centuries after the deluge!

62. Biblical references to antediluvian life are found in Genesis 6:4, Job 40:15–41:34 and Psalm 104:25–26. To these we can add evidence contained in well-preserved French cave paintings, most of which depict human ritual endeavor and animal life in ancient Europe. See the Discovery Channel, "A Cave Beneath the Sea," September 12, 1994; see also "Re-creating a Vanished World," *National Geographic*, March 1972.

63. Despite their long-standing kinship, not all was well between man and beast. A relationship intended to operate on the basis of tender and righteous dominion had deteriorated so that beast regarded man with fear and dread. Having apparently lost the ability to engage in cross-species communication, man saw fraternal emotions replaced by alienation. Eventually the beasts of the field began to shed human blood (see Genesis 9:2, 5).

64. Numbers 13:32–33 indicates that the descendants of Anak were "of great size" and "[came] from the Nephilim." Writing in *The Canopied Earth: World that Was* (Dallas: CFN, 1991), Volume IV of *The Creation Series,* Dennis Lindsay makes the interesting observation that "the giant creatures which once roamed the Earth would not have seemed as awesome and imposing to ancient men if they too were of enormous proportions."

65. *Flavius Josephus' Complete Works*, trans. William Whitson (Grand Rapids: Kregel, 1976), Book I, Chapter 3.9.

66. According to many creation scientists, this golden age robustness may have been due to a protective water vapor canopy that surrounded the earth. (They draw scriptural support for this idea from passages like Genesis 1:6–8, Job 26:8 and 2 Peter 3:5.) Some advocates of this theory claim that the vapor canopy was five to six miles thick and twenty or twenty-five miles above the earth. If such a canopy existed, it would have had several beneficial effects. For one thing, by eliminating temperature variations caused by the uneven heating of the surface of the earth, the canopy would have produced a windless

environment. This, in turn, would have promoted the Genesis 2:6 mist—an important ally of life in the rainless, pre-Flood world.

It may also have resulted in greater atmospheric pressure and protection from harmful radiation—factors that would have enhanced biomass (the total mass of living matter within a given area) and slowed the aging process. In fact, recent discoveries have shown, according to Lindsay, that "air bubbles trapped in [ancient] amber contained a 50 percent higher oxygen concentration than is found today." See Lindsay, *Canopied Earth*, pp. 210, 213; see also pp. 68–71, 97, 107, 122–123, 132, 134, 137, 221, 250.

67. Howard Rheingold, *Virtual Reality* (New York: Touchstone, 1991), pp. 379–382; "Behold the Stone Age," Robert Hughes, *Time*, February 13, 1995. See also John Pfeiffer, *The Creative Explosion: An Inquiry into the Origins of Science and Religion* (Ithaca, N.Y.: Cornell University Press, 1982), and Julien Ries, *The Origins of Religions* (Grand Rapids: Eerdmans, 1994), pp. 43, 50.

68. Rock paintings located near the Zuojiang River in China's Guangxi Province feature hundreds of human supplicants, their arms raised in what appears to be a ritual honoring of the sun (see Ries, *Origins*, p. 72). These and other cave art murals (such as those found at the Cueva de Las Manos Pintadas in Argentina) are most likely post-Flood productions. In some instances, the inclusion of rainbow symbols virtually confirms this assessment (see Ries, *Origins*, p. 42).

69. Terence McKenna, *Food of the Gods: The Search for the Original Tree of Knowledge* (New York: Bantam, 1992), pp. 70–75, 78–79. Others drawing attention to the mushroom motif in the Tassili frescoes include ethnomycologist Jeff Gaines (Boulder, Colorado) and Italian scholar Giorgio Samorini. See "Etnomicologia Nell'arte Rupestre Sahariana (Periodo delle 'Testa Rotonde')," *Boll. Camuno Notizie*, Vol. 6(2):18–22. See also Roger Lewin, "Stone Age Psychedelia," *New Scientist*, June 8, 1991, pp. 30–34.

70. J. Ki-Zerbo, ed., *A General History of Africa: Methodology and African Prehistory* (Berkeley: University of California Press & UNESCO, 1981, 1990), pp. 247–249; Ries, *Origins*, pp. 34–35.

71. Acclaimed French prehistorian Jacques Cauvin has declared his belief that the Genesis accounts of the departure from Eden and the killing of Abel are no mere myth, but rather the account of a true story based on the memory of Near Eastern man. See Jacques Cauvin, "Mémoire d'Orient: la sortie du jardin d'Eden et la néolithisation du Levant," *Cahiers de l'Institut Catholique de Lyon*, No. 17, 1986, pp. 25–40. For mention of possible cave shelters, see Robert Ingpen and Philip Wilkinson, *Encyclopedia of Mysterious Places: The Life and Legends of Ancient Sites Around the World* (New York: Viking Studio, 1990), p. 84; Renfrew, *Archaeology*, pp. 157, 173; and McKenna, *Food*, pp. 79–81.

72. The abandonment of caves for villages, and hunting and gathering for agriculture, was a hallmark of the Natufian civilization. From as late as 8000 B.C., their cultural area had spread between the Nile and Euphrates. See Ries, *Origins*, p. 63.

73. Çatal Hüyük is believed to have been inhabited between 6250–5400 B.C., although some estimates push the origins of the town back as far as 7200 B.C. Of the 139 buildings excavated at this sprawling 32-acre site, nearly a third seem to have been used for ritual purposes. See Gadon, *Goddess*, pp. 25–37; Ingpen and Wilkinson, *Mysterious Places*, pp. 83–87; Ries, *Origins*, pp. 54–71.

74. Hallucinogenic mushrooms once again suggest themselves, owing to the fact that the local cattle cult would have produced an ample supply of the dung necessary to grow the potent fungi.

75. Gadon, *Goddess*, pp. 25, 34, 43; Ingpen and Wilkinson, *Mysterious Places*, pp. 86–87; McKenna, *Food*, pp. 83–85.

76. A mistress who would evolve ultimately into Artemis of the Ephesians (see Gadon, *Goddess*, p. 34).

77. Gadon, *Goddess*, pp. 52–53; Ries, *Origins*, pp. 66–67, 83–84.

78. Genesis 6:5, 11–12.

79. McKenna, *Food*, pp. 64–65, 88–89.

80. Gadon, *Goddess*, p. 11.

81. Genesis 4:17, and later, Genesis 11:4.

Note: Contrary to popular belief, Babel (or Babylon) was not the world's first city—not by a long shot. Impressive human settlements dotted the earth, as archaeological evidence confirms, for at least two or three thousand years before Nimrod launched his famous building boom between the Tigris and Euphrates Rivers. In addition to the well-documented Mesopotamian cities of Eridu, Erech, Susa, Ur, Sippar (Accad), Larsa, Kish and Jemdet Nasr, substantial farming/fishing communities are known to have existed in Turkey (Çatal Hüyük), Palestine (Jericho), Syria (Mureybet), Greece (Nea Nikomedeia), Yugoslavia (Lepenski Vir) and Egypt—where at least some modern scholars think the enigmatic Sphinx stood long before the Flood. See John Anthony West, "Civilization Rethought," *Condé Nast Traveler*, February 1993, p. 100.

82. That the Sethites exchanged their monotheism for perverse idolatry is evidenced by a comparison of Genesis 4:26 with Genesis 6:1–6, 11–12. Also, when Dr. Stephen Langdon excavated Jemdet Nasr (a pre-Flood city 25 miles northeast of Babylon) in 1926, he found pictographic inscriptions indicating this unfortunate decline. Sir Flinders Petrie was said to have uncovered similar evidence in Egypt. See *Halley's*, pp. 49, 62.

83. In Genesis 7:11 we learn that the great Flood began when "all the springs of the great deep burst forth, and the floodgates of the heavens were opened." Something happened, in other words, both *under* and *over* the earth. In the former instance, deep volcanic plumes (or vents) burst through the earth's crust and raised the elevation of the planet's seas. In the latter, a ruptured vapor canopy, like heavenly floodgates, released a torrential downpour on a world that had never known rain. (For evidence that a comet or asteroid strike ruptured the vapor canopy and precipitated underseas volcanic release, see Luis Alvarez, et al., "Extraterrestrial Cause for the Cretaceous-Tertiary Extinction," *Science* 208 [1980], p. 1095; and Emil Venere, "Lava Linked to End of Era," *Seattle Times*, August 14, 1993. See also Roger Larson, "The Mid-Cretaceous Superplume Episode," *Scientific American*, February 1995, Vol. 272, No. 2, pp. 82–86. Larson believes that, among other things, massive explosions on the sea floor created "rising sea levels that [would have] drowned much of what is dry land today.")

84. At that point, life spans that had been cut in half by the immediate effects of the Flood plummeted once again.

85. Compare Genesis 8:20 with Genesis 11:3–4.

86. In one early poem, the god Enki is said to have created all the languages from a single original tongue, while a stone tablet discovered in the holy city of Nippur records that "the people in unison, to Enlil in one tongue gave praise." See Jeremy Black and Anthony Green, *Gods, Demons and Symbols of Ancient Mesopotamia* (Austin: University of Texas Press, 1992, published in cooperation with British Museum Press), p. 179; and "Enmerkar and the Land of Aratta," Nippur fragment, trans. by Samuel Noah Kramer, *From the Tablets of Sumer* (Indian Hills, Col.: Falcon Wing's Press, 1956), p. 259.

87. Merritt Ruhlen, *The Origin of Language: Tracing the Evolution of the Mother Tongue* (New York: John Wiley & Sons, 1994), p. 104.

88. Micah 5:6 refers to the entire region of Assyria as "the land of Nimrod," and the early Assyrian capital of Calah is now known as Nimrud (the Arabic form of *Nimrod*).

89. One reason to explain Nimrod's curious lack of press is that he was deified posthumously and renamed Merodach (see *Halley's*, p. 82). If this is true, this would clarify why a number of Assyrian and Babylonian leaders adopted the title, and why hunting was considered a religious duty of kings (see Saggs, *Greatness*, p. 290). It is also interesting to note that *Merodach* is similar etymologically to *mered*, the Hebrew and Aramaic word for "rebellion." Jan Karnis, *The Nimrod Legacy* (unpublished manuscript), p. 64.

90. Os Guinness, *The Dust of Death* (Downers Grove, Ill.: InterVarsity, 1973), pp. 267–268.

91. Hebrews 2:15 speaks of "those who all their lives were held in slavery by their fear of death." See Green, *Exposing*, pp. 75–76.

92. The stepped-tower ziggurats that dominated many cities of southern Mesopotamia through the fifth century B.C. were generally built of solid brick. Summit shrines were covered in blue glazed tiles and reachable by means of a spiral ramp or exterior triple stairway. While no one knows the precise dimensions of the Tower of Babel, indications are that it was impressive. Ruins of a ziggurat discovered near Babylon reveal a base nearly one hundred yards square. It was here that British archaeologist Sir Henry Rawlinson discovered a cylinder that read: "The tower of Borshippa, which a former king erected, and completed to a height of 42 cubits, whose summit he did not finish, fell to ruins in ancient times" (see *Halley's*, p. 83).

93. Ashe, *Dawn*, p. 109. Ashe also draws attention to the fact that the Tower "was a visual bond, a landmark seen from afar over flat country." At the same time, however, it extended to the heavens and the underworld. To appease the deities of the latter realm, occasional libations were poured down specially installed pipes. See also Mircea Eliade, *The Sacred and the Profane* (Orlando: Harcourt, Brace, 1987), pp. 37; Black and Green, *Ancient Mesopotamia*, p. 53.

In what is possibly a corrupted reference to the Edenic gateway and the mount of assembly where the *beneha elohim*, or "sons of God," are said to congregate, Sumerian creation myths speak of a primal thoroughfare between the earth and a heavenly mountain inhabited by the Anunnaki (a fate-decreeing council of seven gods). This mythology also speaks, with strong biblical overtones, of a vast mountain that rose from primordial waters. Starting out as a single body, it divided subsequently into earth below and heaven above. But the split was not total. A crucial connection remained allowing for traffic between earth and the cosmic abode of the gods.

As a sacral mountain, the ziggurat had seven stories representing the seven planetary heavens. By ascending them, Babylonian kings, priests and consorts reached the summit of the universe. One early Egyptian report insisted that the stepped tower "had been built by giants who wished to climb up to heaven." (In addition to harmonizing with the biblical declaration that "giants were on the earth in those days," the report also suggested that, as a result of the builders' impious folly, many were "afterward unable to recognize each other.") See Boorstin, *Discoverers*, pp. 83–84.

94. Eliade, *Sacred*, pp. 40–41.

95. Saggs, *Greatness*, pp. 307–308. See also Black and Green, *Ancient Mesopotamia*, pp. 52–52, 179; and John Skinner, *Genesis: The International Critical Commentary* (Edinburgh: T & T Clark, 1930), p. 226. For a broader discussion of the role of the "sky ladder" in various international cultures, see Eliade, *Shamanism*, pp. 487–494.

96. Some of these rituals likely also took place in a sacred chamber known as the *Egipar*.

97. Saggs, *Greatness*, pp. 330–332; Black and Green, *Ancient Mesopotamia*, pp. 157–158.

98. The Sumerian ideogram for this title (essentially a divine prostitute) can be inter-preted as either "the lady [who is] a deity" or "the wife of the god." In any case, the Entu was of very high social standing. In fact, several kings, including Sargon of Agade and Nabu'na'id, made their daughters the Entu of particular gods.

The Greek historian Herodotus, who may have visited Babylon in the fifth century B.C., reported that on top of the ziggurat "stands a great temple with a sumptuously-equipped couch in it. . . . No one spends the night there except one Assyrian woman, cho-sen by the god himself; or so say the Chaldeans who are the priests of Bel. These Chaldeans say—not that I believe them—that the god himself comes into the temple and takes his rest on the couch. . . ." See Herodotus, *The Histories*, translated by Aubrey de Sélincourt (New York: Penguin, 1972), Book 1, p. 114; see also Saggs, *Greatness*, p. 305.

99. Although literally hundreds of ziggurats were erected across Mesopotamia in the first three millennia B.C., the original Tower may have been built even earlier. And although practices associated with these temple towers evolved over time, we are nevertheless able to reconstruct a general pattern of belief and behavior that likely applied to Babel.

100. *The Zohar*, 75a, Vol. 1, Harry Sperling and Maurice Simon, trans. (London: Son-cino Press, 1976).

101. Once demons have been drawn to a city, their first order of business is to use whatever wiles they possess to lure additional spiritual targets into the urban web. For this reason Babylon is called the "Mother of Prostitutes" (Revelation 17:5), while Nineveh is referred to as "the mistress of sorceries" (Nahum 3:4).

102. While passages like Ezekiel 38–39 employ *tsaphon* symbolically about other nations, it is still in the context of concentrated—and evil—power. Ezekiel 8:3 also locates the idol of jealousy at the entrance to the North Gate of the inner Temple, while the pri-mary access to the shrine summit of most ziggurats (including the famous structure at Ur) was a great stairway on the northern side. Valuable insights on this subject were pro-vided by Middle East researcher Matthew Hand. See also Black & Green, *Ancient Mesopotamia*, p. 188.

103. But what are we to make of Psalm 48, in which Mount Zion (or holy Jerusalem) is described as being "in the far north" (see verse 2, RSV)? Surely the psalmist was not equating the sanctuary of Yahweh with any generalized "envelope of darkness," nor could he have been referring to Syria's Jebel al-Aqra, which was the recognized abode of Baal. So what did he mean? A natural guess is that he was presenting Mount Zion as a physi-cal place of power directly linked to the heavenly mount of assembly. In this sense it was a replacement for Eden—the Holy of Holies superseding the original center tree as a dimensional gateway. Unlike the cosmic northern mountain of Babylon, Zion is found in the *far north*, well beyond the polluted atmosphere of imaginary gods or fallen angels. Only on Mount Zion could the true God be truly found.

104. At the same time, the north was the direction from which the Aztec ancestors came, and the region where contact was made with powerful deities like Coatlicue. See Tompkins, *Tree*, p. 10; Rudolf Van Zantwijk, "The Great Temple of Tenochtitlan: Model of Aztec Cosmovision," published in *Mesoamerican Sites and World-Views* (Washington, D.C.: Dumbarton Oaks Research Library and Collections, 1981), pp. 75, 78.

105. Cooper, *Traditional Symbols*, pp. 39–40, 112.

Note: A society of Canada's Kwakiutl tribe claim that their power is derived from a can-nibalistic spirit that resides at the north end of the world. See Cushing, *Fetishes*, pp. 16, 30–31; *Spirit World*, pp. 38–39.

106. God also makes clear He is able to bridle these destructive powers for His own sovereign purposes.

107. See Cavendish, *Powers*, p. 177.

108. Ibid., p. 93.

109. It was for this reason that Dositheus, the master of Simon Magus mentioned in Acts 8:9–25, resided in Damascus and claimed to be the messianic star announced in Numbers 24:17. See Damascus Document 7, 14H. See also F. M. Strickert, Damascus Document VII, 10–20; and Qumran Messianic Expectation in *Revue de Qumran* 12 (1986), pp. 327–349; and P. R. Davies, *The Damascus Covenant: An Interpretation of the 'Damascus Document,'* Sheffield 1983 (JSOT, Supplemental Series 25), and J. Daniélou, "L' Etoile de Jacob et la Mission Chretienne a Damas" in *Vigiliae Christianae* 11 (1957), pp. 121–138.

110. While space limitations preclude a comprehensive listing of this evidence, the following summary is worthy of review:

- The Scriptures indicate that both Eden and Lucifer (perhaps before, and certainly after, his fall) were located in the north. Since Eden was an important meeting place between God and man, the enemy conspired to pollute the site.
- The entire postdiluvian population was at one time living in the north—and demonic camps are always pitched in the shadow of human civilization.
- The biblical root word for *north* means "an envelope of darkness."
- Ezekiel 28 and other passages offer descriptions of Lucifer as lofty and gem-encrusted. Mesopotamian and Canaanite gods also lived on northern heights enveloped in precious stones.
- Babylon, a synonym for *north,* is also called the "Gate of the Gods" and the "Mother of Harlots." Neighboring Nineveh is referred to as the "the mistress of sorceries," while the Prince of Persia is presented as a potent spiritual being.
- Cultural mythologies almost universally portray the north as the source of power, revelation and death.
- Shamanism, Goddess worship, divine kingship and astrology all have their origins in the north.
- Most unevangelized people groups are located in the north, as are the headquarters of every major non-Christian religion.

111. *Halley's*, p. 84.

Chapter 5: Out from Babel

1. In fairness to Augustine, it must be said that he did firmly reject the popular notion of an antipodes—a torrid equatorial zone in which rain fell upwards and men's feet were said to be attached in a fashion opposite to that of normal humans. See Boorstin, *Discoverers*, pp. 107, 110.

2. While the exact date of this dispersion may never be known, many scholars are persuaded that the event occurred sometime between 4000 and 2800 B.C. The best biblical clues are linked to the life of Abram and help us primarily with the front end of this projected range. Abram, widely believed to have left Ur of the Chaldees around 2100 B.C., encountered well-established civilizations in Turkey, Canaan and Egypt. In His covenant with Abram, God gave the patriarch land rights to ten (preexisting) nations (see Genesis 15:19–21). Since the peoples and civilizations of Abram's day are widespread and mature, we can only conclude that the division of the nations took place many centuries earlier.

3. William Shakespeare, *The Tempest*, Act 1, Scene 2, line 49.

4. Colin Renfrew, *Archaeology and Language* (New York: Cambridge University Press, 1987), p. 2.

5. Stephen Bertman, *Doorways through Time* (Los Angeles: Jeremy Tarcher, 1986), p. 2.

6. Citizens across Europe, fascinated by the prospect of peering back into the mists of time, flocked to these novel institutions in droves. By the mid-eighteenth century, this robust community of transient spectators had itself given birth to a new word: *tourist.*

7. See Michael Lemonick, "Ancient Odysseys," *Time,* February 13, 1995.

Note: Among the more valuable of these items are engraved stone slabs, known as stelae, that are often found near sacred sites. During a nineteenth-century excavation of Mesopotamia's holy city of Nippur, archaeologists unearthed several stelae, along with a treasure trove of fifty thousand clay tablets, most dating from the third millennium B.C. Shortly thereafter, the famous Weld Dynastic Prism was discovered a few miles north of Ur. Chiseled in 2170 B.C. by a scribe named Nur-Ninsurbur, it is believed to be the first outline of world history. Some scholars think the Prism, found in 1922, was created more than one hundred years before Abraham. See *Halley's,* pp. 43–51.

8. The inability to recover a particular object does not necessarily mean it did not exist. In Central Europe, for example, the earliest actual plow is at least a thousand years younger than images of plows carved in stone by Copper Age artists.

9. Ferreting out and deciphering these weathered clues often requires rigorous detective work. Occasionally, however, researchers get a break when special conditions such as air temperature or soil composition preserve the actual bodies of ancient peoples. One of these mute time-travelers, the so-called Lady of Oplontis (a female victim of the eruption of Mount Vesuvius in A.D. 79), recently yielded a bundle of two-thousand-year-old secrets to the x-rays and CAT scans of modern science. Other examples include the Copper Age "Iceman" discovered by Alpine hikers in 1991, and specimens recovered from Danish and English bogs, the arid deserts of western China and various Altaic and Andean mountain peaks.

10. Not all the lessons are sublime. Some revelations, like this first-century graffiti at Pompeii, serve to remind us how little we have changed over the years: *I wonder, O wall, that you have not fallen in ruins from supporting the stupidity of so many scribblers.*

11. NOVA, "In Search of the First Language," air date December 27, 1994; Ruhlen, *Language,* p. 73.

Note: Although archaeologists like Colin Renfrew caution against making "simplistic use" of protolexicons (prehistoric vocabularies) in historical analysis, they are well acquainted with the benefits of this approach. See Renfrew, *Archaeology,* pp. 77–86, 284–289.

12. For several practical examples, see Ashe, *Dawn,* pp. 31, 44–49.

13. The problem with this approach is that full knowledge of an ancient tongue depends on its having been written down, which in most instances never happened. Even in these circumstances, however, language fragments can still be gleaned from river and place names (which often reflect original, preliterate forms) or through customs that have been recorded by literate neighbors.

14. Renfrew, *Archaeology,* p. 20.

15. When these hymns were written down for the first time, Renfrew notes that they recorded "a whole literature, and an entire early language form, which would otherwise have been lost completely" (*Archaeology,* p. 21).

16. During the Norman period, bards became attached to the aristocracy, their high status coming after a six-year course of study. See Jill and Leon Uris, *Ireland: A Terrible Beauty* (New York: Doubleday, 1975), p. 95.

17. To these genuine traditionalists, truth was paramount. When a Dogon specialist from the Pignari region of Mali was compelled to lie in order to save the life of a hunted

woman he had hidden in his house, he subsequently resigned his office because he no longer fulfilled the conditions required to perform his duties properly. In this sense, masters of knowledge differ from storytellers known as *griots* whose primary function is to entertain. The public does not confuse the two, well aware that griots "are allowed to have two tongues." See Ki-Zerbo, *General History*, pp. 62–72.

18. Ibid., p. 3.

19. While maritime peoples did exist (see Genesis 10:4–5), their seagoing forays were confined to the relative safety of coastal waters.

20. A few of the other Bible references, besides Jonah, to the ships of Tarshish are 1 Kings 10:22 (see NIV text note); 2 Chronicles 9:21 (again, see text note); Psalm 48:7; Isaiah 2:16 (see note), 23:1 and 60:9; and Ezekiel 27:25.

21. Barry Fell, *America B.C.* (New York: Pocket, 1976, 1989), pp. 93–94, 108–110.

22. In addition to fresh evidence from the hard sciences (see Curt Anderson, "Plant Find Links Continents," *Seattle Times*, April 28, 1994), historians point out that a circular disk is the shape associated most often with early maps. Although in medieval times this was ostensibly to preserve the "circle of the earth" referred to in Isaiah 40:22, the form may also have reflected early planetary geology. Adding credence to this theory is the fact that the oldest world map in existence, a Babylonian tablet ascribed to the sixth century B.C., depicts a flat, circular continent surrounded by the "earthly ocean." To the Hebrews, the island of the earth was known as the *tebel*, while the Romans preferred the term *orbis terrarum*, "circle of lands." See Erich Neumann, *The Origins and History of Consciousness* (Boston: Routledge & Kegan Paul, 1954), p. 10, illustration 3; Eckhard Unger, "Ancient Babylonian Maps and Plans," *Antiquity*, Vol. 9, September 1935, pp. 311–322; and John Noble Wilford, *The Mapmakers* (New York, Vintage, 1981), p. 10. Ancient Hindu and Navajo myths present a similar picture, as does the Greek poet Homer. See Ashe, *Dawn*, p. 55; and *The Jain Cosmology* (New York: Harmony, 1981), pp. 26–28.

The idea of a central land mass girdled with water also has roots in the biblical creation account. According to Genesis 1:9–10: "God said, 'Let the water under the sky be gathered to *one place*, and let dry ground appear.' And it was so. God called the dry ground 'land,' and the *gathered waters* he called 'seas' . . ." (emphases added). A primal supercontinent may also be inferred from Genesis 2:10–14, which describes Edenic headwaters as dividing into rivers that flow through Mesopotamia, East Africa (Cush) and possibly India. Since today this would be impossible, given the mountains and seas that separate these lands, we can only assume that the earth was once a far different place.

23. Since the earth was presumably perfect at creation, and life continued to luxuriate even after the Edenic judgment, any geological upheaval must have taken place during or after the Flood. In a possible reference to the draining of the floodwaters that once covered the earth, Psalm 104:5–9 suggests that this kind of upheaval may have included significant continental uplift.

24. Far from being the solid sheath many assume, the earth's crust more accurately resembles crackers floating atop a bowl of hot soup. Known to geologists as *plates*, these "crackers" are constantly shifting. When they collide or slip, the most noticeable consequences are earthquakes and volcanic eruptions.

25. Further evidence of a continental breakup is found in the desolate, mid-Atlantic islets known as the St. Peter-Paul rocks. Instead of comprising uplifted molten material like most oceanic islands, these barren crab haunts reveal features identical to those found in subcontinental mantle. This means that the rocks are geological crumbs left behind from the breakup of the Pangaean loaf. See "Earth Before Pangea," Ian Dalziel, *Scientific American*, January 1995, Vol. 272, No. 1, pp. 58–63. For a related article, see "The

Earth's Mantle Below the Oceans," Enrico Bonatti, *Scientific American*, March 1994, Vol. 270, No. 3, pp. 44–51.

26. Michael Oard offers a plausible case for the land bridge migrations in *An Ice Age Caused by the Genesis Flood* (El Cajon, Calif.: Institute of Creation Research, 1990), pp. 84–86.

27. Either of these theories is plausible, although secular scientists insist that Pangaea drifted apart long before modern man arrived on the scene. Creationists, on the other hand, dispute the assumptions on which secular dating methods are based. As Whitcomb and Morris put it, ". . . The radiocarbon method [of dating] cannot be applied to periods in the remote past because the Biblical doctrine of a universal Deluge calls for a non-uniformitarian history of the earth's atmosphere and thus of cosmic-ray activity and radiocarbon concentrations. The assumptions of this and similar methods of dating . . . are clearly contradicted by the testimony of II Peter 3:3–7" (*The Genesis Flood*, pp. 43–44). In addition, a number of radiocarbon dates have been proven either contradictory or archaeologically unacceptable. In his book *Prehistory and Earth Models* (London: Max Parrish, 1960), former University of Utah professor Melvin Cook writes, "There really are no reliable time clocks despite an overwhelming contrary opinion" (p. xi).

28. While scientists typically contend that the breakup of Pangaea was an imperceptible process occurring over eons, at least one large-scale computer simulation (using a Cray supercomputer at the Los Alamos National Laboratory) showed otherwise. The data in this test demonstrated that, four months after separation, the continents were moving at a speed of nearly 1.7 miles per hour! At this rate, Spain and America would have reached their current positions on opposite sides of the Atlantic in a single year (as opposed to the hundreds of millions of years proposed by evolutionary scientists). See John Baumgardner, "Numerical Simulation of the Large Scale Tectonic Changes Accompanying the Flood," pp. 17–30, published in the "Proceedings of the First National Conference on Creationism," Vol. 2 (Pittsburgh, 1986).

29. The origin myth of the Zuni tribe also draws strong associations with Eden. "In ancient times," the storyteller relates, "all beings belonged to one family. Póshai ank'ia, the father of our sacred bands, lived with his children [disciples] in the City of the Mists, the middle place [center] of the . . . world." See Frank Cushing, *Fetishes*, p. 16; Waters, *Book of the Hopi*, pp. 25–26.

30. William Howells, *Mankind So Far* (New York: Doubleday, 1947), p. 295.

31. Michael Lemonick, "Ancient Odysseys," *Time*, February 13, 1995.

32. Ruhlen, *Language*, pp. 17, 3–4.

Note: One of the most brilliant linguists of our day, Joseph Greenberg has made a career out of upsetting the academic status quo. In the late 1940s, for example, he initiated a decade of research into the classification of African languages that revolutionized African linguistics. His work has also been lauded by anthropologists, geneticists and historical linguists. Although Greenberg's more recent book *Language in the Americas* has provoked vocal criticism for postulating that Native American languages are to be classified into just three families, most of the squawking has come from scholars who have equity in opposing theories. (Unfortunately for these critics, a 1994 monograph published by Cavalli-Sforza reveals that Native Americans fall into three distinct genetic families.)

33. Cavalli-Sforza's project has resulted in the largest database ever assembled on worldwide gene alleles, including traits such as blood groups, proteins and enzymes.

34. Because these discoveries are new, they have never (to my knowledge) been superimposed on the ethno-geographic clues presented in Genesis 10—clues indicating that

the primal fissures in the human race opened up between the descendants of Noah's three sons: Ham, Shem and Japheth.

35. On the basis of Lamentations 4:21 and other evidence, most experts agree that Uz was located in a region south of Edom (Jordan) and west of what is now the great Arabian Desert. Given a liberal northern boundary, the region may once have contained as many as three hundred cities and been traversed by the primary caravan route between Babylon and Egypt.

36. See 1 Chronicles 1:42.

37. Renfrew, *Archaeology*, pp. 143, 173–174.

38. Despite the lack of modern conveyances, their journey may have benefited from the fact that continental drift had not yet torn Arabia loose from the Horn of Africa.

39. Not all dark-skinned peoples are of Hamitic descent. The Dravidian populations of southern India, for example, are more closely related (both genetically and linguistically) to people groups traditionally associated with the Japhethites. At the same time, dark Semitic peoples have long lived in the lands between southern Arabia and Ethiopia (see Ruhlen, *Language*, p. 142). For this reason it can be stated unequivocally that skin color has no relationship to Noah's curse registered in Genesis 9:25–27.

Although idolatry was virulent among the early Hamitic peoples, especially in the cities of Nimrod and the land of Canaan, this has little or nothing to do with the much-debated "curse of Ham." The object of this curse was not an individual or race but a nation (Canaan) that would be subject politically to its neighbors. Finally, those who suggest that the Hamitic peoples are destined to slavery or genetic deficiencies should remember that the mighty Nimrod was himself a great-grandson of Ham.

40. *Methodology*, p. 305. To this day the Horn of Africa represents the most linguistically fragmented region on the entire continent (see pp. 119–120).

41. *Methodology*, pp. 266–271.

42. Ibid., p. 271; Ruhlen, *Language*, pp. 170–177.

43. These include Ethiopia's Gargora shelter and Porcupine Cave, as well as Kenya's Njoro River Cave (near Nakuru) and Keringet Cave (near Molo). See *Methodology*, pp. 207–208.

44. Evidence of the Japhethites' presence in this region was greatly enhanced when, in the late 1980s, independent studies by Colin Renfrew and a pair of Russian linguists, Tomas Gamkrelidze and V. Ivanov, identified eastern Anatolia as the place where the first Indo-European language was spoken. (Indo-European tongues are the standard form of communication among Japhetic peoples and are now spoken by about half of the world's population.)

Although the Russian linguists place the proto-Indo-Europeans in Anatolia around 4,000 B.C., Renfrew sets the date 2,000–2,500 years earlier. If—and this is a very big if—Renfrew's dating is correct, then we are likely talking about a pre-Flood population. In this scenario we can only surmise that the language was carried through the Flood by Noah's family and simply represented one of the linguistic alternatives after Babel. See Renfrew, *Archaeology*, pp. 174, 266, 269.

45. Although the earliest farming settlements in Europe have been dated to 6500 B.C., these are likely antediluvian traces. Post-Flood peoples had occupied nearly all of Europe, except the extreme north, by 3000 B.C. See Renfrew, *Archaeology*, p. 30.

46. Renfrew, *Archaeology*, pp. 168, 159–161.

47. Depending on the reliability of radiocarbon datings, the Andronovo culture arose sometime between 3000 and 1800 B.C. (The earlier date is cited by J. P. Mallory.) It is possible they were an offshoot of the so-called Afansievo folk, whose remains archaeologists

have discovered to the northwest. An alternative explanation places the Afansievo in the pre-Flood era.

48. J. P. Mallory, *In Search of the Indo-Europeans* (New York: Thames & Hudson, 1989), p. 229.

49. The contents of this library were recorded on palm leaves, Chinese paper and wooden tablets.

50. Renfrew, *Archaeology*, pp. 63–67.

51. Other Tocharian inscriptions have since been found painted in caves in the foothills west of Urumchi. Next to the inscriptions are paintings of swashbuckling knights wielding long swords. The knights are depicted with full, red beards and European faces!

52. This evidence includes textile fragments similar to samples recovered from roughly the same time period at sites in Germanic Europe, and pieces of wooden wagon wheels virtually identical to wheels found in the Ukraine as far back as 3000 B.C.. Leather and wood horse-riding equipment have been found decorated with an image of the sun similar to tattoos found on some of the mummies. See Evan Hadingham, "The Mummies of Xinjiang," *Discover*, April 1994, pp. 68–77.

53. At least one scholar, W. B. Henning, has argued that the proto-Tocharians were none other than the Guti, a people documented in Babylonia at the end of the third millennium B.C. If Henning is correct, it means "their nearest relatives among the Indo-Europeans would be the Hittite nations of Asia Minor." See W. B. Henning, "The First Indo-Europeans in History," *Society and History, Essays in Honour of Karl August Wittfogel*, G. L. Ulmen, ed. (The Hague: Mouton, 1978), pp. 215–230.

54. While investigating the origins of these peoples, Arizona State University professor Christy Turner recently added another interesting wrinkle: They have different teeth! Having noted that distinct differences in dental characteristics (specifically crown and root features) can help distinguish between prehistoric families, Turner proceeded to examine a number of ancient Asian skeletons. He found that the teeth of Indo-Europeans and Southeast Asians (later called *Sundadonts)* bore a startlingly different pattern than those of North Asians and Native Americans (whom Turner dubbed *Sinodonts).* So consistent was this difference that Turner concluded the Sundadonts likely *had nothing to do with the peopling of northeastern Asia or the Americas.* See Brian Fagan, *The Journey from Eden* (New York: Thames & Hudson, 1990), pp. 196–198, 232–233.

55. Ruhlen, *Language*, p. 164.

56. Not only does this help explain the isolation of the Dene-Caucasian remnants, but it offers a reason other language families would present more abundant and more transparent cognates.

57. Another explanation is that some of today's Dene-Caucasian speakers—notably the Tibetans and various Native American groups (such as the Haida, Tlingit and Navajos)—were once pastoral nomads on the steppes north of China. At one point and for some unknown reason, they apparently broke off from their relatives and embraced the tongues of their Dene-Caucasian-speaking neighbors. Whereas the Tibetans picked up a Sino-Tibetan language (probably from Dene-Caucasian remnants in Mongolia), the Native American tribes adopted Na-Dene (possibly from the same group, or the more northerly Yeniseians). That they did not absorb their genes as well is explained by the fact that the Tibetans subsequently took off for the hinterlands of southwestern China, while the Na-Dene-speaking Native Americans migrated across the Bering Strait to Alaska. See Ruhlen, *Language*, pp. 166, 100, 169–170.

It is also possible that the Tibetans and Native Americans derived their languages from a single culture (from which they subsequently split off). As Fagan observes in *The Jour-*

ney from Eden, "The Afontovo Gora-Oshurkovo tradition was once thought to be a purely local Siberian culture, confined to the Yenesei River Valley, but now appears to have flourished over an enormous area of northern Asia, perhaps from the Altai to the Amur River" (p. 194).

58. Here Ruhlen cites the case of the Basques: "Despite their completely distinct language, which bears virtually no similarities to any other European languages, there has certainly been significant gene flow between the Basques and a later migration of people who moved into Europe . . . replacing all of the languages previously spoken [there]—except for Basque—with Indo-European languages" (*Language,* pp. 165–166). Cavalli-Sforza adds, "Two populations that have separated begin a process of differentiation of both genes and languages." And while "later events such as gene flow or language replacement . . . may blur the genetic and the linguistic picture, our conclusion is that they do not obscure it entirely" (pp. 153–154).

59. It is silly to reason, as some do, that the Bible could not be the inspired Word of God since it merely echoes stories that were known and discussed years earlier. As Otto Whittaker rightly asks, "What else would we expect?" If the people at Babel migrated out into new homelands because they were suddenly unable to understand their neighbors' speech, would they have forgotten to tell such a thing to their progeny? While it is true, as Whittaker points out, that man often "applies his imagination to things he retells," it is also true that "God revealed to Moses the truths from which 'oral traditions' had wandered. And he told Moses to put them into writing." See Otto Whittaker, "Didn't They Tell the Kids?", *World,* July 18, 1992, Vol. 7, No. 11, p. 21.

60. This dim reminiscence of a lost Eden is supported by the fact that nearly all traditional mythologies contain aspects of a golden age. Although recollections of this age differ, the fact that they exist at all, and that they are so widespread, is strong evidence of something real. Ashe, referring to the golden age, notes that the term, if not the idea, was first coined by the Greek poet Hesiod in the eighth century B.C. In the poet's grand scheme, there were five epochs, each with its own human species. The golden race flourished in the first of these ages, when Cronus was the chief of the elder deities known as Titans (giants). "The golden people lived carefree lives, feeding on nature's gifts," Ashe wrote, ". . . without disease or decrepitude." In the Hindu record, the golden age is known as the *Krita Yuga,* an extremely ancient era in which "all beings were righteous, wise, prosperous, and healthy, and fulfilled the laws of their nature . . ." (Ashe, *Dawn,* pp. 1–3; see also Cowan, *Fire,* p. 197; Eliade, *Shamanism,* p. 99; cf. pp. 171, 431, 486, 492–93, 508).

In *Liber Null and Psychonaut: An Introduction to Chaos Magic* (York Beach, Me.: Samuel Weiser, 1987, 1991), British occultist Peter Carroll writes: "Shamanism once guided all human societies and kept them in equilibrium for thousands of years. All occultism is an attempt to win back that lost wisdom" (p. 169).

61. According to Mircea Eliade, "The mystical experience of primitives is equivalent to a journey back to the origins, a regression into the mythical time of the Paradise lost . . . [and] the most representative mystical experience of the archaic societies, that of shamanism, betrays the nostalgia for Paradise, the desire to recover the state of freedom and beatitude before 'the Fall', the will to restore communication between Earth and heaven . . ." (*Myths, Dreams and Mysteries* [New York: Harper & Row, 1960], p. 66; see also Ashe, *Dawn,* pp. 28, 30, 144).

62. Ashe, *Dawn,* pp. 13, 16–17; and Fagan, *Journey,* pp. 192–194. While the cold and remote Altai may seem an improbable seedbed for cultural motifs that would eventually manifest themselves in the great civilizations of Mesopotamia, India, Greece and the Americas, the evidence for such a claim is compelling. (See especially Geoffrey Ashe's

Dawn Behind the Dawn.) Not only do we find the raw ideological material used in the construction of nature-based deceptions; we also find historical references to a northerly people—such as the northern Kurus and Hyperboreans—whose descriptions fit the location and practices of Altaic shamans. (Although the former are technically the product of Hindu and Greek legends, many scholars consider them based in fact. This was certainly the sentiment of the Greek explorer Aristeas who, in the seventh century B.C., set out to locate the Hyperboreans. While his success is a matter of debate, he seems at least to have reached the southern reaches of the Altai [perhaps Kyrgyzstan near the Dzungarian Gate]. Here he claimed to have encountered the "People from Beyond the North Wind," who taught him the art of spirit flight.) See Rutherford, *The Druids,* p. 133; and Ashe, *Dawn,* pp. 169–183 (especially pp. 173–175).

63. In the words of former Cambridge University ethnologist A. C. Haddon: "A migration induced by an attraction is rare as compared with that produced by an expulsion, for as a rule people are loath to leave their fatherland. . . ." See *The Wanderings of Peoples* (Washington, D.C.: Cliveden, 1984), p. 2.

64. As Michael Oard writes in *An Ice Age Caused by the Genesis Flood,* "The earth may be expected to have continued tectonically unstable, with a high level of volcanism, for years after the Flood . . ." (p. 67). At least one French geologist has hypothesized that exaggeratedly overturned rock folds high in the Alps were formed during violent world quakes. See Steven Austin, *Catastrophes in Earth History,* ICR Technical Monograph 13 (El Cajon, Calif.: Institute for Creation Research, 1984), pp. 153–154.

65. Historically such catastrophes have been attributed to the deities of fate-decreeing stars. The very word *disaster* is derived from the Latin *astrum,* or "star," and means literally "ill-starred."

66. W. C. Gussow, "Salt Diapirism: Importance of Temperature, and Energy Source of Emplacement," in *Diapirism and Diapirs,* J. Braunstein and G. D. O'Brien, eds. (Tulsa: American Association of Petroleum Geologists, Memoir 8), pp. 16–52. See also *Guinness Book of World Records,* P. McWhirter, ed. (New York: Bantam, 1995), 34th edition, p. 156.

67. Lightning strikes one hundred times each second. See Kendrick Frazier, *The Violent Face of Nature: Severe Phenomena and Natural Disasters* (New York: Morrow, 1979).

68. As Roger Larson noted in "The Mid-Cretaceous Superplume Episode," early volcanic activity on the earth "dramatically altered the terrestrial climate [and] surface structure. . . ."

69. According to Suzuki, surrounding desiccation is the only explanation for the population growth in these four valleys. Many other big river valleys in the world at the time did *not* see corresponding development.

70. Suzuki also noticed that most of these ancient civilizations collapsed about 3500 years ago—the same time the prime latitudes experienced a sudden drop in temperature (three degrees Celsius). When added to the prevailing dryness, these lower temperatures had an adverse impact on cultivation; most of the migrations recorded during this period, not surprisingly, were southward. What caused the thermometer to drop? Scientists speculate it may have been the eruption of Thera volcano on Santorini Island in the Aegean Sea. See Hideo Suzuki, *The Transcendent and Environments* (Yokohama, Japan: Addis Abeba Sha, 1981), pp. 53–54, 116–117, 127; Robert Kates, "Sustaining Life," pp. 115–116.

71. Blood flukes and parasitic worms were major problems in ancient China and Egypt, and likely Mesopotamia and the Indus River valley as well. See William McNeill, *Plagues and Peoples* (New York: Anchor, 1976), pp. 38–41. Based on the fact that early cities were

few and small, McNeill believes that epidemics spread by person-to-person contact could not have established themselves much before 3000 B.C. (pp. 37, 55–56).

72. Abraham Udovitch, "Egypt: Crisis in a Muslim Land," reproduced in William L. Bowsky, *The Black Death: A Turning Point in History?* (New York: Holt, Rinehart & Winston, 1971), p. 124. Skeletons from the so-called Stone Age and the Egyptian Old Kingdom also reveal evidence of tubercular damage (the tuberculosis bacilli being among the oldest on earth). See McNeill, *Plagues,* p. 156.

73. McNeill, *Plagues,* pp. 103–104.

74. Quoted by Beverley Raphael in *When Disaster Strikes: How Individuals and Communities Cope with Catastrophe* (New York: Basic, 1986), pp. 12–13. Another work that highlights both the internal and external horrors of the plague is Albert Camus' classic novel *The Plague.*

Note: It is frightening, of course, to think that such devastation could be caused by a virus—an entity so small it cannot be seen with the unaided eye. While rationalists look condescendingly at the ancients' tendency to link pestilence with supernatural forces, perhaps our forefathers were not so far off. Could something so dangerous and unnatural have originated in anything other than a demonic workshop?

75. A comparison of two Chinese census figures taken in A.D. 2 and A.D. 742 reveals that the overall number of households (or hearths) dropped during this period from 12.3 million to 8.9 million. During the same period Buddhism spread to the Han empire and won converts in high places. See McNeill, *Plagues,* pp. 119–121.

76. McNeill, *Plagues,* pp. 143–144, 168.

77. A new tool in the detection of early environmental disasters is called paleoliminology (the study of lake sediment). Silt from rivers and streams collected in lake bottoms carries evidence that can provide a time-ordered history of a region. The disappearance of tree pollen, for instance, is a strong indicator of deforestation. Large quantities of ash from burned buildings is a marker for warfare or environmental catastrophe such as volcanic eruptions. According to Patrick Kirch of the University of California at Berkeley, this type of research has "revolutionized our understanding of the past." See Thomas Maugh II, "Plunder of the Earth Began with Man," *Los Angeles Times,* June 12, 1994.

78. In supporting his claim, Raikes cites the lack of settlements in the area near the mouth of the river, and also the fact that the fossil beaches are many miles inland from the present coast. If the route of the river to the sea had been suddenly blocked by an uplift of land near the mouth, its liquid cargo would necessarily have backed up into a large lake that could have inundated the Harappan area. See Robert Wenke, *Patterns in Prehistory* (New York: Oxford University Press, 1984), pp. 316–317.

79. Ibid.; Saggs, *Greatness,* pp. 60–61.

80. Ingpen and Wilkinson, *Mysterious Places,* p. 235.

Note: According to John Barrat of the Smithsonian Museum's Office of Public Affairs, environmental archaeologists have concluded recently that the demise of the Clovis people—among North America's oldest known inhabitants—resulted from a severe drought.

81. Thomas Maugh II, "New Ideas About 'People with No Name,'" *Los Angeles Times,* June 12, 1994.

82. The Mongols were not the only ones to strike terror in the hearts of early men and women. At other times and in other places, mothers silenced their misbehaving children by invoking the reputation of nearby Assyrians, Philistines, Huns, Visigoths, Scythians, Celts, Vikings and Pawnee.

83. Kai Erikson, *A New Species of Trouble: The Human Experience of Modern Disasters* (New York: Norton, 1994), pp. 228–230. Erikson goes on to note that "in classical medical usage 'trauma' refers not to the *injury* inflicted but to the *blow* that inflicted it, not to the *state of mind* that ensues but to the event that provoked it. The term 'posttraumatic stress disorder' is an accommodation to that medical convention." At the same time, Erikson believes, "It is *how people react to them* rather than *what they are* that gives events whatever traumatic quality they can be said to have."

84. Ibid., pp. 230–231, 234, 237. Erikson speaks of traumatized communities as distinct from assemblies of traumatized persons: ". . . Something of the sort can also happen to whole regions, even whole countries."

85. This assessment was passed on to me by a consortium of credentialed Christian therapists and pastors on the East Coast of the United States.

86. Raphael notes that "definitions of disaster are often related to crisis concepts. Both are characterized by rapid time sequences, disruption of usual coping responses, perceptions of threat and helplessness, major changes in behavior, and a turning to others for help" (*Disaster*, p. 6).

87. Reciprocal vows often involve making a pilgrimage; offering a sacrifice at a holy place as a symbol of submission; extending charity; refraining from certain actions or from some specially desired food; or constructing or donating toward a building in the name of the deity. See Surinder Bhardwaj, "Single Religion Shrines, Multireligion Pilgrimages," *The National Geographic Journal of India*, Vol. 33, Part 4, December 1987, pp. 105–115.

88. Ki-Zerbo, *General History*, pp. 291, 293.

Note: Painted or etched mythograms offer some of the earliest indicators of how covenanted communities once paid tribute to their spiritual overlords. While these ancient records punctuate the landscape of every continent, few collections are as impressive as those found near Val Camonica and Val d'Aosta in northern Italy. Over three hundred thousand images have been discovered here; and if archaeological datings are correct, the earlier versions were almost certainly left behind by Indo-European-speaking tribes traveling westward out of Anatolia. (According to Julien Ries: "It is reasonable to suppose that the Indo-Europeans reached the alpine valleys around 3200 B.C." [*Origins*, p. 71]. See also Emmanuel Anati's piece "Valcamonica: A Center of Creativity" in *People of the Stone Age: Hunter-Gatherers and Early Farmers*, Göran Burenhult, ed. [New York: HarperSanFrancisco, 1993], pp. 120–121.) The paintings themselves display two recurring elements: a radiant sun disk (often shown as the head of a cosmological being) and praying human figures. The latter are depicted with their arms raised skyward or linked with other figures in a circular dance formation. Considered in tandem with cup marks carved prominently into the surrounding rock, these images strongly suggest offering rites to an early astral deity.

89. Ibid., p. 261.

90. Heliopolis, a Greek designation meaning "City of the Sun," was known to the Egyptians themselves as Onou. In Genesis 41:45 and 46:20 it is called On.

91. Several years into his reign, Amunhotep IV changed his name to Akhenaten ("Well-Pleasing to Aten"). See Finegan, *Myth*, p. 57; *Larousse Encyclopedia of Mythology*, Félix Guirand, ed. (New York: Barnes & Noble, 1994), p. 29.

92. *Larousse Encyclopedia*, p. 43.

93. Notice the striking similarity in language between this text and the passage in Isaiah 14:13–14.

94. Pyramid Texts §§ 1652–54 (quoted in Finegan, *Myth and Mystery*, p. 52). Another adulation of the solar deity—this one contained in spell #15 of the *Book of Going Forth by Day*—removes all doubt as to his place in the universal scheme (Finegan, *Myth and Mystery*, p. 59): "Hail to thee, Ra at his rising, Atum at his setting. . . . Thou art lord of sky and earth, who made the stars above and humankind below, sole God, who came into being at the beginning of time. . . ."

95. Iconographically Mata is often represented as a yellow woman sitting on a water lily, dressed in red and suckling an infant. Her shrines are usually found outside villages, under trees or in groves. Cholera, another disease that has long ravaged India, is represented by several goddesses, most notably Hulka Devi (the impersonation of vomiting), and the dread Mari Mai, or "Mother Death," who is said to be Sítala's sister.

96. E. Osborn Martin, *The Gods of India: Their History, Character and Worship* (Delhi: Indological Book House, 1988), pp. 252–256; Bhardwaj, "Single Religion Shrines," pp. 105–115.

97. Lars Skrefsrud (a Norwegian) and his Danish colleague Hans Børreson were the forerunners of what would become the Norwegian Santal Mission.

98. Don Richardson, *Eternity in Their Hearts* (Ventura, Calif.: Regal, 1981), pp. 34–40. Subsequent migrations brought them still farther east, where they became the modern Santal people. Here, in the vicinity of present-day Calcutta, they progressed into sorcery and even sun worship. Happily, spiritual deliverance reached the Santal in the late 1900s, largely as a consequence of the enlightened preaching of Lars Skrefsrud.

99. Lilly de Jongh Osborne, "Pilgrims' Progress in Guatemala," *Bulletin of the Pan American Union*, March 1948, p. 135.

100. Tierney, *Altar*, pp. 165–166.

101. Ibid., pp. 105–106.

102. According to Machi Juana's assistant Felipe Painén, this was done "because the serpent Cai Cai Filu is hungry for blood. It comes out of the ocean searching for food. Only after getting blood will it go back into the depths and leave the world alone" (Tierney, *Altar*, p. 133).

The Mapuches' belief that a hungry water spirit was responsible for their desperate plight invites comparison with an August 1986 eruption of Cameroon's Lake Nyos (during which a deadly cloud of carbon dioxide rose from the depths to asphyxiate more than seventeen hundred people). According to research scientist Curt Stager, "Numerous explanations for the disaster circulated around the highlands. One involved 'Mammy Water,' a spirit woman who inhabits lakes and rivers. Some Cameroonians suspect there was an angry Mammy behind the Nyos explosion." At the forefront of those seeking rapprochement with the Mammy and other lake spirits were secret ritual societies like the Ndengo. Rowing out into the deep waters, they positioned their boats over mystic power points. There, while chanting songs in a secret language, they proceeded to pour out libations consisting of sacrificial chicken blood mixed with herbal medicines. Local myths tell of angry outbursts by lake spirits, giving clues to more ancient disasters. See Curt Stager, "Silent Death from Cameroon's Killer Lake," *National Geographic*, Vol. 172, No. 3, September 1987, pp. 404–420.

Pacts with other nature spirits, especially mountain spirits, are often signed with human blood. Chapter 18 of Patrick Tierney's book *The Highest Altar* features a chilling account of a Peruvian *yatiri* (shaman) named Maximo Coa who sacrifices humans in order to seal provisional pacts with a demonic power called Tiu Lucífugo Rofocal. In Ecuador, mountain spirits such as Cerro Puntas and Cerro Guacamayos are believed to hold the blood of sacrificial victims in inkwells. Responsibility for refilling these inkwells belongs to the *compactado*—families and communities that have entered into special relationships with these spirits.

103. At this point in the ceremony, Machi Juana announced, "Here are my two black sheep." Suddenly two naked men jumped out from behind a bush and began dancing with spears. According to Tierney, "The use of the archaic spears, the nakedness of the dancers, and their identification with the most common animal victim—black sheep—indicated the primitive origin of the ritual" (*Altar*, pp. 173–175).

104. Tierney, *Altar*, pp. 104, 108–109, 173–178. See also p. 184 for a description of Machi Juana's spirit connections.

105. This phenomenon became a routine part of my visits to various temples and monasteries. Although in every other setting my tape recorder functioned normally, conversations were eerily cut off in mid-sentence every time I entered one of those sacred complexes. As I stepped across the exit thresholds, the audio abruptly returned.

106. The later date corresponds to Tibetologist Françoise Pommaret's assertion that Chang Ganka Lhakhang was built in the fifteenth century by a descendant of Lama Phajo Dugom Shigpo, widely considered the father of the present Bhutanese faith. See Françoise Pommaret, *Bhutan* (Hong Kong: Odyssey, 1994), p. 162. Kunzang Delek, on the other hand, suggests that the temple was built as early as the thirteenth century. In either case, Chang Ganka is one of the oldest temples in the Thimphu valley.

107. Human conflicts at the time were between independent principalities associated with major ethno-religious groups that had settled the country's central valleys from the north.

108. Powerful and invisible local deities, *mi-ma-yin* can offer protection but not enlightenment.

109. Territorial deities, according to Delek, can be either *local protectives* brought into the country from somewhere else (in this case, Tibet) or *natural deities* summoned from nearby mountains or jungles by presiding lamas and essentially given a promotion.

110. When I inquired how many years of preparation it takes these lamas to discern the deities physically, Delek responded: "As a rule, it takes approximately twenty years before they can hear the *mi-ma-yin,* and another decade to really see them."

111. Which is not to say God does *not* punish—for otherwise the universe would be under the power of the lawless. But if divine patience is not inexhaustible, it does possess astonishing elasticity.

112. As Michael Green has noted, Milton dealt with much the same issue in *Paradise Lost.*

Chapter 6: Enchanting the Lie

1. Nigel Dennis, *Cards of Identity* (New York: Vanguard, 1955).

2. Walter Truett Anderson, *Reality Isn't What It Used to Be* (San Francisco: HarperSanFrancisco, 1990), p. 105.

3. As Athanasius once observed, "It is very easy for the Enemy to create apparitions and appearances of such a character that they shall be deemed real and actual objects." Quoted by Richard Cavendish, *Man, Myth and Magic*, Vol. 1 (London: Purnell, 1970–72), p. 95; see also *Powers*, p. 198.

4. Quoted by Everett Ferguson, *Demonology of the Early Christian World*, Symposium Series, Vol. 12 (New York: Edwin Mellon, 1984), p. 116.

5. C. S. Lewis, *The Lion, the Witch and the Wardrobe* (New York: Macmillan, 1950), pp. 84, 38.

6. Green, *Exposing,* pp. 63–64.

7. 1 Corinthians 10:13 presents temptation as a countervailing influence to righteousness. It is up to us to decide which influence will prevail.

8. See Michael Heim, *The Metaphysics of Virtual Reality* (New York, Oxford University Press, 1993), p. 134.

9. Cytowic, *Shapes,* p. 133.

10. For a comprehensive and sobering perspective on visualization techniques employed by Tibetan Buddhists, see Stephan Beyer, *Magic and Ritual in Tibet—The Cult of Tara* (Delhi, India: Motilal Banarsidass, 1988), pp. 66–92.

11. Conceived by Dr. John Lilly in 1954, this device suspends subjects in a dark tank filled with water maintained at precisely 93° F., the temperature at which the body feels neither hot nor cold. Deprived of all external stimuli, subjects quickly move into trance-like, often hallucinatory states while remaining fully conscious.

12. *Harper's Encyclopedia of Mystical and Paranormal Experience* (Edison, N.J.: Castle, 1991), pp. 208–209.

13. Richard Smoley, "Man as God and Creator," *Gnosis,* Summer 1993, p. 60.

14. Cavendish, *Powers,* p. 256.

15. Gersi, *Faces,* p. 4.

16. See Job 32:8; Proverbs 20:27; Ezekiel 36:26; John 3:6; 4:23–24.

17. Nee, *Latent Power,* pp. 20, 45.

18. *Sounds True* catalog, Vol. 8, No. 2, fall-winter 1996.

19. Michael Winkelman, "Shamans and Other 'Magico-Religious' Healers: A Cross-Cultural Study of Their Origins, Nature, and Social Transformations," *Ethos,* Vol. 18, No. 3, September 1990, p. 324.

20. DHEA (Dehydroepiandrosterone) is a steroid hormone produced naturally by the adrenal glands. Most people produce plentiful amounts of DHEA until they reach age thirty, at which point production levels begin to decline. Recent studies have shown that people with chronic and degenerative diseases have far lower levels of DHEA in their bloodstreams. One such study cited in the May-June 1996 issue of *Consumer's Digest* was conducted by Samuel Yen, an endocrinologist at the medical school of the University of California at San Diego. In the study, Yen found a correlation between low DHEA levels and death from cardiovascular disease. He also concluded that the restoration of DHEA was associated with a "remarkable increase in perceived physical and psychological well-being" defined as "the ability to cope, increased mobility, less joint pain and sounder sleep." See Ruth Winter, "The Truth about Anti-Aging Products," *Consumer's Digest,* Vol. 35, No. 3, pp. 20-24, May-June 1996.

21. Fox Network "Sightings," November 18, 1994.

22. One of the more famous personalities to have grappled with the powers of the human mind in recent years is Nobel-Prizewinning researcher John Eccles. While conducting a series of experiments at the Australian National University in Canberra during the 1970s, Dr. Eccles made an interesting discovery: Milliseconds *before* a person carries out a willed action, certain neurons in the cerebral cortex discharge an electrical signal preparing other parts of the brain to respond appropriately. In a later set of experiments with similar results, Dr. Benjamin Libet of the University of California at San Francisco hooked up healthy subjects to an EEG machine (which monitors brain waves) and instructed them to flex a finger at the moment of their choosing. In case after case, the EEG readings indicated that the subjects' brains displayed neural activity a full third of a second *before* they decided to act (or became conscious of the decision).

What these experiments did not resolve was the question of what prompts the readiness signal. (While most neuroscientists are persuaded that consciousness resides somehow in the electrochemical signal traffic within the brain's neurons, they cannot explain how otherwise nonsentient cells can "know" what the signals they transmit represent.) Dr. Eccles hypothesizes that *psychons,* or "will influences," somehow gain access to the physical brain via a specialized liaison area in the cortex—a proposition startlingly reminiscent of Andrew Murray's earlier idea of the soul as a meeting place, or point of union, between body and spirit. Although Dr. Eccles' psychons have thus far eluded scientific observation, if he is right, it means that every human action is literally a feat of mind over matter (matter in this case being the brain itself). See John Horgan, "Can Science Explain Consciousness?" *Scientific American,* Vol. 271, No. 1, July 1994, pp. 88–94.

23. Single neurons (brain cells), like the bulbs in a scoreboard, can participate in many different patterns (or thoughts). See Restak, *Brain,* pp. 252–253; George Johnson, *In the Palaces of Memory* (New York: Vintage, 1992), p. 73.

24. Johnson, *Palaces,* pp. 20–22.

25. Quoted in *Secrets of the Inner Mind,* p. 118.

26. As studies by Dr. Matsumoto and others have shown, our most potent memories are never erased (see Freedman, *Brainmakers,* p. 113).

Note: According to Candace Pert, a former National Institutes of Health pharmacologist who now heads her own research firm, "Emotions are neuropeptides attaching to receptors and stimulating an electrical charge on neurons." See Joel Swerdlow, "Quiet Miracles of the Brain," *National Geographic,* Vol. 187, No. 6, June 1995, pp. 24–25.

27. Other emotionally charged events such as imbibing pornography or being traumatized by sexual or verbal abuse can produce the same effect.

28. Synapses are electrochemical "bridges" that allow signal traffic to move between brain cells.

29. These findings were later confirmed in a hostile replication by University of Illinois psychologist William Greenough (see Johnson, *Palaces,* pp. 40, 57–58). Another interesting discovery has shown that repeated exposure to a given stimuli will greatly sensitize, or strengthen, neural pathways. This condition, known as long-term potentiation, or LTP, permits specific memories to be recalled easily over long periods of time. Although scientists examining the LTP effect have known for some time that stimulated tissue contains more receptors than non-stimulated tissue, they did not begin to discover until the early 1980s how this process works. For more on this subject see Johnson, *Palaces,* pp. 36, 42, 44, 58.

30. In the words of C. S. Lewis, "It seems much more likely that human thought is not God's, but God-kindled" (*Miracles,* p. 29).

31. Beyer, *Magic,* p. 85.

32. Michael Harner, ed., *Hallucinogens and Shamanism* (New York: Oxford University Press, 1973), p. xi.

33. As Harner notes, "The use of hallucinogenic agents to achieve trance states for perceiving and contacting the supernatural world [was] evidently an ancient and widespread human practice." Unfortunately, many discovered too late that once you give a charlatan power over you, you almost never get it back (*Hallucinogens,* p. xiv).

34. Harner, *Hallucinogens,* pp. xi, xiv.

35. Eliade, *Shamanism,* pp. 509–510.

36. Cowan, *Fire,* pp. 8–9. Os Guinness, supporting this assumption, insists that "any general principles or experiences must be interpreted in the light of the set and setting

of the user, his character and the circumstances in which he takes the drug" (*Dust*, pp. 236–237).

37. According to UCLA research professor Ronald Siegel, "These images can be evoked by simply remembering, or they may erupt in spite of conscious efforts to avoid them. Such eruptions are common in hallucinations, especially in those induced by drugs. They form a type of involuntary reminiscence, complete with many of the feelings and emotions that were present when the image was first recorded" (Siegel, *Fire in the Brain*, pp. 30–31).

38. See Harner, *Hallucinogens*, pp. xii-xiv.

Note: Although few contemporary or recent historical cultures of Europe and the Old World show a central religious preoccupation with hallucinogenic substances, Marlene Dobkin De Rios and Michael Winkelman point out that "there is widespread evidence for . . . the ancient use of hallucinogens." Ritual consumption of potent mind-altering agents has been documented in early Egyptian, Persian, Aryan, Scythian, Greek and Roman cultures; and small, mushroom-shaped objects have been found in the former Yugoslavia and at numerous pre-Columbian sites throughout Mesoamerica. Those sites, according to one scholar, have yielded hundreds of mushroom stones, usually not more than a foot tall. One field near Uxmal in the Yucatán was full of those stones. See Marlene Dobkin De Rios and Michael Winkelman, "Shamanism and Altered States of Consciousness: An Introduction," *Journal of Psychoactive Drugs*, Vol. 21(1), January–March 1989, p. 4.

39. *Did You Know?* p. 91.

40. McKenna, *Food*, p. 100; see also H. D. Griswold, *The Religion of the Rigveda* (London: Oxford University Press, 1923).

41. McKenna, *Food*, pp. 110, 98.

42. Ibid., pp. 101, 120.

43. Ibid., p. 120.

44. Wasson further speculated that, among certain lower castes, *Stropharia cubensis* might have something to do with the inclusion of cow urine and dung in the Vedic sacrifice of *pancagavya*. See R. Gordon Wasson, *Persephone's Quest: Entheogens and the Origins of Religion* (New Haven: Yale University Press, 1986), p. 135.

45. In nearly every dream incubation site, sensory aids like incense and religious artwork were employed to create an "atmospheric narcotic." See Gadon, *Goddess*, pp. 64–65; Robin Lane Fox, *Pagans and Christians* (New York: HarperCollins, 1986), pp. 152–153. See also Mara Lynn Keller, "Eleusinian Mysteries: Ancient Nature Religion of Demeter and Persephone," *The Journal of Feminist Studies in Religion*, No. 1, 1987.

46. Howard Bloom, *The Lucifer Principle* (New York: Atlantic Monthly Press, 1995), p. 101.

47. Ibid., p. 98.

48. Ibid., p. 101. Each of these memes is the equivalent of the dynamic "kernel" metaphors of Scripture—i.e., the "grain of wheat" and "mustard seed faith."

49. Ibid., p. 99. In Marx' poem entitled "The Fiddler," he writes: "The hellish vapours rise and fill the brain/Till I go mad and my heart is utterly changed./See this sword? The prince of darkness sold it to me." Richard Wurmbrand, *Was Marx a Satanist?* quoted by Green, *Exposing*, pp. 164–165.

50. See Otis, *Giants*, pp. 35–37.

51. Ibid., pp. 49–52.

52. Bloom, *Lucifer*, pp. 126, 131, 138.

53. For information on trauma as a crafter of community tradition, see Erikson, *Trouble*, pp. 231–232. For more on memes as problem-solving devices, see Bloom, *Lucifer*, pp. 128–132.

54. While these "deities" appear to lead autonomous lives, their bloody and perverse ways are carefully choreographed by the prince of darkness.

55. Green, *Exposing*, p. 45. See also John 8:44.

56. Tompkins, *Tree*, pp. 59–63.

Note: Tezcatlipoca, one of the foremost gods of ancient Mexico, was known as *The Shadow*, or "He Who Is At the Shoulder." Like many other Mesoamerican deities, Tezcatlipoca required blood (lots of it) and human hearts. His "red" aspect was known as Xipe Totec, the flayed god of agriculture and penitential self-mutilation. The Aztecs reasoned that, just as Tezcatlipoca gave humans food by being skinned (in the sense that corn is husked), his festival should be celebrated by skinning captives alive. See Richard Carlyon, *A Guide to the Gods* (New York: Quill, 1981), pp. 51, 54.

57. According to German playwright Carl Zuckmayer, the city of Vienna experienced comparable spasms during its formal annexation by the Nazis in March 1938: "It was as if the underworld had opened its gates and let loose its lowest, most revolting, most impure spirits. The city was transformed into a nightmare painting by Hieronymous Bosch, the air filled with [the] incessant, savage, hysterical screeching [of] hate-filled triumphs." Quoted by Alan Bullock in *Hitler and Stalin: Parallel Lives* (New York: HarperCollins, 1991), p. 628.

58. Quoted in Cavendish, *Powers*, p. 38.

59. Green, *Exposing*, p. 164.

60. A terror that continued under Milton Obote.

61. Barbara Rudolph, "Unspeakable Crimes," *Time*, January 18, 1993, p. 35.

62. From an interview conducted by U.S. Assistant Secretary of State for Human Rights John Shattuck in July 1995. "CIA: Photos Show Atrocities," *Seattle Times*, August 10, 1995.

63. "The Evil at the Dragon's Feet," *Time*, June 1995, p. 66; "Perspectives," *Newsweek*, April 25, 1994, p. 19.

Chapter 7: The Art of Shadow-Ruling

1. *Wayang* in the modern Indonesian language translates loosely as "puppet." *Kulit* means leather, the material from which the figures are carved. While the Javanese hold that *wayang* originates from the word *bayang*, which means "shadow," their Balinese neighbors believe the term originates from two early Sanskrit words that suggest a homecoming of family spirits. (To the Hindu, a person's shadow holds a portion of the spirit. Recreating the shadow allows part of that spirit to appear with it.)

2. In *Facing the Powers* (Monrovia, Calif.: MARC, 1991), Thomas McAlpine offers a useful appendix (pp. 87–89) listing definitions and occurrences for New Testament words for spiritual powers. See also Clinton E. Arnold, *Powers of Darkness: Principalities and Powers in Paul's Letters* (Downers Grove, Ill.: InterVarsity, 1992), p. 218.

3. The term *kosmokratores*, which Paul employs in Ephesians 6:12, is found nowhere else in Scripture. According to Clinton Arnold, it appears the apostle took it out of prevailing magical/astrological tradition and reinterpreted it for his Christian readers. It seems that, in the context of his communication with the Ephesians, Paul saw the *kosmokratores* as subordinate but powerful demons that animated deities associated with the forces of nature, particularly heavenly bodies. See Clinton E. Arnold, *Ephesians: Power and Magic* (Grand Rapids: Baker, 1992), pp. 65–68.

4. The writers of the Upanishads expressed the concept of "I" or "ego" through the use of the word *atman.*

5. The forest folk were, not surprisingly, the first cultures to adopt a cyclical view of history. (Hindu literature records droughts in the fifth and third centuries B.C. that may have played a role in transforming India's forests into the present-day savannas.) On balance, their environmental experiences differed considerably from those of the monotheistic cultures of the Middle East and North Africa—cultures that emerged in proximity to the desert, where dry, sun-bleached bones gave death a sense of earthly finality. See Suzuki, *Transcendent,* pp. 64–67.

6. Stuart Piggot, *The Druids* (London: Thames & Hudson, 1961), p. 115. Piggot records an interesting account of the Romans' encounter with a Celtic sacred grove in southern France (p. 79).

7. Tierney, *Altar,* p. 222.

8. Ibid., pp. 62–63, 96–97.

9. For more on the Andean practice of "feeding the earth," see Tierney, *Altar* (multiple chapters), and Joseph Bastien, *Mountain of the Condor* (Prospect Heights, Ill.: Waveland Press, 1985), pp. 37–50. For more on Hinduism's metaphorical linkage between the human body and nature, see Amita Sinha, "Nature in Hindu Mythology, Art, and Architecture," *National Geographic Journal of India,* Vol. 39, Nos. 1–2 (special issue), 1993.

10. This universal power is similar to the Eastern *tao,* the Indian *brahman* and the Polynesian *mana.* See Cowan, *Fire,* pp. 46–47; Joan Halifax, *Shaman: The Wounded Healer* (New York: Crossroad, 1982), p. 11.

11. Raffi, "Our Dear, Dear Mother," *Evergreen Everblue,* Troubadour Records, Ltd., 1990.

12. Marcia Starck, "The Dark Goddess: Inanna, Lilith, Hecate, Pele, Kali," *Proceedings of the Seventh International Conference on the Study of Shamanism and Alternate Modes of Healing,* Ruth-Inge Heinze, ed. (Berkeley: Independent Scholars of Asia, 1990), p. 298.

13. McKenna, *Food,* pp. 40–41.

14. In recent years a new scientific discipline has enabled us to learn much more about how and what ancient peoples observed in the heavens, and in what manner they integrated this astronomical knowledge into their religion and mythology. Known as archaeoastronomy, it combines the specializations of archaeology, astronomy and art history. See John Carlson, "American's Ancient Skywatchers," *National Geographic,* Vol. 177, No. 3, March 1990, pp. 84–86.

15. As we noted in chapter 4, many archaic peoples attempted to connect themselves to this cosmic entrance by way of a "binding post"—which in different places and times took the form of trees, poles, mountains and towers. See Ashe, *Dawn,* p. 34; Eliade, *Shamanism,* pp. 260–263; Henry Michael, ed., *Studies in Siberian Shamanism* (Toronto: University of Toronto Press, 1972), pp. 50–51.

16. Ashe, *Dawn,* pp. 46–48, 51. This worship was also strong among the Mongols. See Walter Hessig, *The Religions of Mongolia,* trans. Geoffrey Samuel (Boston: Routledge and Kegan Paul, 1980), pp. 46, 81–84.

17. The Druids also worshiped the moon and stars, but as the destinations of departed souls. They believed that the soul progressed from one heavenly body to another on its way to increasingly exalted states of existence. So convinced were they of "the existence of a future life in the stars," according to astrology expert Christopher McIntosh, "that they lent money to one another on the understanding that it would be repaid in the other world." *A Short History of Astrology* (New York: Barnes & Noble, 1969), p. 3.

18. Carlson, "Skywatchers," p. 86.

19. In Book II of his *Tetrabiblos,* Ptolemy referred to this category of prognostication as "general" or "universal" astrology (McIntosh, *Astrology,* p. 23).

20. To determine how these modified forces might affect everyday life, early astrologers divided the heavenly dome into twelve, thirty-degree "houses" (or sectors) that were associated with matters such as physical appearance, money, friendships, travel, sorrow, work, ideals, sex, health and death. By examining the relative position of planets, signs and houses (each sign moves into a new house approximately every two hours), astrologers could "predict" daily events or lifetime destinies. The earliest known horoscope was cast for a Babylonian child born in 410 B.C. See McIntosh, *Astrology,* pp. 27, 133; Saggs, *Greatness,* p. 445.

21. *Stoicheia* is used in Colossians 2:8, 20 and Galatians 4:3, 9. While scholars are divided as to whether the term should be interpreted as "spirit beings" or "elemental principles," Arnold leans toward the former as "the most compelling view." In support of this position, he cites its widespread use as a term for astral spirits in the second and third centuries A.D. See *Powers of Darkness,* pp. 53–54.

22. Arnold, *Powers of Darkness,* p. 48.

23. McIntosh, *Astrology,* p. 22.

24. Quoted in McIntosh, *Astrology,* p. 63.

25. Arnold, *Powers of Darkness,* p. 59.

26. Worship of the Queen of Heaven was seen in the streets of Jerusalem, the towns of Judah and Lower and Upper Egypt.

27. See Zephaniah 1:4–5. In Acts 7:42, another reference to Israel's early idolatry, we read that God eventually did turn away and "[give] them over to the worship of the heavenly bodies."

28. Cavendish, *Powers,* p. 80.

29. The problem of syncretism, it must be admitted, extended far beyond astrological influences and Gentile churches. In a 1925 study on the religious background of early Christianity, Samuel Angus called the Jewish synagogues of the day "fruitful seedpots of syncretism." At the same time, he noted that "when pagans began to rush into the Christian Church . . . they brought with them magical or quasi-magical conceptions which infected Christian theology and worship." Illustrating the effects of this trend, Robin Lane Fox reports that, by the fourth century, Christian men of letters were seeking dreams and advice in hillside shrines that paralleled pagan oracular centers. See Samuel Angus, *The Mystery Religions and Christianity* (New York: Citadel, 1966), pp. 193, 252; Fox, *Pagans,* pp. 678, 676.

30. Aquinas held that the stars governed human bodily appetites and desires, while Dante admitted in his *Purgatorio* (through the spirit Marco Lombardo) that "the heavens set your impulses in motion." In the *Paradiso,* Dante described an ascent through nine heavens ruled by the planets (or Roman gods). See McIntosh, *Astrology,* pp. 59–61, 66–68.

31. The ancient Egyptians found this imagery so compelling that their pantheon was dominated by a menagerie of jackals, cats, crocodiles, birds, hippos, cattle and serpents. As an acknowledgment of the divine status of these creatures, they had many of these creatures mummified and interred in special cemeteries (Finegan, *Myth and Mystery,* pp. 43–44).

32. Joan Halifax, *Shamanic Voices: A Survey of Visionary Narratives* (New York: Dutton, 1979), p. 5; see also *The Spirit World,* The American Indians Series (Alexandria, Va.: Time-Life, 1992), pp. 19, 49–83.

Note: In similar fashion, and reminiscent of ancient dream incubation temples, the Beaver Indian culture of North America has long been influenced by *nachene yine*, or dreamers' songs—so-called because they are brought back from the spirit world by an entranced shaman dreamer. The songs, which are also revelatory messages, are believed to emanate from heavenly animals and ancestral sages. See Robin Ridington, "Beaver Dreaming and Singing," in Sam Gill, *Native American Traditions* (Belmont, Calif.: Wadsworth, 1983), pp. 25–26; see also Stanley Krippner, "The Use of Dreams by Tribal Shamans," *Proceedings of the Fifth International Conference on the Study of Shamanism and Alternate Modes of Healing*, Ruth-Inge Heinze, ed. (Berkeley: Independent Scholars of Asia, 1989), p. 299.

33. Cowan, *Fire*, p. 118. A similar image of shaman and horned serpent appears in a three-thousand-year-old rock painting in southern Utah (*Spirit World*, p. 26).

34. David Freidel, Linda Schele and Joy Parker, *Maya Cosmos: Three Thousand Years on the Shaman's Path* (New York: Quill, 1993), pp. 140, 51.

35. Krippner, "Use of Dreams," pp. 297–298.

36. Debra Carroll, "Power Animals and Allies," *Proceedings of the Fifth International Conference on the Study of Shamanism*, pp. 346–347.

37. Carl Jung, *Archetypes and the Collective Unconscious*, Part I, Vol. 9 of *Collected Works* (Boston: Routledge and Kegan Paul, 1959), pp. 195–196.

38. Given the context, we might add the suffix *as gods*.

39. Ashe, *Dawn*, pp. 167, 158. Cybele is spoken of in the Sibylline Books as the Great Mother. She was represented in her Roman temple by a black meteorite and was honored in an annual festival, the Megalensia, at which eunuchs known as *Galli* marched through the streets beating on hollow drums and cymbals. In another ceremony called the *taurobolium*, a priest stood in a trench and was washed by the blood of a bull slain in Cybele's honor. See Finegan, *Myth and Mystery*, pp. 193–196.

40. Ibid., p. 13.

41. Gaia has more recently been associated with the hypothesis, put forward in the early 1970s by British biologist James Lovelock, that the earth and its inhabitants are a single living organism. (While Lovelock has insisted that Gaia is not sentient, his New Age readers have continued to use his work in support of their own theories.)

The Goddess has had other names as well. Ancient Slavic tribes paid homage to Mati-Syra-Zemlya ("Moist Mother Earth"), while the Algonquin Indians worshiped the Goddess as Nokomis. In South America she is still known as Pachamama, while Nepalese Sherpas venerate Mount Chomolungma as "goddess mother of the world."

42. Gadon, *Goddess*, panel 8.

43. For the most part, this Goddess was earth- and not heaven-centered; immanent (or within) rather than transcendent (or from above). Early female figurines found in Europe, Africa and Asia are typically shaped with a downward point, indicating they were staked into the ground as symbols of fertility. See Gadon, *Goddess*, pp. xii-xiv; Suzuki, *Transcendent*, p. 52.

44. Aidan Kelly, "Why a Craft Ritual Works," *Gnostica*, Vol. 4, No. 7, March-May 1975, p. 33.

45. While Goddess syncretism is pervasive in many Catholic cultures (especially those of Latin America, southern Europe, Poland and the Philippines), my mention of this fact should not be construed as a general indictment of Catholicism. Many Catholics have rejected pagan cultural trappings and retained a biblical perspective on the Person of Christ. Some have adopted beliefs that are more thoroughly evangelical than those

espoused by certain Protestants. To view these evangelical Catholics as anything less than full members of the Body of Christ is to dishonor the Holy Spirit.

46. Gadon, *Goddess*, pp. 57–68, 87–107.

47. Revelation 2:15 (see also verse 6); E. O. James, *The Cult of the Mother-Goddess* (New York: Barnes & Noble, 1994), pp. 192, 194, 201.

48. The great Byzantine general Heraclius sailed his fleet under the protection of an icon of the Mother of God, which (it was claimed) "had not been made by human hands" (Esmond Wright, ed., *History of the World: Prehistory to the Renaissance* [Feltham, England: Bonanza, 1985], p. 358). See also James, *Mother-Goddess*, pp. 209–213, and Gadon, *Goddess*, pp. 194–218.

49. Diane Knippers and Jane McDermott, "Woodstock for Women: Sixteen Days in the Land of Goddesses," *United Voice*, November 1995, pp. 7–9.

50. Cited in Margot Adler, *Drawing Down the Moon* (Boston: Beacon, 1979), p. 174.

51. Cowan, *Fire*, pp. 117–118, 59. According to Cowan, homosexual relations were rather common among Celtic men. In support of this assertion, he cites the Roman historian Diodorus Siculus, who wrote in the first century B.C.: "Although [Celtic males] have good-looking women, they pay very little attention to them, but are really crazy about having sex with men. They are accustomed to sleep [sic] on the ground on animal skins and roll around with male bed-mates on both sides."

52. Ashe, *Dawn*, p. 28; Eliade, p. 125 (see also pp. 257–258, 351–352, 461).

53. Cowan, *Fire*, pp. 58.

54. The Enares, who served as soothsayers and judges among upper-class Scythians, represented yet another group in this category. Both Herodotus and Hippocrates described them as biological males who dressed as women. Saggs, *Greatness*, pp. 303–304, 371–373; Ashe, *Dawn*, p. 162; "Diana" in Cavendish, *Man, Myth*, p. 632.

55. First popularized among French explorers, the term *berdeche* refers to Native Americans who assume the role and status of the opposite sex.

56. Quoting from *Visionary Love* by Mitch Walker, he went on to explain "that a door can be opened when you have psychic knowledge of male and female united within yourself. You then form a oneness that connects you with the sexuality of nature creation." See Adler, *Moon*, pp. 344–345, 348.

57. While most supernatural activity seems to occur as a direct response to human behavior (such as prayer, fasting or cursing), other phenomena are apparently instigated with the intent of arousing attention. Incidents of this sort often fall into categories like location hauntings, light phenomena, UFOs and crop circles.

We must not forget, as we investigate such things, that God also uses nature to speak. In addition to the fact that the heavens routinely declare His glory (Psalm 19), He has also communicated through a burning bush (to Moses in Exodus 3:2 ff.), a donkey (to Balaam in Numbers 22:28 ff.), a whirlwind (to Job in Job 38–41), a northern windstorm (to Ezekiel in Ezekiel 1:4 ff.) and a star (to the Magi in Matthew 2:1–2, 9–10).

58. Quoting the lost work of the historian Ctesias, who lived in the Persian court in the fourth century B.C., the Christian apologist Arnobius of Sicca referred to an ancient "wizard's war" between the Assyrians and Bactrians—a conflict that was fought "not only . . . with the sword and with brawn, but even with the esoteric arts of the Magi and the Chaldeans. . . ." See *Arnobius of Sicca, The Case Against the Pagans*, 1.5, George McCracken, trans. (New York: Newman, 1949).

59. Tierney, *Altar*, p. 153.

60. "Rather than creating everything directly," Pratney says, "God commanded the earth and the waters, themselves His creations, to participate in the creation of even

higher structural forms" (*Healing the Land*, p. 22). As scientists now know, natural systems allow for chaos within a deterministic environment. Thus, while nature follows general structural rules, there is no way of telling where a water molecule at the top of a waterfall will end up. (Weather changes that fool meteorologists are another example of this.)

61. Lewis, *Miracles*, p. 66 (see also pp. 67–68). In *Genesis in Space and Time*, Francis Schaeffer adds, "The universe is not an extension of the essence of God, but in all its parts it does speak of him" (p. 61).

62. Ephesians 2:2 and John 14:30 (the operative term in this latter passage is the Greek *kosmos*). See also Ezekiel 31:11—an interesting passage in which Egypt is turned over to the "ruler of the nations" for destruction.

63. Green, *Exposing*, p. 84.

64. The Scriptures employ terms like *principalities, powers* and *thrones* to describe both human rulers (see Luke 12:11; Acts 4:26) and the spiritual forces that lie behind them (see Romans 8:38; Ephesians 6:12; Colossians 1:16; 2:15). See Green, *Exposing*, pp. 84–85; Ferguson, *Demonology*, pp. 151–152.

65. Daniel 10; Revelation 18:2; Ezekiel 28; Revelation 2:10, 13; Acts 19:23–28; John 8:44; Revelation 2:9. Speaking of the politico-religious dynamics that led to Christ's crucifixion, Green writes: "Organized religion [and] politics were there at the cross: but behind Herod and Pilate, the earthly rulers (*archontes*) lay the invisible powers (*archontes*) and it was they who crucified the Lord of glory (1 Corinthians 2:8)." See *Exposing*, p. 93.

Another important passage is Deuteronomy 32:8, although its true meaning appears to have been obscured by a late rabbinical error. While Masoretic-based translations suggest that God "set up the boundaries for the peoples according to the number of the sons of Israel (*bene elohim*)," the Dead Sea scrolls, Greek Septuagint, Latin Vulgate and older Syriac sources all seem to contradict this reading. According to scholars like F. F. Bruce, C. Peter Wagner, Rick Moore and Michael Green, the more appropriate rendering of this latter phrase is *according to the number of the sons (or angels) of God*. See C. Peter Wagner, *Warfare Prayer* (Ventura, Calif.: Regal, 1992), pp. 90–91; and Green, *Exposing*, p. 79.

66. Other biblical terms for these ruling demons include the Hebrew *sar* (used in Daniel to describe the prince of Persia) and the Greek *archontes* (rulers), *exousiai* (authorities or powers) and *archai* (ruling principalities). Gary Greig, associate professor of Old Testament at Regent University's School of Divinity, argues that this continuity between the gods and their earthly representatives is an established spiritual principle. In support of this position, he cites Herbert Niehr, "3 Götter oder Menschen—Eine Falshe Alternative: Bemerkungen zu Psalm 82:2," *Zeitshrift für die Altestamentliche Wissenschaft 99* (1987), pp. 94–98. See also E. T. Mullen, "The Divine Council in Canaanite and Early Hebrew Literature," *Harvard Semitic Monographs 24* (Cambridge: Harvard University Press, 1980), p. 228, note 195, and p. 236; H. J. Kraus, *Psalms 60–150: A Continental Commentary* (Minneapolis: Fortress, 1993), p. 156; D. F. Payne, "King," *The International Standard Bible Encyclopedia*, Vol. 3, G. W. Bromiley, ed. (Grand Rapids: Eerdmans, 1986), p. 23.

67. See also Exodus 12:12.

68. Green notes (*Exposing*, p. 81) that "it was very widely accepted in antiquity that behind the rulers of the state lay their *daimones*. . . ."

69. These details were passed on to me during a 1988 interview in Alexandria, Virginia.

70. Otis, *Giants*, p. 89.

71. While regal megalomania was much in evidence in ancient Babylon and Egypt, the cult may have reached its height in the reign of Nero, when the unstable leader ordered his military corps to create a thousand-pound statue of him. See Saggs, *Greatness*, pp. 312, 59, 128, 311, 314–319; Finegan, *Myth and Mystery*, pp. 44–45, 49, 212–214.

72. See Black and Green, *Ancient Mesopotamia*, pp. 170–171.

73. Also reminiscent of Ezekiel's angelic creatures is the Chinese dragon king. A supernatural consort of emperors, he issued his commands by moving in all four directions simultaneously.

74. *Halley's*, pp. 46–47.

75. Among the Tibetans these *nagas* are known as *klu* (see chapter 3). According to anthropologist Stan Mumford, "There is an ancient relationship between Buddhist societies and serpent deities of the underworld." So important was this alliance that, in earlier times, the king's ordination was held at the same shrine where the serpents were given offerings. See *Himalayan Dialogue: Tibetan Lamas and Gurong Shamans in Nepal* (Madison, Wis.: University of Wisconsin, 1991), p. 95.

76. Huxley, *Dragon*, p. 61; *Larousse Encyclopedia*, p. 47; Freidel, Schele and Parker, *Maya Cosmos*, pp. 185, 190–191.

77. Thorn EMI video, "Amin, The Rise and Fall," 1982 Intermedia Productions in association with the Film Corporation of Kenya; Hassanain Hirji-Walji, *Bittersweet Freedom* (Monticello, Minn.: Building Bridges, 1981, 1993), pp. 24–25, 28–29.

78. From an interview conducted in Minneapolis on March 17, 1995.

79. October 8, 1995, correspondence from Indonesian prayer leader in Jakarta; Loveard, "Journey," pp. 37–39.

80. See Ruth-Inge Heinze, *Trance and Healing in Southeast Asia Today* (Bangkok: White Lotus, 1988), pp. 183–206.

81. This Shinto ritual, known as the Daijosai, was performed on the grounds of the imperial palace. For a comparison with Babylon's sacred marriage ceremony, see Otis, *Giants*, p. 93.

82. Tom Sawicki, "Inside the World of the Mystic Healers," *The Jerusalem Report*, January 27, 1994, p. 11.

83. King Fahd himself, after being warned by a soothsayer that he would meet his end in the capital of Riyadh, has spent an increasing amount of his time in Jeddah and the provinces. Fahd was also told he would die if he did not view the face of his son, Prince Abdul Aziz, at least once a week. Accordingly, the king has reportedly bequeathed his entire fortune (estimated at forty billion dollars) to Aziz and placed his three half-brothers under 24-hour surveillance to ensure that no harm provoked by jealousy comes to him. See Shyam Bhatia, "Occult Power Behind the Saudi Throne," Observer News Service, March 7, 1995.

84. Former Colombian president Ceasar Gaviria has likewise admitted that both he and several of his cabinet ministers received advice from an astrologer.

85. Andres Oppenheimer, "Many Latin American Leaders Follow Advice of Fortunetellers," *The State* (Columbia, S.C.), June 27, 1993.

86. Curiously, Noriega's betrayer, Colonel Roberto Diaz Herrera, moved against his former boss on advice received from a California-based psychic and the Indian guru, Satya Sai Baba.

87. Before becoming chancellor of England, for example, Sir Francis Bacon was initiated into a society that worshiped the Greek goddess Pallas Athene. In neighboring France, America's revolutionary ally, the Marquis de Lafayette, was an active member of the Nine Sisters Masonic Lodge—a lodge that also claimed Benjamin Franklin as a member.

88. Michael Howard, *The Occult Conspiracy: Secret Societies: Their Influence and Power in World History* (Rochester, Vt.: Destiny, 1989), pp. 74, 78–79, 105, 118–119, 123; Trevor Ravenscroft, *The Spear of Destiny* (York Beach, Me.: Samuel Weiser, 1973, 1982), p. 117.

Note: The Kaiser's spiritual confidant was the brilliant but demonized Houston Steward Chamberlain. According to author William Shirer *(The Rise and Fall of the Third Reich)*, "Chamberlain was given to seeing demons" who appeared to him in dreams, fevers and apparitions. After observing this behavior, Ravenscroft reports *(Spear,* p. 119), army chief of staff General Helmuth von Moltke "had no doubt at all that Chamberlain was in the hands of demonic intelligences who sought to influence and disrupt the course of European history." Czar Nicholas, on the other hand, was under the spell of the mystic monk Grigori Rasputin. In addition to possessing healing powers (which he employed on behalf of the czar's hemophiliac son), Rasputin was reputed to have a hypnotic hold over women—including, and perhaps especially, the Czarina Alexandra.

89. Ken Anderson, *Hitler and the Occult* (Amherst, N.Y.: Prometheus, 1995), pp. 13–14, 150, 208–209, 212; Ravenscroft, *Spear,* pp. 244, 246.

90. Anderson, *Hitler,* pp. 132–137; Howard, *Conspiracy,* pp. 131–132.

91. Howard, *Conspiracy,* pp. 78, 82, 90.

92. While such things are hardly new—virtually every English royal court since 1066 has had an astrologer—it is further evidence of how pervasive the powers' influence has become.

93. Almost immediately after this story broke, administration spin doctors went out of their way to mainstream Houston's techniques and minimize her influence on the first lady. Despite their efforts, however, many damaging revelations leaked out. Among them was the fact that Houston—who runs the Foundation for Mind Research in Pomona, New York, and the Mystery School in Port Jervis, New York—often goes into extended trance, using the goddess Athena as her focusing image. According to an NBC investigation, Houston's relationship with the Clintons began when she was invited to an intimate convocation of self-help gurus at Camp David in 1994. From there she quietly became a regular guest at the White House, often staying for up to a week at a time. Her effect on the first lady was apparently significant. On one occasion, when Mrs. Clinton seemed particularly upbeat, her chief of staff, Maggie Williams, was heard to remark, "Hillary's clicking today; she's had her Jean fix." See NBC "Dateline," June 26, 1996; Lawrence Goodman and Helen Kennedy, "Jean Houston: 'I'm Really Boring,'" *Seattle Times,* June 24, 1996.

94. See Arnold, *Powers of Darkness,* p. 204.

95. 2 Corinthians 4:4.

96. Arnold, *Powers of Darkness,* p. 204.

97. Nebuchadnezzar's Babylon, like Nimrod's Babel, has become a synonym for independence, greed and arrogance—a reflection of the ambitions and character of their prime patron. (In 1 Peter 5:13, the apostle's reference to Babylon is made not in relation to the physical city on the Euphrates, but her metaphorical successor in Rome.) For more on Babylon as an archetype of idolatrous cities, see James Charlesworth, *The Old Testament Pseudepigrapha* (New York: Doubleday, 1985), Vol. 2, p. 931 (index).

98. Saggs (*Greatness,* p. 318) describes how Babylon's temple foundation stones (or bricks) were dedicated to and blessed by the gods. Imbued with supernatural power, these sacred blocks and the process that produced them were seen as upholding the very well-being of the city.

99. The influence of dark powers over modern business and technology is every bit as strong as it is in the realm of politics. This is seen not only in the occult worldviews of many leading physicists, engineers and computer scientists, but in the practices of scores of multinational corporations. To ensure success and ward off misfortune, some construction firms build idols into the walls of their high-rise office buildings and hotels. Other companies, like Coca-Cola, employ spiritualists and shamans to the same end.

(One Christian ethnographer actually lived with one of these shamans in Indonesia.) In Japan one of Boeing's leading subcontractors inaugurated its production line with elaborate Shinto ceremonies involving the participation of leading Seattle executives. Even international air carriers have gotten into the act. From the day its inaugural flight was charted by astrologers, Thai Airlines has been linked to spiritual forces. The acquisition of each new plane is accompanied by ceremonial rites during which the "Supreme Patriarch," head of Thailand's Buddhist community, personally anoints "the nose cone, cockpit, entrances, and exits with lustral water" ("The Story of Thai," *Sawasdee*, May 1992, p. 72).

100. Scripture is unclear on the question of whether the beast of Revelation 13 represents a system, an individual or both. A hypothesis for the former is contained in chapter 9 of Otis, *Giants*.

101. Revelation 12:9 and 20:2 identify the dragon as Satan, the ancient serpent. His relationship with the Antichrist represents the ultimate co-conspiracy against the purposes and people of God.

102. Schaeffer, *Genesis*, p. 80.

103. The word for *idol* in both Hebrew and Greek indicates "phantom" or "mere appearance" (see 1 Corinthians 8:4).

104. In a commentary on Paul's observation that "the sacrifices of pagans are offered to demons" (1 Corinthians 10:20), the second-century apologist Athenagoras wrote, "The demons who hover about matter, greedy of sacrificial odors and the blood of victims, and ever ready to lead men into error, avail themselves of these delusive moments of the soul; and taking possession of their thoughts cause to flow into the mind empty visions as if coming from the idols" (quoted in Ferguson, *Demonology*, p. 115).

In fact, the Greek rendering of Psalm 96:5 declares that "all the gods of the Gentiles are demons" (see also Leviticus 17:7, Deuteronomy 32:17 and Psalm 106:37). For Arnold's comments on the subject, see *Ephesians: Power and Magic*, pp. 67–68, and *Powers of Darkness*, p. 93.

105. "We hold," said Origen, "that the worship which is supposed among the Greeks to be rendered to the gods at the altars, and images, and temples, is in reality offered to demons" (*Against Celsus* VII. 69; cf. VII. 65). See also Margaret Schatkin, "Culture Wars: How Chrysostom Battled Heresy, Superstition, and Paganism," *Christian History*, Vol. XIII, No. 4, p. 35; Ferguson, *Demonology*, pp. 111–113.

106. Saggs, *Greatness*, p. 309.

107. Pratney, *Healing*, pp. 149–150.

108. Hindu convert Rabi Maharaj describes how during daily meditation sessions he "began to have visions of psychedelic colors, to hear unearthly music, and to visit exotic planets where the gods conversed with [him], and encouraged [him] to attain ever higher states of consciousness." In this trance state, he remembers encountering "the same horrible demonic creatures that are depicted by the images in Hindu, Buddhist, Shinto, and other religious temples." Rabi Maharaj, *Death of a Guru* (Eugene, Ore.: Harvest House, 1984), p. 57.

109. Cavendish, *Powers*, pp. 234–235.

110. Quoted in Wagner, *Warfare Prayer*, pp. 90–91. See also Daniel 10:13, 20 ff.; 12:1 ff.; Ezekiel 28; Mark 5:10.

111. Michael Cheilik, *Ancient History* (New York: HarperCollins, 1969), p. 14; *Larousse Encyclopedia*, p. 10.

Note: Regional deities were also rife among the Assyrian deportees to Samaria. 2 Kings 17:29 reveals that "each national group made its own gods in the several towns where they settled"; and Jeremiah lamented over the backslidden tribes of Israel, "You have as many gods as you have towns, O Judah" (Jeremiah 2:28; 11:13).

112. In defining the nuances of this Semitic title, William Robertson Smith writes: "When a god is simply called 'the Baal,' the meaning is not 'the lord of the worshipper' but the possessor of some place or district, and each of the multitude of local Baalim is distinguished by adding the name of his own place." Melcarth is thus the Baal of Tyre, while Astarte is the Ba'alat (feminine) of Byblos. See William Robertson Smith, *The Religion of the Semites: The Fundamental Institutions* (New York: Schocken, 1972), pp. 92, 94–96; Cavendish, *Powers*, p. 237. See also Helmer Ringgren, *Religions of the Ancient Near East* (Philadelphia: Westminster, 1973), pp. 131–132.

113. Rudolf van Zantwijk, "The Great Temple of Tenochtitlan: Model of Aztec Cosmovision," *Mesoamerican Sites and World-Views*, p. 81.

114. Although these sanctuaries typically assumed the form of temples and shrines, natural settings were not unusual. Some Minoan deities, for example, seemed to prefer caves, while the gods of the Syrians sat atop great mountains. Ancient Celts paid homage to their local spirits at a variety of wells, trees and bogs.

115. During an August 1992 interview with Dr. Tokutaro Sakurai and Yoshimasa Ikegami, I learned that every Japanese village clan or people has its own set of deities, known as *ugigami*. Attached more to people than to geography, the *ugigami* are distinct from the *ubusuna*, which are local deities associated with an individual's birthplace.

116. According to Diane Coccari, *dih* is a generic term for a village guardian deity. In most instances, a *dih* (like a Baal) will also have a proper name. Derived from the Persian *deh*, the term in its Indian context carries a broad range of meanings that include "haunt, the site or ruins of a deserted village, the dwelling of the ancestors, a mound of earth, the place where worship of the village gods takes place, and simply village gods." As head of a village, the *dih* performs functions similar to those of the human official, except his realm of authority extends to spirits and magical energies. See "Protection and Identity: Banaras's Bir Babas as Neighborhood Guardian Deities," *Culture and Power in Banaras*, Sandria Freitag, ed. (Berkeley: University of California Press, 1989).

According to ancient Indian texts known as the *Silpasastras,* planning for new communities was based on explicit linkage "between gods, men, and [religious] rites." See Rana Singh, *Where Cultural Symbols Meet: Literary Images of Varanasi* (Varanasi, India: Tara Book Agency, 1989), p. 157. See also Kevin Lynch, *A Theory of Good City Form* (Cambridge, Mass.: MIT Press, 1981).

117. Coccari, "Protection and Identity," pp. 137–142; Mumford, *Himalayan Dialogue,* p. 118.

118. In a manner reminiscent of the Arabian goddess Al-'Uzza—whom early Qurayash tribesmen believed was incarnate in a cluster of three acacia trees on the road from Mecca to Medina—the *alijanu* are believed to patrol specific roads and live in chew-stick trees. See Ralph Faulkingham, "The Spirits and Their Cousins: Some Aspects of Belief, Ritual, and Social Organization in a Rural Hausa Village in Niger," Research Report No. 15, Department of Anthropology, University of Massachusetts, October 1975, pp. 13–18; *The Encyclopedia of Religion,* Vol. 1, Mircea Eliade, ed. (New York: Macmillan, 1987), p. 364.

119. Medicine Grizzlybear Lake, *Native Healer: Initiation into an Ancient Art* (Wheaton, Ill.: Quest, 1991), pp. 135–136.

120. This lifting and settling of symptoms, according to Williams, occurred on three separate occasions.

121. Adapted from a June 1994 interview.

122. Beyer, *Magic*, pp. 299–300.

123. Max Beauvoir, quoted by Wade Davis in *The Serpent and the Rainbow*, p. 93.

124. Some disagreements can be bridged through a simple adjustment in our semantics or perspective. A good example of this is the distinction between *territorial spirits* and *spiritual territoriality*. Whereas some Christians are uncomfortable with the idea that demonic powers exert a controlling influence over specific locations, almost no one questions the fact that the enemy's deceptive strategies are routinely and uniquely tailored to the far-flung cultures they are aimed at. (Witness the divergent means employed by the enemy in the cities of Mecca and Hollywood.) While we may squabble over emphasis, the bottom line is the same in both instances: deceptive strategies administered by demons in territorially diverse settings.

125. Bel (also known as Marduk) was the patronal god of Babylon from the Third Dynasty of Ur—and quite possibly earlier. His cult was closely connected to Babylon's mercurial rise from a major city-state to the capital of an empire. See also Jeremiah 51:44, 52; 50:38.

126. 1 Kings 20 offers a vivid illustration of how belief in territorial spirits (or gods) influenced an entire military campaign—in this case, between Israel and the king of Aram, Ben-Hadad.

127. Smith adds, "As the heathen gods are never conceived as ubiquitous, and can act only where they or their ministers are present, the sphere of their permanent authority and influence is naturally regarded as their residence" (*Semites*, pp. 92, 95).

128. In *Taoist Ritual and Popular Cults of South-East China* (Princeton: Princeton University Press, 1994), author Kenneth Dean presents a pattern of evidence over the past millennium that deities and temples in China's Fujian Province are attached to territorially based lineage groups.

Chapter 8: Territorial Dynasties

1. People who exhibit these symptoms suffer from a syndrome known as Seasonal Affective Disorder, or SAD. In communities situated at extreme latitudes or under chronic overcast, SAD can affect upwards of 25 percent of the population. See Angela Smyth, *Seasonal Affective Disorder* (New York: Thorsens, 1990), pp. 2–3, 9–30, 54–55, 58–61.

2. One research factor used in both physical and spiritual mapping is population density. As we noted earlier, demons are where people are.

3. Since many of the oldest pacts between peoples and demonic powers were transacted in Asia, and since Asia now hosts the greatest population centers of the planet, it should not surprise us that the continent presently dominates the great unreached frontier known as the 10/40 Window. Population and pact longevity both have much to do with the territorial entrenchment of spiritual darkness.

4. "From Child-Killing to Mysticism," *Christian History*, Vol. XIV, No. 3, p. 25.

5. August 6, 1992, interview with Dr. Yoshihiro Tanaka, president of Japan's Matsuri [Festival] Society in Nagoya; Yoshihiro Tanaka, "Festivals and Folk Art," *Matsuri News* 186, special issue, summer 1976, Matsuri Society, Nagoya, Japan, p. 19; Cooper, *Traditional Symbols*, p. xiii.

6. Nowruz is an ancient Persian New Year festival with links to Zoroastrianism. See Alex Tizon, "Area Persians Greet New Year with Old Ways," *Seattle Times*, March 21, 1996.

7. "Hindus Defy Guerrillas to Make Trek," *Seattle Times*, September 3, 1995.

8. Quoted in J. C. Cooper, *The Dictionary of Festivals* (London: Thorsons, 1995), p. xiii.

9. Quoted in Abd al-Masih, *The Occult in Islam* (Villach, Austria: Light of Life, n.d.), p. 40.

10. The ceremony, also known as the Bahatara Turun Kabeh, is always held during the full moon. While most of the festivities center around the Hindu Mother Temple, animal sacrifices are tossed into the steaming caldera of nearby Mount Agung.

11. This popular pageant takes place on the last Sunday in July and is intended to celebrate the community's long history of witchcraft.

12. In his book *The Sacred and the Profane: The Nature of Religion* (Orlando: Harcourt, Brace, [1959], 1987), Mircea Eliade notes that many religious festivals are perceived as the reactualization of creative acts by divine beings. Accordingly, so long as the festival is underway, participants believe themselves to be living in another time, sometimes becoming the contemporaries of the gods (see pp. 80–91).

13. The Maha (or mega) Kumbh Mela, located near the city of Allahabad, is held every twelve years and is believed to be the largest periodic assemblage of people anywhere on earth. The festival lasts for six to eight weeks. See D. P. Dubey, "Kumbh Mela: Origin and Historicity of India's Greatest Pilgrimage Fair," *National Geographic Journal of India*, Vol. 33, Part 4, December 1987, pp. 117–136. See also Tony Heidere, "India's Maha Kumbh Mela: Sacred Space, Sacred Time," *National Geographic*, Vol. 177, No. 5, May 1990, pp. 106–116.

14. Cambridge lecturer Carmen Blacker, who observed this farewell from the shore of Lake Matsue in 1972, recalls seeing thousands of flickering lights float past, "uncannily like a great host of spirits." Gradually the little spirit boats receded into the darkness of the other side of the lake, where "one by one they quivered and went black." See Blacker, *Catalpa Bow*, pp. 46–47. See also Tokutaro Sakurai, "Japanese Festivals: Annual Rites and Observances," *Understanding Japan 60* (Tokyo: The International Society for Educational Information, 1991), pp. 57–61.

Note: Elsewhere in the world returning ghosts are celebrated during "the Days of the Dead," possibly the most important religious period of the year in Mexico; and on "the Days of Released Souls," observed by Zoroastrians during the last ten days of the year. This latter holiday, like the Japanese O-bon season, is a time when departed spirits and their guardians *(fravashis)* draw near to this world and are invited to dwell in temporary "gardens" (or flower arrangements).

15. Samhain was considered the Lord of Death by the Celts, who held annual festivals to ward off his evil.

16. Assuming Halloween to be a time when ghosts return to roam the earth, the Celts put on frightening costumes and carved grotesque masks out of gourds to ward off evil spirits. (The masks were also offered as sacrifices in exchange for a successful harvest and protection from the upcoming winter.) In similar fashion, the ancient Romans protected themselves from evil spirits by carving out gourds and placing lighted candles inside. Others left out supplies of bread and water to nourish the visiting ghosts (see Cowan, *Fire*, p. 55).

17. Freidel, Schele and Parker, *Maya Cosmos*, pp. 257–269.

18. Once a year, for example, the Huichol Indians of northern Mexico set out on the Wirikuta, a solemn pilgrimage to the mythical place of their origin. During this ritual journey, daylight hours are spent gathering peyote, which they consider sacred, and reserve the nights for mystical rendezvous with gods and ancestors. The pilgrimage is led by a *mara'akáme*, or shaman, whose first act is to instruct participants in the coded vocabulary and protocols that must be observed during the Wirikuta. Received through spiritual dreams, these complex terms result in a strange, reversible world in which eyes become tomatoes, tobacco is referred to as ant droppings and men shake feet instead of hands. "This is how it is," explains one *bikuritámete* (peyote pilgrim). "It must be as it was

said in the beginning, in ancient times." See Ramon Medina Silva, "How the Names Are Changed on the Peyote Journey," an appendix to Barbara Myerhoff, "Return to Wirikuta: Ritual Reversal and Symbolic Continuity on the Peyote Hunt of the Huichol Indians," in *The Reversible World: Symbolic Inversion in Art and Society,* Barbara Babcock, ed. (Ithaca, N.Y.: Cornell University Press, 1978), pp. 236–239.

19. Corn pollen is a sacred symbol that traditional Navajos often scatter during prayers.

20. Bill Donovan, "News of Navajo Deities' Visit Draws Thousands to Site," *The Arizona Republic,* May 28, 1996; Michelle Boorstein, "Sacred Site Draws Navajos Despite Skeptics," *Los Angeles Times,* June 30, 1996; July 1996 telephone interview with Kay Courtney at Navajo Gospel Mission field office in Hard Rock, Arizona.

Note: Although debate continues over the authenticity of the Big Mountain visitation, no evidence of fraud had been uncovered as of late 1996. Many Navajo believers and local mission workers are persuaded that the visitation was demonic in origin—a reasonable conclusion in light of the far-reaching impact of the event.

21. Akemi Nakamura, "Town Makes Pact with Devils, Demons in Bid to Revitalize," *Japan Times,* December 20, 1994.

22. These ancient rites take place every May and include special processions and offerings at the Shimogamo and Kamigamo shrines.

23. Julia Wilkinson, "Spirit Island," *Sawasdee,* May 1992, pp. 15–18.

Note: A similar and equally ancient ritual is found in the Bolivian town of Toracari. Known as *tinku,* it involves bands of villagers who fight one another with fists and stones. In an attempt to explain this practice, which was once widespread throughout the Andes, one villager declared: "The blood that is shed and the lives which are lost are offerings to Pachamama (Earth Mother) and the mountain gods. The more that is sacrificed, the better the harvest." See Johan Reinhard, "Sacred Peaks of the Andes," *National Geographic,* March 1992, pp. 95–98.

24. While communities can and often do make pilgrimages, they are generally attached to festivals that focus on collective need.

25. Jere Van Dyke, "Long Journey of the Brahmaputra," *National Geographic,* November 1988, pp. 680–681.

26. Qur'an XXII:27–28.

27. Ni'mah Nawwab, "Hajj: The Journey of a Lifetime," *Aramco World,* Vol. 43, No. 4, July–August 1992, pp. 24–35; Heidi Tawfik, *Saudi Arabia: A Personal Experience* (San Jose: Windmill Publishing, 1991), pp. 69–79; Gai Eaton, "The Hajj," *Parabola,* Vol. IX, No. 3, August 1984, pp. 18–25.

28. Much of this information was gleaned from a May 1992 interview with Dr. Rana Singh in Varanasi, India. See also Rana P. B. Singh, "The Pilgrimage Mandala of Varanasi: A Study in Sacred Geography," *The National Geographic Journal of India,* Vol. 33, No. 4, December 1987, pp. 493–524; Rana P. B. Singh, "Peregrinology and Geographic Quest," in *Trends in the Geography of Pilgrimages,* R. L. Singh and Rana P. B. Singh, eds., The National Geographic Society of India, Research Publication Series #35, Banaras Hindu University, 1987, pp. 173–177; Robert Stoddard, "Pilgrimages along Sacred Paths," *National Geographic Journal of India,* Vol. 33, Pt. 4, December 1987, pp. 96–102; Santha Rama Rau, "Banares: India's City of Light," *National Geographic,* Vol. 169, No. 2, February 1986, pp. 241–243.

29. Paul Hensley, "Thaipusam in Malaysia," assignment report for Phenomenology and Institutions of Folk Religions, Fuller Theological Seminary, November 15, 1984, pp. 1–4.

30. Percival Lowell, *Occult Japan: Shinto, Shamanism and the Way of the Gods* (Rochester, Vt.: Inner Traditions, 1990 [orig. 1894, Houghton-Mifflin]), pp. 223–229.

Note: Unlike that of Mount Fuji, Ontake's summit is squat and jagged, having lost its symmetrical cone to a series of volcanic explosions. A string of circular craters, each filled with the green waters of a lake, presently crown its brow. (It is here, many believe, that the dragon deity Hakuryusan lives.) The three routes to the summit are each divided into ten stages. The lower of these pass through exquisite forests of pine and cryptomeria, while the middle latitudes (which start about the sixth stage) are dominated by a crawling shrub known as *haimatsu*. From the eighth stage onward, all vegetation vanishes and the pilgrim is enveloped in a thick mist saturated with pungent, sulfurous fumes (the breath, it has been suggested, of what sleeps beneath). The pathway along the lunar landscape of the summit is dotted with the eerie gray outlines of furious Buddhist idols. At least three primary shrines present themselves, all of which are in frequent use during midsummer trance rituals. The Ontake ko hold séances here for the purpose of being possessed by, and extracting information from, the Ontake Okami, a trinity of gods comprising: 1) the mythological creator of the nation; 2) the goddess associated with the royal family; and 3) the deity that rules the world of the dead.

31. Much of the wall space inside the lodge was devoted to photos of the annual Gojinkasai Festival, a local event whose main feature is a magic bonfire fueled by small prayer request sticks known as *gomagi*. Held every August 6–7, the Gojinkasai is the largest festival associated with Mount Ontake. Other photos depicted group séances at the summit.

32. Don Belt, "Israel's Galilee: Living in the Shadow of Peace," *National Geographic*, Vol. 187, No. 6, June 1995, pp. 62–87. For more information on *baraka* and the veneration of saints within the world of folk Islam, see Bill Musk, *The Unseen Face of Islam* (Eastbourne, England: MARC/Monarch, 1989), pp. 45–59.

33. Davis, *Serpent*, p. 209.

Note: Irrational or unfounded traditions that modify people's behavior are often called superstitions. Ancient Babylonians, for instance, believed that eating garlic on the first day of the month of Tashrit would invite a scorpion sting, while partaking of pig-meat on the fifth day was sure to bring on a lawsuit. Even today the taboo-ridden people of Tonga insist that headaches can be caused by either stress or by ancestors whose bones are troubled by the roots of casuarina trees.

34. Edward Albert Shils, *Tradition* (Chicago: University of Chicago Press, 1981), pp. 50–52.

35. Bern Williams, quoted in *Reader's Digest*, "Quotable Quotes," May 1996.

36. On the Melanesian island of New Ireland, secluded (and ritually dead) boys are carried back to the village by masked figures representing certain deceased ancestors. See Bodrogi, "New Ireland Art," p. 24.

37. Eliade, *Myths, Dreams*, pp. 192–195.

38. Ibid., p. 199. In a similar fashion, Omagua Indian girls in Peru are traditionally sewn into hammocks suspended from the ceilings of their huts. There they must remain motionless for eight days. See *Did You Know?*, p. 240.

39. The Dagara homeland is spread across the West African nations of Burkina Faso, Ghana and Côte D'Ivoire.

40. Somé reveals that a spiritual tether was provided during his years at the seminary, in the form of visionary appearances by his shaman grandfather. "He was always there at the major intersections of my life," Somé recalls. "He kept me in touch with my ancestors."

41. Primal language is a manner of speech that traditional elders, shamans and sorcerers learn to accomplish their duties. Believed to be a "language of creation," it has the power in certain circumstances to manifest what is uttered. It can be extremely dangerous. Somé recalls the first time he heard his grandfather speak it: "He used it as a retaliatory weapon against a vulture who had defecated on his bald head. He faced the tree where the bird was sitting, uttered a few sentences, and the poor thing came crashing to the ground. When I rushed over to grab it, it was ash."

42. "Traditional education," according to Somé, "consists of three parts: enlargement of one's ability to see, destabilization of the body's habit of being bound to one plane of being, and the ability to voyage transdimensionally and return."

43. See chapter 4 segment on "The Dimensional Gate."

44. Shortly after this unfortunate incident, a second of even greater proportion was recorded when the elders failed to retrieve an initiate at all.

45. Here Malidoma became convinced that somebody was breathing for both him and itself. "I had the feeling," he says, "that I was caught in the middle of a vast intelligence. Something knew I was there and wanted me to do something."

46. Malidoma Patrice Somé, *Of Water and Spirit: Ritual, Magic, and Initiation in the Life of an African Shaman* (New York: Jeremy Tarcher / Putnam, 1994), pp. 162–169, 174–180, 192–205, 213, 226–248, 295–298; Somé, "Rites of Passage," *Utne Reader,* July–August 1994, pp. 67–68. See also Frederick Butt-Thompson, *West African Secret Societies: Their Organizations, Officials, and Teachings* (Westport, Ct.: Negro Universities Press [1970], reprint of 1929 ed.), and Isaiah Oke, *Blood Secrets: The True Story of Demon Worship and Ceremonial Murder* (Buffalo, N.Y.: Prometheus, 1989).

Note: Similar initiations take place throughout Africa. Among the Diola tribe of Senegal's Casamance region, the ritual is called the Bakut and may be held only once every decade or two. Other tribal initiations are held annually or at periods ranging from three to seven years. The length of these exercises ranges from three weeks to six months.

47. For centuries the Maya have also planted small stone pillars in the ground before sacred pyramids and hills where protective ancestors are believed to reside. Here sacrifices are offered at least every 260 days (see Freidel, Schele and Parker, *Maya Cosmos,* p. 188). In the American Southwest, Hopi clan members make pilgrimages to specific ruins in order to commune with the spirits of their ancestors, while Indians of the Altiplano consider certain rocks the petrifaction of mythical ancestors.

48. Faulkingham, "The Spirits," pp. 17, 36; Harry McArthur, "The Role of the Ancestors in the Daily Life of the Aguacatec (Maya)," XLIII International Congress of Americanists, University of British Columbia, Vancouver, Canada, August 10–17, 1979, pp. 7–13.

49. Edward Whitley, "Trains, Tortoises, and Turning the Bones," *Seattle Times,* February 21, 1993.

50. Linda Stone, "Illness Beliefs and Feeding the Dead in Hindu Nepal," *Studies in Asian Thought and Religion,* Vol. 10 (Lewiston/Queenston, Canada: Edwin Mellen Press, 1988), pp. 116–123, 133–148.

51. Ki-Zerbo, *General History,* pp. 17–18. Among several African peoples (notably the Bafulero of Zaire, the Banyoro of Uganda and the Mossi of Burkina Faso), the tribal chief is the mainstay of collective time. His death constitutes a break in both time and taboos. In 1992 Dr. Tokutaro Sakurai informed me that since most Japanese cannot trace their lineage beyond ten generations, corporate ancestors (idealistically imagined as ancient royalty) are often created to fill the void and offer at least mythological roots.

52. Even Scripture informs us that "faith cometh by hearing" (Romans 10:17, KJV).

53. A high or incarnate lama will typically possess multiple initiations. These are passed on from his masters, from teachers he visits on pilgrimage and from traveling lamas who pass through his monastery. The basic initiation process involves three phases: 1) the *wang* or empowerment stage, in which the initiate is introduced to the god and his characteristics; 2) the *lung* or authorization stage, in which the student is read the relevant texts associated with the deity; and 3) the *tri* or explanation stage, during which the initiate is taught secret ritual procedures, including visualization techniques necessary to invoke the deity. This period of largely solitary work lasts for three years, three months and three days. Before the monk can direct the deity's power to any end, he must recite its mantra as many as ten million times and learn to vividly visualize himself as the god.

54. Tibetan Buddhist lineages are based on mentors rather than relatives. See Beyer, *Magic*, pp. 20–27, 36–38; May 1992 interview with Mina Tulku at the Bhutan National Museum in Paro, Bhutan.

55. Quoted in Freidel, Schele and Parker, *Maya Cosmos*, pp. 208–209.

56. In this latter instance, the traditions of the conqueror are typically impressed on its new subjects not by the sword, but through the charismatic force associated with ascendant power. See Edward Albert Shils, *Tradition* (Chicago: University of Chicago Press, 1981), pp. 250–251.

57. Unpublished report by Bernard and Elisabeth Piaget, April 1996.

58. Ries, *Origins*, p. 70.

59. Jill and Leon Uris, *Ireland*, p. 30.

60. Until A.D. 664, the center for this mystical, syncretistic religion was the monastery school of Lindisfarne on Holy Island. See Thompson, *Evil*, pp. 8–9.

61. Although the original name of the goddess was translated "Serpent Woman," colonial historian Fray Bernardino de Sahagún (himself a Catholic) informs us that the Aztecs later called her Tonantzin, which means "Our Mother." When the Church of Our Lady of Guadalupe was built on Tepeyac hill, de Sahagún claims that the Marian image became synonymous with Tonantzin. See *A General History of the Things of New Spain*, Florentine Codex (Santa Fe, N.M.: School of American Research, 1950), Book 1, chapter 6, and Book 11, appendix 7.

Note: A similar cult has risen up around Guatemala's Black Christ of Esquipulas, a dark wood image whose origins date back to an idolatrous, pre-Columbian stronghold. See Lilly de Jongh Osborne, "Pilgrims' Progress in Guatemala," *Bulletin of the Pan American Union*, March 1948, p. 136.

62. William Cormier, "Halloween Haunts Mexican Holiday," *Seattle Times*, November 1, 1992.

63. Robert Randall, "Return of the Pleiades," *Natural History*, Vol. 96, No. 6, June 1987, pp. 42–52.

64. Joseph Murphy, *Santería: An African Religion in America* (Boston: Beacon, 1988), pp. 28–34.

Note: Similar examples of Christo-pagan syncretism can be found in Filipino street pageants, which routinely transform pagan gods into patron saints; the Ratana Movement, which blossomed among New Zealand's Maoris in the 1920s; and the Africa-based Celestial Church of Christ. The latter claims fifteen thousand parishes in Africa, Europe and the Americas, and holds services in which prayers are offered in traditional Islamic poses, and worship is often accompanied by a pulsating merengue beat. "We are rooted in Christian traditions," says evangelist David Harrison-Adeove, "[but] we also take the best of all religions." See Cecila Farrell, "Church Rooted in Africa Mixes 'Best of All Religions' into One," *The Washington Post*, August 24, 1991.

65. In *Myth and Mystery* (p. 44), Finegan notes that both pyramid and obelisk have their origins in the respective hieroglyphic signs for the primeval hill and the Benben stone.

66. According to Tibetan scholar Tashi Tsering, when Buddhism was introduced in the Himalayas between the seventh and ninth centuries A.D., the Tibetan people accepted the philosophy of Buddhism but retained the ritual practices of Bön. See Per Kvaerne, "Tibet Bön Religion," *Iconography of Religions XII*, 13, Institute of Religious Iconography, State University Groningen (Leiden), 1985, pp. 3–5.

67. Tierney, *Altar,* pp. 38–39.

68. In addition to worshiping Hubal, locals venerated three female deities: al-Lat, al-'Uzza and Manat (which some have suggested were the three daughters of Allah). There were many others. The black stone still immured in one of the walls of the Ka'bah (or cube) that is now established as the centerpiece of the Grand Mosque is an extremely ancient cult object.

69. Nabih Amin Faris, ed., *The Arab Heritage* (Princeton, N.J.: Princeton University Press, 1946), pp. 52–53.

Note: While official Islam decries idolatry, pagan remnants have still infiltrated its symbols and practices (as they have those of traditional Christianity).

70. E. O. James, *Mother-Goddess*, pp. 182–183.

71. Estimates range from seventy to eighty percent.

72. The time periods associated with traditional and folk practices are arbitrary.

73. In many areas of North Africa, Islamic orthodoxy emerged slowly as it moved against a strong animist tide. (A 1922 study from the Sudan actually characterized local Islamic healers as able to "bilocate" or engage in soul flight.) In time peoples such as the Fulani, Hausa and Tuareg synthesized Islamic and indigenous traditions, with the former losing its purity and the latter acquiring many Islamic aspects. See Michael Winkelman, "Shamans and Other 'Magico-Religious' Healers," *Journal of the Society for Psychological Anthropology,* Vol. 18, No. 3, September 1990, p. 343. For more on folk Islam, see Bill Musk, *The Unseen Face of Islam;* George Braswell Jr., *Islam: Its Prophets, People, Politics and Power* (Nashville: Broadman & Holman, 1996), pp. 74–77; and *Muslims and Christians on the Emmaus Road,* J. Dudley Woodberry, ed. (Monrovia, Calif.: MARC, 1989), pp. 45–61.

74. Japanese "New Religions" refers to an amalgam of syncretistic sects that have formed in the twentieth century. The so-called *New* New Religions have sprung up in the years since 1980.

75. These new movements have also sprouted because Japan lacks an authorized system of thinking. (World War II put an end to Shinto as the state religion.) At the same time, democratic individualism was introduced to the society by the Americans—a development that proved a two-edged sword. Although it enabled people to escape traditional straitjackets, it paved the way for them to get snagged by new dangers.

76. From interviews with Ryu Oyama and Yoshi Kaneko, research associates with the Chuo Academic Research Institute, and Tadashi Takatani, assistant program officer with the Niwano Peace Foundation, Tokyo, August 1, 1992. Many young people have moved toward New Age thinking because Buddhism is seen as too rigid and next-worldly. New Age and the New Religions, by contrast, are very much this-worldly. The primary difference between the two: New Age is oriented toward the individual, while the New Religions are geared toward the group. A third philosophical stream in Japanese society is called "New Moral Thinking." The root of this thinking is not new at all—it is actually Confucianist—but the motto of the ideology, officially called Moralology, is "Old Ideas,

New Package." See also Christal Whelan, "Japan's 'New Religion,'" *Seattle Times,* May 13, 1995; "A New Religion in Japan," *The Church Around the World,* Vol. 22, No. 4, 1992; interview with Moriya Okano, senior editor, Shunjusha Publishing Company, Tokyo, July 31, 1992.

77. Fetcho, "Shipwrecked Stars," pp. 25–30. See also the 1992 *SCP Journal* double issue entitled "Alien Encounters: UFOs and the Realm of Shadows" (Vols. 17:1 and 2).

78. In the summer of 1690, the armies of Protestant king William of Orange defeated Catholic James II at the famous Battle of the Boyne—a victory that assured Protestants a political foothold on the Emerald Isle.

79. Indicative of its violent legacy, Ulster's provincial shield bears the emblem of a bloody severed hand.

80. Jill & Leon Uris, *Ireland,* pp. 179–185.

81. The latter offense is estimated to have cost some twenty million young people their freedom as they were sold into slavery in the plantations of the New World. Millions more died in transit. During a March 1996 Parliamentary debate on African reparations, Britain's Lord Gifford stated that this action was "without doubt, in the fullest sense of the term, a crime against humanity." And the aftermath, as is the case with most crimes, will affect victims, offenders and their progeny for generations until it is made right.

82. Braswell, *Islam,* p. 257.

83. Samuel Zwemer, *Raymond Lull: First Missionary to the Moslems* (New York: Funk & Wagnalls, 1902), pp. 52–53.

84. Braswell, *Islam,* pp. 258, 261.

85. Other passages referencing the "voice" of oppression or injustice include Exodus 2:23–24; 3:7–9; Psalm 9:12; 72:14; and James 5:4.

86. Among the hundreds of examples are sites associated with murders, fatal fires, mine disasters and battlefields (such as those found in the Scottish Highlands and at Gettysburg).

87. In brief, the hypothesis of morphic resonance suggests that the form of a physical structure or system becomes present to subsequent systems with similar form. The leading advocate of this theory is British scientist Rupert Sheldrake, whose book *A New Science of Life* has been called "an important scientific inquiry into the nature of biological and physical reality." Although Sheldrake has New Age tendencies, his scientific credentials are impressive: Harvard and Cambridge. To learn more about morphic resonance, see *A New Science of Life* (Rochester, Vt.: Park Street Press, [1981] 1995), pp. 71–74, 76–77, 93–102,132.

Note: If forms produced by ancient actions *can* be reconstituted, Sheldrake may be alluding to the physics employed (or manipulated) by demons—a physics that, at present, remains under the heading of *supernatural events.*

88. Gadon, "Sacred Places of India: The Body of the Goddess," in Swan James, ed. *The Power of Place and Human Environments* (Wheaton, Ill.: Quest, 1991), pp. 82–83.

89. Vasudeva Sharana Agrawala, *Ancient Indian Folk Cults* (Varanasi, India: Prithivi Prakashan, 1970), p. 185.

90. Stalinist Communism, introduced by Enver Hoxha, became the country's predominant ideology in 1944.

91. Dusko Doder, "Albania Opens the Door," *National Geographic,* Vol. 182, No. 1, July 1992, pp. 74–93; Catherine Field, "Vendetta: Gruesome Custom Re-emerging in Albania," *Seattle Times,* April 13, 1992; Larry Luxner, "Albania's Islamic Rebirth," *Aramco World,* Vol. 42, No. 4, July–August 1992, pp. 38–47; James Pandeli, *Oh Albania, My Poor Albania,* self-published manuscript, 1988, p. ii.

92. Ann and James Tyson, "Villagers Put Gods Before Marx," *Christian Science Monitor,* August 12, 1992.

Note: Another of China's primal forces is seen in the clans or lineages that hold large celebrations regularly to worship their ancestors. See Ann and James Tyson, "Family Clans Reemerge as Loyalties Go Local," *Christian Science Monitor,* August 12, 1992.

93. Tierney, *Altar,* pp. 222, 279, 356–357, and numerous other segments.

94. Otis, *Giants,* pp. 109–112. For speculation on the nature and role of the biblical Gog, see pp. 212–213.

95. Niwat Kongpien, "A Trip to the Great City," *Thai Accent,* October 1993, p. 75.

Note: During a March 1995 prayer journey that took them to Angkor Wat and the ancient pact site of Ba Phnom, veteran prayer leaders John Robb and the late Kjell Sjöberg made significant progress penetrating this mystery.

96. Lawrence Harrison, "Voodoo Politics," *The Atlantic Monthly,* June 1993, pp. 101–107.

Chapter 9: Rising Stakes

1. At the forefront of these technologies are video (the *Jesus* Film), shortwave radio and satellite television. Other new technologies (such as the Internet, personal computers and jet aircraft) have affected every evangelistic means from Bible translation to missionary mobilization and global networking.

2. The Justin Long statistic (which is adjusted for defections) derives from a June 1996 telephone conversation with Brian Kooiman of Global Harvest Ministries; see also "Worldscene," *Christianity Today,* November 9, 1992, p. 64.

3. Lance Morrow, "Evil," *Time,* June 10, 1991, pp. 52–53.

4. Green, *Exposing,* p. 97. A similar situation manifested itself in the last few decades before the Spanish conquest of Mesoamerica. Mayan and Aztec priests, sensing the approaching end of their culture, called for an increase in human sacrifices, while symbols of death began to predominate in art. See *The Seasons of Humankind,* P. Van Dongen, ed. (Den Haag: Rijksmuseaum Voor Volkenkunde, 1987), p. 101.

5. The Catholic Church, for example, has recorded a dramatic increase recently in the number of requests for exorcisms.

6. Notable exceptions to this rule include South Korea, where God's work has been hindered primarily through disunity between various churches and their leaders; Argentina, where revival fires have been cooled by the moral failure of a leading pastor; and Germany, where great gains were set back by a highly publicized sex abuse case involving a pastoral team in Nürnberg (the trial of this godly couple was based on trumped-up charges).

7. During this special season of grace, the Saudi Church enjoyed a relaxation of internal security, an unprecedented influx of Christian literature and a wave of supernatural visions and healings.

8. Elisabeth Farrell, "Saudi Arabian National Is Beheaded," *News Network International,* November 25, 1992, pp. 23–25; Barbara Baker, "Court Hearing Still Pending for Four Filipino Christians," *News Network International,* November 22, 1994, pp. 8–10.

9. David Stravers, executive vice president of the Bible League. See Kim Lawton, "The Suffering Church," *Christianity Today,* July 15, 1996, p. 58.

10. Lawton, "Suffering," pp. 57–58.

11. "Religion in China," *Wall Street Journal,* September 19, 1996. See also William Kazer, "Rise in Religion Seen as Threat," *Seattle Times,* August 12, 1996.

12. As of the mid-1990s, tens of thousands of Algerian nationals had been killed in the nation's vicious politico-religious struggle. See "Priest, Nun Killed by Islamic Radicals," *Christian Century*, Vol. III, No. 20, June 29–July 6, 1994, p. 638; Barbara Baker, "Security of Christians Deteriorates after Murder of Priests," *News Network International*, January 16, 1995, pp. 6–8; Willy Fautre, "Two More Catholic Nuns Assassinated," *News Network International*, September 22, 1995, pp. 11–12.

13. For more on Islamic vigilance, see Otis, *Giants*, pp. 78–79. According to one veteran missionary in South Asia, Christian incursions into the Tibetan Buddhist world are monitored by an agency known as Tibet International Network.

14. Lawton, "Suffering," p. 60. Michael Horowitz presently serves as a senior fellow at the Hudson Institute, a conservative political think tank.

15. These facts were compiled through a series of interviews conducted with various missionaries and Bible translators between October 1993 and October 1996. The conversations took place in Mussorie, India; Kathmandu, Nepal; Lynnwood, Washington; and Arlington, Texas. Certain names are withheld for security reasons.

16. Details verified via February 23, 1994, correspondence with ULS director Hallett Hullinger.

17. This brother was released miraculously after two weeks because of a dream that frightened his captors.

18. Francis Frangipane, *The Three Battlegrounds* (Marion, Iowa: Advancing Church Publications, 1989), p. 7.

19. Both apostles (see James 4:6 and 1 Peter 5:5) quote from Proverbs 3:34.

20. Jesus declared to the Pharisees, "You belong to your father, the devil" (John 8:44). For individuals who prided themselves on their devotion to prevailing religious orthodoxy, it is hard to imagine a more stinging indictment. Like Lucifer, the Pharisees had become infatuated with themselves—their knowledge, their pomp, their position. By valuing such things, they (like many religious intellectuals) had become "ignorant of God's righteousness" (Romans 10:3, NKJV). Their "zeal [was] not according to knowledge" (verse 2, NKJV). They had missed the point—that godly beliefs should translate into godly character.

The Christian world is still full of religious legalists who cannot resist parading their interpretations as biblical orthodoxy. To them, truth is validated by the standards of age (tradition is sacred) and popularity (often disguised as consensus), and they conveniently overlook the fact that Jesus' message clearly failed such standards. What matters to them is conformity to *core doctrines and practices*. In the process of defending this orthodoxy, however, gross deception sets in. These religious legalists view themselves as a kind of "palace guard," their mentalities turning increasingly adversarial. Who people *are*—the object of God's great affection—becomes less important than what they *believe*. Relational bridge-building is replaced with theological litmus tests and passwords. Eventually such legalists, like the Galatians before them (see 5:15), turn into Christian attack dogs, "biting and devouring" those who stand opposed to the "truth."

21. C. Peter Wagner, "Territorial Spirits and World Missions," *Evangelical Missions Quarterly*, Vol. 25, No. 3, July 1989, p. 286.

22. Jaki Parlier, "Dabbling with the Enemy," *In Other Words*, Vol. 18, No. 6, September–October 1992, pp. 1–2.

23. And procrastination! See James 4:17.

24. Although God often limits or deflects the devil's barbs, as He did with Job and Daniel, there is evidence that, in special cases of martyrdom, He grants His servants supernatural grace (see Acts 7:55–60).

25. In the autumn of 1993, I had the privilege of confirming this account through first-hand interviews with both mother and daughter, now a beautiful young lady.

26. Although my original conversation with Pastor Sandrup took place in Thimphu, Bhutan, there are reports he has since been deported from the country on account of his Nepalese ethnicity. Please pray for him and the church he has shepherded.

27. Chöd, or the "Mystic Banquet," is viewed by its practitioners as a shortcut to enlightenment (a state that typically requires thousands of lifetimes to attain). After mastering advanced visualization techniques (a process that can itself take several years), the disciple sets out to empty himself of ego by "feeding" his dismembered body parts to demons. The ritual, nearly always conducted in private, is carried out at places like caves and cremation grounds where demons are believed to congregate.

Upon arriving at the site, the practitioner goes into deep trance. A Daikini spirit conjured through visualization takes a scimitar and slices off the top of the head. The skullcap is then enlarged supernaturally for use as a serving container. For the next several hours, the practitioner's other organs and body parts are dismembered in the same manner and placed in the skullcap. Finally, when nothing remains of the corporeal entity, the practitioner invokes roaming demons to feast on the severed parts by blowing on a (real) hollowed-out human thighbone. This is the most dangerous moment in the entire ritual. Those who have not prepared themselves sufficiently for this gruesome manifestation can (and do) die of fright. Many others succumb to a condition known as "religious madness." (I had occasion to meet one of these victims on the day after my visit to the chöd master's private monastery in 1992.)

28. From a January 1997 interview with Pete Beyer (now recovered and wiser), and two conversations with Phil and Bev Westbay, his Singapore hosts.

29. Linda Williams, "The Curse of the Devil Worshiper," *Physician*, May-June 1994, pp. 18-20.

30. But also, as Francis Frangipane has said, "We must take off sin before armor can be put on and protect us."

31. Carol Shields, quoted in *Reader's Digest*, "Quotable Quotes," March 1996.

32. Kraft, *Christianity*, pp. 32-33.

33. Siegel, *Fire in the Brain*, pp. 126-127, 122.

34. See also Hebrews 13:17.

35. In the midst of this wrenching experience, Lisa and I found great comfort in the words of Psalm 57:1-3: "I will take refuge in the shadow of your wings until the disaster has passed. I cry out to God Most High, to God, who fulfills his purpose for me . . . rebuking those who hotly pursue me."

36. See Otis, *Giants*, pp. 260-265.

37. Other Christians attend church not because they want to enhance their relationship with Christ, but because they are afraid of losing their salvation. In the end, however, they are rejected by the very One they thought they were serving (see Matthew 7:21-23).

38. Otis, *Giants*, p. 263.

39. Kraft, *Christianity*, p. 135.

40. Jamie Buckingham, "The Risk Factor," *Charisma & Christian Life*, January 1989, p. 106.

41. Jack Deere, "Why Does God Do Miracles?", *Charisma*, September 1992, pp. 36.

42. "Terra X," The Discovery Channel, July 30, 1996.

43. Ed McGaa, *Mother Earth Spirituality: Native American Paths to Healing Ourselves and Our World* (San Francisco: HarperSanFrancisco, 1990), p. 90.

44. Howard Brant, "Toward an SIM Position on Power Encounter," SIM Position Paper, p. 7.

Note: Tibetan missionary Stephen Hishey, agreeing with Brant's position, added the following comment on ministry within his own culture: "We are dealing with a people group who walk with prayer beads in their hands. They will even take them into the toilet. In the marketplace, they have the beads going in the left hand while their right hand is doing business. It is a prayer culture, and if we try to enter it unprepared, if we have not personally adopted prayer as a lifestyle, then we simply will not be successful."

45. Kayanja traveled to Soroti (located northeast of Lake Kyoga) with the Echoes of Grace Choir from Eden Revival Church, pastored by Morris Bukenya and George Kyamuzugu.

46. This account was gathered through an August 1994 interview conducted by Ed Delph at the Diplomat Hotel in Kampala, Uganda.

Chapter 10: Spellbending

1. Lewis, *Lion*, p. 113.

2. Spiritual inroads into enemy territory are nearly always the result of godly initiatives rather than heathen invitations. See Otis, *Giants*, p. 264.

3. Although the prospect of spirits assuming animal form may seem farfetched, Choeden is not the first person to claim to have seen a red dog. Patrick Tierney reports, for example, that in 1953 "a Chilean court exonerated a twenty-seven-year-old Mapuche woman named Juana Catrilaf for murdering her grandmother. Juana Catrilaf was controlled by a force greater than her own reason, the court ruled, because she believed her grandmother, a *machi* with a penchant for black magic, was responsible for killing Catrilaf's twenty-one-day-old baby—through the agency of a malevolent spirit shaped like a red dog" (*Altar*, p. 103).

4. Bhutan is the only country in the world besides Tibet devoted to the Tantric form of Mahayana Buddhism.

5. Wearing turquoise earrings, one is better equipped to buy water after death, when it is sought to quench a soul's burning thirst.

6. The Jowo, one of the most sacred statues (idols) in Bhutan, resembles an image found in the Jokhang Temple in Lhasa, Tibet.

7. Jesus made a similar prayer commitment to Simon Peter in Luke 22:31: "Simon, Simon, Satan has asked to sift you as wheat. But I have prayed for you, Simon, that your faith may not fail."

8. Otis, *Giants*, p. 92.

9. Wink, "Demons and DMins," p. 505.

10. Bloom, *Lucifer*, p. 9.

11. Gordon Rupp, *Principalities and Powers*, cited in Green, *Exposing*, pp. 106–107.

12. Thigpen, "Power of the Spirit," p. 22.

13. Gerry Spence, *How to Argue and Win Every Time* (St. Martin's Press), quoted in *Reader's Digest*, "Quotable Quotes," December 1996.

14. Robert Priest, Thomas Campbell and Bradford Mullen, "Missiological Syncretism: The New Animistic Paradigm," *Spiritual Power and Missions: Raising the Issues*, Evangelical Missiological Society Series #3, pp. 70–75.

15. Reckless claims and dubious practices are not unique to the present generation. In the third century, for example, the Catholic Church routinely conducted pre-Easter masses, or "scrutinies," in which catechumens seeking admission to the Church were

exorcised. The scrutinies included a rite known as "exsufflation," in which the priest blew into the candidate's face to express contempt for the demons and drive them away. See Russell, *Prince*, pp. 120–122.

16. Barry Chant, "Spiritual Warfare," unpublished college text, Tabor College, Sydney, Australia, p. 1.

17. Miranda Ewell, "An Unholy Row in San Francisco," *Seattle Times*, November 1, 1990.

18. This outlandish event is outdrawn only by Pasadena's venerable Rose Parade on New Year's Day.

19. Tom White, "A Model for Discerning, Penetrating and Overcoming Ruling Principalities and Powers," paper presented at Lausanne II Congress on World Evangelization in Manila, July 1989, pp. 3–4.

20. When Paul talked about pulling down strongholds, he used the word *dunamis*—a word that means not just power, but power released to outward action.

21. See also Matthew 12:29.

22. Matthew 18:18 is often cited as evidence of unqualified authority to "bind" and "loose," but the passage has nothing to do with spiritual warfare. And those Scriptures that apparently do talk about binding evil spirits (see Matthew 12:29; 16:19; Mark 3:27) offer no promise that this action will result in permanent liberation. To achieve long-term relief from demonic enchantment, individuals and communities must repent of their sins—an action made easier by the temporary lifting of demonic deception.

23. To be led by the Spirit involves more than acknowledging the general scope of God's will. It is also recognizing that He is the Lord of the details, that only He can reveal the *how* and *when* of our particular mission.

Once this is said, it is important that we draw a distinction between the strategic initiatives discussed in this chapter and the deliverance of demonized individuals. The latter kind of spiritual warfare, which C. Peter Wagner calls "ground level," is something *all* Christians have been authorized to pursue (see Matthew 10:8; Mark 16:17).

24. John Hutchinson, "Warfare Praying in the Psalms," special research paper, summer 1994.

Note: Hutchinson is well aware of the fact that some of these psalms are imprecatory.

25. An interesting exception is Psalm 82, in which God speaks through Asaph against the "gods" (territorial spirits and, presumably, their corresponding earthly representatives). While the psalmist does address the enemy directly in this case, he does so as an oracle of judgment, speaking God's words in God's timing. See M. Tate, *Word Biblical Commentary: Psalms 51–100* (Waco, Tex.: Word, 1990), p. 328 ff.

Gary Greig, associate professor of Old Testament at Regent University's School of Divinity, notes that while some conservative evangelicals interpret the "gods" in this psalm as human judges (because of Jesus' reference in John 10:34–35), the internal evidence of the psalm itself makes it clear that it is dealing with demonic rulers (see reference to Deuteronomy 32:8 in endnote #65, chapter 7) and their earthly representatives.

26. Although earnest or persistent prayer is mentioned often in Scripture (see Genesis 32:26; 1 Chronicles 16:11; Daniel 6:10; Luke 11:5–10; Hebrews 11:6; James 5:16), this does not mean we must transform ourselves into pagan ascetics in order to attract God's attention (see Matthew 6:7–8). If our hearts are right before the Lord, breakthroughs can come speedily. Other factors affecting response time: the degree of spiritual entrenchment, the number and quality of people praying and issues relating to divine sovereignty.

27. Morrow, "Evil," p. 49.

28. Interview with Emeka Nwankpa on February 14, 1997, in Colorado Springs.

29. Arnold, *Powers of Darkness*, p. 204.

30. To learn how you can obtain these calendars, contact The Sentinel Group at P.O. Box 6334, Lynnwood, WA 98036. You can also e-mail us at SentinelGp@aol.com.

31. Report by Francisco Galli at the Ibero-American Conference on Spiritual Warfare in Antigua, Guatemala, on November 3, 1995.

32. "Church Seeks Forgiveness," *Seattle Times,* August 29, 1992.

33. John Dart, "Historic Step for Southern Baptists," *Seattle Times,* June 21, 1995.

Chapter 11: Lights in the Labyrinth

1. See chapter 2.

2. See Matthew 13:58; Luke 22:67; John 12:37; Acts 14:2.

3. Henry Mirima, "International Tribunal on Hutus Is Hypocrisy," *The Exposure,* No. 59, August 1994, printed in East Africa online at http://library.ccsu.ctstateu. edu/~history/world_history/archives/africa055.html.

4. It is common in Africa to see people yield themselves to whatever deity they perceive to have triumphed in a particular power encounter.

5. Robert Kayanja was interviewed by Ed Delph in August 1994 at the Diplomat Hotel in Kampala, Uganda.

6. Mama Jane's divination techniques included the use of ashes, dark cloths and even the Bible, which she would pretend to lay on people, receiving a "word from God."

7. This "death zone" stretched for about five hundred meters (more than fifteen hundred feet) to a nearby post office.

8. Thomas also told me in 1996: "An important target of our prayer effort has been the rampant alcoholism in Kiambu. When we first came here, it seemed that everyone was bound to *changaa* (a local brew). Now this has changed. Three bars near the church have been closed through prayer. One of them, the Bahamas Bar, used to play music so loudly that we could not sleep. Less than a month after we took the matter to God in prayer, it burned down. Another bar, the Diplomat Bar, is now a church. In fact, our own new church facility is being built in a ravine that was once a notorious bootlegging center."

9. This is based on estimates from the U.S. Drug Enforcement Administration. Colombia is also a major producer of marijuana and heroin. See "Colombia Police Raid Farm, Seize 8 Tons of Pure Cocaine," *Seattle Times,* October 16, 1994.

10. Pollard, Peter, "Colombia." Britannica Online: Book of the Year: World Affairs. 1995. Online. Encyclopedia Britannica. Available on the World Wide Web: http://www.eb.com :180/cgi-bin/g?DocF=boy/ 96/J03830.html. March 11, 1997.

11. To keep tabs on their operations, cartel founders Gilberto and Miguel Rodriguez Orejuela installed no fewer than 37 phone lines in their palatial home.

12. Interviews were via correspondence and telephone, the latter conducted on November 26, December 13 and 31, 1996.

13. The Association of Christian Evangelical Ministers of Vie. (Vie is the political department that hosts the city of Cali.)

14. Documenting the dimensions of Colombia's national savagery, Bogota's leading newspaper, *El Tiempo,* cited fifteen thousand murders during the first six months of 1993. This gave Colombia, with a population of 32 million people, the dubious distinction of having the highest homicide rate in the world (eight times that of the United States). See Tom Boswell, "Between Many Fires," *Christian Century,* Vol. III, No. 18, June 1–8, 1994, p. 560.

15. Two years earlier, as a Christmas "gift," the Rodriguez brothers had provided the Cali police with 120 motorcycles and vans.

16. This unique group comprises Colombian police, army personnel and *contra* guerrillas.

17. The June 1995 campaign also included systematic neighborhood searches. To ensure maximum surprise, the unannounced raids usually occurred at four A.M. "Altogether," MacMillan reported, "the cartel owned about twelve thousand properties in the city. These included apartment buildings they had constructed with drug profits. The first two floors would often have occupied flats and security guards to make them look normal, while higher-level rooms were filled with rare art, gold and other valuables. Some of the apartment rooms were filled with stacks of hundred dollar bills that had been wrapped in plastic bags and covered with mothballs. Hot off American streets, this money was waiting to be counted, deposited or shipped out of the country."

The authorities also found underground vaults in the fields behind some of the big haciendas. Lifting up concrete blocks, they discovered stairwells descending into secret rooms that contained up to nine million dollars in cash. This was so-called "throwaway" money. Serious funds were laundered through banks or pumped into "legitimate" businesses. To facilitate wire transfers, the cartel had purchased a chain of financial institutions in Colombia called the Workers Bank.

18. Dean Latimer, "Cali Cartel Crackdown?", *High Times*, August 8, 1995, online. Available at http://www.hightimes.com/ht/mag/958/calicar.html. March 6, 1997.

19. After being welcomed by the mayor of Cali, the intercessors who got inside were led in prayer by local pastors, with each session focusing on specific municipal and national strongholds.

20. After serving six months of his sentence, Santacruz embarrassed officials by riding out of the main gate of the maximum-security prison in a car that resembled one driven by prosecutors.

21. As the authorities probed the mountain of paperwork confiscated during government raids, they discovered at least two additional "capos" of the Cali cartel. The most notorious of these, Helmer "Pacho" Herrera, turned himself in to police at the end of August 1996. The other, Justo Perafán, had not been linked by authorities to the Cali operations until November 1996 because of a previous connection with the Valle cartel.

22. This well-publicized anti-corruption campaign is referred to by locals as *Processo Ocho Meyo*, or "Process Eight Thousand."

23. These reelection contributions totaled approximately six million dollars.

24. Juan Tamayo, "Colombian President Formally Charged," *Seattle Times*, February 15, 1996.

Note: Many of these politicians had thousands of dollars they could not legally account for. Although initially they denied any involvement with the drug lords, they were eventually implicated when police raids of cartel properties turned up copies of endorsed checks.

25. In December 1996 the Colombian legislature passed a powerful bill allowing the government to confiscate property gained through illegal means, primarily narcotics trafficking. (One narco clique had more than 1,100 deeds on properties located in Cali, New York, Paris and other international locations.) The legislation, retroactive to 1974, includes a provision forbidding the transfer of property to family members.

26. Quoted in Juanita Darling, "Cali Is a City for Sale Now that Drug Lords Are Gone," *Seattle Times*, September 8, 1996.

27. "Gracias a Dios No Explotó," *El Pais*, November 6, 1996; "En Cali Desactivan un 'Carrobomba,'" *El Pais*, November 6, 1996.

28. The number of days is derived by multiplying thirteen numbers and twenty day names (the latter of which are mostly animals).

29. Freidel, Schele and Parker, *Maya Cosmos*, p. 107.

30. On December 29, 1996, an agreement formally ending Guatemala's 36-year civil conflict was signed in Guatemala City by President Alvaro Arzu and leftist rebel leaders.

31. A dual reference to the area's six divine hills and the classic Maya name for the central "world tree."

32. Lisbeth Hernández Sum, "Momostenango, in the Middle of the Hills," *El Regional Huehuetenango*, June 15, 1995; Freidel, Schele and Parker, *Maya Cosmos*, pp. 169–172.

33. Freidel, Schele and Parker, *Maya Cosmos*, p. 51.

34. Similar ritual prayers will be offered at the New Year's dawning. See Paul Townsend, "Ritual Rhetoric from Cotzal, Guatemala," Instituto Linguistico de Verano, 1980.

35. Zunil is a 25- to 30-minute drive from Quetzaltenango on one of the major roads linking the Guatemalan highlands with the Pacific coast.

36. In an article in Guatemala's *Cronica Semanal*, Mario Roberto Morales suggests that the much-feared deity is also "a material image of Kukulkan, the Feathered Serpent" ("La Quiebra de Maximon," del 24 al 30 de Junio 1994, p. 19). See also E. Michael Mendelson, "Maximon: An Iconographical Introduction," reprinted from *MAN*, No. 87, April 1959.

37. Some scholars have speculated that the practice of placing tobacco products in the Maximon's mouth is an allusion to the *Popol Vuh* heroes, who smoked cigars in the House of Gloom. Many traditional Maya interpret shooting stars as cigar stumps smoked by agricultural deities.

38. Literally *ajkun*. See Mendelson, "Maximon," p. 19.

39. While he frolics in the dance room, Maximon's "throne"—actually an old wooden barber's chair—is kept warm by a smaller, doll-sized image.

40. Juanita Darling, "New Faiths for Latin America," *Los Angeles Times*, February 5, 1996.

41. Ibid.

42. The Morales article (see endnote #36) was forwarded to me by C. Peter Wagner on October 17, 1994.

43. Morales, "La Quiebra," pp. 17, 19–20.

44. Other named prayer efforts that I have heard about include "Morning Glory" and "Operation Prayer Storm." In the early 1990s a group of Japanese intercessors rented six railroad coaches, which they dubbed the "Glory Train," and rode the mobile prayer platform through all of Japan's prefectures.

45. I do not mean to suggest that prayer can alter God's essential nature or that human requests are always the linchpin for divine action. God's nature is unchanging and His will sovereign. I am suggesting, however, that selfless prayers, which God Himself inspires, are routinely collected and in some mysterious way inhaled or absorbed by the Almighty (see Revelation 8:4). When this occurs, God is released to be "impartially partial" in the lives of lost and needy people. He is changed in the sense that He has absorbed something—a fragrant prayer—that has originated, at least in part, outside of Himself. Because God's Spirit abides in us, our prayers are not tangential to, but synchronous with, the purposes of heaven (see Matthew 6:9–10; John 15:7).

Selected Bibliography

Ancient Religions

Agrawala, Vasudeva Sharana. *Ancient Indian Folk Cults.* Varanasi, India: Prithivi Prakashan, 1970.

Angus, Samuel. *The Mystery-Religions and Christianity.* New York: Citadel, 1966.

Finegan, Jack. *Myth and Mystery.* Grand Rapids: Baker, 1989.

Fox, Robin Lane. *Pagans and Christians.* San Francisco: HarperSanFrancisco, 1986.

Griswold, H. D. *The Religion of the Rigveda.* London: Oxford University Press, 1923.

Jacobsen, Thorkild. *The Treasures of Darkness: A History of Mesopotamian Religion.* New Haven: Yale University Press, 1976.

James, E. O. *Prehistoric Religion.* New York: Harper & Row, 1988.

Meyer, Marvin, ed. *The Ancient Mysteries: A Sourcebook.* San Francisco: Harper & Row, 1987.

Ries, Julien. *The Origins of Religions.* Grand Rapids: Eerdmans, 1994.

Ringgren, Helmer. *Religions of the Ancient Near East.* Philadelphia: Westminister, 1973.

Saggs, H. W. F. *The Greatness that was Babylon.* London: Sidgwick & Jackson, 1988.

Smith, William Robertson. *The Religion of the Semites: The Fundamental Institutions.* New York: Schocken, 1889, 1972.

Archaeology, Language and Prehistory

Ancient Tibet (research materials from the Yeshe De Project). Berkeley: Dharma Publishing, 1986.

Ashe, Geoffrey. *Dawn behind the Dawn.* New York: Henry Holt, 1992.

Bertman, Stephen. *Doorways through Time*. Los Angeles: Jeremy Tarcher, 1986.

Cheilik, Michael, and Anthony Inguanzo. *Ancient History*. New York: HarperCollins, 1969.

Cook, Melvin. *Prehistory and Earth Models*. London: Max Parrish, 1966.

Fagan, Brian. *The Journey from Eden: The Peopling of Our World*. New York: Thames & Hudson, 1990.

———. *World Prehistory: A Brief Introduction*. Boston: Little, Brown, 1979.

Fell, Barry. *America B. C.* New York: Pocket, 1989.

Grayson, Donald. *The Establishment of Human Antiquity*. New York: Academic, 1983.

Göran, Burenhult, ed. *People of the Stone Age: Hunter-Gatherers and Early Farmers*. New York: HarperSanFrancisco, 1993.

Haddon, A. C. *The Wanderings of Peoples*. Washington, D.C.: Cliveden, 1984.

Howells, William. *Mankind So Far*. New York: Doubleday, 1947.

Ingpen, Robert, and Philip Wilkinson. *Encyclopedia of Mysterious Places: The Life and Legends of Ancient Sites around the World*. New York: Viking Studio, 1990.

Kang, C. H., and Ethel Nelson. *The Discovery of Genesis*. St. Louis: Concordia, 1979.

Ki-Zerbo, J., ed. *Methodology and African Prehistory*. Berkeley: University of California Press, 1990.

Mallery, J. P. *In Search of the Indo-Europeans*. New York: Thames & Hudson, 1989.

Oard, Michael. *An Ice Age Caused by the Genesis Flood*. El Cajon, Calif.: Institute for Creation Research, 1990.

Pfeiffer, John. *The Creative Explosion: An Inquiry into the Origins of Science and Religion*. Ithaca, N.Y.: Cornell University Press, 1982.

Rahtz, Philip. *Invitation to Archaeology*. Oxford: Basil Blackwell, 1985.

Renfrew, Colin. *Archaeology and Language*. New York: Cambridge University Press, 1987.

Richardson, Don. *Eternity in Their Hearts*. Ventura, Calif.: Regal, 1981.

Rouse, Irving. *Migrations in Prehistory: Inferring Population Movement from Cultural Remains*. New Haven: Yale University Press, 1986.

Ruhlen, Merritt. *The Origin of Language: Tracing the Evolution of the Mother Tongue*. New York: John Wiley & Sons, 1994.

Saggs, H. W. F. *The Greatness that was Babylon*. London: Sidgwick & Jackson, 1988.

Van Dongen, P., ed. *The Seasons of Humankind*. Den Haag: Rijksmuseaum Voor Volkenkunde, 1987.

Wenke, Robert. *Patterns in Prehistory.* New York: Oxford University Press, 1984.

Whitcomb, John, and Henry Morris. *The Genesis Flood.* Phillipsburg, N.J.: Presbyterian & Reformed Publishing, 1961.

White, Randall. *Dark Caves, Bright Visions: Life in Ice Age Europe.* New York: American Museum of Natural History, 1986.

Consciousness and the Human Brain

Bandler, Richard. *Using Your Brain for a Change.* Moab, Utah: Real People Press, 1985.

Barrow, John, and Frank Tipler. *The Anthropic Cosmological Principle.* Oxford: Clarendon Press, 1986.

Cytowic, Richard. *The Man Who Tasted Shapes.* New York: Warner, 1993.

Johnson, George. *In the Palaces of Memory.* New York: Vintage, 1992.

McKellar, Peter. *Imagination and Thinking: A Psychological Analysis.* New York: Basic, 1957.

Moss, Thelma. *The Probability of the Impossible: Scientific Discoveries and Explorations of the Psychic World.* Los Angeles: Jeremy Tarcher, 1974.

Nee, Watchman. *The Latent Power of the Soul.* New York: Christian Fellowship Publishers, 1972.

Penrose, Roger. *The Emperor's New Mind: Concerning Computers, Minds and the Laws of Physics.* Oxford: Oxford University Press, 1989.

Restak, Richard. *The Brain: The Last Frontier.* New York: Warner, 1979.

Secrets of the Inner Mind. Alexandria, Va.: Time-Life, 1993.

Siegel, Ronald. *Fire in the Brain.* New York: Plume, 1992.

Watkins, Mary. *Invisible Guests: The Development of Imaginal Dialogues.* Hillsdale, N.J.: Analytic, 1986.

Demons, Dragons and the Devil

Cavendish, Richard. *The Powers of Evil.* New York: Dorset, 1993.

Crapanzano, Vincent, and Vivian Garrison. *Case Studies in Spirit Possession.* New York: Wiley, 1977.

Delbanco, Andrew. *The Death of Satan: How Americans Have Lost the Sense of Evil.* New York: Farrar, Straus and Giroux, 1995.

De Plancy, Collin, and Jaques Albin Simon. *Dictionary of Demonology.* New York: Philosophical Library, 1965.

Ferguson, Everett. *Demonology of the Early Christian World.* New York: Edwin Mellen, 1984.

Gettings, Fred. *Dictionary of Demons: A Guide to Demons and Demonologists in Occult Lore.* North Pomfret, Vt.: Trafalgar Square, 1988.

Huxley, Francis. *The Dragon.* London: Thames & Hudson, 1979.

Kernot, Henry. *Bibliotheca Diabolica*. New York: Scribner, Welford & Armstrong, 1874.

Kinnaman, Gary. *Angels Dark and Light*. Ann Arbor, Mich.: Vine, 1994.

Kreeft, Peter. *Angels and Demons*. San Francisco: Ignatius, 1995.

Langton, Edward. *Essentials of Demonology*. New York: AMS Press, 1981.

MacGowan, Kenneth, and Herman Rosse. *Masks and Demons*. New York: Harcourt, Brace, 1923.

Nebesky-Wojkowitz, Rene de. *Oracles and Demons of Tibet*. The Hague: Mouton & Co., 1956.

Robbins, Rossell Hope. *The Encyclopedia of Witchcraft and Demonology*. New York: Crown, 1959.

Russell, Jeffrey Burton. *The Prince of Darkness*. Ithaca, N.Y.: Cornell University Press, 1988.

Watson, Lyall. *The Dreams of Dragons*. Rochester, Vt.: Destiny, 1992.

Disaster and Trauma

Austin, Steven. *Catastrophes in Earth History*. El Cajon, Calif.: Institute for Creation Research, 1984.

Bowsky, William L. *The Black Death: A Turning Point in History?* New York: Holt, Rinehart & Winston, 1971.

Erikson, Kai. *A New Species of Trouble: The Human Experience of Modern Disasters*. New York: W. W. Norton, 1994.

Frazier, Kendrick. *The Violent Face of Nature: Severe Phenomena and Natural Disasters*. New York: William Morrow, 1979.

McNeill, William. *Plagues and Peoples*. New York: Anchor, 1977.

Preston, Richard. *The Hot Zone*. New York: Random House, 1994.

Prisco, Salvatore. *An Introduction to Psychohistory: Theories and Case Studies*. Lanham, Md.: University Press of America, 1980.

Raphael, Beverley. *When Disaster Strikes: How Individuals and Communities Cope with Catastrophe*. New York: Basic, 1986.

Simpson-Housley, Paul, and Anton Frans de Man. *The Psychology of Geographical Disasters*. North York, Ont.: Atkinson College, York University, 1987.

Spitz, Lewis William, and Richard Lyman, eds. *Major Crises in Western Civilization*. New York: Harcourt, Brace, 1965.

Suzuki, Hideo. *The Transcendent and Environments: A Historico-Geographical Study of World Religions*. Yokohama: Addis Abeba Sha, 1981.

VandenBos, Gary and Brenda Bryant, eds. *Cataclysms, Crises, and Ca-tastrophes: Psychology in Action.* Washington, D.C.: American Psychological Association, 1987.

Divination and Occultism

Anderson, Ken. *Hitler and the Occult.* Amherst, N.Y.: Prometheus, 1995.

Buckland, Raymond, and Kathleen Binger. *The Book of African Divination.* Rochester, Vt.: Inner Traditions, 1992.

Campion, Nicholas. *An Introduction to the History of Astrology.* London: ISCWA, 1982.

Crowley, Aleister. *Magick in Theory and Practice.* Paris: Lecram, 1929.

Fontenrose, Joseph. *The Delphic Oracle.* Berkeley: University of California Press, 1978.

Gasson, Raphael. *The Challenging Counterfeit.* Plainfield, N.J.: Logos, 1966.

Gilchrist, Cherry. *Divination: The Search for Meaning.* London: Dryad Press, 1987.

Godwin, Joscelyn. *The Theosophical Enlightenment.* Albany, N.Y.: State University of New York Press, 1994.

Howard, Michael. *The Occult Conspiracy.* Rochester, Vt.: Destiny, 1989.

Matthews, John, ed. *The World Atlas of Divination.* London: Headline, 1992.

McIntosh, Christopher. *A Short History of Astrology.* New York: Barnes & Noble, 1969.

Nebesky-Wojkowitz, Rene de. *Oracles and Demons of Tibet.* The Hague: Mouton & Co., 1956.

Pennick, Nigel. *Secret Games of the Gods.* York Beach, Me.: Samuel Weiser, 1992.

Wasserman, James. *Art and Symbols of the Occult: Images of Power and Wisdom.* Rochester, Vt.: Destiny, 1993.

Eastern Religions

Albrecht, Mark. *Reincarnation.* Downers Grove, Ill.: InterVarsity, 1982.

Beyer, Stephan. *Magic and Ritual in Tibet: The Cult of Tara.* Delhi: Motilal Banarsidass, 1988.

Brooke, Tal. *Lord of the Air: Tales of a Modern Antichrist.* Eugene, Ore.: Harvest House, 1990.

Carmody, Denise, and John Carmody. *Eastern Ways to the Center: An Introduction to the Religions of Asia.* Rev. ed. Belmont, Calif.: Wadsworth, 1992.

Chang, Garma. *The Practice of Zen.* New York: Perennial, 1959.

Cozart, Daniel. *Highest Yoga Tantra.* Ithaca, N.Y.: Snow Lion Publications, 1988.

Daniélou, Alain. *Hindu Polytheism.* Boston: Routledge & Kegan Paul, 1964.

———. *The Myths and Gods of India.* Rochester, Vt.: Inner Traditions, 1991.

Dean, Kenneth. *Taoist Ritual and Popular Cults of South-East China.* Princeton: Princeton University Press, 1994.

Earhart, H. Byron. *Japanese Religion: Unity and Diversity.* Belmont, Calif.: Wadsworth, 1982.

Evola, Julius. *The Yoga of Power: Tantra, Shakti, and the Secret Way.* Rochester, Vt.: Inner Traditions, 1992.

Hartsuiker, Dolf. *Sadhus: India's Mystic Holy Men.* Rochester, Vt.: Inner Traditions, 1992.

Kvaerne, Per. *Tibet Bön Religion.* Leiden, Germany: Institute of Religious Iconography, State University Groningen, 1985.

Lowell, Percival. *Occult Japan: Shinto, Shamanism and The Way of the Gods.* Rochester, Vt.: Inner Traditions, 1990.

Martin, E. Osborn. *The Gods of India: Their History, Character and Worship.* Delhi: Indological Book House, 1988.

Needleman, Jacob. *The New Religions.* New York: Pocket, 1970, 1972.

Nishitani, Keiji. *Religion and Nothingness.* Berkeley: University of California Press, 1982.

Raj, Sunder. *The Confusion Called Conversion.* New Delhi: Traci Publications, 1988.

Smith, Huston. *The Religions of Man.* New York: Perennial, 1958.

Snelling, John. *The Buddhist Handbook: A Complete Guide to Buddhist Schools, Teaching, Practice, and History.* Rochester, Vt.: Inner Traditions, 1992.

Waddell, Austine. *Tibetan Buddhism.* New York: Dover, 1972.

General History

Boorstin, Daniel. *The Discoverers.* New York: Vintage, 1983.

Carey, John, ed. *Eyewitness to History.* New York: Avon, 1987.

Grun, Bernard. *The Timetables of History.* New York: Simon & Schuster, 1979.

Herodotus: The Histories. London: Penguin, 1972.

Meltzer, Milton. *Slavery: A World History.* New York: Da Capo Press, 1993.

Mumford, Lewis. *The City in History.* Orlando: Harcourt Brace, 1961.

Wilford, John. *The Mapmakers.* New York: Vintage, 1981.

Wright, Esmond, ed. *History of the World: Prehistory to the Renaissance.* Feltham, England: Bonanza, 1985.

Goddess History and Theology

Adler, Margot. *Drawing Down the Moon.* Boston: Beacon, 1979.

Beane, Wendell Charles. *Myth, Cult and Symbols in Sakta Hinduism: A Study of the Indian Mother Goddess.* Leiden: E. J. Brill, 1977.

Bolen, Jean Shinoda. *Goddesses in Everywoman: A New Psychology of Women.* San Francisco: Harper & Row, 1984.

Bonanno, Anthony, ed. *Archaeology and Fertility Cult in the Ancient Mediterranean.* Amsterdam: B. P. Gruner, 1985.

Budapest, Zsuzsanna Emese. *The Holy Book of Women's Mysteries.* Vol. 1. Oakland, Calif.: Susan B. Anthony Coven 1, 1986.

Downing, Christine. *The Goddess: Mythological Images of the Feminine.* New York: Crossroads, 1984.

Gadon, Elinor. *The Once and Future Goddess.* San Francisco: Harper & Row, 1989.

———. *The Goddesses and Gods of Old Europe: Myths and Cult Images.* Berkeley: University of California Press, 1982.

Gimbutas, Marija. *The Language of the Goddess.* San Francisco: Harper-SanFrancisco, 1991.

Griffen, Susan. *Women and Nature.* New York: Harper & Row, 1978.

Harding, M. Esther. *Women's Mysteries: Ancient and Modern.* New York: Harper & Row, 1971.

Iglehart, Hallie. *Womanspirit: A Guide to Woman's Wisdom.* San Francisco: Harper & Row, 1983.

James, E. O. *The Cult of the Mother-Goddess.* New York: Barnes & Noble, 1994.

Kjos, Berit. *Under the Spell of Mother Earth.* Wheaton, Ill.: Victor, 1992.

Luhrmann, T. M. *Persuasions of the Witch's Craft.* Cambridge, Mass.: Harvard University Press, 1991.

Moss, Leonard, and Stephen Cappannari. *Mother Worship.* Chapel Hill, N.C.: University of North Carolina Press, 1982.

Neumann, Erich. *The Great Mother.* Princeton: Princeton University Press, 1955, 1963.

Olsen, Carl. *The Book of the Goddess Past and Present: An Introduction to Her Religion.* New York: Crossroads, 1983.

Perera, Sylvia Brinton. *Descent to the Goddess.* Toronto: Inner City Books, 1981.

Sjöö, Monica, and Barbara Mor. *The Great Cosmic Mother.* New York: Harper & Row, 1987.

Spencer, Aída Besançon, Donna F. G. Hailson, Catherine Clark Kroeger and William David Spencer. *The Goddess Revival.* Grand Rapids: Baker, 1995.

Starhawk. *The Spiral Dance: A Rebirth of the Ancient Religion of the Great Goddess.* San Francisco: Harper & Row, 1979.

Stone, Merlin. *When God Was a Woman.* New York: Dial, 1976.

Streep, Peg. *Sanctuaries of Power: The Sacred Landscapes and Objects of the Goddess.* Boston: Little, Brown, 1994.

Von Cles-Reden, Sibylle. *The Realm of the Great Goddess: The Story of Megalith Builders.* Englewood Cliffs, N.J.: Prentice-Hall, 1962.

Walker, Barbara G. *The Women's Encyclopedia of Myths and Secrets.* Edison, N.J.: Castle, 1983, 1996.

Whitmont, Edward. *Return of the Goddess.* New York: Crossroads, 1982.

Hidden Forces and Other Dimensions

Abbott, Edwin. *Flatland.* New York: HarperCollins, 1994.

Barrow, John, and Frank Tipler. *The Anthropic Cosmological Principle.* Oxford: Clarendon Press, 1986.

Barrow, John. *Theories of Everything: The Quest for Ultimate Explanation.* Oxford: Oxford University Press, 1991.

Burger, Dionys. *Sphereland.* New York: HarperCollins, 1994.

Davies, Paul. *The Mind of God: The Scientific Basis for a Rational World.* New York: Touchstone, 1992.

Hawking, Stephen. *A Brief History of Time.* New York: Bantam, 1988.

Kaku, Michio. *Hyperspace.* New York: Oxford University Press, 1994.

Lewis, C. S. *The Lion, the Witch and the Wardrobe.* New York: Macmillan, 1950.

Russell, Robert John, William Stoeger and George Coyne, eds. *Physics, Philosophy and Theology: A Common Quest for Understanding.* Vatican City: Vatican Observatory, 1988.

Sheldrake, Rupert. *A New Science of Life: The Hypothesis of Morphic Resonance.* Rochester, Vt.: Park Street Press, 1995 (1981).

Wilbur, Ken, ed. *Quantum Questions.* Boulder, Colo: New Science Library, Shambhala, 1984.

Idols, Gods and Symbols

Black, Jeremy, and Anthony Green. *Gods, Demons and Symbols of Ancient Mesopotamia.* Austin, Tex.: University of Texas Press, 1992.

Carlyon, Richard. *A Guide to the Gods.* New York: Quill, 1981.

Cooper, J. C. *An Illustrated Encyclopaedia of Traditional Symbols.* New York: Thames & Hudson, 1987.

Lurker, Manfred. *Dictionary of Gods and Goddesses, Devils and Demons.* London: Routledge & Kegan Paul, 1988.

Martin, E. Osborn. *The Gods of India: Their History, Character and Worship.* Delhi: Indological Book House, 1988.

Wasserman, James. *Art and Symbols of the Occult: Images of Power and Wisdom.* Rochester, Vt.: Destiny, 1993.

Magic, Superstition and the Paranormal

Beyer, Stephan. *Magic and Ritual in Tibet: The Cult of Tara.* Delhi: Motilal Banarsidass, 1988.

Brooke, Tal. *Lord of the Air: Tales of a Modern Antichrist.* Eugene, Ore.: Harvest House, 1990.

Bryan, C. D. B. *Close Encounters of the Fourth Kind: Alien Abduction, UFOS, and the Conference at M.I.T.* New York: Alfred Knopf, 1995.

Cornwell, John. *The Hiding Places of God.* New York: Warner, 1991.

Dailey, Timothy J. *The Millennial Deception: Angels, Aliens and the Antichrist.* Grand Rapids: Chosen, 1995.

Evans, H. *Visions, Apparitions, Alien Visitors.* Wellingborough, England: Aquarian Press, 1984.

Gersi, Douchan. *Faces in the Smoke.* Los Angeles: Jeremy Tarcher, 1991.

Guiley, Ellen Rosemary. *Harper's Encyclopedia of Mystical and Paranormal Experience.* Edison, N.J.: Castle, 1991.

Heinze, Ruth-Inge. *Trance and Healing in Southeast Asia Today.* Bangkok: White Lotus, 1988.

Hurwood, Bernhardt. *Supernatural Wonders from Around the World.* New York: Barnes & Noble, 1972.

Kiev, Ari, ed. *Magic, Faith, and Healing.* New York: The Free Press/Macmillan, 1974.

Moss, Thelma. *The Probability of the Impossible: Scientific Discoveries and Explorations of the Psychic World.* Los Angeles: Jeremy Tarcher, 1974.

Musk, Bill. *The Unseen Face of Islam.* Eastbourne, England: MARC/Monarch, 1989.

Somé, Patrice Malidoma. *Of Water and the Spirit.* New York: Jeremy Tarcher/G. P. Putnam's Sons, 1994.

Memes and the Forces of History

Anderson, Walter Truett. *Reality Isn't What It Used to Be*. San Francisco: HarperSanFrancisco, 1990.

Barber, Benjamin. *Jihad vs. McWorld*. New York: Times, 1995.

Bloom, Howard. *The Lucifer Principle: A Scientific Expedition into the Forces of History*. New York: Atlantic Monthly Press, 1995.

Bork, Robert. *Slouching towards Gomorrah: Modern Liberalism and American Decline*. New York: ReganBooks, 1996.

Cavendish, Richard, ed. 7 vols. *Man, Myth and Magic*. London: B. P. C. Publishing, 1970–1972.

Delbanco, Andrew. *The Death of Satan: How Americans Have Lost the Sense of Evil*. New York: Farrar, Straus and Giroux, 1995.

Long, Zeb Bradford, and Douglas McMurry. *The Collapse of the Brass Heaven*. Grand Rapids: Chosen, 1994.

Thompson, William Irwin. *Evil and World Order*. New York: Harper Colophon, 1976.

Myths and Mythology

Ashe, Geoffrey. *Dawn Behind the Dawn*. New York: Henry Holt & Co., 1992.

Bierlein, J. F. *Parallel Myths*. New York: Ballantine, 1994.

Caldecott, Moyra. *Myths of the Sacred Tree*. Rochester, Vt.: Destiny, 1993.

Campbell, Joseph. *The Masks of God: Occidental Mythology*. New York: Viking, 1959.

———. *The Mythic Image*. Princeton: Princeton University Press, 1983.

———. *The Power of Myth*. New York: Doubleday, 1988.

Eliade, Mircea. *Myths, Dreams and Mysteries*. New York: Harper & Row, 1960.

———. *The Sacred and the Profane*. Orlando: Harcourt Brace, 1987.

Frazer, James. *The Golden Bough*. New York: Macmillan [1922], 1974.

Guirand, Félix, ed. *The Larousse Encyclopedia of Mythology*. New York: Barnes & Noble, 1994.

Leach, Maria, and Jerome Fried, eds. *Funk & Wagnalls Standard Dictionary of Folklore, Mythology, and Legend*. San Francisco: Harper & Row, 1984.

Leeming, David Adams. *The World of Myth*. New York: Oxford University Press, 1990.

Markman, Roberta, and Peter Markman. *The Flayed God: The Mythology of Mesoamerica*. San Francisco: HarperSanFrancisco, 1992.

Reed, A. W. *Aboriginal Legends*. Chatswood, Australia: Reed, 1978.

The Rider Encyclopaedia of Mythology. London: Rider, 1989.

The Epic of Gilgamesh. New York: Penguin, 1960.

Schwartz, Howard. *Lilith's Cave.* New York: Oxford University Press, 1988.

Walker, Barbara G. *The Women's Encyclopedia of Myths and Secrets.* Edison, N.J.: Castle, 1996 (1983).

Prayer and Spiritual Warfare

Alves, Beth. *The Mighty Warrior.* Bulverde, Tex.: Canopy, 1987.

Anderson, Neil, and Charles Mylander. *Setting Your Church Free.* Ventura, Calif.: Regal, 1994.

Arnold, Clinton. *Ephesians: Power and Magic.* Grand Rapids: Baker, 1992.

———. *Powers of Darkness.* Downers Grove, Ill.: InterVarsity Press, 1992.

Bounds, E. M. *Power through Prayer.* Grand Rapids: Zondervan, 1987.

Bryant, David. *Concerts of Prayer.* Rev. ed. Ventura, Calif.: Regal, 1988.

———. *The Hope at Hand.* Grand Rapids: Baker, 1995.

Dawson, John. *Taking Our Cities for God.* Lake Mary, Fla.: Creation House, 1989.

Duewel, Wesley. *Mighty Prevailing Prayer.* Grand Rapids: Francis Asbury, 1990.

Eastman, Dick. *Love on Its Knees.* Tarrytown, N.Y.: Chosen, 1989.

———. *The Hour that Changes the World.* Grand Rapids: Baker, 1978.

Christenson, Evelyn. *What Happens When Women Pray.* Wheaton, Ill.: Victor, 1975.

Frangipane, Francis. *The Three Battlegrounds.* Marion, Iowa: Advancing Church Publications, 1989.

Green, Michael. *Exposing the Prince of Darkness.* Ann Arbor, Mich.: Vine, 1981.

Hawthorne, Steve, and Graham Kendrick. *Prayerwalking: Praying on Site with Insight.* Lake Mary, Fla.: Creation House, 1993.

Hayford, Jack. *Prayer Is Invading the Impossible.* New York: Ballantine, 1977, 1983.

Jacobs, Cindy. *Possessing the Gates of the Enemy.* Grand Rapids: Chosen, 1991.

Kinnaman, Gary. *Angels Dark and Light.* Ann Arbor, Mich.: Vine, 1994.

Kraft, Charles H. *Christianity with Power.* Ann Arbor, Mich.: Vine, 1989.

Lewis, C. S. *Letters to Malcolm: Chiefly on Prayer.* Glasgow, Scotland: Fontana, 1963, 1966.

———. *The Screwtape Letters.* New York: Macmillan, 1961.

Long, Bradford Zeb, and Douglas McMurry. *The Collapse of the Brass Heaven*. Grand Rapids: Chosen, 1994.

McAlpine, Thomas. *Facing the Powers*. Monrovia, Calif.: MARC, 1991.

Murphy, Ed. *The Handbook for Spiritual Warfare*. Nashville: Thomas Nelson, 1992.

Murray, Andrew. *The Ministry of Intercession*. Springdale, Pa.: Whitaker House, 1982.

Nee, Watchman. *The Latent Power of the Soul*. New York: Christian Fellowship Publishers, 1972.

Otis, George Jr. *Spiritual Mapping Field Guide*. Lynnwood, Wash.: The Sentinel Group, 1995.

———, ed. *Strongholds of the 10/40 Window*. Seattle: YWAM Publishing, 1995.

———. *The Last of the Giants*. Grand Rapids: Chosen, 1991.

Reidhead, Paris. *Beyond Petition*. Minneapolis: Dimension, 1974.

Sheets, Dutch. *Intercessory Prayer*. Ventura, Calif.: Regal, 1997.

Sherman, Dean. *Spiritual Warfare for Every Christian*. Seattle: YWAM Publishing, 1990.

Strong, Gary. *Keys to Effective Prayer*. Basingstoke, England: Marshall Pickering, 1985.

Torres, Hector. *Desenmascaremos: Las Tinieblas de Este Siglo*. Nashville: Betania, 1996.

Wagner, C. Peter, ed. *Breaking Strongholds in Your City*. Ventura, Calif.: Regal, 1993.

———. *Confronting the Powers*. Ventura, Calif.: Regal, 1996.

———, ed. *Engaging the Enemy*. Ventura, Calif.: Regal, 1991.

———. *Prayer Shield*. Ventura, Calif.: Regal, 1992.

———. *Warfare Prayer*. Ventura, Calif.: Regal, 1992.

———, and F. Douglas Pennoyer, eds. *Wrestling with Dark Angels*. Ventura, Calif.: Regal, 1990.

Warner, Timothy. *Spiritual Warfare*. Wheaton, Ill.: Crossway, 1991.

White, Tom. *The Believer's Guide to Spiritual Warfare*. Ann Arbor, Mich.: Servant Publications, 1990.

———. *Breaking Strongholds: How Spiritual Warfare Sets Captives Free*. Ann Arbor, Mich.: Vine, 1993.

Religious Festivals and Pilgrimages

Agrawala, Vasudeva Sharana. *Ancient Indian Folk Cults*. Varanasi, India: Prithivi Prakashan, 1970.

Anderson, Mary. *The Festivals of Nepal*. London: Allen & Unwin, 1971.

Bodde, Derk. *Festivals in Classical China: New Year and Other Annual Observances During the Han Dynasty.* Princeton: Princeton University Press, 1975.

Brown, Alan, ed. *Festivals in World Religions.* New York: Longman, 1986.

Casal, U. A. *The Five Sacred Festivals of Ancient Japan.* Rutland, Vt.: Charles Tuttle, 1967.

Cooper, J. C. *The Dictionary of Festivals.* London: Thorsons, 1995.

Crumrine, N. Ross, and Alan Morinis, eds. *Pilgrimage in Latin America.* New York: Greenwood, 1991.

Dunkling, Leslie. *A Dictionary of Days.* New York: Facts On File, 1988.

Eickelman, Dale, and James Piscatori, eds. *Muslim Travellers: Pilgrimage, Migration, and the Religious Imagination.* London: Routledge & Kegan Paul, 1990.

Festivals in Asia. Tokyo: Kodansha, 1975.

Harrowven, Jean. *Origins of Festivals and Feasts.* London: Kaye & Ward, 1980.

Johnson, Russell, and Kerry Morgan. *The Sacred Mountain of Tibet: On Pilgrimage to Mount Kailas.* Rochester, Vt.: Park Street, 1989.

Lai, Kuan Fook. *The Hennessy Book of Chinese Festivals.* Kuala Lumpur: Heinemann Asia, 1984.

Lincoln, Louise, and Tibor Bodrogi. *Assemblage of Spirits: Idea and Image in New Ireland.* New York: George Braziller, Minneapolis Institute of Arts, 1987.

MacNeill, Mary. *The Festival of Lughnasa: A Study of the Survival of the Celtic Festival of the Beginning of Harvest.* London: Oxford University Press, 1962.

McPhee, Colin. *A House in Bali.* New York: Oxford University Press, 1980.

Nag, Sunil Kumar, ed. *Popular Festivals of India.* Calcutta: Golden, 1983.

Pennick, Nigel. *The Pagan Book of Days: A Guide to the Festivals, Traditions, and Sacred Days of the Year.* Rochester, Vt.: Inner Traditions, 1992.

Shemanski, Frances. *A Guide to World Fairs and Festivals.* Westport, Conn.: Greenwood, 1985.

Singh, R. L., and Rana P. B Singh, eds. *Trends in the Geography of Pilgrimages.* Varanasi, India: National Geographic Society of India, 1987.

Singh, S. B. *Fairs and Festivals in Rural India: A Geospacial Study of Belief Systems.* Varanasi, India: Tara Book Agency, 1989.

Snelling, John. *The Sacred Mountain.* London: East-West Publishers, 1983.

Welbon, Guy, and Glenn Yocum, eds. *Religious Festivals in South India and Sri Lanka.* New Delhi: Manohar Publications, 1982.

Sacred Sites and Places of Power

Ahlback, Tore, ed. *Old Norse and Finnish Religions and Cultic Place-Names.* Stockholm: Donner Institute for Research in Religious and Cultural History, Almqvist & Wiksell, 1990.

Bernbaum, Edwin. *Sacred Mountains of the World.* San Francisco: Sierra Club, 1990.

Cowan, James. *Sacred Places in Australia.* Sydney: Simon & Schuster, 1991.

Devereux, Paul. *Earth Memory.* St. Paul: Llewellyn Publications, 1992.

———. *Places of Power.* London: Blandford, 1990.

Dowman, Keith. *The Power Places of Central Tibet: The Pilgrim's Guide.* London: Routledge & Kegan Paul, 1988.

Earth's Mysterious Places. Pleasantville, N.Y.: Reader's Digest, 1992.

Freitag, Sandria, ed. *Culture and Power in Banaras: Community, Performance, and Environment, 1800–1980.* Berkeley: University of California Press, 1989.

Harpur, James, and Jennifer Westwood. *The Atlas of Legendary Places.* New York: Weidenfeld & Nicolson, 1989.

Harpur, James. *The Atlas of Sacred Places.* New York: Henry Holt, 1994.

Joseph, Frank, ed. *Sacred Sites: A Guidebook to Sacred Centers and Mysterious Places in the United States.* St. Paul: Llewellyn Publications, 1992.

Locke, Raymond Friday. *Sacred Sites of the Indians of the American Southwest.* Santa Monica, Calif.: Roundtable Publishers, 1991.

Lowell, Percival. *Occult Japan: Shinto, Shamanism and the Way of the Gods.* Rochester, Vt.: Inner Traditions, 1990.

McPherson, Robert. *Sacred Land, Sacred View: Navajo Perceptions of the Four Corners Region.* Provo, Utah: Brigham Young University, Signature, 1992.

Osmen, Sarah. *Sacred Places: A Journey into the Holiest Lands.* New York: St. Martin's Press, 1990.

Peterson, Natasha. *Sacred Sites: A Traveler's Guide to North America's Most Powerful, Mystical Landmarks.* Chicago: Contemporary, 1988.

Proudfoot, Peter. *The Secret Plan of Canberra.* Kensington, Australia: University of New South Wales Press, 1994.

Singh, R. L., and Rana P. B. Singh, eds. *Environmental Experience and Value of Place.* Varanasi, India: National Geographic Society of India, 1991.

———. *Trends in the Geography of Pilgrimages.* Varanasi, India: National Geographic Society of India, 1987.

Singh, Rana P. B. *Where Cultural Symbols Meet: Literary Images of Varanasi.* Varanasi, India: Tara Book Agency, 1989.

Singh, S. B. *Fairs and Festivals in Rural India: A Geospacial Study of Belief Systems.* Varanasi, India: Tara Book Agency, 1989.

Snelling, John. *The Sacred Mountain.* London: East-West Publishers, 1983.

Sopher, David. *The Geography of Religions.* Englewood Cliffs, N.J.: Prentice-Hall, 1967.

Streep, Peg. *Sanctuaries of Power: The Sacred Landscapes and Objects of the Goddess.* Boston: Little, Brown, 1994.

Swan, James, ed. *The Power of Place and Human Environments.* Wheaton, Ill.: Quest, 1991.

Vogt, Evon. *Zinacantan: A Maya Community in the Highlands of Chiapas.* Cambridge, Mass.: Belknap Press, Harvard University Press, 1969.

Walters, Derek. *Chinese Geomancy.* Shaftesbury, England: Element, 1991.

Shamanism and Traditional Religions

Bastien, Joseph. *Mountain of the Condor.* Prospect Heights, Ill.: Waveland, 1985.

Blacker, Carmen. *The Catalpa Bow.* London: Unwin Hyman, 1989.

Butt-Thompson, Frederick. *West African Secret Societies: Their Organizations, Officials, and Teachings.* Westport, Conn.: Negro Universities Press, 1970 (1929).

Cowan, Tom. *Fire in the Head: Shamanism and the Celtic Spirit.* San Francisco: HarperSanFrancisco, 1993.

Cushing, Frank Hamilton. *Zuni Fetishes.* Las Vegas: KC Publications, 1990.

Davis, Wade. *The Serpent and the Rainbow.* New York: Warner, 1985.

Eliade, Mircea. *Shamanism: Archaic Techniques of Ecstacy.* Princeton: Princeton University Press, 1972.

Faris, James. *The Nightway.* Albuquerque: University of New Mexico Press, 1990.

Frazer, James. *The Golden Bough,* New York: Macmillian [1922], 1974.

Freidel, David, Linda Schele and Joy Parker. *Maya Cosmos: Three Thousand Years on the Shaman's Path.* New York: Quill, 1993.

Gersi, Douchan. *Faces in the Smoke.* Los Angeles: Jeremy Tarcher, 1991.

Halifax, Joan. *Shamanic Voices: A Survey of Visionary Narratives.* New York: E. P. Dutton, 1979.

————. *Shaman: The Wounded Healer.* New York: Crossroad, 1982.

Harner, Michael, ed. *Hallucinogens and Shamanism.* New York: Oxford University Press, 1973.

————. *The Way of the Shaman.* New York: Bantam, 1980.

Hart, Mickey. *Drumming at the Edge of Magic.* San Francisco: Harper-San Francisco, 1990.

Heinze, Ruth-Inge. *Trance and Healing in Southeast Asia Today.* Bangkok: White Lotus, 1988.

————. *Shamans of the 20th Century.* New York: Irvington Publishers, 1991.

Hessig, Walter. *The Religions of Mongolia.* Geoffrey Samuel, trans. Boston: Routledge & Kegan Paul, 1980.

Kalweit, Holger. *Dreamtime and Inner Space: The World of the Shaman.* Boston: Shambala, 1988.

Lake, Medicine Grizzlybear. *Native Healer.* Wheaton, Ill.: Quest, 1991.

Lincoln, Louise, and Tibor Bodrogi. *Assemblage of Spirits: Idea and Image in New Ireland.* New York: George Braziller, Minneapolis Institute of Arts, 1987.

Lowell, Percival. *Occult Japan: Shinto, Shamanism and the Way of the Gods.* Rochester, Vt.: Inner Traditions, 1990.

McGaa, Ed. *Mother Earth Spirituality: Native American Paths to Healing Ourselves and Our World.* New York: HarperSanFrancisco, 1990.

McKenna, Terence. *Food of the Gods: The Search for the Original Tree of Knowledge.* New York: Bantam, 1992.

————. *True Hallucinations.* San Francisco: HarperSanFrancisco, 1993.

Mumford, Stan Royal. *Himalayan Dialogue: Tibetan Lamas and Gurung Shamans in Nepal.* Madison, Wis.: University of Wisconsin Press, 1991.

Nicholson, Shirley, ed. *Shamanism.* Wheaton, Ill.: Theosophical Publishing House, 1987.

Oke, Isaiah. *Blood Secrets: The True Story of Demon Worship and Ceremonial Murder.* Buffalo: Prometheus, 1989.

Piggot, Stuart. *The Druids.* London: Thames & Hudson, 1961.

Ray, Benjamin. *African Religions.* Englewood Cliffs, N.J.: Prentice-Hall, 1976.

Reichard, Gladys. *Navajo Religion.* Princeton: Princeton University Press, 1977.

Rutherford, Ward. *The Druids: Magicians of the West.* Wellingborough, England: Aquarian Press, 1983.

Shils, Edward Albert. *Tradition.* Chicago: University of Chicago Press, 1981.

Somé, Patrice Malidoma. *Of Water and the Spirit.* New York: Jeremy Tarcher/G. P. Putnam's Sons, 1994.

The Spirit World. Alexandria, Va.: Time-Life, 1992.

Taylor, Rogan. *The Death and Resurrection Show.* London: Anthony Blond, 1985.

Tierney, Patrick. *The Highest Altar.* New York: Viking, 1989.

Tompkins, Ptolemy. *This Tree Grows Out of Hell.* San Francisco: HarperSanFrancisco, 1990.

Wasson, R. Gordon. *Persephone's Quest: Entheogens and the Origins of Religion.* New Haven: Yale University Press, 1986.

Signs, Wonders and Power Evangelism

DeArteaga, William. *Quenching the Spirit.* Lake Mary, Fla.: Creation House, 1996 (1992).

Greig, Gary, and Kevin Springer, eds. *The Kingdom and the Power.* Ventura, Calif.: Regal, 1993.

Kinnaman, Gary. *And Signs Shall Follow.* Old Tappan, N.J.: Chosen, 1987.

Kraft, Charles H.. *Christianity with Power.* Ann Arbor, Mich.: Vine, 1989.

Lewis, C. S. *Miracles.* New York: Macmillan, 1947.

Pytches, David. *Spiritual Gifts in the Local Church.* Minneapolis: Bethany, 1985.

Springer, Kevin, ed. *Power Encounters among Christians in the Western World.* San Francisco: HarperSanFrancisco, 1988.

Wagner, C. Peter and F. Douglas Pennoyer, eds. *Wrestling with Dark Angels.* Ventura, Calif.: Regal, 1990.

White, John. *When the Spirit Comes with Power: Signs and Wonders among God's People.* Downers Grove, Ill.: InterVarsity, 1988.

Williams, Don. *Signs, Wonders and the Kingdom of God.* Ann Arbor, Mich.: Vine, 1989.

Wimber, John, and Kevin Springer. *Power Evangelism.* Rev. ed. San Francisco: HarperSanFrancisco, 1992.

———. *Power Healing.* San Francisco: HarperSanFrancisco, 1987.

Woodberry, J. Dudley. *Muslims and Christians on the Emmaus Road.* Monrovia, Calif.: MARC, 1989.

Index

George Otis Jr. is the founder and president of The Sentinel Group, a multifaceted Christian research and information agency headquartered in Colorado Springs. In the 1980s his research expertise in restricted-access lands led to his selection as a senior associate with the Lausanne Committee for World Evangelization. More recently Mr. Otis was appointed co-coordinator of the A.D. 2000 & Beyond Movement's United Prayer Track, a position that includes leadership responsibilities for the Track's Spiritual Mapping Division. He is also a founding director of the new World Prayer Center, and serves as an advisor to Women's Aglow International and the Lydia Prayer Fellowship.

Mr. Otis has authored several books over the years, including *The Last of the Giants* and *Strongholds of the 10/40 Window.* He is also a frequent speaker, and his ministry calling has taken him to nearly 100 nations. Mr. Otis lives near Seattle, Washington, with his wife, Lisa, and their four children.

The Sentinel Group is a Christian research and information agency dedicated to helping the Church mobilize prayer and ministry resources intelligently during the latter stages of world evangelization. Specific helps include a monthly prayer digest called *World InSight,* an annual trend-watch seminar called CompassPoint and a variety of spiritual mapping support services. The organization's reach is worldwide with special emphasis placed on the United States and the 10/40 Window. For more information on The Sentinel Group, or a complete product list, contact:

The Sentinel Group
P.O. Box 62040
Colorado Springs, CO 80962
phone: (719) 534-9193
e-mail: SentinelGp@aol.com